MORE
KINDERGARTEN
RESOURCES

Josephine Newbury

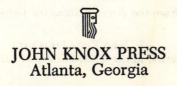

JOHN KNOX PRESS
Atlanta, Georgia

ABOUT THIS BOOK

This text grew out of a need for an expansion of the curriculum anthology *Church Kindergarten Resource Book*. It is supplementary to it both in content and in the rationale for the suggested activities. This text is also cross-referenced to the earlier volume for specific recommended additional resources.

Since the *Church Kindergarten Resource Book* provides adequate materials for celebrating Christian festivals as well as a wealth of Bible stories and readings, prayers, and songs for use in religious instruction, this volume was planned as an expansion of suggested teaching materials needed in other phases of the curriculum. These volumes together provide a rich anthology of original teaching materials as well as a vast collection of resources which have been brought together from a wide selection of publications.

The contents have been organized in ways which make them readily available for the teacher's use.

A large number of the poems, stories, songs, and finger plays included in this text were created by students in the kindergarten education program, student teachers, and the four- and five-year-olds in the Demonstration Kindergarten of the Presbyterian School of Christian Education in Richmond, Virginia.

To all
the student teachers
and the four- and five-year-old
boys and girls who have lived and
learned together in the Demonstration Kindergarten
of the Presbyterian School of Christian Education

Library of Congress Cataloging in Publication Data

Newbury, Josephine, comp.
  More kindergarten resources.

  Supplement to the author's Church kindergarten resource book.
  Includes bibliographies.
  1. Kindergarten—Methods and manuals. 2. Religious education of preschool children. I. Newbury, Josephine. Church kindergarten resource book. II. Title.
LB1169.N53   372.1'9   73-5349
ISBN 0-8042-1360-7

Scripture quotations are from the *Revised Standard Version of the Bible*, copyrighted 1946 and 1952.

FOREWORD

This book is planned to help persons working with young children to have a ready source of teaching materials for meeting their individual and group needs. It provides resources for realizing teaching objectives in both the affective and cognitive domains. One specific chapter deals with ways of nurturing a positive self-image. Other curriculum suggestions allude to this objective through the ways in which the materials are used in meeting the children's needs.

One chapter takes a quick look at the kindergarten child—what he is like in his overall development, what his general needs and interests are, and what the implications of these are for building an effective curriculum for this age child.

There are materials which suggest activities designed to help the young child develop his ability to solve problems and to develop sensory and perceptual acuity. Teachers will also find a wealth of resources for helping the young child develop skills in language usage and in developing math and science concepts essential for later learnings.

Materials relating to other aspects of the kindergarten curriculum found in this anthology are: art activities, play, music and movement, games and finger plays, songs and singing games, and poetry and stories.

The first chapter includes a collection of inspirational materials for teachers and parents to use as individuals and at staff meetings or for parent gatherings at the kindergarten.

The last chapter encourages the teacher to develop the "squirrel habit" of collecting scrap and other discarded materials and recycling them for a variety of uses with the children in the kindergarten program.

Most of the chapters, particularly the last one, include an extensive bibliography of additional resources of teaching aids and materials useful for the teacher's own personal and professional growth.

This text is planned to serve teachers and administrators working with young children in public or private kindergartens, child development and day care centers, weekday programs sponsored by local churches, or in any situation where young children are brought together for group care.

Parents of young children will find it a welcome resource of activities and materials for use in the home.

First-grade teachers can also make use of the wealth of stimulating materials for their children, particularly for those who have not attended kindergarten prior to their first-grade enrollment.

—Josephine Newbury

353549

Contents

1
Spiritual Enrichment
for Teachers and Parents
of Young Children

TEACHER[1]

resource person
guiding, caring, ever learning,
always open to Truth
Communicator!

—*Mary Jean McFadyen*

BITS OF CONVERSATION WITH MOTHER

Child: "I know my teacher *by heart.*"
Mother: "Now what do you mean by that?"
Child: "Well, I *understand* her—
and I *love* her—
and I *won't ever forget* her!"

MY TEACHER IS . . .[2]

My teacher is to smile.
She sounds always yes,
When she
Comes her Hello starts
Everybody happy.

My teacher is to listen.
All my "ifs" and "whys"
She hears,
She hears also the "buts"
I cannot say.

I learn, I learn because
"We'll try" and "Let us find"
Says she,
Always it is us and we
When things are doing.

My teacher is to see.
So far, so near, this long
She looks
Until she shows a pattern
Full of sparkle.

My teacher is to sing.
Like dancing, like Christmas
She fills
My heart full of tunes
To sing all day.

—*Lorna Kray*

TO MY TEACHER[3]
(You Are My Friend)

You are my friend because . . .
You understand. When things go right, or when
mistakes are in the making,
You understand.

You are my friend because . . .
You listen. To all the little things, as well as to
those of great importance,
You listen.

You are my friend because . . .
You make me happy. Even as I brush aside a
tear,
You make me happy.

You are my friend because . . .
You give. You give the most important things
. . . encouragement, love, and best of all, it
is yourself
You give.

You are my friend because . . .
You make me want to do my best. Accepting all
the bad, you seek and praise the good, and
so,
You make me want to do my best.

[1]Used by permission of the author.
[2]Reprinted by permission of the United Church Press
from *Children's Religion,* February 1956. Copyright 1956
by the Pilgrim Press.
[3]Used by permission of the author.

Because you are my friend,
I want to reach up to the stars and touch them
    with my hands.
I want to change all sadness into joy, all dark-
    ness into light.
I want to live and grow and share the beautiful
    ... to laugh and love and lift.
But first of all, I want to thank you for the gift
    ...
Of Friendship ...
Because you *are* my friend.

                              —*Jane Carpenter*

GIVE US THE EYES TO SEE THIS CHILD[4]

Give us the eyes to see this child
    As thou dost see him, whole;
See through his mask of need and doubt,
    Of fear within and noise without,
        Till we can reach his soul.

Give us the ears that we may hear
    More than his words alone,
And find, within, his deep desires
For truth and love, as he aspires
    To be indeed thine own.

Give us the hands to do our task
    With sympathy and skill;
To reach, and touch, and hold him fast
    Delighting in thy will.

Give patience, too, through weeks of drought
    When labor seems in vain,
        Content to wait refreshing showers
When thou shalt send renewing powers—
    Help us to try again.

Give us the grace to know our need,
    Our constant need of thee;
So children both, this child and we
    May eagerly draw nigh to thee,
    And blessed together be. Amen.

                          —*Miriam Dewey Ross*

THE TEACHER ASKED OF THE CHILD[5]

The teacher asked of the child,
"What would you have of me?"
And the child replied,
"Because you are you, only you know some of
    the things
I would have of you.
But because I am I,
I do know some of what
I would have of you."

The teacher asked again,
"What would you have of me?"
And the child replied,
"I would have of you what
You are and what you know.
I would have you speaking and silent,
Sure and unsure, seeking for surety,
Vibrant and pensive.

I would have you talking and letting me tell,
Going my way with my wonderings and en-
    thusiasms,
And going your way that I may know new curi-
    osities,
I would have you leading step by step
Yet letting me step things off in my own fash-
    ion."

"Teach me," said the child,
"With simplicity and imagination—
Simply that the paraphernalia and the gadgets
Do not get between us;
Imaginatively that I may sense and catch your
    enthusiasm,
And the quickening thrill of never having been
    this way before.

"Too, I would have you watching over me, yet
    not too watchful,
Caring for me, yet not too cautiously,
Holding me to you, yet not with bindings,
So when the day comes, as it must, that we,
    each, go our separate ways,
I can go free.
Let me take you with me not because I must,
    but because I would have it so.
Let me take you with me because you have
    become, in me,
Not just today—
Tomorrow!"

[4]From *Fifteen New Christian Education Hymns,* copyright 1959 by the Hymn Society of America; used by permission.
[5]From *Childhood Education,* Nov. 1961, p. 152. Reprinted by permission of Leland Jacobs and the Association
for Childhood Education International, 3615 Wisconsin
Ave., N.W., Washington, D.C. Copyright © 1961 by the Association.

THE GIFTS OF CHILDREN[6]

They are not bought
With silver or with gold
The gifts of little children.
They give them freely
Asking no riches in return.

Laughter they bring
Voices that shout and sing
With gladsome living,
Bodies that dance and swirl
With all the joy of movement,
Eyes that sparkle
Lips that smile
Feet that run and skip
Into our very beings.

They bring their magic
And their wonder
Their deep and tender feelings,
Their sorrows and their tears,
Hearts big enough
To hold the Universe
They bring us.
No prejudice is theirs.
Love they give
To all living creatures
Asking only loving in return.

They bring their questioning,
Their Whats and Hows and Whys,
Their eagerness for learning,
Their confidence that
Answers can be found.

What greater gifts
Than these the children bring us—
They bring themselves.

—*Laura Hooper*

BEATITUDES FOR PARENTS[7]

Blessed are the parents who make their peace
with spilled milk and with mud, for of such is
the kingdom of childhood.

Blessed is the parent who engages not in the
comparison of his child with others, for precious
unto each is the rhythm of his own growth.

Blessed are the fathers and mothers who have
learned laughter, for it is the music of the child's
world.

Blessed and wise are those parents who understand the goodness of time, for they make it not
a sword that kills growth but a shield to protect.

Blessed and mature are they who without anger
can say no, for comforting to the child is the
security of firm decisions.

Blessed is the gift of consistency, for it is heart's-
ease in childhood.

Blessed are they who accept the awkwardness
of growth, for they are aware of the constant
perilous choice between marred furnishings
and damaged personalities.

Blessed are the teachable, for knowledge brings
understanding, and understanding brings love.
Blessed are the men and women who in the
midst of the unpromising mundane give love,
for they bestow the greatest of all gifts to each
other, to their children, and—in an ever widen-
ing circle—to their fellowmen.

—*Marion Kinneman*

A PARENT'S GIFT[8]

Gold and silver have I none.
What gift then can I give my son?

I can endow him with a sense of worth.
    I can deepen his inner security by develop-
        ing self-esteem.
    I can encourage natural talents and special
        qualities.
    I can show an understanding of other cul-
        tures and other peoples.

I can stimulate his sense of adventure.
    I can present to him a wide variety of ex-
        periences.
    I can feed his natural curiosity.
    I can help him to develop an awareness of
        all life around him.

---

[6]From *All Children Have Gifts,* ACEI Bulletin No. 100
(1958), p. 4. Reprinted by permission of Laura Hooper and
the Association for Childhood Education International.
  [7]Used by permission of the author.
  [8]Reprinted with permission from *Young Children,* Vol.
24, No. 4, March 1970. Copyright © 1970, National Association for the Education of Young Children, 1834 Connecticut
Ave., N.W., Washington, D.C. 20009.

I can enrich his vocabulary.
>   I can talk with him of many things, as opposed to talking "at" him.
>   I can listen to him and welcome his unique expression of ideas.
>   I can read to him from fact and fancy, poetry and prose.
>   I can sing with him old songs and new.

I can ignite the spark of his creativity.
>   I can kindle his imagination.
>   I can accept his new ideas.
>   I can appreciate his efforts.
>   I can provide him the raw materials with which to work.
>   I can give him time to dream.

I can communicate moral and spiritual values.
>   I can set a worthy example for him to follow.
>   I can motivate him toward achieving honest goals.
>   I can be reverent and hold certain values sacred.
>   I can laugh with him when life tests us both.
>   I can offer him love.

—*Pauline Crabb*

A CHILD'S PLEA [9]

"Touch me, please," is what I say
When I begin to act that way.
"Hold me please, I'll make a mess,
But all I want is tenderness."
You offer me love I'm denied,
And though I've all your patience tried—
Just stop a while and let me sap
The sweetness from your flowing tap.
Don't judge my rough defiant say
As expressions of my chosen way.
But see my open wound and heed;
It's love and warmth I want and need.

—*Judith Hynd Bowling*

UNCERTAINTY [10]

So small the hand
That clings for aid,

So bright the eyes
That search for truth,
So quick the mind
That's unafraid,
So soon the child
Becomes a youth.

How short our time
To guide the heart,
How quick the days
Of leading go;
How much I helped
Or did impart,
How well I taught
I may not know.

—*Mary Jackson Cathey*

PRAYER [11]

—Upon entering
>   the classroom—
Your life is here,
>   In these I see,
May I teach them
>   As they teach me.

Our lives are meshed
>   As thoughts compare,
Help each to grow
>   As days we share.

—*Mary Jackson Cathey*

IF A CHILD LIVES WITH . . . [12]

If a child lives with criticism
>   He learns to condemn
If a child lives with hostility
>   He learns to fight
If a child lives with ridicule
>   He learns to be shy
If a child lives with jealousy
>   He learns to feel guilty
If a child lives with tolerance
>   He learns to be patient
If a child lives with encouragement
>   He learns confidence
If a child lives with praise
>   He learns to appreciate
If a child lives with fairness
>   He learns justice
If a child lives with security
>   He learns to have faith
If a child lives with approval
>   He learns to like himself

---

[9]Used by permission of the author.
[10]Used by permission of the author.
[11]Used by permission of the author.
[12]From *Baptist Leader*, July 1972. Used by permission of the American Baptist Board of Education and Publication.

If a child lives with acceptance and friendship
He learns to find love in the world
—*Dorothy Law Nolte*

IF YOU LOOK AT THE WORLD
WITH THE EYES OF A CHILD [13]

If you look at the world with the eyes of a child,
There is joy in the simplest thing,
From the green of a leaf on the earliest tree
To the curve of a bird on the wing.

If you look at the world with the eyes of a child,
There are miracles filling each day,
From the grass which mysteriously sways in the
    wind
To the gold in the sun's friendly ray.

If you look at the world with the eyes of a child,
There is wonder beyond any measure,
From the stars and the moon in the evening sky
To the sparkle of a dewdrop treasure.
—*Gail Brook Burket*

RECIPE FOR THE INNER SMILE [14]

A cook, whether cautious or carefree,
At times wants to try a new recipe.
With tongue in cheek
And mind in gear,
Check the following ingredients.
Do you find yourself here?

Mix:

> The essence of humor
> The moisture of one tear
> Three teaspoons of pleasure
> A dash of Don't Care
> One cup full of manners
> Two cloves of opinion
> A world full of challenge
> An air of dominion
> A swirl of excitement
> The yeast of sharing
> The sparkle of being loved
> The tolerance of caring
> The citrus of business
> The herb of poise
> The spice of anticipation
> The salt of all joys.

Combine:

> A red splash of spirit
> A yellow ray of mirth and goodwill

A blue drop of memory
A green sprig of hope, your life to fulfil

Fold in:

All dreams for the future.

Sprinkle with ambition, and
Cover with a full measure of faith.

Bake until you can see:

> The upside of courage
> The downside of fear
> The inside of valor
> The outside of cheer.

> Do not ice or use frosting!
> Let the ingredients show through;
> Then viewers will recognize
> The composite of YOU.

Serve generously to all you meet.
—*Reba Dunn Westbrook*

IF I COULD USE WORDS [15]

If I had in my mouth words to say . . . if I had the knowledge of my needs to put into these words . . . these are some of the things I'd like to say to you . . . the grown-ups in my life:

When I am so little . . . give me food to nourish me; and shelter; and sleep that I may grow in health. Let me enjoy my five senses and enrich my world with a knowledge of God's great wonders. So please give me plenty of things to handle, to feel, to smell, to touch, to hear—and some that I may break.

I cannot grow unless I practice. Let me try out my powers as my body develops . . . to sit, to creep, stand, walk, climb, and jump when I am ready. This "God Mansion" of mine must be the best, else life is harder to bear.

But . . . don't mix up the natural needs of my body with your emotions and mind. I need from you . . . warm and comforting security in your love. Don't make me experience too much, too many, too long.

Do not punish me when learning how to live makes me fight and cry and kick at life. I'm

---

[13]Used by permission of the author.
[14]From *Preschool Leadership*, January, February, March 1971. © Copyright 1970 The Sunday School Board of the Southern Baptist Convention. All rights reserved. Used by permission.
[15]Used by permission of the author.

learning. Or when I've been disappointed or deprived . . . It is bad enough as it is.

There are so many things I have to learn; training my body, learning to use my hands, learning to speak, learning how to get along with you and the dog and the cat and children and people and . . . with myself. Learning to trust you and then to turn you loose. Learning to understand you and them and me and my world and God and His world and find my place in it. And I WANT to learn.

Help me . . . even when I fight you . . . for I'm scared . . . there's so much to know . . . and sometimes you make me so angry!

Speak to me with your heart and your hands; I do not understand your words. Surround me with kindly people, gentle people, nice-to-me people to whom I belong, just like I am.

Give me peace in which to grow . . . a corner in your home all my own . . . with my share of attention and consideration. If you let me feel that I am wanted . . . that I am important to you . . . then you free me to be friendly and loyal to others. When you prove to me that a promise is a promise . . . I learn faith. When family planning includes my little part . . . I want to learn to cooperate.

Let me question, and answer me honestly . . . but not with more information than I can bear.

Let me experiment . . . to find out things myself.

Encourage my efforts to do things even when I cannot do them very well. I die without your approval . . . for then I have no self-respect either. Without these, how can I believe that I am a child of God who can do my job in His world?

Let me have fun with little things . . . no matter how foolish they may seem to you. Be patient with my little messes . . . it is so hard to learn everything about my world.

Let me share responsibilities, too, measured to my size. Let me learn to take my turn in a game, a reward, or a task . . . but believe in me while I'm learning to be unselfish. Watch my play and let me tell you in it how hard I am trying to learn to live like you and to solve my hard problems.

When you tell me this or that, tell me why. I learn that way, too. Let me stay sensitive to beauty. I must see it first through your eyes . . . whether it is beauty of nature or music or words.

Let me learn, bit by bit, to bear pain, to want, to postpone, to do without you, to look forward to pleasures, to feel strongly, but to learn to govern my temper.

Please, please, don't nag me . . . I need a friend who is mature and who can understand that I want to grow . . . I really do . . . but sometimes I want to quit, too, but I want your support and belief in me or everything will be too hard.

Don't keep me your baby . . . helpless . . . when I want to feel grown up, but stay nearby for I weary so quickly. Don't be so demanding that I am afraid of losing your love. And don't add your fears to mine. I've enough already. See my child's point of view . . . try . . . and see that I love you. To me you are the greatest people in all the world. Is God really as smiling and strong and gentle as you are . . . does he really love me like you do? Does He? Then He must be awful nice!

—*Alice M. Kousser*

AN INCHWORM SQUIRMS OUT OF KINDERGARTEN[16]

I'm a very small creature
    that God has made,
But I can go where I choose
    without being afraid.

An Inchworm I'm called
    by people, you see,
For I hump along slowly
    but surely and free.

I've learned lots about people,
    for every day
I move in and out where
    young children play—

On a kindergarten yard with
    a teacher to tell
Where the children must stay
    till they hear the bell.

Today they ran and laughed
    with glee

[16]Used by permission of the author.

Then the teacher yelled, "Come
    here to me!"

"Inside you must go," as she
    pushed Ted in line.
So I climbed on Sue's shoe—
    the life saved was mine.

On Sue's shoe I stayed for the
    short ride
If you're ready, I'll tell you
    what happened inside.

The chairs for the children were
    so close to the table
I moved from Sue's shoe as
    soon as I was able.

"Now it's Arithmetic time," the
    teacher announced.
"You children must learn
    about a quart and an ounce."

"We'll measure this room from
    wall to wall
And the number of feet and inches
    you are tall."

A small piece of paper was
    given each child.
"Copy all these numbers,"
    said the teacher with a smile.

The children looked tired.
    Some began to wriggle.
Bret copied not a number
    But did scribble, scrabble, scribble.

Then after arithmetic came the
    alphabet, too.
There was A and B and C and
    finally Q.

They said them, they sang them,
    they wrote them on a line,
No matter how they looked
    the teacher said, "That's fine."

For perfect papers all neat
    and clean
The teacher gave a star—gold
    or red or green.

Some children were proud
    for the rest of the day.
Others, quite discouraged,
    threw their papers away.

Next came the art period—
    it must be on time,
For today the class was to
    color within the line.

Tommy disliked being told
    what to make,
So he turned his paper over
    and drew a purple snake.

"Tommy Buchanan, I'm surprised
    at you!"
And turning to the class, the
    teacher said, "What shall we do?"

"I know, teacher," answered
    perceptive little Joyce,
"Tommy won't get to go to the
    college of his choice."

And so went the morning with
    its work, work, work.
It was woe be to any who dared
    shirk, shirk, shirk.

I was sorry for each child
    who came to that place.
So inch by inch, I moved
    to outer space.

And I thought as I moved,
    "I'm glad as can be
God in his wisdom made an
    Inchworm of me."

—*W. Mae Fariss*

THE INCHWORM TURNS[17]
(A sequel to "An Inchworm Squirms
Out of Kindergarten")

In the starry span of space,
    the Inchworm roamed about.
He chanced to meet an Astroworm
    a'wandering in and out.

---

[17]Used by permission of the author.

"Hello my friend," the Inchworm cried.
   "Hello yourself," said he.
His Astro-ship screeched to a stop,
   "Come on and ride with me—

"What brings you into Outer Space?"
   The Inchworm lost his smile—
But told his new friend of the school
   he had visited for a while.

"Well, come with me, I know a place—
   you won't believe your eyes.
It's just two zips and half a loop
   across the starry skies."

Within a wink the two were there
   and hopped on a janitor's broom.
Then, later from the closet floor
   crept softly to the room.

Oh, such a place he'd never seen,
   so warm, so light and gay.
The teachers smiled as they prepared
   activities for the day.

The Inchworm saw a puzzle here,
   a game and crayons too—
Each learning center in the room
   held something fun to do.

"Here they come," said Astroworm,
   as the children began to arrive.
Friendly greetings and eager minds
   soon had the place alive.

Some children to the blocks first went,
   some painted or played a game.
One working with large letters
   even spelled his name.

The Inchworm smiled, "I like this school,
   they just have fun all day."
"Don't be deceived," said Astroworm,
   "they are learning as they play."

Later in the morning
   they gathered on the floor,
They heard a story, sang a song,
   then talked and sang some more.

Oh what a happy time they had,
   even till the end,
When Mom or Dad would come to school
   And take them home again.

The Inchworm sighed, "Astro friend,
   my heart would sing with glee,
If in such a free and happy school
   every child could be!"
                    —*Judith Hynd Bowling*

THE SEARCH[18]

I watched the ways of children in their work
   and play
And longed to find a magic to transform
And guide their steps into a joyful day . . .
Any child . . . Whatever his gifts or emptiness be
To allow expression, a sense of fulfillment
As he discovers his talents acceptable to Thee.

I searched the schools . . . the programs . . . the
   many goals
For the bright . . . the slow . . . the restless
   . . . the quiet . . .
Handicapped . . . hungry . . . unloved or alone
And found resources, techniques, materials not
   a few,
A dream world, in fact, so much it cluttered my
   view
And reduced to complacency my restless urge
   . . . until . . .
   I saw along the way . . .
      Some left behind with empty hands . . .
         Naught but time and space, anger
            or defeat . . .
            Children yet, but no joy for
               their day!

I searched the theories, both old and new
From Freud to Piaget, insight I gained
In emotions, special teaching, it's true . . .
Enough to turn a robot into a perfect whole! . . .
What value the theories if communication fail
To lead the child, new discoveries to unfold?

I look to the world, both east and west
The systems tried of regiment, structure,
Freedom, creativity, to find out what was best.
Indeed, no stone unturned, they all were trying
Their own goals with perfection to see,
But how many denied the child the right to BE.

---

[18]Used by permission of the author.

I searched the heart of a child at last.
Deep into his sparkling eyes I gazed, asking,
"What can I do for you? . . . Help me!"
With enthusiasm his hand grasped mine
    Exploring, new discoveries to find—
        A bug, an ant hill, the wind, the sky,
          A cluttered street, water rushing by,
            A smile of knowing who I am
            and why;
My search ended and the answer found . . .
"If I am to walk with him . . . a light to
be . . .
First, let me find again the child in me!"
                —*Sylvia H. Boyer*

THE MINISTRY OF TEACHING

We are joined together in a common ministry;
We are called to communicate the gospel with
  young children.
    We need each other.
    The children need each of us.
    We need the children.

We will move among them with joy;
    Joy in living;
    Joy in being the people of God!
    Joy in living and learning with young chil-
    dren.

We will move among them with love;
    Love of God;
    Love for each other;
    Love for young children.

We will move among them with sensitivity;
    Sensitivity to their needs;
    Sensitivity to our own needs;
    Sensitivity to God at work in the world.

We are joined together in a common ministry.
We are called to live among children in ways
  that speak to the good news of God's love.
              —*Source unknown*

A CHILD'S GARDEN[19]

We have the loveliest garden,
It's called a Kindergarten.
We've variety and profusion
(Though some would say confusion!).
Variety provides the spice they say;
Our garden is new each day.

We cannot predict a bloom—
Here in their own special room,
These little ones sprout at will.
Each sign of growth brings a thrill—
This pattern is His design;
Not our plan, but His divine.

This is our task, our privilege rare:
The Master Gardener's work to share.
With His guidance give our best;
Though we stumble, still find rest
In faith secure: God's great love
Directs their growth from above.
              —*Catherine Rogers*

A CHALLENGING QUOTE[20]

    Let's give today's children vital opportuni-
ties for learning that lasts. . . . It stands to reason
that depth of involvement leads to depth of
meaning, that depth of meaning leads to
greater understanding, that greater understanding leads to more workable concepts, that
more workable concepts lead to more available
linkage to new learnings. When these are un-
derwritten by involvement of the five senses,
the new ideas are etched in.
              —*Alice V. Keliher*

THANK YOU[21]

For days of teaching, thank you, Lord,
    The joy,
    The pain,
        The self ignored,
    A sign,
        A song,
            A story read,
All things by which the mind is fed.

For children trusted to my care,
    The shy,
        The bold,
            The plain,
              The fair,
    Hostile,
        Humble,
          Stubborn,
            Proud,
Each variation you allowed.

---

[19]Used by permission of the author.
[20]From *Childhood Education*, January 1967, p. 251.
[21]Used by permission of the author.

For times of sharing, thank you, God,
   The smile,
     The touch,
       The knowing nod,
A word,
   A look,
     A friendly face,
Reminds me you are in this place.

For skill and patience, Lord, I ask,
   For zest,
     For verve
       To do my task,
For strength,
   For insight,
     And for love
To help them know you, God above.

—Mary Jackson Cathey

2
The Kindergarten Child

LISTEN . . . A CHILD SPEAKS[1]

I am a child.
You have seen me
searching for the ticking of a clock,
reaching for wiggly, creeping things,
pulling velvet petals from tall stems,
catching dancing dust in shafts of sunlight,
chasing an elusive shadow,
weaving dreams into the great expanse of
    space.

I am a child.
You have heard me
crying in the darkness of the night,
squealing with unbridled joy,
sobbing over hurts and hurting,
laughing at funny, fumbling clowns,
chatting with real, but invisible friends.

I am a child.
You have seen me
You have heard me
But have you understood?
Have you seen only the tykes and bikes and
    dolls and one-eyed teddy bears?
Or have you seen and heard
the tagging sisters
the teasing brothers
the bossy friends
the nagging do's and don'ts
the perplexing rules
the aching loneliness
the stiffening fears
the births, the deaths
the love, the hate,
the pain of growing?

I am a child.
You think your adult world is different from my
    world.
But you are wrong.

You say—Children play; adults work.
Children have fun; adults have problems.
Children are learning; adults know.
Children are preparing to live; adults are in-
    volved in living;
But you are wrong.

I am a child.
I do play, but I play out the social scene as I see
    it—
Baddies, goodies
Hiding, shooting
Shopping
Phoning
Gulping coffee
Reckless driving
Packing
Moving
Spanking baby.
I do play, but in my life of play I meet
"Truck drivers" who get in my way
Problems on the "block-construction crew"
Times when everyone wants to be "mother"
Children who want their own way
Children who push and pull
Children who do not want to be my friends.

I am a child.
I do have fun, but remember . . .
sometimes friends get angry
parents interfere with plans
teachers do not understand how hard I tried to
    master that new skill
and I live with hurts and hurting.

I am a child.
I am learning—more things than you will ever
    know—

[1]From *Baptist Leader,* May 1965. Used by permission of
the American Baptist Board of Education and Publication.

but I live with you in an unknowable world
Our earth is now a launching pad for satellites
   —rockets
spaceships and nuclear weapons.
Who knows what our earth will be next?
Not I—nor you . . .
Each new discovery only makes us aware of
   something else we do not understand.

I am a child.
I am preparing to live, but my here-and-now
   days are full of living—
the birth of babies, puppies, kittens
the death of pets and grandpas
"being mad" and making up
conquering fear of darkness and strange
places . . .

I am a child.
You think your adult world is different from my
   world,
But you are wrong.
We all have feelings of love and hate, joy and
   sadness.
We all know the anxiety of frustration and the
   joy of fulfillment.
We all are searching for our place in the world.
We all are struggling with the same gnawing
   questions:
Who am I?
What is my world like?
Who are you?
Who is God?
What are we to do in this world?

I am a child.
You see and hear me everywhere
But do you understand?

I am a child.
Listen to me with your whole being.
Listen and respond in love.
                   —*Florence Wangner*

THE FIVE-YEAR-OLD

A kindergarten class will contain as many

different five-year-olds as there are children in
the class.

Since a child's home life and environment
have important bearing on his development and abilities the children may differ
greatly in their readiness for group living,
their use of school materials, their recep-
tivity to teacher authority, and their re-
sponsiveness to ideas and possibilities for
creativity.[2]

However, it is possible, remembering that
each child is a unique individual, to recognize
certain identifiable similarities that exist among
children who have had their fifth birthdays.

By the time a child is five he has usually
developed a rather definite personality. He
gives evidence of the type of person he is
becoming, both in physical appearance and in
the way he responds to life about him.

Physically, he has entered a period of
growth which is generally much slower than
during his preceding early years. This growth is
also somewhat uneven. His legs are growing
longer and more rapidly than other parts of his
body. His heart also is developing at a rapid
rate, but his lungs are still relatively small. He
is normally farsighted and his eye-hand function still lacks good coordination.

The five-year-old has usually established his
handedness. He knows the hand with which he
eats, paints, draws, and cuts, although he may
not be able to identify the right and left members of his body.

His gross motor activity is quite well developed. He can walk and run with good coordination. He can climb and descend steps; he can
skip, alternating feet with comparative ease.

His fine muscles, however, are not as well
developed, limiting him in activities requiring
fine muscle function.

His special skills are beginning to become
apparent, as are his intellectual potentialities.

The five-year-old enjoys general good
health but is still subject to respiratory infections. With all the different immunizations for
young children today, there is little chance of
the kindergarten child contracting the common communicable diseases which beset young
children in the past.

The five-year-old is still quite an active

[2]Marguerita Rudolph and Dorothy H. Cohen, *Kindergarten—A Year of Learning* (New York: Appleton-Century-
Crofts, 1964), p. 18.

child, although he may appear more restrained in his activity than when he was a four-year-old. His activity is much more purposeful, and he can remain with an activity for extended periods of time, depending on his interest in what he is doing.

His play is predominantly physical—vigorous and noisy, but it is beginning to show some organization. Leadership ability in this area begins to be evident as we observe a child who "takes over" a play activity, giving directions as to "who" each is to be and "where" and "what" he is to do.

The five-year-old prefers rigorous, big-muscle play, and he tires quite easily. He needs to have his strenuous play activity balanced with quiet activity and rest. Irritability and crossness are often the result of fatigue.

He enjoys a variety of table games as well, and is developing skill in following directions and waiting his turn. He functions better when no more than four children are involved in the game and when the game has simple rules and progresses rapidly toward completion.

The kindergarten child enjoys his play with other children and is beginning to display some ability to cooperate with his peers. He is making a good beginning at taking turns and respecting the rights and property of others. He is now more inclined to *ask for* rather than snatch or grab from others that with which he wishes to play. He will still fight when provoked and will be the aggressor, but he is learning to handle difficult situations in more socially acceptable ways.

Much of the five-year-old's play is of the dramatic, imaginative type. He plays out situations which he knows or situations which may have been puzzling to him. This is one way he has for better understanding his environment and the experiences in which he finds himself. It is also one way he has of dealing with the problem of *being little*.

Someone has very aptly termed the kindergarten child a scientist. He is constantly probing for answers that will help him become better acquainted with the world around him. This seems to be a way of life for him—exploring, experimenting, and asking questions to satisfy his curiosity. He is constantly pushing back the horizon of his knowledge. He continues to make discoveries on his own through the use of his five senses. According to Piaget, the young child's thought "tends to be dominated by his perceptions."[3]

Occasionally a five-year-old can be observed making a penetrating observation, asking questions of the most profound nature, and even reasoning brilliantly. But by and large he is not yet capable of dealing with abstract ideas and logical thought.

He is in a period of very rapid language development. He has lost much of his infantile articulation. For the most part he is quite a conversationalist, though he is prone to make unreliable statements. This is due in part to his lack of judgment as well as to the fact that he does not always have a grasp of the meaning of the vocabulary he uses. It could be due also to the fact that the English language is often confusing. One word can have many different meanings, depending on the way it is used.

Imagine the young child's confusion as he hears the word *light* used in conversation in a number of different situations: "*Light* the campfire. Turn out the *light*. Moon*light*, sun *light*, star*light*. The package is *light*. The minister said, 'Jesus, the *light* of the world.' . . . The teacher said, 'See, the prism made a rainbow of colors from the *light* coming through the window.' Daddy said, 'We will leave for the country tomorrow morning as soon as it is *light* enough to drive without *lights*. The bird will *light* on the tree. She is *light* on her feet. Don't make *light* of what I say. We wear *light* clothing in warm weather."[4]

As well as making unreliable statements, the kindergarten child is also given to making grammatical errors. He usually is able to convey his message, however, as can be noted in the following statement made by a five-year-old one morning in kindergarten when he realized he had failed to return with a signed note from home: "Uh-oh, I learned my note what I bringed home last tomorrow!" Five's usually define things in terms of their usage: "A chair is to sit on." "A spoon is to eat with."

The five-year-old enjoys stories, particularly about the *here and now* things with which

---

[3]Millie Almy, *et al.*, *Young Children's Thinking: Studies of Some Aspects of Piaget's Theory* (New York: Teachers College Press, 1966), p. 13.

[4]Thelma C. Adair and Rachel S. Adams, *When We Teach 4's and 5's* (Philadelphia: The Westminster Press, 1963), p. 27.

he is familiar. He likes imaginative stories, especially if they are about animals. He is not old enough for unreal and fantastic fairy stories. He is still having problems coping with reality.

Poems and jingles delight him, particularly when he can help supply the rhyming words.

He enjoys creating and dictating short stories and poems and then hearing them read back to him and his friends.

Basically, the five is a happy, well-poised child. He will cry easily, but usually bounces back with a great deal of resilience. He is developing an interesting sense of humor. He enjoys jokes on others, but cannot laugh at himself too well.

He bids for affection and approval of adults and displays jealousy if he thinks he has too much competition for the affection he desires from the grown-ups in his life. At this age the child experiences a very real fear of losing his parents, particularly his mother. Though to a lesser degree than the four-year-old, the five still has some very real fears—night sounds, darkness, storms, and sirens. Individual children will harbor special fears that have grown out of frightening experiences, but these are usually temporary.

Five is the age when the developing conscience is becoming apparent. It is the time when bad dreams and even frightening nightmares plague the child in his sleep. These dreams usually contain wild animals and strange people chasing the child or harming him in some gruesome manner.

The five may still hold on to one or more of his tensional outlets, especially at nap or bedtime. Thumb-sucking still occurs with many five's when the child is unhappy or unoccupied. Cuddly, stuffed animals play the same role of support with some children.

If the five-year-old does something wrong or that he really did not intend to do, he is more than apt to place the blame on some object or someone else. He is apt to accuse the nearest person at hand. "You made me do it; it's your fault," he will exclaim.

"In general the emotional life of the five-year-old suggests good adjustment within himself and confidence in others."[5] All in all, he is comfortably at home in his world.

If the five-year-old has been free from undue adult pressures and demands made upon him in his earlier years, he will display a good deal of independence. He finds joy and satisfaction in doing things on his own—and often in his own way. He has become quite capable of caring for his personal needs—eating, toileting, bathing, and dressing himself (except, generally, for tying his shoestrings). He still needs encouragement and reminders and, on occasion, adult help with some of his daily routines.

Although he is striving for increased independence, he experiences some ambivalence, for he still recognizes his dependence on his parents and teachers for supplying his basic needs.

He is growing in his ability to perform simple tasks at home and at kindergarten. He likes being trusted and having special responsibilities. He delights in performing jobs which he can accomplish on his own. He may at times, however, shrink from a simple routine responsibility with the explanation "I'll do it some other time." And he will.

The five-year-olds' curiosity and eagerness for information, their hunger for companionship, their readiness to grow in independence and competency, their ability to reason and think, make it desirable that such potential for growth be nurtured by professional, planned guidance within our schools. Such professional guidance can be given in good kindergartens, kindergartens that promote health, stimulate many interests, and provide a year of learning.[6]

This year of learning will be planned basically in light of the knowledge of the general developmental characteristics common to most children, but with the awareness of the individual differences and special needs of each child.

CHILDREN[7]

ever changing
growing, discovering, learning
constellations of gifts and abilities
Challenge!
—*Mary Jean McFadyen*

---

[5]Arnold Gesell and Frances Ilg, *The Child from Five to Ten* (New York: Harper & Brothers, Publishers 1946).
[6]Rudolph and Cohen, *Kindergarten—A Year of Learning*, p. 24.
[7]Used by permission of the author.

IMPLICATIONS OF DEVELOPMENTAL CHARACTERISTICS FOR CURRICULUM PLANNING

1. Knowing that kindergarten children are very active, the teacher provides for the best use of both the indoor and outdoor space. He or she will "take stock" of all the furniture and large equipment to ascertain the importance of the roles which they play in the "good life" of the children. This may mean that in order to give the children adequate play space, some of the tables and chairs should be dispensed with. Movable equipment and that which can be used creatively in numerous ways allows for diversity of activities and more freedom of movement. (Fifty to sixty square feet per child is adequate floor space indoors, while 100 to 200 square feet is essential for the outdoor play area.)

2. To meet the child's need for vigorous, gross motor activity, the kindergarten should provide large, sturdy equipment for climbing. Equipment for balancing plays an important role in meeting this need of the five-year-old, as do wheel toys such as tricycles of different sizes and Irish mails. The teacher will plan for daily experiences in creative rhythmic movement and many other bodily expressions which the children enjoy inventing as they create or interpret music.

3. Realizing that the five's large muscles are developing more rapidly than the fine muscles, the teacher will provide large play and work materials for the children: large blocks, large balls, large chunks of clay, large crayons and colored chalk, large easel brushes, and large sheets of paper on which to express their thoughts and feelings. The teacher will avoid using activities which require too much eye-hand coordination and fine muscle usage, such as "coloring in" pictures, cutting out intricate figures, using small pegboards, working with sewing cards, and the like. The teacher will help the left-handed child to be comfortable in the use of materials, and will have available left-handed, blunt-end scissors for his use.

4. Knowing that the kindergarten child spends much time in dramatizing life about him, the teacher will provide an abundance of resource materials for this play. This will mean, besides the basic equipment in the home and block centers, there will be available interesting dress-up clothes and play accessories such as a fireman's hat, doctor's kit, toy cash register, large flat paint brushes and painter's cap, squares of cloth, red bandanna handkerchiefs, tire pump, ad infinitum.

5. Mindful that five's are ego-centered and seek attention and praise, the teacher will be accepting of them as they are and will establish a warm, supportive relationship with them. The teacher will also make every effort to help each child have satisfying experiences which merit approval and special attention, and will try hard not to be annoyed by the attention-getting techniques the children use.

6. Knowing that the five-year-old fatigues easily, the teacher should balance the active times with periods of quiet activities throughout the session, maintaining a consistent sequence and rhythm of both types of activities.

7. Responding to the natural curiosity expressed by the kindergarten child, the teacher will provide a rich environment of resources which will stimulate questioning. The variety of ways with which the teacher deals with the children's questions will help them begin to develop ways of discovering answers for themselves.

8. Aware of the child's interest in and rapid development of language skills, the teacher should provide an environment that stimulates and encourages conversation and discussion. He or she should provide a wealth of good picture books, use poetry with individuals and the group, tell stories, and encourage and record children's creative stories. The teacher will be more concerned about the child's spontaneity and creativity in verbal expression than the grammatical accuracy which he employs. Correct grammatical forms will come with time and exposure to good speech models. (See chapter on Language Development for a detailed discussion of this subject.)

9. Recognizing that five's are becoming increasingly interested in and capable of small group play, the teacher will provide a number of learning centers in response to the children's interests and needs. These centers will allow for small groups of boys and girls to play together according to their individual interests and with peers of their own choosing. The teacher will

not expect real cooperation among the children all the time, for she knows that the "i" in "child" is still a capital "I"! She will be alert to situations where the children need a bit of adult help. For example, a group had built a train as a cooperative venture, but were having trouble in their play that followed. The teacher, noting that the cooperative spirit was about to disintegrate, entered the play with some scraps of colored construction paper, a play watch, and a pair of hole-punchers. Her comments to the group were: "You might need to make and sell tickets for the passengers, and then you might want to have a conductor to take up the tickets and punch them when the train is on its way." This timely suggestion, with the added play resources, gave the experience the boost the group needed. (The children had seen a filmstrip about a train ride several days before and were somewhat familiar with the roles of some of the railroad workers.)

Here is another example of how a kindergarten teacher helped a child make her way more easily into the play of a small group in the home center. Knocking at the home center, the teacher introduced the child, saying, "This is Mrs. Jones who has come over to help you with the children. She heard the baby is sick." The play picked up in interest for all involved, and the child who was brought into it was able to make a contribution to the experience.

10. The teacher is continually aware of evidences of the child's growing independence, and will meet his need for doing things for himself by seeing that there are individual cubbies, lockers, or special places for the child's personal things. Low open shelves for work materials and toys make it possible for the child to select the materials which he wishes to use. It is important for the children to be able to put the equipment away without adult help. Responsibility charts for each day might include such routines as feeding the fish and other pets, watering the plants, preparing for snacks, and leading the calendar activities for the day. The teacher will also allow for individual responsibility in toileting, hand-washing, and general housekeeping activities in the kindergarten room. To make this easier for the children, child-size clean-up equipment should be made

easily accessible to the children at all times. They can then take the responsibility for cleaning up spills and other messy situations as they occur.

11. Aware of the five-year-old's need to make appropriate choices, the teacher will provide an environment in which choice-making is encouraged. The organization of the day's activities, the selection of materials and equipment, will offer the child numerous opportunities to select his own activities and to make discoveries on his own and to put his thinking into action. The teacher's respect for the child's ability to have his own ideas and to choose the types of learning experiences of interest to him is essential for the child's self-respect and confidence. "The overly structured or highly adult-directed program does not allow the young child to develop his own potential or discover his own ability to think and plan."[8]

12. Knowing the young child's susceptibility to respiratory infections, the teacher has the responsibility of helping the children to form good health habits such as:

Washing hands after toileting and before eating.

Keeping fingers and toys out of mouth.

Drinking at the water fountain without touching the fixture with his mouth.

Not eating part of another child's food.

Covering coughs and sneezes with a paper handkerchief and disposing of it immediately after using.

Wearing warm outer clothing and caps which cover ears during cold, windy weather.

The teacher will also be certain that the room temperature ranges between 68° and 72° and that the children are never in a draft in the room. He or she will also keep a change of clothes for each child in order to meet any emergency which otherwise would mean that the child would have to wear wet shoes or clothes while at school.

13. In order to provide the security five's need in group living, the teacher sets firm but appropriate limits for behavior. He or she will help the children understand that certain rules for behavior must be enforced for the sake of the safety of every member of the group. The children must know that the limits set will be enforced consistently but with love and, when necessary, with firmness. This, however, does

---

[8]Adair and Adams, *When We Teach 4's and 5's*, p. 29.

not preclude times flexibility is necessary in order to meet special needs of individual children.

Having limits set and adhered to gives the child a sense of security. He knows that he can depend on the teacher to provide boundary lines within which he can test more freely his ideas and his developing powers.

14. Being aware of the young child's capacity for wonder and awe, the teacher is sensitive to the child's responses and will provide opportunities for him to develop his sense of wonder. Wonder and awe are, for the young child, the beginnings of worship.

15. Knowing the kindergarten child's need for the assurance that he is loved and needed and valued as an individual, the teacher will offer a warm, friendly, accepting relationship and a challenging environment in which the children and the teacher may live and learn and grow together.

PROVIDING FOR INDIVIDUAL DIFFERENCES

Having dealt briefly with a few of the general likenesses found among five-year-olds, it is of equal importance to recognize some of the differences that are apparent within this one-year age group and the implications these differences have for the teacher.

Although there may be only a few months difference in the chronological ages of the children in a kindergarten class, the teacher will find a wide span of variance in physical growth and development, mental ability, and social and emotional maturity. There will be diversity among the children in interests and performance, in language usage, imagination, creative expression, sensory perception, motor control, and behavior in problem-solving situations.

Specifically, the implication of this knowledge for the teacher is that he or she must know each child—his needs and interests, his strengths and weaknesses, and in the light of such knowledge plan a program that will allow each child to progress at his own rate and in his own way. The teacher will provide centers of learning that allow for a wide range of interests. They should offer challenges to the children at whatever level of maturity they may be operating. For example, the inlay puzzles should range in difficulty from a few puzzles with no more than six or eight pieces to those with eighteen to twenty-five pieces.

This is true for other manipulative equipment. One or two soft, cuddly stuffed animals should be available for times when less mature individuals might need a bit of "added security" to help them through a difficult situation.

To accommodate to the children's physical differences, the kindergarten should provide equipment of varying sizes, such as tricycles, chairs, etc. (The chain-driven trike is perhaps easier for the smaller child to manage.)

A large portion of the daily session will be spent in free activity, so that the child can find satisfaction in working independently or with varying small groups in the centers of his choice.

The teacher will refrain from ever making comparisons of the children's achievements and will offer encouragement and praise as deserved.

The teacher will make opportunities for each child to "shine" in some way and to realize a personal pride in the success of his undertaking.

If there is a child in the group with a physical handicap, care must be taken to help him live with his handicap without giving in to it. Whatever accommodations that are essential for his participation in the group should be made. However, he needs to become as self-sufficient as is possible within his limitations. He needs to feel that he is a part of the group, participating and enjoying achievement and making contributions to the group in ways in which he is physically capable.

Whatever the child's limitation, the teacher will strive to help him develop a mental outlook and forms of response which will make for his own happiness and his social and emotional adjustment in the group.

As the teacher recognizes the differences which make each child a unique person, he or she will plan the curriculum to best meet the developmental needs and interests of the individuals. With respect for the individual, the teacher will give each child the affection, support, and guidance he requires in proportion to his needs.

The teacher will accept each child where he is in his development, recognizing that growth is continuous, but that each child has his own growth rate and unique pattern. The teacher is aware that the child may evidence periods of regression which are usually triggered by some crisis situation in his life. Unless there is a serious problem, the child experiences only a temporary setback.

So with patience and understanding the teacher strives to provide an educational environment and a program which stimulate and promote the realization of the development of each child's full potential for his present stage of maturity.

Throughout this chapter the term "teacher" in the singular has been used. This is not to say that there would be only one teacher for a kindergarten class. There should be at least two adults; perhaps one may be considered an aide. Aides serve much as a "second teacher" in the group in their relationships with the children and in working as teammates with the teacher.

BIBLIOGRAPHY

Adair, Thelma C., and Adams, Rachel S. *When We Teach 4's and 5's*. Philadelphia: The Westminster Press, 1963.

Axline, Virginia M. *Dibs: In Search of Self*. Boston: Houghton Mifflin Co., 1966.

Fraiberg, Selma H. *The Magic Years*. New York: Charles Scribner's Sons, 1959.

Hymes, James L., Jr. *Behavior and Misbehavior*. Englewood Cliffs, N.J.: Prentice-Hall, 1955.

————. *A Child Development Point of View*. Englewood Cliffs, N.J.: Prentice-Hall, 1955. (Out of print, but available in libraries.)

————. *The Child Under Six*. Englewood Cliffs, N.J.: Prentice Hall, 1963. (Out of print, but available in libraries.)

————. *Understanding Your Child*. Englewood Cliffs, N.J.: Prentice-Hall, 1952.

Jenkins, Gladys G., *et al. These Are Your Children*. 3rd ed. Chicago: Scott, Foresman & Co., 1966.

Mussen, Paul H., *et al. Child Development and Personality*. 3rd ed. New York: Harper & Row, 1969.

Schulman, Anne Shaaker. *Absorbed in Living—Children Learn*. Washington, D.C.: National Association for the Education of Young Children, 1967.

3
Nurturing the Young Child's Self-Concept

One very important part of the young child's development with which teachers must be vitally concerned is a wholesome feeling of self-worth—sometimes spoken of as "self-regard," "self-image," or "self-concept."

The young child needs to develop a feeling of self-confidence and well-being—to feel good about himself—if he is to achieve and be motivated to learn. And, by the same token, if he is *unable* to enjoy some measure of success in his living at home and in his kindergarten, his self-image will suffer.

The teacher of young children will want to help each child develop a growing understanding of who he is—and to accept himself and be glad *he is who he is.*

The young child needs opportunities to discover satisfying answers to these questions:

Who am I?
What can I do by myself?
What am I really like?

It is hoped that some of the child's answers will be:

There is no one else just like me.
I do not look like anyone else.
I can have my own thoughts and feelings.
I am growing and learning every day.
I am an important person.
I am *Me*. I am glad I am *Me* and I like *Me*.

Overarching all the ways and means for helping the young child to come to these understandings is the teacher's close, warm, accepting relationship with each child in the group.

Nonverbal communication is a very important part of this relationship. It may be expressed by facial responses in looking directly at the child—eyeball to eyeball; through physical contact expressed in an affectionate pat on the shoulder or holding the child's hand; and by allowing him to touch the teacher for comfort or security as needed.

As important as nonverbal communication is, it must be supported by verbal communication that conveys the same message to the child. This may be accomplished through giving directions or explanations and in conversations in which the teacher listens patiently and attentively to the child.

Kindergarten children come to school in all states of mind. Some are fearful, hesitant, apathetic, and shy. Some are upset and frustrated even to the point of rage or despair.

At the early ages of four and five there are some children who already feel that they are worthless—complete failures—so unsure about themselves that they can't even look up or speak. They have a very blurred sense of self.

As the teacher reaches out to them to meet this challenge which they present, he or she must receive each child with unconditional acceptance. This acceptance of the child must encompass the truisms that each child is a person of worth in his own right and is a unique individual with needs and interests that are his alone.

[1]Gladys Andrews, *Creative Rhythmic Movement for Children*, p. 19. © 1954. Reprinted by permission of Prentice-Hall, Inc., Englewood Cliffs, N.J.

Such acceptance will allow each child the freedom to be himself and to know that his teacher appreciates him and loves him just as he is.

The need for this freedom is very aptly stated in the "Bill of Rights" for children by Gladys Andrews. It is a request from a child himself, as it were.

Let me grow as I be
And try to understand why I want to grow like
    me;
Not like my Mom *wants* me to be,
Nor like my Dad *hopes* I'll be
Or my teacher thinks I *should* be.
Please try to understand and help me grow
Just like me![1]

It is essential that the young child be helped to be realistic about his strengths and weaknesses, his abilities and disabilities. And he should be respected for his individual differences and receive his measure of the teacher's attention and concern in the fulfillment of his needs.

What does it mean for the teacher to meet the needs of individual children for developing a healthy, *positive* self-image?

KINDERGARTEN ENVIRONMENT

Flexibility of the entire kindergarten setting and a permissiveness which allows the child to explore, experiment, and make judgments on his own level of ability is basic to respect for individual differences. In such a situation the child feels challenged to learn and at the same time feels valued as a person with his own special needs and interests.

The room arrangement and the variety of activities which the teacher provides take into consideration a knowledge of and respect for individual differences within the group. The teacher expresses concern for individuals by offering activities and resources requiring differing degrees of ability and skills.

WELCOME UPON ARRIVAL

As each day begins, a warm and friendly personal welcome to each child helps him to feel safe and welcome and more at home in his classroom. This enhances the child's feeling of self-esteem.

TEACHER'S AVAILABILITY

The teacher's availability for helping individuals who need encouragement and adult support gives evidence of concern for individuals and their needs. And as the teacher is able to help a child follow through on an activity he has begun, he or she is helping him to develop competence and the feeling of self-satisfaction so essential to a good self-image.

DESERVED PRAISE GIVEN

The teacher gives praise and expressive admiration freely, but of course honestly, for any deserving achievement—no matter how small it may be. A thoughtful teacher may be overheard speaking to individuals in ways such as:

"You finished your puzzle all by yourself this time, Bryan. I'm proud of you."

"You waited very patiently for the prism, Alice."

"My! What a good housekeeper you are! You've cleaned the paint brushes so well today!"

USE OF THE CHILD'S NAME

A child's self-concept is very closely associated with his name. Therefore, it should be used as extensively as possible throughout the school year. Besides the use of the child's name in speaking with him, the teacher will print his name in manuscript in situations calling for labeling of his work, his coat locker, and listing his name on the daily responsibility charts.

Teachers can also use songs that lend themselves to name situations. Hearing his name sung in connection with group activities enhances the child's self-image. Some of these might be:

"We Have a Good Friend," page 87
" 'M' Is for Mary," page 85
"Resting Song," page 35
"Where Is Our Friend?" page 35.

PHYSICAL AWARENESS

A young child's developing self-concept is dependent in part on his awareness of his physical self. Action songs, finger plays, and simple games are helpful, in the spirit of play, to alert the child to the awareness of his body. Examples of these are relaxation games and songs such as "Simon Says," "Heads and Shoulders, Knees and Toes," "On My Head My Hands I Place."

The song "I'm Very Happy with All of Me" refers to various body parts and the fact that the child is "very happy with all of me."

Footprints, Handprints, and Fingerprints

There's nothing quite so revealing to the child in understanding his uniqueness than the making of his footprints, handprints, and fingerprints. As he compares his prints with the prints of other children in his group, he can readily see that there really is no one exactly like himself. (Directions for making these are given at the end of the chapter.)

The Child's Silhouette

Making a silhouette of each child is another very graphic way of showing the children that each has physical features that are alike in general to all other children, but with each there are the special, unique characteristics which make him himself. (Directions for making these are given at the end of the chapter.)

Life-Size Self-Pictures

When the kindergarten child is given the opportunity of painting a life-size self-picture, he gains a better concept of his physical size. Much of the young child's world is filled with big people and things which make him aware of his "littleness." When he sees his picture of himself hanging on the wall, he will invariably exclaim, "Look how big I am! Am I really that tall?" (Directions are given at the end of the chapter.)

A Full-Length Mirror

A full-length mirror in the kindergarten is also helpful in conveying to the child his identity and body size. He sees his own physical likeness and can then better understand how he looks to others. Hand mirrors are also useful in this respect.

Teacher's Reflection

But the most telling reflections come from the teacher, who can convey them nonverbally by a smile, a frown, turning away from a child and ignoring him, or by a gentle pat on the shoulder or a nod of approval.

Equally important is the teacher's consistency in mirroring his or her concept of the child through conversation with him.

The following poem indicates how confused a young child can become over the inconsistent reflections of himself that come from the adults in his life. In this case it is his mother.

Today I asked my mother if I could whittle;
That's what I did.
"Why, no, my child. You're too little."
That's what she said.

But when I fell and bumped my head,
I cried, I did.
"Why, you're too big a boy to cry,"
My mother said.

"Why can't I cry, if I am little?"
I ask again,
"Or, if I'm big, why can't I whittle?"
I want to know.

—*Author unknown*

One of the problems of growing up for the young child is in understanding his feelings and knowing how to deal with them in socially acceptable ways.

He first needs to identify his various feelings and to know that it is all right to have those feelings. He needs the security of knowing that he is loved and accepted no matter how he feels.

The young child needs help situationally to understand his feelings, particularly his bad feelings. He also needs opportunities for draining off his bad feelings in ways that give him emotional and physical release without danger to himself or others around him. This is essential for upholding his self-respect.

Appropriate classroom discipline is most effective in helping individuals maintain a healthy self-image. First of all, the child must be separated from the offense. He needs the assurance that his teacher loves and respects him no matter what he says or does, even though he or she disapproves of his actions.

As the child tries to deal with his difficulty and work through it to a satisfactory solution, he needs the concerned support of his teacher. He must be treated with courtesy and respect at all times. At no time should there ever be ridicule, comparison of children's behavior, or embarrassment for any child.

The resource section at the end of this chapter includes teaching tools and materials such as pictures, songs, poems, and filmstrips for use in helping children with their feelings.

Tape Recording Children's Conversations

Recording the children's conversations on tape and letting them listen to themselves and identify each other by voice builds self-esteem as well as promoting verbal self-expression.

Making Colored Slides of the Children

From time to time many teachers take colored slides of their kindergarten children as they are involved in various classroom activities. A showing of the slides brings much joy to the children as they see themselves on the screen. This is just one more way of adding to the child's self-awareness and helps him in building a healthy self-image.

Family Snapshots

At the beginning of the school year, as the teacher is collecting pupil information and health forms, he or she can request a recent snapshot of each child's family. These can be mounted and placed along the wall at the children's height so that they may see themselves with their families and enjoy looking at the families of the other members of the group.

Kindergarten children never tire of pointing out their pictures and explaining, "That's me!" or "Here I am!" Sometimes a child, experiencing a moment of loneliness or frustration, will be observed standing in front of his family's picture. And in one situation, a rather insecure little boy chose to have his mat right under his family's picture at rest time each day for weeks.

PHYSICAL GROWTH

1. *Periodic weighing of the children.* It is sometimes hard for the young child to understand that he is growing—that there is a regular pattern for this which he can expect. He is apt to think of himself as he now is as his past, present, and future status as far as size is concerned.

Periodic weighing and measuring—perhaps in September, January, and May—can show graphically the fact of his physical growth. Records may be kept in any way satisfactory to the teacher, just so each child is made aware of how much taller he is and how many pounds he has gained from September until May.

2. *Children's baby pictures.* Later in the year some kindergarten teachers have the children bring one of their baby pictures to share with each other and to see if they can recognize one another.

3. The book *The Growing Story* by Ruth Krauss conveys to the child the fact of *his* body growth, even though it is slower in comparison to the plant and animal world he sees about him.

4. A collection of a child's clothing from infancy to five years displayed against an outline of a kindergarten-age child's figure is a very concrete way of showing physical growth.

5. A child's birthday is an excellent time to help with the understanding of growth and taking pride in it. This is an extremely important occasion for the young child, and a wise celebration of each birthday can nurture his good self-concept. He feels important when the class sings to him, when he is allowed to select a special activity for the group, when he is chosen for some special responsibility during the morning, and then perhaps hears a story about himself at together time with his friends. For this the teacher can check with the birthday child's mother to obtain the highlights of his growing up, from his birth to his present age. The teacher can work these into a story which will fascinate him.

A NEW BABY IN THE FAMILY

A new baby arriving in the family of a four- or five-year-old can be an event which threatens the young child's self-assurance and even his sense of worth as a member of his family. He can become filled with all kinds of fears and anxieties. "Will they love me now, or will they trade me in for the new model?" he may think.

There are any number of ways of helping the child through this shaky time for his self-image.

He will enjoy bringing the baby's first picture to show his school friends. The large classroom calendar can be marked with a small picture of a baby to indicate the day of the baby's birth. This can be referred to from time to time to determine how many days old the new baby is. Poems and songs about new babies add to the interest of the group and also lend support to the new big brother or sister. Stories such as *Peter's Chair* by Ezra Keats, *Baby Sister* by Valerie Grayland, and *Amy and the New Baby* by Myra Brown will help the child identify with the storybook children and their feelings and attitudes about their new baby at home.

The following story endeavors to point out to the *big brother* or *big sister* that he or she was once just like the new baby in his home and that his parents did all those extra things for him when he was a tiny new baby.

A STORY ABOUT YOU

(This story would be much more effective if it were made into a large scrapbook with pictures to illustrate the various activities. Magazine pictures or pictures from baby-gift wrapping paper provide good sources.)

A long time ago you were a little new baby boy (girl). Your mother and your daddy were so proud of you and loved you so very much. And they kept right on loving you more and more as you grew.

When you were a tiny new baby, you slept most of the time. You would wake up and want something to eat. At first you just drank milk.

You ate and slept and ate and slept and grew and grew. That's the way it is with all babies. The doctor's scales showed you weighed more each time your mother took you to see him.

Soon you were able to pull up and stand in your crib. Sometimes you would cry and cry. This was your way of saying you were hungry, or you needed dry clothes, or maybe you were just lonesome.

Your mother or daddy would come to your bed and take you up in their arms. They would do for you whatever you needed. This was one way they had of showing you how much they loved you.

Days went by and you grew and grew. Soon you were big enough to sit in your high chair and try to feed yourself. You liked to play in your food while you ate. Sometimes before your mother could catch your hand, you would dump your food out of your little feeding dish. You were messy. You would often get more of your oatmeal on your face than in your mouth. But you were learning. And your mother just laughed and washed your face. "I love my little 'messcat'," she would say. "I know he'll (she'll) do better some day." And you did.

You kept right on growing and growing. When you were about a year old, you began to stand up and walk. How proud you were! And how proud your mother and daddy were too. Just think, their little boy (girl) could walk! Of course you had to have help. It was easier if you could hold on to Mother or Daddy's finger. You would walk them all through the house.

You kept on growing a little every day. You began talking, that is, saying lots of words like "bye," "cookie," "go ride," "daddy," "mommie," and many more—new words every day.

In no time, it seemed, you were two years old. You could run around and play and get into all kinds of trouble in the house. Someone had to watch you all the time to see that you didn't get hurt or eat something you shouldn't. Your parents didn't mind, because they loved you and they enjoyed watching you grow. They knew you would be three years old soon, and then you could do more things for yourself.

By the time you were three years old you had learned to play with your toys, look at your books, dig in your sandbox, and do many more interesting things. You were kept busy every day playing and growing.

Then you had another birthday. You were four years old. That was a year of growing and playing with your friends and learning to do things to help your mother and daddy at home. You could do so many things now that you couldn't do when you were only three! But that's what growing is all about. And your parents kept right on loving and enjoying you every day.

And now that you are five you are such a big boy (girl) in so many ways. And something special has happened to you. You are now a *big brother (sister)* because you have a new baby brother (sister) in your home. He (she) is very new and very tiny yet. He (she) will need lots of loving and caring for from your mother and daddy, just as you did when you were a tiny new baby. But the new baby in your home has someone else special to love and care for him (her). That someone is *you.* We are all happy that you have a little new brother (sister) and that now you have become a *big brother (sister).*

GIVING RESPONSIBILITIES

A sense of importance comes when the young child is assigned responsibilities such as being host or hostess at snack time, watering the flowers, feeding the fish, or fixing the calendar for the day. The children will assume many responsibilities situationally, as needs become evident in the group. Every day each child should be able to "sparkle" a little in some way. Then he may, in time, come to feel as a kindergarten boy commented about himself one day: "I feel just like a Cracker Jack box." When asked how a Cracker Jack box feels, he replied, "I don't know, but it always has a *good prize in it!*"

As a part of nurturing confidence and self-respect, teachers offer the child experiences which will help develop the skills he needs for cognitive growth, new skills in the use of his body, and successes achieved in discovering and creating on his own.

It is of utmost importance to remember also that if a child develops a healthy, positive self-concept without the competences to uphold it, then the teacher has failed and the child's self-image will come tumbling down.

In all living and learning that takes place in the kindergarten, the teacher must constantly be aware of just what kind of image of the self each child has. Is it a positive one of self-assurance and self-respect, or are the expectancies of his home and school out of reason for his age and abilities? Are the pressures to achieve so much for the child that he begins to think of himself as a failure or of little worth?

The children themselves will give the teacher the clues if he or she keeps the focus where it rightly belongs—on the individual child and how he sees himself. For the way a child feels about himself is crucial in determining much of what he thinks and says and does —and in reality, to what extent he is able to learn and live comfortably with his peers.

POEMS

SUPPOSE[2]

Suppose that you lived in a bird's nest,
Or lived in a hive with the bees;
Or lived in a hole like a rabbit,
Or just like a squirrel—in the trees.

Suppose that you lived like a turtle,
And carried your house on your back;
Or suppose that you
Were a small kangaroo,
And your mother carried you in her sack.

Suppose that you lived like a tiger,
Who roars in his cage at the zoo;
Or suppose like a bear,
A cave was your lair,
And you slept there the whole winter through.

Suppose that you lived like a goldfish,
In a bowl for all to see;
You could swim and play
All night and day;
What a pleasant life that would be!

But you're not like any of these, you know,
You live in a house instead;
You eat at the family's table,
And sleep in your very own bed.

You live with people who love you,
And do things that you like to do;
God planned for you to be different.
You're special—there's no other YOU!
                              —*DeVere M. Ramsay*

WAYS I FEEL[3]

Sometimes I feel so happy
Sometimes a little sad
Then there are times when
I feel very mad.

There are times when I feel I'm growing—
Growing too big and tall.
But there are times when I look around
And feel, oh so small!

Sometimes I feel quite grown-up
Sometimes helpful, too
Then sometimes I feel like just thinking
About the things I like to do.

Always I feel thankful
And I say so in my prayers,
Because no matter how I feel,
I know God loves me and cares.
                          —*Roberta Parker Martin*

I AM ME

I am so happy that I am me;
For that is who I want to be.
                              —*Josephine Newbury*

GLAD I AM ME

I am as glad as glad can be
That I am no one else but me.

I like myself—my funny nose,
My ears and eyes and wriggly toes;

My hands and feet that help me go
And I like the ways in which I grow.

I don't always like the things that I do
But I still like me and hope you do too.
                              —*Josephine Newbury*

I'M GLAD[4]

I'm glad I've got this body.
These arms and legs are fine.
Fingers, toes, and ears and nose—
I'm glad they all are mine.

It's good to have an elbow
When you want to throw a ball,
And how could you learn to whistle
If your mouth wasn't there at all?

---

[2] © DeVere M. Ramsay 1974. Used by permission of the author.
[3] Used by permission of the author.
[4] From *Nobody Else Is Just Like Me—Teaching Units,* by Florence Schulz, p. 67. © Marshall C. Dendy 1966. Used by permission of John Knox Press.

THANK YOU, GOD![5]

I see a daisy on the hill,
I hear the wind that won't be still,
I smell the honeysuckle fair,
I feel the warm sun everywhere,
I taste a berry from its stem,
My senses five—for each of them
I thank you, God, that I can be,
I thank you, God, that I am me!

—*Mary Jackson Cathey*

THERE ARE MANY CHILDREN IN THE WORLD[6]

There are many children in the world:
    Some with chubby cheeks and dimples,
    Some with curly hair and freckles,
    Some with braids and big, round eyes,
    Some with long, strong arms and bodies,
    Some with scratches on their legs,
But nobody else is just like me.

There are many children in the world:
    Some can roller-skate quite well,
    Some can't seem to skate at all,
    Some climb trees and some can swim,
    Some keep secrets, some do not,
    Some can skip and some can whistle,
But nobody else is just like me.

There are many children in the world:
    Some live out on farms and ranches,
    Some in houseboats on a river,
    Some in very tall skyscrapers,
    Some in houses in a row,
But nobody else is just like me.

There are many children in the world:
    Some have many sisters and brothers,
    Some have none and some are twins,
    Some don't have a mother with them,
    Some have grandmas and grandpas,
But nobody else is just like me.

There are many children in the world:
    They look different,
    They do different things,

They live in different places,
They have different families,
Different people love them,
But nobody else is just like me.

But something is the same about us all:
God loves us.
He made us so that we can love him,
And so that we can love each other.

—*Florence Schulz*

Note: Teachers should discover enough information about the children so that they can make changes in the above lines to fit the children, making it personally meaningful to them.

THE MANY FACES OF BARNABY[7]

I have a great big smile that looks quite cheerful on my face,
    But every now and then it seems to go some other place,

Because my little brother Joe does things that make me mad.
    He's just about the worst child that a family ever had.

He takes my things and breaks them, and I have to let him go,
    Because my mother says he's young; he really doesn't know.

My chin begins to push my mouth into a thin, straight line;
    My forehead makes my eyes come down—this face doesn't look like mine!

After a while this angry face begins to feel too tight.

I'm sorry for myself, and sad, and nothing goes quite right.

But then, if I remember that my chin belongs to me,

That I can make my mouth go just where I want it to be,

That God created me to think and make up my own mind,

That *I* decide how I will be—angry, sad, or kind,

I think it over for a while, and then I change my face.

I make my chin go down again; *I* put it in its place.

My smile comes back, I'm glad again because I really know

My brother, too, will change and learn; we *all* change as we grow.

Note: Stick puppets made of each of these faces adds to the effectiveness of the poem.

SOME FUN [8]

I look into the mirror
  And whom do I see?
Somebody that looks
  Just like me.

When I smile
  That somebody smiles too,
He seems to follow
  Everything I do.
I jump and he jumps,
  I clap and he claps,
I bend and he bends,
  I tap and he taps.

And if I run away,
  He'll follow rapidly.
Do you know the reason?
  Because he's really me.

I'M VERY GLAD [9]

I'm very glad
I have two ears
To hear what people say;
I'm very glad
I have two eyes
To see with every day.

I'm very glad
I have two lips,
(I'm even glad they're pink);
They help my mouth
To talk and sing
And yawn and eat and drink!

I'm very glad I have a nose;
I don't need more than *one!*
It helps me smell
The nicest things
And have so much more fun!

—*Vivian Gouled*

GROWING BIGGER [10]

Oh, the things
That I can do:
Wash my hands,
And hunt my shoe,
Hang up my coat
And dress myself,
Put all my toys
Upon the shelf,
Play alone

---

[8] From *Be My Friend and Other Poems for Boys and Girls,* by Edith Segal, p. 36. New York: The Citadel Press, 1952. Used by permission.

[9] *Nursery Days,* Graded Press, copyright © 1968. Used by permission.

[10] *Nursery Days,* Graded Press, copyright © 1967. Used by permission.

On a rainy day,
Mind the sitter
When Mother's away.
I'm growing bigger
And bigger, you see,
Because my mother
Depends on me.

—*Elaine M. Ward*

HOW DO YOU KNOW YOU GROW?[11]

How do you really know you grow?
Because your mother told you so?

Or is there a way to watch and see
Our sizes change from two to three?

A mirror can help to show us how
We looked yesterday—and now.

Eyes and ears and noses grow,
And mouths can form a bigger "O."

Fingers grow, and feet do too.
It's time to buy a bigger shoe!

Last year's mittens fit too tight,
And last year's hat does not look right.

You used to have to use a stool
To see the children go to school.

But just today it wasn't so.
Did the window shrink, or did you grow?

Your big brother is a person who
Is tall and strong and bigger than you.

Now what do you suppose it means
When you can wear his outgrown jeans?

You're right—it means it's really true!
You're *growing* into a big, tall YOU!

—*Frances Williams*

AREN'T YOU GLAD?[12]

Aren't you glad
    You have a nose

To smell the flowers in bloom?
Aren't you glad
    You have two feet
    To dance around the room?
Aren't you glad
    You have two eyes
    To see new life in spring?
Aren't you glad
    You have a mouth
    So you can talk and sing?
Aren't you glad
    You have two hands
    To climb and hold and clap?
Aren't you glad
    You have a mother
    Who hugs you on her lap?
Aren't you glad
    For family and friends,
    And for Father too?
Aren't you glad
    Yes, aren't you glad,
    Oh, aren't you glad you're you!

—*Elaine M. Ward*

MY FIVE SENSES[13]

I have five senses, Mother says;
I've learned their names to tell.
You know them, too, there's *sight* and *sound*,
And *touch* and *taste* and *smell*.

That each has brought me many joys
Is now quite plain to see.
But I shall name you just a few
That seem the best to me.

Sight

An orchard full of pink peach blooms,
A bluebird darting by,
A glowing cloud at sunset,
The rainbow in the sky.

Sound

A baby's laughter, chuckling, sweet;
Clear silvery notes that swell
And pour from my canary's throat;
A violin, a bell.

Touch

The feel of my wee puppy's coat,
So soft and warm and sleek;
My cool clean bed at night time,
A baby's silken cheek.

[11] *Nursery Days*, Graded Press, copyright © 1967. Used by permission.
[12] *Nursery Days*, Graded Press, copyright © 1969. Used by permission.
[13] From *The Kindergartner*, Graded Press, copyright © 1969. Used by permission.

Taste

Strawberries red and peach ice cream
And tiny chocolate cakes;
Golden pancakes, honey-topped,
The kind my mother makes.

Smell

The clean sweet smell of summer rain,
Of snowy, new-washed clothes,
A fresh-plowed earth, a lilac tree,
A spicy yellow rose.

How pleasant are my senses all!
They truly serve me well—
My sense of *sight*, my sense of *sound*,
Of *touch* and *taste* and *smell!*

—*Beth Robertson*

NEW BABY[14]

We have a brand-new baby
At our house! Come look and see—
He's small and soft, and Mommy says
He sort of looks like me.

We waited and we planned for him;
We're glad as we can be.
I hope he will be happy, too,
With his big brother—me!

—*Carolyn Joyce*

I'M GLAD I'M WHO I AM[15]

I'm glad I'm who I am,
I like to be myself.
Even when I do the wrong thing,
I know I am the right person.

—*Jessie Orton Jones*

SONGS

RESTING SONG

(Tune: "The Bear Went Over the Mountain")
I see that *Tommy* is resting,
I see that *Alice* is resting,
I see that *Teddy* is resting
And *Mary* is resting too.

—*Josephine Newbury*

"ALL OF ME" (This song is found on page 87.)

"SOMETIMES I'M HAPPY" (This song is found on page 89.)

FINISH MY RHYME[16]
Naming the Parts of the Body
(Tune: "Twinkle, Twinkle Little Star")

If a bird you want to hear,
You have to listen with your *(ear)*.

If you want to dig in sand,
Hold the shovel in your *(hand)*.

To see an airplane as it flies,
You must open up your *(eyes)*.

To smell a violet or a rose,
You sniff the fragrance through your *(nose)*.

When you walk across the street,
You use those things called your *(feet)*.

East and West and North and South,
To eat or talk you use your *(mouth)*.

When all these things we said get dirty
You jump in the tub and make yourself purty!

WHERE IS OUR FRIEND?
(Tune: "Pawpaw Patch")

Where, oh where is our friend, Tommy?
Where, oh where is our friend, Tommy?
Where, oh where is our friend, Tommy?
Right over there with a striped shirt on.
or
Where, oh where is our friend, Mary?
Where, oh where is our friend, David?
Where, oh where is our friend, Alice?
We're glad they're here with us today.

(This last stanza may be used when it is necessary to call each child's name.)

FINGER PLAYS

MY FINGERS AND I[17]

One, a stick
Two, a "V."

---

[14]From *The Kindergartner*, Graded Press, copyright © 1970. Used by permission.
[15]From *Secrets*, by Jessie Orton Jones. Viking Press, 1945. Used by permission of the author.
[16]From *Parent-Teacher Guide #2 to Sesame Street* (Dec. 15, 1969). © Children's Television Workshop, 1970. Used by permission.
[17]From *Nursery Days*, Vol. 2, No. 3 (Nov. 9, 1969). Used by permission.

Three, and my hand
Looks like a tree.

Four fingers up—
It makes a fan.
All five, and look
There's just my hand!

—*Bette Killion*

TEN LITTLE FINGERS

I have ten little fingers,
And they all belong to me.
I can make them do things—
Would you like to see?

I can shut them up tight
Or open them out wide,
I can put them together
Or let them all hide.

I can make them jump high,
I can make them jump low,
I can lay them gently in my lap,
And leave them there just so.

—*Author unknown*

RELAXATION ACTIVITY

HANDS ON SHOULDERS

Hands on shoulders, hands on knees,
Hands behind you, if you please;
Touch your shoulders, now your nose,
Now your hair and now your toes;
Hands up high in the air,
Down at your sides, now touch your hair;
Hands up high as before,
Now clap your hands, one, two, three, four.

—*Author unknown*

RESOURCES

Directions for Making Silhouettes

The teacher selects a place in the room where a piece of newsprint (12″ × 18″) can be taped at the level of the child's head. The child stands in front of the paper with his left shoulder against the wall.

The teacher shines a bright light on the child, making a distinct shadow of the child's head. Holding the child's head very still, the teacher draws around his shadow, beginning with the facial features.

In order that the silhouette be an accurate likeness of the child, the teacher will need to place the drawing of the shadow on a piece of black construction paper and cut out her drawing. The black silhouette may then be pasted on white poster board with rubber cement.

This is a useful aid in helping the children recognize their distinct differences that make them unique individuals. The silhouettes also make very welcome gifts to the parents.

Directions for Making Hand and Footprints

Materials needed: Large cellulose sponge placed in a square cake pan; tempera paint (blue makes interesting prints); white construction paper.

Mix the tempera paint to a consistency that will be absorbed into the sponge. Experiment by trying your own hand first, placing it palm-side upon the sponge, and then with fingers loosely spread apart, placing it upon the paper. If the paint is the correct consistency, the lines in the hand will show in the print.

The method is identical for making the footprints. It usually works better if the child sits on a little chair in front of the sponge paint pad and places his bare foot on the pad without too much pressure. He can then lift his foot and put it carefully on the white paper. Experimenting will show each teacher what is needed to get the most effective prints.

Directions for Making Life-Size Self-Portrait

The child lies on his back on a large piece of heavy brown wrapping paper. The teacher draws around the child's body. This gives the child an outline of himself. He paints himself as he sees himself in a mirror.

As most four- and five-year-olds cannot manage scissors well enough for such a large cutting job, it is wise for the teacher to cut out the painted figure. The self-portrait makes a nice surprise for the child's family.

Collage

Cut out interesting pictures of young children doing all kinds of things and expressing a variety of feelings. Make a collage of these on a large piece of cardboard. (One side of a large corrugated box makes a sturdy background.)

Place a mirror in the middle of the finished collage. As the children view other children and their expressions, they can also see themselves. They may enjoy trying to imitate and identify children pictured in the collage.

"Every child possesses a basic urge to grow —a basic striving to become what he can become, to be more of himself, to become a fuller and more complete self. This becoming occurs within each individual's own private world; and the quality of the becoming depends on the richness of relationships, conditions and experiences characterizing this private world."[18]

BIBLIOGRAPHY

Children's Books

Brawley, Eleanor Riggins. *Lisa's Spring Baby*. Richmond: John Knox Press, 1969.

Brown, Myra Berry. *Amy and the New Baby*. New York: Franklin Watts, Inc., 575 Lexington Ave. 10022, 1965.

Cook, Melva. *The Thinking Book*. Nashville: Broadman Press, 1966.

Eng, Rita. *When You Were a Baby*, rev. ed. New York: Golden Press, 1961.

Fritz, Jean. *Growing Up*. Chicago: Rand McNally & Co., 1956.

Grayland, Valerie. *Baby Sister*. Chicago: Rand McNally & Co. 1965.

Green, Mary McBurney. *Is It Hard? Is It Easy?* New York: William R. Scott, 1960.

Keats, Ezra J. *Peter's Chair*. New York: Harper & Row, 1967.

Krasilovsky, Phyllis. *The Very Little Boy*. Garden City, New York: Doubleday & Co., 1958.

———. *The Very Little Girl*. Garden City, New York: Doubleday & Co., 1962.

Krauss, Ruth. *The Growing Story*. New York: Harper & Bros., 1947.

Lenski, Lois. *When I Grow Up*. New York: Henry Z. Walck, 1960.

McRoberts, Agnesann. *Two New Babies*. Racine, Wisconsin: Whitman Publishing Co., 1967.

Schlein, Miriam. *The Way Mothers Are*. Chicago: Albert Whitman & Co., 1963.

Schulz, Florence. *Nobody Else Is Just Like Me*. Richmond: John Knox Press, 1966.

OTHER RESOURCES

Audio-Visual Materials

Filmstrips—*Who Am I?*:
  "Joy of Being You"
  "Nothing Is Something to Do"
  "People Packages"
  "All Kinds of Feelings"
  "Do You Believe in Wishes?"

Available from:
Scholastic Kindle Filmstrips
902 Sylvan Ave.
Englewood Cliffs, N.J. 07632

Coronet Sound Filmstrips—*Discovering Your Senses*:
  "Your Eyes Are for Seeing"
  "Your Ears Are for Hearing"
  "Your Skin Is for Feeling"
  "Your Tongue Is for Tasting"
  "Your Nose Is for Smelling"
  "Your Senses Work Together"

Available from:
Coronet Films and Filmstrips
65 E. South Water St.
Chicago, Ill. 60601

Flat Pictures

Moods and Emotions
  This set of eight study prints is in full color, on cards sturdy enough to stand up on a picture rail. They are 13″ × 18″.

Available from:
The Child's World
P.O. Box 681
Elgin, Ill. 60120

Moods and Emotions (same title, but different pictures)

  This set is less expensive, but not all sixteen of the pictures are in full color. The size of these photographs is 12¼″ × 17″. A 40-page manual accompanies this picture set.

Available from:
David C. Cook Publishing Co.
School Products Division
Elgin, Ill. 60120

Songbook

Mister Rogers' Songbook by Fred Rogers. New York: Random House, 1970.

Recordings

Inslee, Joseph. *I Can*. Philadelphia: Fortress Press, 1969. (Record accompanies book.)

Hamilton, Lawrie. *The Growing-Up Book*. Philadelphia: Fortress Press, 1970. (Record accompanies book.)

Getting to Know Myself, by Hap Palmer

Available from:
Educational Activities
Freeport, N.Y. 11520

Movie

"Headstart to Confidence," 16 mm, black and white. This is a helpful movie to use with teachers and parents.

Available from:
Modern Talking Pictures Service Inc.
2000 "L" St., N.W.
Washington, D.C. 20036

---

[18]Gerthon Morgan, "Building Self-Esteem at Home and School." *Childhood Education*, Feb. 1962, p. 278.

4
Language Development

CREATIVE EXPRESSION AND LANGUAGE

"The spontaneous language of [young] children is often poetic in nature. Dorothy, telling about the little bird that had fallen out of the nest, said, 'The little bird was shivering with scaredness.' "[1]

The following are other examples which bear out the above quote:

"This is a very disappeary day. The snow is disappearing my sleeves."

"Waves are like weaving. They go over and under, over and under."

"Those clouds in the sky are hanging up to dry."

"My teeth stepped on my tongue."[2]

"A flood is when water gets real deep up."

To a teacher who had had laryngitis, a child asked, "Is your sound back?"

Commenting about a piece of instrumental music the class had just heard, a child said, "That sounded like marshmallow music."

"It is so many tomorrows ago I've forgotten when our baby was born."

After working a wooden inlay picture puzzle a child said, "I want to button up another one."

Having difficulty skipping, a child com-

---

[1] Sarah Hammond Leeper, *et al, Good Schools for Young Children,* rev. ed. (New York: The Macmillan Company, 1968), p. 199.

[2] Maryland State Department of Health and Mental Hygiene, Division of Maternal and Child Health. Child Care Guidelines No. 21, January 1972. Used by permission.

mented, "My feet have got the hiccups."

Leaning up against the teacher, a child commented, "You are so soft and fluffy."

Another child commented, "I am so excited my heart tickles."[3]

Kindergarten children need the encouragement of adults in expressing freely their thoughts and feelings verbally. They need to have the experience of dictating their thoughts to an adult who will manuscript their stories for them. The child who has his story written down for him begins to feel that what he has to say is important. He can also see what his ideas look like on paper, though he cannot read them. He looks forward to the time when he can write down his own thoughts. He begins to understand that the stories the teachers read from books are someone else's ideas.

If the adult ratio is sufficient, each child may have his own booklet containing his original stories, poems, and songs, with his own illustrations. This is one service parents can render in the group as volunteer aides.

An electric typewriter makes it possible for those children who are interested to type their stories after they dictate them to an adult. (For details, see the item in this chapter on the use of the typewriter.)

If individual storybooks cannot be made, a large class storybook on chart paper will serve many purposes. It will preserve for the group and their parents some of the special activities which they have enjoyed. The teacher will see that each child makes at least one contribution of a story or a poem for the book. Group efforts at creativity should also be included. This book might include pictures which the children have drawn or painted to illustrate the written accounts.

The teacher will manuscript the children's creative expressions for the book, using the same type of letter formation which the children will learn in first grade. This book will be read to the children just as any other storybook is read. At the end of the year the stories in this class book may be mimeographed and made into booklets to give to the parents—a cherished gift.

"Children cannot create out of a vacuum," says Natalie Cole. "They must have something to say and be fired to say it."[4] He must first have experiences of doing and being and feeling. These may be experiences the child has with his parents on some special occasion or experiences enjoyed by the group at school. Seasonal activities and those surrounding special days spark many literary creations among the children.

"Shared reading experiences by teacher and children make a major contribution to the classroom climate in their development of an interest in and enthusiasm for ideas and the imaginative use of language."[5]

The following are samplings of children's work, individual and group efforts.

(This trip was planned as a special treat for David while his mother was in the hospital with his new baby sister.)

MY TRIP TO WILLIAMSBURG[6]
by David Douthit

From Richmond we went to Surry. Then we went to the dock to get on the ferry. We rode all the way across to the other side of the James River.

Then we got to Williamsburg. First we parked at the movie house and saw the movie. The movie told us all about Williamsburg.

We got on a little bus and rode all about Williamsburg.

I liked the movie best, because I hadn't seen a cannon shoot before.

They shot a cannon outside. It really made a lot of noise.

Then we came home. My daddy and Aunt Madeline didn't have to cook supper. We went to a restaurant to eat.

Seasonal activities stimulate many kinds of expressions. Paige especially enjoyed the colors of the autumn leaves. She composed a tune for these words. It became a favorite song for the group for days.

---

[3]Quotes from children in the Demonstration Kindergarten of the Presbyterian School of Christian Education, Richmond, Virginia.

[4]Natalie Cole, *The Arts in the Classroom* (New York: The John Day Co., 1940), p. 3.

[5]Leonard Marsh, *Alongside the Child: Experiences in the English Primary School* (New York: Harper & Row, 1972), p. 96.

[6]Permission granted by David and his mother, Mrs. Nathan Douthit.

AUTUMN LEAVES[7]
by Paige Coffey

Leaves are falling,
Leaves are falling,
Turning colors, too.
Red and yellow,
Brown and orange,
They are pretty, too.

The little girl in the following story was really the author, Tessie, telling about her experiences on a warm day in Spring.

A SPRING STORY[8]
by Tessie Vries

Once upon a time there was a little girl named Jenny. She loved her poodle Ruff. One day they went outdoors to play. Ruff saw two butterflies and chased them. But they went so fast and so high that Ruff couldn't catch them.

When it was dark Jenny took Ruff and they went inside and played a game with her daddy.

This was a happy day.

The days before Halloween are filled with the products of the children's imaginations in their search to understand the mystery surrounding this special celebration.

THE WITCH AND THE PUMPKIN[9]
by Karis Berge

Once upon a time there lived a witch and a pumpkin in an old castle. And once when it was Halloween, the pumpkin went outside and saw some friends. Then the old witch came out and said, "Pumpkin, come in. It's time for Halloween."

And the pumpkin said, "Here comes another pumpkin we can play with."

They played Halloween and never stopped doing it, because they thought is was so much fun. So they had Halloween all the time in the castle.

Why not Christmas for the animals? Bryant's imagination expanded his world, as was evidenced by one of his stories.

CHRISTMAS FOR THE RABBIT AND DUCK[10]
by Bryant Childress

There was a duck who lived in a little cottage in the woods. One day he stopped to get a drink of water in the pond. Then he wanted to go back home because he was tired. Just then he heard a noise—Thump! He saw a little rabbit.

They became friends. Then it was Christmas and that snowy day they made a snowman. They went in the house to have hot chocolate.

It was soon night. They went under the couch to go to sleep. Then Santa Claus came. He brought the rabbit a bunch of carrots. He brought the duck a whole bunch of fish.

PAMELA'S FAMILY[11]
by Pamela Dent

Julie, my sister, goes to her school. I go to my school. It is kindergarten. Julie goes to nursery school.

Daddy goes to work and mother writes the checks. Mother puts on her lipstick and we go for little rides in the car.

We have a dog at home named Cider.

Julie and I play games and work puzzles. We also have books, a puppet, and dishes.

MY VISIT TO UNCLE SAM'S FARM[12]
by Holly Graham

This summer I went to visit my Uncle Sam. He had two horses, ten cows, and one bull. I rode on the horse. His name was Prince and he was a Tennessee Walking horse. The other horse's name was Thunder, just like ours in the kindergarten.

Uncle Sam had seven hens. He kept them in a hen house. It was a middle-sized house with a sign on the door. It said "Ladies."

I had a good time on the farm.

One day in early March a kindergarten teacher planned outdoor experiences which would help the children become more aware of the wind as a force of nature. She also wanted them to enjoy playing with the wind.

The children felt it blow in their faces, blow their hair, ripple streamers of crepe paper, and wave silk scarves as they ran against the wind.

---

[7]Used by permission of Paige's parents, Dorothy and John Coffey.

[8]Used by permission of Tessie's mother, Mrs. Britt Vries.

[9]Used by permission of Karis' father, Mr. Paul Berge.

[10]Used by permission of Bryant's mother, Mrs. Faye M. Childress.

[11]Used by permission of Pamela's mother, Mrs. W. H. Dent, Jr.

[12]Used by permission of Holly's mother, Mrs. Anne S. Graham.

They watched it tossing a kite. They observed that the branches of the trees waved about in the wind. They saw it blowing leaves and paper along on the ground. They discovered that the wind was everywhere and that it was strong.

After their romp in the wind, the children had a quiet time back in their classroom. They talked about what they had seen the wind doing and how it made them feel.

The teacher used the following poem to gather together and rephrase some of the children's thoughts.

THE WIND AT PLAY
by Anne Halladay

I like to push against the wind
When it goes blustering by.
I shut my eyes and duck my head
As leaves whirl to the sky.

It puffs at me and bumps at me—
Of course, 'tis all in fun—
Sometimes it gets in back of me,
And I just have to run.

This was just the needed stimulation for some of the children to express their thoughts in poetic form.

The following are samples of children's creations after such an outdoor experience on a windy, windy day:

I know the wind is there
It blows the trees,
And blows my hair.

—Cheryl Foster[13]

Wind, wind, blow my kite
In the air
And out of sight.

—Brian Wayne Epps[14]

Experiences with bubble-blowing stimulate conversation and monologues filled with picturesque, poetic language.

Such was the case with a small group of kindergarten children as they blew bubbles. Their spirits were high as they watched the bubbles bobbing about in the air, landing here and there, and disappearing. After the bubble blowing the children were still talking about their bubbles. The teacher, sensing their enthusiasm, picked up on one of the statements she

overheard: "bubbles, bubbles in the air."

"That sounds like the way a poem about bubbles would start," she commented. "Could anyone think of something else about the bubbles to add to 'bubbles, bubbles in the air'?"

The following poem was the result of the group's effort:

BUBBLES[15]

Bubbles, bubbles in the air;
Bubbles, bubbles everywhere.
Little bubble, where did you go?
I wish you'd stay
'Cause I loved you so!

—Kindergarten Class, Title I Program
Chesterfield County, Virginia

RAIN[16]

The rain is falling down,
It makes a drizzly sound,
Going drip, drop, drip, drop,
Tapping on the roof tops
And falling on the ground!

The next two examples of group efforts in creative writing in a kindergarten grew out of experiences centering around Thanksgiving.

The first was an effort to express gratitude to God for his creation:

WE ARE THANKFUL[17]

God is great and God is good—
He has made the world.
He has made the sun for daytime
And the moon and stars for nighttime.
We enjoy the things he has made.
We are glad and
We are thankful.
—*Kindergarten Class*
 Demonstration Kindergarten
 Presbyterian School of Christian Education
 Richmond, Virginia

---

[13]Used by permission of Cheryl's father, Mr. Camm G. Foster, Jr.
[14]Used by permission of Brian's mother, Mrs. Walter Epps.
Note: These two poems were created in the Matoaca Laboratory Kindergarten at Virginia State College, Petersburg, Virginia, Mrs. Jimmie L. Battle, teacher.

[15]Used by permission of the teacher, Mrs. Mary Elizabeth Jonas.
[16]Bristol Township School District, Pa. Kindergarten class, Wanda Guokas, teacher, 1970. Used by permission.
[17]The children began this psalm of praise with the first line of a familiar table blessing: "God Is Great and God Is Good."

The following "Thanksgiving Psalm" was composed by the children of a kindergarten class to have for use with their families at some appropriate time on Thanksgiving day. It was mimeographed, and the children mounted it on colored art paper. A letter of explanation accompanied the psalm. Those who wished to drew or painted pictures illustrating it.

PSALM OF THANKSGIVING [18]

Give thanks to God, for he is good.
He has made the earth and sky;
He gives rain for the earth.
He gives the sun for the day and the moon and
    stars for the night.
He has made all that lives on the earth.
Give thanks to God, for he is good.
We are his people;
We are children of God.
Give praise to him.
Tell of his love to all people.
Give thanks to God, for he is good.
Sing praises to him.

Besides producing stories and poems, young children need to become involved in creating other types of printed communication:

1. Recording special events such as an excursion or the celebration of a holiday or a child's birthday.
2. Dictating class news to be used in a news sheet for parents.
3. Dictating thank-you letters to persons who helped the group with some activity.
4. Making greeting cards: birthday, get well, or others.
5. Dictating notes to send to sick members of the class.
6. Dictating a get-acquainted letter to send to a new child in the kindergarten class.
7. Preparing invitations for some special occasion at kindergarten.
8. Dictating captions for child's art work.

---

[18]Kindergarten Class, Demonstration Kindergarten, Presbyterian School of Christian Education, Richmond, Virginia.
[19]Helen F. Robinson and Bernard Spodek, *New Directions in the Kindergarten* (New York: Teachers College Press, Columbia University, 1965), p. 187.
[20]Marguerita Rudolph and Dorothy H. Cohen. *Kindergarten—A Year of Learning* (New York: Appleton-Century-Crofts, 1964), p. 20.

Robison and Spodek have this to say about young children's creative language experiences:

"When children help to compose a letter, story, or book, the relationship between spoken language and written symbols seems more immediate and visible and children remember and understand better material which incorporates their own language."[19]

SPEAKING VOCABULARIES

Teachers in kindergarten capitalize on the children's interest in words:

    rhyming words,
    descriptive words,
    nonsense words, and
    action words.

As models for the children, teachers make use of good literature, both prose and poetry, in the classroom. They surround the children with a wealth of all kinds of words—big words, tongue-tickling words, singing words, words that make no sense, and words that open doors to new ideas and whet the listener's curiosity.

Along with a lush offering of stories and poems, the teacher needs to provide for the children opportunities "to exercise their expanding speech power . . . to experiment and be inventive with language, to engage in rhyming and to indulge in joking . . . to have opportunity for easy conversations with each other and with teachers, to do some arguing, and to express their ideas."[20]

ENLARGING VOCABULARY

Using a touch book or a box of scraps of materials, have the children use words telling how the materials feel to them. Responses will be varied as each child reacts to his sense of touch. After feeling a piece of corduroy cloth (with their eyes closed), a small group of children responded with the following descriptive words:

    scrubby
    furry
    curvy

bumpety
striped
slickish
soft
fuzzy
wavy
smoothish
ridgy

Playing with Descriptive Words

Let the children make up descriptive phrases using such word starters as:

"quiet as"
"slow as"
"soft as"
"fast as"
"heavy as."

Children will come up with interesting similies such as these:

"quiet as the stars coming out"
"quiet as a bunny's nose wriggling"
"quiet as the sunshine"
"quiet as a snowflake on my nose"
"quiet as a bubble blowing up"
or
"soft as a puppy's ear"
"soft as soapsuds all over you"
or
"heavy as a moonboot"
"heavy as an elephant's foot"
or
"slow as getting bigger"
"slow as my birthday"
"slow as catsup to put on my hamburger."

Rhyming Activities

Young children should have experiences in rhyming words. They need to hear lots of good poetry and to share in providing the rhyming words as poems are read to them.

Games may be created to "play with" words that rhyme. The teacher may say a word and let the children respond with a word that rhymes such as bat/cat, mother/brother, or dish/fish.

The following is an example of rhyming jingles in which the children supply the rhyming words:

ANIMAL BABIES[21]

One little kitten
    curled up on a mat
She is the baby of old mother _____ .
                    (cat)

Two furry cubs—
    a mischievous pair
They are the twins of mother _____ .
                    (bear)

Three curly-tailed piglets
    dancing a jig
Are the squealing babies of mother_____ .
                    (pig)

Four fluffy chicks
    scratching in a pen
They are the babies of old mother _____ .
                    (hen)

Five wriggly tadpoles
    swimming near a log
They are the babies of Mrs. _____ .
              (Bullfrog)

—Josephine Newbury

Conversation

Conversation thrives on experience. Children have to have something to talk about and a patient, interested listener to engage them in conversation.

As children arrive in the morning, many will have something to tell their teachers and their peers. The teachers need to be free to listen attentively to each child and *hear what he says.* But teachers should not always assume that all their children have adequate experiential backgrounds needed for good conversational practices.

Robison and Spodek suggest that "many children will require more interesting subjects for conversation, more first-hand experiences, more understandable absorbing ideas, before the forms of information exchange, discourse, and conversation can be improved."[22]

Work and play materials in learning cen-

---

[21]Used by permission of the author.
[22]Helen F. Robison and Bernard Spodek, *New Directions in the Kindergarten* (New York: Teachers College Press, 1965), pp. 171–172.

ters in the kindergarten encourage the children to talk with each other.

Puppets stimulate conversation and are particularly helpful with the more shy, self-conscious child. He forgets himself and talks for the puppet. In fact, he becomes the puppet.

Puppetry not only encourages the child to engage in conversation with other puppets, but gives him an opportunity to express his feelings as well.

Use of Telephones

Play telephones as well as real ones encourage conversation among children. It is imperative to have two phones of each kind. A young child will often carry on a one-sided conversation on a play telephone in the home center, sometimes talking for a long time. And then when he hangs up the receiver, he explains to the nearest person exactly what the "other person" said.

The battery operated telephones or walkie-talkies allow for real exchange of thoughts. Some local telephone companies have school demonstration sets of real telephones which may be borrowed for a period of time.

From time to time the teacher may telephone the children at home and engage them in a brief conversation. They delight in being called to the telephone and having someone think enough of them to take time to call them. Most young children do not get enough experience in talking over the telephone.

MATCH-MAKER[23]
(An activity to stimulate conversation)
Number of Children: Two.

Preparation: Fill each of two bags with exactly the same objects.
Procedure: Child 1 puts his hand into one bag and finds something. He does not take it out; he does not look at it. He begins to describe how it feels. Child 2 puts his hand into the other bag and tries to find something that matches the description being given by his partner.

When Child 2 thinks he has the right object, he takes it out of the bag. The first child does the same, and they check to see if the objects match.

Using Action Words

The following poem is a good one to use when having the children listen for the "doing" (action) words.

After identifying the words ("sleeping," "creeping," "nibbling," and "scamper"), they will enjoy dramatizing the poem as the teacher reads it again to them. The words of this poem are also set to music. The song "The Old Gray Cat" is found on p. 115 in the song chapter of this text. At another time the children may be introduced to the song. The teacher may even prefer to use the musical version first.

THE OLD GRAY CAT[24]

The old gray cat is sleeping,
  sleeping, sleeping.
The old gray cat is sleeping in the house.

The little mice are creeping,
  creeping, creeping.
The little mice are creeping
  through the house.

The little mice are nibbling,
  nibbling, nibbling.
The little mice are nibbling
  in the house.

The little mice are sleeping,
  sleeping, sleeping.
The little mice are sleeping
  in the house.

The old gray cat comes creeping,
  creeping, creeping.
The old gray cat comes creeping
  through the house.
The little mice all scamper,
  scamper, scamper.
The little mice all scamper
  Through the house.

[23]John A. Wood and David K. Kravit, "Talking the Way to Reading—Conversation Pieces," printed in *Early Years*, November 1971, p. 43.
[24]Traditional.

Word Games

Word pairs with opposite meanings:

Different word games may be used as a brief transition activity.

Opposites: One game could deal with opposites. The teacher would suggest a word and someone in the group would give the opposite. Examples could be:

up/down	night/day
hot/cold	big/little
in/out	over/under
near/far	easy/hard
long/short	stop/go
high/low	

Words that begin alike

Initial sounds: No formal instruction is given in phonics, but children will pick up sounds informally in many different activities as the situations arise.

Games are an informal way to help the children become aware of the sounds in the words they speak.

The teacher may explain that he or she is going to say a word and wants the children to think of a word that begins in the same way. At first the teacher may need to illustrate by saying several words with the same initial sound. Examples might be:

> box, boy, boat
> hat, house, hand
> cat, coat, cow

The song " 'M' Is for Mary," on page 85 in the song chapter of this text, can be used in this way. See the directions given with the song.

Picture matching—initial sound

Print the alphabet in large capital letters on nine strips of cardboard (3 letters each to 8 boards). The letters should be scrambled.

Paste on cards at least 4″ × 6″ pictures of things beginning with the initial sounds of the letters. (Avoid the consonant blends such as cheese, tree, or clock.)

The children may line the cardboards out on the floor and then place the cards under the correct letter, matching the initial sound of the object pictured with the letter on the card as:

rat	boat	top	puppy	kite
rabbit	ball	tent	pig	kitten
radio	bird	typewriter	pie	kitchen

Cinquain

CLOUDS [25]

Very fragile
Slowly passing by
Cotton balls of white
Fluffy

—Vay Saurs

CAT EYES [26]

Bright
Intently Staring
Looking carefully about
Watching every move made
Glowing

—Vay Saurs

THE LION [27]

Ruler
Fierce hunter
Attacks on sight
King of the jungle
Majestic

—Vay Saurs

GRASS [28]

Emerald green
Short and stubby
Cold, crisp, and crunchy
Delightful

—Vay Saurs

Cinquain, pronounced sin-kān, is a five-line form of poetry:

> first line—one word which may be the title
> second line—two descriptive words
> third line—three action words
> fourth line—four words expressing feeling
> fifth line—a synonym of the first word.

---

[25] and [26]Used by permission of the author and her mother, Mrs. Rosetta Saurs.

[27] and [28]Used by permission of the author and her mother, Mrs. Rosetta Saurs.

LISTENING SKILLS

"To listen well is as powerful a means of influence as to talk well, and is as essential to all true conversation."—Proverb.

Just as young children vary widely in their abilities to communicate with words, they also vary decidedly in their listening skills.

The child's listening skills play an important role in his language development. It is through listening that he acquires much of his vocabulary, learns acceptable enunciation and inflection, and picks up proper sentence structure.

Because of this the kindergarten program should provide opportunities for helping each child to sharpen his skill in purposeful and thoughtful listening. The teacher will endeavor to meet each child's needs in developing good listening habits and will provide daily opportunities for different kinds of listening:

for directions,
for information, and
for pleasure.

The following are representative of activities which will sharpen the child's listening skills:

playing games developed for sharpening listening skills
listening for likenesses and differences in sounds
following directions
listening to stories and poems
participating in dramatic play
listening to sounds indoors and outdoors
listening to music
participating in group discussions
listening to recorded materials at the listening post
using telephone and walkie-talkie
participating in conversation with peers and teachers
listening to directions for a game
recording on tape their voices and listening to themselves
engaging in participation songs.

EXPERIMENTING WITH LETTERS

By the time many children are five years old, they have had play experiences with letters of the alphabet. Such experiences might have been with alphabet blocks or with the alphabet printed on their own chalkboard. They may have had a large alphabet picture book or played with magnetic letters and a metal board such as those produced by commercial toy companies.

Television has contributed its share in making young children more aware of the letters of the alphabet.

Whatever their background, kindergarten children enjoy playing with letters.

Commercial sets of both upper and lower case letters are available in large sizes, easily manipulated by small hands. These letters are made of a variety of materials—wood, felt, rubber, plastic, cardboard, and sandpaper.

Some letters will stand up, some may be used on felt boards, while others are magnetized for use on metal boards.

For good manipulative experiences with these three-dimensional letters, the children should have opportunities to play with different types of letters. They should be free to just "mess around" with the letters in ways that interest them.

They will begin to make exciting discoveries on their own, as one five-year-old did when he had laid the letters on the floor in alphabetical order. "Come quick, everybody! There's a word right in the middle of the alphabet!"

Everyone crowded around to see the word "NO" which had just been discovered "right in the middle of the alphabet"!

One of the first things a child will do will be to try to make his own name using the letters. He may then find other children's names on responsibility charts and try to "spell" these names too.

The more ambitious child will then look about the room for other words to make with the letters. He may see the traffic signs being used in the block building center. He will look at a label under a child's painting which might read "My pet."

Then there is the child who seeks out an adult, asking how to spell "mother" or "I am having fun."

This is the beginning of reading printed symbols for this child, for it is believed now that the child "writes" before he reads.

Plastic Magnetized Letters

Large plastic magnetized letters are easy for the kindergarten child to manipulate. They can be purchased in a single color or in white. The teacher can make several metal boards so that a group may play together at a table, helping each other. Large *tin* cookie sheets are excellent for this activity. The teacher should cover the playing side of the cookie sheet with plain contact paper of a dark color. This eliminates the glare from the plain tin sheet and is, of course, more attractive and makes a good contrast in background for the letters.

Sandpaper Letters

The teacher may cut letters from coarse sandpaper and mount them on heavy cardboard or pieces of masonite. As the children finger these letters they have the added tactile sensory experience to support their visual understanding of the shapes of letters.

Matching Outline Letters

Cards with the outline of the large wooden or rubber letters are useful for the child in matching the letter to the outline. This also helps develop the child's sense of spatial relationships.

Electric Typewriter

The electric typewriter may be used for exploring letters, in matching them, and in typing brief stories which the child first dictates to an adult. The adult manuscripts the child's story for the child to copy in type. The typewriter should have large, Primer face type—letters in manuscript writing.

Games may also be played with letters of the alphabet. The following is an example of a game the teacher can make:

Alphabet Lotto

Two different sets may be made—one for upper case letters and the other for lower case letters.

Materials needed: 4 pieces of heavy cardboard cut 9″ × 9″ and ruled off into 9 equal squares, 3″ each.

A package of cardboard letters about 2″ high, available from educational equipment companies.

Directions for making: With a felt pen, draw around a different letter on each section of the playing boards as shown here:

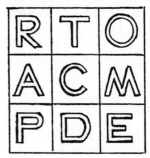

Directions for playing: This game is limited to four players, each with a playing board. The letters are placed in a box or a bag so that they can not be seen. Each child in turn draws a letter, identifies it, and matches it to the letter outline on his board if he has it. If not, he places the letter in another container to be put back in the drawing receptacle when it is empty. Or, to move the game faster, if a child draws a letter he does not have on his board, he may place it on the board of the player who has the letter.

CATEGORIZING

The young child needs many different kinds of experiences in categorizing materials. This activity is also treated in the chapters on science and math.

The kinds of things which the child can categorize are limited only by his environment and his knowledge of it.

A group project might deal with the four basic food groups. The Dairy Council produces materials to help young children understand the values of eating from the "basic four foods" each day. The children may be asked to bring magazine pictures of meat and poultry, fruits and vegetables, milk and milk products and eggs, and breads and cereals. Four large sheets of paper may be taped in a place convenient for the children to work on. They may paste the pictures of the kinds of foods found in each group on the appropriate sheets of paper.

Greeting Cards

Another type of categorizing may be done with used greeting cards—birthday, Christmas, Valentine. Be sure that there is a clearly identifiable symbol in addition to the printed words on each card.

Shoe boxes may be labeled with pictures indicating the type of card for each box. Several children may participate in this activity at a time, then they may check each other to be sure each card was placed in the correct box.

Seasonal Pictures

The children's parents may be notified of the need for magazine pictures representing cold weather and warm weather scenes. They can encourage and help their children look for the pictures.

Two large sheets of wrapping paper may be placed so that they are easily accessible to the children. They may tape the pictures where they think they belong. This kind of activity stimulates small group conversation, and may be used to let the children who worked on the categorizing report to the class why they made the selections which they did.

Booklets

Pages from large wallpaper sample books may be removed and stapled together to make individual booklets of eight or ten pages.

One booklet might be for pictures of *things that move on wheels.*

Another booklet might be on *fruits,* while another might be on *babies.*

Individual booklets might include *colors*— a different color for each page. The child could use a box of kindergarten crayons and make a different colored mark on each page. He would then hunt for pictures to go on each page according to the color.

Matching "Go-Togethers"

Pictures of objects may be pasted on cards and the cards mixed up. The child has to find the things that go together and place them side by side. Pictures might include:

ball/bat
shoe/sock
knife/fork
cup/saucer
letter/postage stamp

Rebus Story

The teacher manuscripts the story on large chart paper, leaving out words that can be replaced by pictures of the person, place, animal, or object in the story.

The pictures are then inserted in the right places in the story. This not only makes an interesting looking story, but the children, reading the pictures, can fill in the omitted words as the teacher reads the story. (The pictures may be outline drawings or pictures cut from magazines or catalogs.)

Word Pictures

Children will enjoy thinking about words. The teacher may ask them to tell *what they think of* or *what they see* when they hear a word. Examples:

winter/wind
sticky/soft
hand/circus

"I'm Thinking of . . ."

The child who is chosen the leader thinks of an object that is in plain sight in the room. He whispers it to the teacher. Then he begins to describe it without giving its name or looking at it.

The children try to see how quickly they can guess the name of the object the leader is thinking of. The first one to guess correctly becomes the leader and thinks of and describes another object for the group to guess. An example:

"I'm thinking of something that is square. It has to be plugged into electricity to make it run. You put something round on it and you hear a story or sometimes music." (record player)

Riddles

Making up riddles helps children to describe something accurately without giving its name. They become more familiar with words describing shape, texture, size, and locomotion. Examples are:

I am big.
I have a coat of fur.
I eat berries and fish.
I sleep all winter in a cave.

(bear)

I am little.
My coat is made of fur.
I have a long, bushy tail.
I hide nuts for winter.
I live in the trees.

(squirrel)

I am round.
I am different colors.
Children like to play with me.
I can roll and I can bounce.

(ball)

Naming Parts of the Body

Children sit in a circle. The leader begins by touching a part of his body and naming it, saying, "This is my thumb." Everyone imitates the leader. He then calls the name of another child who touches a different part of his body and says its name. The group does as he does. And the game progresses. Children should be encouraged to speak in sentences.

This is a good game to plan at the beginning of the school year while the children are learning each other's names.

As the children try to think of different names of the body parts, they will become more aware of themselves.

The vocabulary for this simple game might include: thumb, thumbnail, finger, hand, wrist, arm, elbow, shoulder, neck, head, forehead, cheek, jaw, eye, nose, mouth, hair, ear, chest, back, hip, leg, knee, ankle, foot.

BOOKS FOR YOUNG CHILDREN

Books stir the imagination and help the child to retain an open receptive attitude to ideas, but above all they enrich his imagination and encourage him to extend his awareness of feelings. Books are in this sense companions, and the teacher, provided that he is also a reader in the classroom, can join forces with the book and accompany children into experiences just as valuable as those arising at first hand.[29]

Books are . . .
Pictures   Color
People   Excitement
Places   Recognition

Books DELIGHT when
—illustrations are lively
—humor is based on what children know
—they excite curiosity about what happens
—they play upon a fascination with words
Books REASSURE children when
—they are read by a warm and interested adult
—they present the familiar and the real
—they can be looked at and heard again and again
—they can be talked about
—they give children time to form ideas and concepts
Books TELL young children about
—themselves
—the world
—the feelings and thoughts of others
Books HELP young children to
—clarify, associate, and extend ideas
—expand vocabulary
—talk about ideas and feelings.[30]

Of greatest importance in the classroom environment for stimulating the child's interest in books and reading is the teacher and his or her attitude toward books and reading. By showing pleasure and appreciation for books and interest in reading, the teacher is setting a worthy example for the child to emulate.

The teacher will arrange in a light, cheerful corner of the kindergarten room a library center for the children. Near the shelves on which the books are displayed there should be a small table around which several children may gather and enjoy "reading" and discussing their picture books. The teacher exercises judgment in the number and kinds of books that are available for the children at one time. Once or twice a week, the teacher will also put out books which are new to the children. Books of which the children have tired should be put away for a while.

Occasionally, when a child asks questions about something, the teacher will go to a book and, through pictures and a story, help the child

---

[29]Leonard Marsh, *Alongside the Child: Experiences in the English Primary School* (New York: Harper & Row, 1972), p. 79.
[30]Maryland State Department of Health and Mental Hygiene, Division of Maternal and Child Health. Child Care Guidelines No. 21 (January 1972), p. 1. Used by permission.

discover the answer. In this way the child begins to understand that besides finding enjoyment in books, we also gain information we need from them.

Many of the best books for young children have been recorded on tape and records. A listening post affords a number of children the opportunity to listen to the story as they look at the book. The headphones make it possible for the children to listen to the story with all other noises blocked out. And children working in other learning centers are not disturbed by the story.

As the child hears fascinating stories read from books, and as he himself looks at books, he comes to realize that books provide fun, and that within their pages new and exciting experiences await him. His curiosity is thus aroused to discover the meaning of printed symbols.

Helen Heffernan says, with regard to stimulating the child's interest in reading:

> The good teacher fosters esthetic enjoyment in countless situations, but again and again she will turn to the right book or story to enhance or crystallize a group experience, to afford outlet for mood or emotion, to intensify a new interest.
>
> It is through such functional beginnings that children learn to delight in literature. Thus before they can read for themselves they taste the satisfaction of adventuring imaginatively within the covers of a book, a taste which sometimes whets an insatiable appetite of lifelong duration.[31]

Picture Books (not included in other listings)

Alain. *The Elephant and the Flea.* New York: McGraw-Hill, 1956.

Beskow, Elsa. *Pelle's New Suit.* New York: Harper & Row, 1929.

Bryant, Bernice. *Let's Be Friends.* Chicago: Childrens Press, 1954.

Burton, Virginia Lee. *Mike Mulligan and His Steam Shovel.* Boston: Houghton Mifflin Co., 1939.

Cerf, Bennett. *Bennett Cerf's Book of Laughs* (1959), *Bennett Cerf's Book of Riddles* (1960), *More Riddles* (1961). Westminster, Md.: Beginner Books.

---

[31]Helen Heffernan, ed., *Guiding the Young Child* (Boston: D. C. Heath & Co., 1959), p. 130.

Eastman, Phillip D. *Are You My Mother?* Westminster, Md.: Beginner Books, 1960.

Flack, Marjorie. *Ask Mister Bear.* New York: The Macmillan Co., 1958.

———. *The Story About Ping.* New York: The Viking Press, 1933.

———. *Wait for William.* Boston: Houghton Mifflin Co., 1935.

Friskey, Margaret. *Johnny and the Monarch.* Chicago: Childrens Press, 1961.

———. *Mystery of the Gate Sign.* Chicago: Childrens Press, 1958.

———. *Mystery of the Magic Meadow.* Chicago: Childrens Press, 1968.

Gag, Wanda. *Millions of Cats.* New York: Coward-McCann, 1938.

Hawkinson, Lucy. *Picture Book Farm.* Chicago: Children's Press, 1971.

Keats, Ezra Jack. *A Letter to Amy.* New York: Harper & Row, 1968.

———. *The Little Drummer Boy.* New York: The Macmillan Co., 1968.

———. *Peter's Chair.* New York: Harper & Row, 1967.

———. *Whistle for Willie.* New York: The Viking Press, 1969.

Lakritz, Esther. *Randy Visits the Doctor.* Nashville: Broadman Press, 1962.

Lenski, Lois. *Davy Goes Places.* New York: Henry Z. Walck, 1961.

———. *When I Grow Up.* New York: Henry Z. Walck, 1960.

McCloskey, Robert. *Make Way for Ducklings.* New York: The Viking Press, 1941.

Wolff, Janet. *Let's Imagine Being Places.* New York: E. P. Dutton & Co., 1961.

Woods, Ruth. *Little Quack.* Chicago: Follett Publishing Co., 1961.

Zion, Gene. *Harry the Dirty Dog.* New York: Harper & Row, 1956.

Books for Children

Baer, Edith. *The Wonder of Hands.* New York: Parents' Magazine Press, 1970.

Borten, Helen. *Do You Know What I Know?* New York: Abelard-Schuman, 1970.

Brawley, Eleanor Riggins. *Lisa's Spring Baby.* Richmond: John Knox Press, 1969.

Brown, Margaret Wise. *A Pussycat's Christmas.* New York: Thomas Y. Crowell Co., 1949.

Bulla, Clyde Robert. *What Makes a Shadow?* New York: Thomas Y. Crowell Co., 1962.

Daly, Eileen. *Butterfly: A Story of Magic.* Racine, Wisconsin: Western Publishing Co., Inc., 1969.

Garelick, May, and Weisgard, Leonard. *Where Does the Butterfly Go When It Rains?* New York: Scholastic Book Services, 1970.

Gibson, Myra Tomback. *What Is Your Favorite Smell, My Dear?* New York: Grosset & Dunlap, 1964.

Hoban, Russell. *A Baby Sister for Frances,* New York: Harper & Row, 1964.

Holland, Vicki. *We Are Having a Baby*. New York: Charles Scribner's Sons, 1972.

Keats, Ezra Jack. *Pet Show!* New York: The Macmillan Co., 1972.

Krauss, Ruth. *The Growing Story*. New York: Harper & Row, 1947.

Palazzo, Tony. *Let's Go to the Circus*. Garden City, N.Y.: Doubleday & Co., 1961.

Prokofieff, Serge, and Palazzo, Tony. *Peter and the Wolf*. Garden City, New York: Doubleday & Co., 1961.

Rand, Ann and Paul. *I Know a Lot of Things*. New York: Harcourt Brace Jovanovich, 1956.

Schlein, Miriam. *Laurie's New Brother*. New York: Abelard-Schuman, 1961.

———. *The Way Mothers Are*. Chicago: Albert Whitman & Co., 1963.

Scott, Ann Herbert. *Sam*. New York: McGraw-Hill, 1967.

Tresselt, Alvin R. *I Saw the Sea Come In*. New York: Lothrop, Lee & Shepherd Co., 1954.

Tudor, Tasha. *Pumpkin Moonshine*. New York: Henry Z. Walck, 1962.

Woodard, Carol. *It's Nice to Have a Special Friend*. Philadelphia: Fortress Press, 1970.

Zaffo, George J. *The Giant Nursery Book of How Things Change*. Garden City, N.Y.: Doubleday & Co., 1968.

Zemach, Harve, ed. *Mommy, Buy Me a China Doll*. Chicago: Follett Publishing Co., 1966.

Zolotow, Charlotte. *Wake Up and Goodnight*. New York: Harper & Row, 1971.

———. *William's Doll*. New York: Harper & Row, 1972.

FORMAL READING

Kindergarten teachers are frequently under pressure by parents and the community to teach the children to read. Popular publications guarantee that even baby can be taught to read!

Quite a few children do learn to read at age four or five. But the question should be raised, "Is this the wisest use of the child's time at this age?"

Kindergarten children are "reading" constantly in their own way as five-year-olds—reading their environment, observing likenesses and differences and relationships. They "read" pictures in books and their favorite television programs. They "read" magazine covers, the calendar, illustrated displays in the supermarket or corner drug store. Observant, curious young children begin to read such signs as "stop," "go," "hot," "cold," "in," "out," "push," "pull." They read the names of their favorite breakfast cereals and the signs on the filling stations their parents patronize.

Teachers need to capitalize on what the children are ready for *now* and tailor language activities to fit their needs. Providing the children with a learning environment in which to enjoy those experiences for which they are now ready will mean that the children live richly each today. This is the best utilization of the child's time and energies in the important days before he is ready to read printed symbols on the pages of books.

A wise program for five-year-olds will have no time for "reading readiness" workbooks and hectographed exercises and drills. Such materials as those which have the child color the little house red or put a mark on the tallest boy in the row or draw a circle around the ducks that are just alike are artificial activities which waste the school's money and the children's and teachers' time. In the day's program they displace the good learning activities which five's could be enjoying. They crowd out those enriching experiences which the children should be having *now* because they are ready for them *now*.

A good kindergarten program offers the children a variety of firsthand and vicarious experiences. Paul Witty points out the following contribution which these experiences make to the children's formal reading activities:

"Experiences help children understand the material they are going to read in school. The more understanding and information a child can *bring to a book*, the more he will *get out of it*. The more varied a youngster's experiences, the more meaning there will be in what he reads."[32]

OTHER RESOURCES

Puppets

All kinds of puppets are useful in stimulating conversation among young children. There are face puppets, hand puppets, finger puppets, and stick puppets.

Hand puppets may be made of socks or paper bags. They may be made with Styrofoam heads. Stick puppets may be made on tongue depressors or dowels, using flat pictures of the

[32]Paul Witty. *Helping Children Read Better*. Chicago: Science Research Associates, p. 11.

characters or stuffing paper bags and inserting the dowels. Finger puppets may be made on the fingers cut from women's gloves, or paper puppets may be attached to a small length of masking tape made into a roll with the sticky side out. The tape slips over the puppeteer's fingers and holds the paper puppet in place.

Recorded Stories

Recorded stories may be used by an individual child or a small group at the listening post, or may be enjoyed by the entire group.

The following sound filmstrips have accompanying records which may also be used in the listening center, with or without books.

Sound Filmstrips of Children's Literature

"Andy and the Lion," by James Daugherty
"Angus and the Ducks," by Marjorie Flack
"The Biggest Bear," by Lynd Werd
"Blueberries for Sal," by Robert McCloskey
"Brown Cow Farm," by Dahlov Ipcar
"Caps for Sale," by Esphyr Slobodkina
"Danny and the Dinosaur," by Syd Hoff
"Harold and the Purple Crayon," by Crockett Johnson
"Lentil," by Robert McCloskey
"Make Way for Ducklings," by Robert McCloskey
"Mike Mulligan and His Steamshovel," by Virginia Lee Burton
"Peter's Chair," by Ezra Jack Keats
"The Snowy Day," by Ezra Jack Keats
"The Story About Ping," by Marjorie Flack
"The Tale of Peter Rabbit," by Beatrix Potter
"A Tree Is Nice," by Janice May Udry
"Where Does the Butterfly Go When it Rains?" by May Garelick
"Whistle for Willie," by Ezra Jack Keats.

The above are a few of the sound filmstrips available from:

Weston Woods
Weston, Conn. 06880

A number of the above named books have also been made into 16 mm films by Weston Woods. They are usually available for loan from local and state departments of education.

Activity Records (with directions)

Learning Basic Skills Through Music, Vol. 1, by Hap Palmer
Learning Basic Skills Through Music—Building Vocabulary, by Hap Palmer

Available from:
Educational Activities, Inc.,
Freeport, L.I., N.Y. 11520

Wooden Inlay Puzzles

Puzzles of varying difficulty to allow for the differences of ability in the group and the growth that takes place.

Sequence Puzzles

Complete stories cut into separate episodes for the children to arrange into meaningful sequence.

Available from:
General Learning Corporation
Early Learning Division
310 N. Second St.
Minneapolis, Minn. 55401

Flannel Board

Flannel letters or textured-backed cardboard letters.

Letters of the Alphabet

Rubber, wooden, plastic, or magnetized—upper and lower case.

Magnetic Board

Telephones

Real or battery powered.

Tell-Again Story Cards

Level II. Louise Binder Scott. Webster Division, McGraw-Hill Book Co., 1967. (May be used to tell the story—later allow children to arrange the picture cards in correct sequence.)

Tape Recordings

Commercial and teacher-made.

Pictures for Categorizing

Typewriter

With Primer typeface (large-size type).

Chart for Printing Children's Original Stories

Language Games

5
Experiencing Music and Movement with Young Children

The nimble foot, the hankering hand,
The itching mind, the yearning heart,
The vibrant voice, the scintillating eye,
The creative spirit—the child![1]

There is nothing more constant in the life of the young child than sound and movement. Consequently, there is no time in which music is so integrated with life as in the early years.[2]

With ease and naturalness music can flow in and out of the day's program for young children. Emphasis is on the *joy* which the music experiences bring the young child; performance and the achievement of techniques and perfection are never the aim with this age group.

Good music experiences for young children include a balanced combination of sound, movement, song and story, and drama. Many music experiences are spontaneous and may occur any time during the day. In order that this

may happen, the teacher provides ample space, varied materials for sound-making, props for dramatization, and offers freedom for exploring the vast possibilities of music forms.

The teacher will be aware of the spontaneous opportunities for using music with the children, but will also plan carefully for several different kinds of music activities for each session. He or she provides for variety and new experiences as well as the "old favorites" the children always enjoy.

SINGING

When children feel free and comfortable, they will just bubble into song or chant as they work and play. On occasion the teacher might record a child's spontaneous song and use it with the group at some later time. However, as

[1]Gladys Andrews, *Creative Rhythmic Movement for Children,* © 1954. Reprinted by permission of Prentice-Hall, Inc., Englewood Cliffs, N.J.
[2]Mary J. Nelson in *Music for Children's Living* (Washington, D.C.: Association for Childhood Education International, 1955), p. 11.

Emma Sheehy says:

> It is important that these beginnings of music making should focus on the constant encouragement of this *way of expressing himself* and not on the product itself. . . . What is important is not the preservation of any special song that a child creates, but the preservation of a way of life that will keep on inspiring him to experiment freely.[3]

Conversational singing has special appeal for young children. Sometimes the teacher can save a child or a group from a tense situation by singing lightly brief counsel or comments. With a little ingenuity and imagination, the teacher can improvise these chants with ease. Musical questions by the teacher will frequently stimulate a child to "set his answer to a tune." The more creative the teacher is in the use of songs, the more creativity the children evidence in their responses.

There is such a wealth of good songs for young children's singing today that the teacher can help the group build an interesting repertoire that will serve them well in school and out.

There are songs relating to all aspects of the child's life: there are nonsense songs and story songs, musical finger plays and action songs, as well as simple folk-dance songs and dramatic songs—all of which add to the young child's "growing edge" in the developmental process in which he is so vigorously involved.

In selecting songs for young children to sing, the first consideration should be given to the range of the melody. It should generally fall between middle C and D above high C. The following criteria may be used in selecting songs for use with this age group:

1. The song should be truly artistic.
2. It should be short and simple.
3. It should have a definite and unchanging rhythm, with some phrase repetition.
4. The music should fit the mood and thought of the words.
5. It should carry one main idea.
6. It should relate to the child's experiences.

---

[3]Emma Sheehy, *There's Music in Children* (New York: Henry Holt & Co., 1952), p. 56.

Teaching a New Song

When a song which is to be taught is in line with the mood and interest of the group, there is little need to talk about it. Often introductory discussions detract from the song itself. A new song should be sung to the children from beginning to end without accompaniment. It should be sung correctly and distinctly, so that the children hear the right melody along with the words. The children will often respond with an enthusiastic request, "Sing it again!"

The teacher may suggest that as the children listen this time, they might look for the word pictures they hear in the song. Or they may listen for the action words. For example, "What do you hear the cat in the song doing?" (Purring, creeping, etc.)

The teacher's own voice is the most effective way of insuring that the children will respond in light, relaxed voices.

Much of young children's singing should be done without accompaniment. It is easier for the children to match the teacher's voice than an instrument; then, too, they are apt to become too dependent upon the instrument. After the children have become quite familiar with the song, they will enjoy singing it with the piano, autoharp, guitar, or violin. For teachers who have difficulty keeping on pitch, there are albums of recordings of the songs from most kindergarten songbooks in music education series published today.

Creative Songs by the Group

Sometimes an occasion arises when the group will create a tune for a jingle or a short poem.

This is what happened one morning in a kindergarten class in early spring. A child brought in a daffodil. After the group had talked about its being the first spring flower they had had in the kindergarten, the teacher repeated the following poem:

> A little yellow cup,
> A little yellow frill,
> A little yellow star,
> And that's a daffodil.
>
> —*Source unknown*

The children were fascinated and begged her to "Say it again." This time the teacher asked one of the children to point to each part of the daffodil as she repeated the poem.

Aware of the children's keen interest in the flower and the poem, she suggested, "Perhaps we can say it together this time—you and I."

Their response was enthusiastic, so the teacher thought she would push the experience one step further.

"That was fun," she commented. "You said it so well. Did you notice that the poem almost sings along as it describes the daffodil? I wonder if we couldn't make a tune for the poem so we could sing it? Let's think of the words, 'A little yellow cup,' and perhaps a tune for the words will come to someone's mind."

There was a moment's silence; then one of the children sang his tune. The teacher picked it up on the piano and quickly wrote it down. The same procedure was followed with each of the next two phrases.

The teacher then asked the children to listen carefully as she sang the first three phrases together so that they could think of a tune to finish the song.

Almost without hesitation, one little boy added the melody for the last phrase.

Below is the composite creation.

It is important for the teacher to remember that for young children singing is essentially an activity for fun and satisfaction. Keeping this in mind, as well as the developmental level of the young child, the teacher will not expect too much of the individuals in a group.

The teacher will accept the fact that some of the children will not have acquired much control of their singing voices and will never tell a child he cannot sing or eliminate him from the singing activities of the group. Rather, he or she will accept what the child is able to do and will give him encouragement and support while trying to help him raise his own standard

of achievement in ways that will build his self-esteem and his love for music.

Young children enjoy activities which involve them in distinguishing and responding to changes in the pitch of an instrument or a voice. They may indicate with their hands, by moving them in high and low motions to corresponding high or low notes as they are struck on the piano, resonator bells, or xylophone. A variation in response might include stretching their bodies high or bending down low in recognition of the level of pitch.

Activities in tone-matching help children to raise their singing voices. Such activities should never become formal music drills, but should always be used as fun games. One of the simplest of these is calling the children's names and having the group echo back just as the teacher sings them.

When the children become familiar with singing each other's names in this way, then the individual child may respond with "I am here," matching the tones used with his name as the teacher sings it.

Singing Games

Singing games have universal appeal for young children. They combine song, movement, and the elements of a simple group game into a musical fun activity.

Some of the favorites are: "The Farmer in the Dell," "Looby Loo," "Punchinello," "Fly, Little Blue Bird," "Here We Go 'Round the Mulberry Bush," and "London Bridge Is Falling Down."

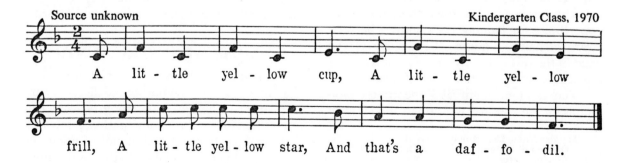

With those dances which involve the children in more vigorous activity, it is better to use recorded music. Young children experience shortness of breath with the physical activity of the game. This makes it difficult for them to sing while they dance.

Very simple square dances such as "Bingo," "Seven Jumps," and "The Hokey Pokey" may be used with the recordings. These dances help the child to orient himself in space, to follow directions, to participate in a group activity, and, best of all, to have fun with his friends.

LISTENING ACTIVITIES

The young child needs to develop skill in listening in order that he may become aware of sounds about him and learn to identify them accordingly.

Listening activities not only provide pleasure for the child, but also help to develop his auditory discrimination. As the group listens to various musical selections, the children will have opportunities for determining whether the music is sad or happy, slow or fast, loud or soft.

Children enjoy closing their eyes and guessing whether several children are marching or hopping, walking or skipping. The teacher may also ask the group to listen to several rhythm instruments playing at once and try to tell which ones are being played. They may also listen to a brief instrumental recording and see what "pictures" or stories they hear. They may respond with interpretations through bodily movement.

Listening to music stimulates the children's imagination. A five-year-old once responded to a light and airy composition by saying, "That sounded like marshmallow music."

The teacher will take advantage of every opportunity for helping the children become aware of nature's music—the melody of the wind in the trees, the rhythm of raindrops, the noises of insects, and the songs of birds.

The teacher might also record on tape sounds for the children to listen to and identify —such sounds as a bouncing ball, typing, clapping hands, pouring water, a ringing bell, a beating drum.

The records which accompany Margaret Wise Brown's books *The City Noisey Book* and *The Country Noisey Book* are entitled *Muffin in the City* and *Muffin in the Country*, respectively. These recordings are filled with familiar sounds found in the child's environment. It is exciting for him to be able to identify sounds without being able to see the objects making the sound.

Another listening activity which promotes growth in the child's auditory perception is the discovery of rhythm in words. To begin with, the teacher would help the children to recognize the number of syllables in their names. This is done by clapping as the name is called.

> Tom—one clap
> Betty—two claps
> Josephine—three claps
> Elizabeth—four claps

Rhythm sticks or the tone block may be used instead of or along with the clapping.

A rhythmic pattern may evolve by chanting two or more of the children's names along with the clapping as: Bet-ty, Jo-se-phine, Bet-ty, Jo-se-phine (__ __, __ __ __, __ __, __ __ __).

To involve the children more completely in this "listen-respond" activity, the teacher may suggest that they use their feet as well as their hands. Then they may add their heads to the movement.

After the children have enjoyed hearing the "beats" in their first names, their last names may be added. This will make a different rhythmic pattern. A game may be made out of this activity by having one child call the name of a friend. As he does, the group beats out the syllables. Then the child whose name was called calls out another child's name. The game proceeds until all the children have had a turn.

MUSICAL INSTRUMENTS

Instruments both commercial and home-made, are for the purpose of discovery and experimentation with seeing, hearing, handling; for discovery of vibration, pitch, tone quality, different techniques of usage; for experimentation with rhythm and sound.[4]

[4]Maryland State Department of Health and Mental Hygiene, Division of Maternal and Child Health. *Child Day Care Guidelines: Much About Music*, No. 14, April 1967.

Using musical instruments does not mean that there should be a rhythm band "so that the children can learn to keep time." If children have opportunities to use their bodies freely in creative rhythmic activities, and if they have instruments to use as individuals and in small groups in ways that are interesting to them, then they will not have to *learn* to keep time. They *will* keep time.

Rhythm band activities which train young children to function together in set patterns tend to make it difficult for the children to use instruments creatively. Rhythm band activities do for children what "coloring in" hectograph pictures does—they stifle imagination, impose adult standards upon the children, and limit the individual's response according to his own feelings.

Musical instruments make a significant contribution to the music experiences of kindergarten children in many ways.

The following are given only to suggest a few activities which teachers might provide. A creative teacher and group will discover many more.

1. Children enjoy experimenting with instruments in the music center. They will discover likenesses and differences in pitch and resonance.

2. Children may use instruments as sound effects in dramatizing stories such as "The Boy and His Goats." This will mean that the children should first have the opportunity to discover which instruments make the appropriate sounds to accompany each character in the story.

3. A child may beat on the drum a rhythmic pattern to which a group of children may respond with clapping or body movement. The teacher might pick up the child's rhythm and improvise an accompaniment on the piano, sometimes using only the black keys for this.

4. The teacher may use a selected group of instruments which "talk to the children." For example, before beating the drum or the tone block, he or she may explain to the group that the instrument will tell them how to move about the room. The teacher may make short little taps in a fast tempo, beat out a slow, heavy pattern, or mix the tempo and the weight of the beat. Stopping suddenly adds interest to this activity and helps the child to gain control of his body in response to the music.

Young children enjoy responding to the "directions of the tambourine" in moving parts of their bodies, then in total body response. The teacher may suggest that the children move as the tambourine speaks to them. He or she may "tap-shake," "shake-tap," or give continuous taps or continuous shakes. The children should be free to respond in motions as they hear the message of the instrument.

Resonator bells, a xylophone, or the piano may be used to give direction for the levels of bodily movement as high/low, up/down. Beginning with the children down on the floor "as low as they can get," the teacher may tap out the notes of an octave, say from middle C to high C. The children respond by gradually rising, a little with each note, to their tallest height. Then the order may be reversed. By sliding the finger over the keys or a mallet over the xylophone, a continuous motion is suggested. Tapping middle C then high C and back to middle C with pauses in between helps the children not only to hear but to feel the difference in pitch as they respond with appropriate bodily movements.

5. Sometimes a small group may use a few appropriate instruments to accompany a song. An example might be the song "Hickory, Dickory, Dock." Tapping rhythm sticks or a tone block might represent the ticking of the clock. The striking of the cymbal could represent the clock striking one o'clock, and the running of the mallet down the scale on the xylophone would represent the little mouse's quick retreat.

Maracas, large seed pods, or shakers containing rice could be used to accompany a song about rain.

6. If allowed to experiment with the instruments, young children will soon create interesting short melodies. Resonator bells provide excellent means for this type of experimentation. The teacher should number the bars of the bell set 1 through 8 according to the scale.

Here are examples of ways the bells may be used in creating simple tunes to original "lyrics" or short jingles.

7. Young children find real satisfaction in playing instruments to a short instrumental recording. After listening to the music, the chil-

dren should decide which instruments would sound best with the recording. As one small group uses the instruments, another group might respond with body movement.

It should be remembered that musical instruments may be used indoors and out, and the creative use of them will provide endless fun and all kinds of learnings for the children.

Commercial Instruments

Piano—not essential, but offers a dimension to music activities unequaled by any other instrument.

Record player—three speed; tempo control.

Autoharp—excellent for accompanying children because it "fills in" and supplements their voices as they carry the melody.

Drums of several types—tub drum, hand drum, and tom-tom.

Resonator bells—preferably chromatic set (20 bars). The 8-bar diatonic set has many uses, but is more limited than the larger set.

Toneblocks—hardwood square toneblock; gourd tone block.

Tambourine

Triangles

Cymbals

Finger cymbals

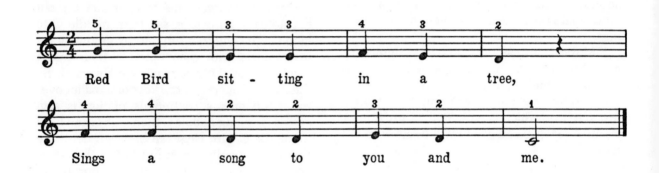

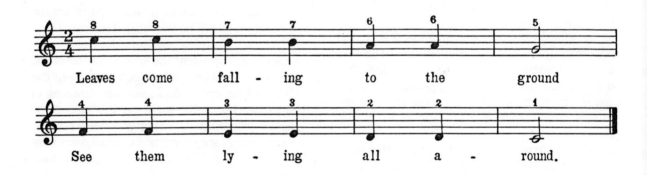

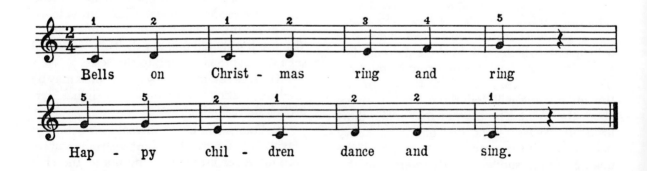

Ankle bells and wrist bells
Finger castanets
Hand bells of varying sizes and tone quality
Cowbell
Rhythm sticks and claves

Instruments from other cultures which add richness and variety to the music experiences in the kindergarten:

Africa:

Kalimba—hand-sized sound box with spring steel strips producing diatonic melodies—easily played by teacher or child. Called a hand piano.

India:

Brass bells

Mexico:

Bongo drum
Maracas
Guiros

Trinidad:

Steel drum

Hawaii:

Puili sticks—(21″ bamboo poles split into narrow strips which create a swishing sound when struck against floor or body)
Coconut shells cut in half

All the above mentioned instruments are usually available from local music stores or may be ordered from educational equipment distributors. (See listings at the end of the chapter.)

Some kindergartens will not be able to have too many of these instruments. But groups of classes could have a musical instrument center and pool their resources. The instruments could be available on a loan basis to those participating, much as books are checked out from a library. Kindergarten classes in public elementary schools would have access to many such instruments belonging to the school music library or center.

But every kindergarten should have available for the children such basic instruments as drum, maracas, rhythm sticks or claves, triangle, cymbals (hand and finger), tone block, tambourine, and bells of various kinds.

Noncommercial Instruments

Noncommercial instruments which the teacher can make should in no way take the place of good quality commercial musical instruments. They do, however, offer an added dimension of tones for creative uses with different music forms and activities. The variety of homemade musical instruments is limited only by the teacher's initiative and creativity.

The following are samples of homemade musical instruments:

Wooden bucket drum.

Materials needed: a wooden bucket or small keg, secondhand drum head, and upholstery tacks. Music companies often have large, damaged drum heads for sale at reasonable prices.

This drum head should be soaked in warm water for about an hour. The usable part of the drum head is then stretched tightly over the bucket and nailed securely. In order to be certain the head is stretched properly, it is essential that the hide be nailed from opposite sides, back and forth, all around the bucket. It is better for two people to do this so that the skin will be stretched evenly. A round fishing cork with a ¼ inch dowel run through it makes an effective drumstick. A felt-head drumstick or lamb's-wool-head mallet will produce better tones.

Automobile brake drums

Brake drums from automobile scrap parts dealers make excellent musical instruments. It is essential to collect five or six from different makes of automobiles. The drums will thus vary in size and shape. This is what gives the difference in pitch and quality of tone. The drums will probably need to be soaked in a strong detergent and then cleaned with steel wool. Spraying the drums with an anti-rust solution will keep them looking like new for years. Three-quarter inch dowels in 10″ lengths make good drumsticks.

To play these drums, place them on the floor, rim side down, and arrange them in a semi-circle. With a dowel in each hand, tap the drums one at a time in whatever rhythmic pattern desired. An oriental sounding melody can be created in this way. The child playing the brake drums can set the beat for others to pick up with other instruments or with body movements.

Clay flowerpots

Select clay flowerpots of different sizes. Tap them gently to discover their musical tones. By selecting carefully, you can find four or five notes of the scale.

In order to be played, they should be hung from a broom handle propped between two chairs. Each pot should hang freely so as not to touch the pot next to it. A piece of wire attached around the center of a nail and pulled through from the inside of the pot will keep it secure and not cut down on the resonance of the flowerpot. The pots may be tapped lightly with a dowel or drumstick.

Tuned bottles or glasses

Tuning glasses or bottles is an activity in which the children can participate. They will discover that the amount of water in the glass will determine the pitch the glass produces when it is tapped lightly. It is fun for them to match the tone of the glass to that of a note on the piano. When the glasses are tuned, they may be arranged in order of pitch and played like a xylophone. Unless the glasses or bottles are capped when not in use, the water will evaporate and the pitches will change.

Rhythm sticks

Very effective rhythm sticks can be made of twelve-inch lengths of three-quarter inch dowels. Old broom handles may be used also, but you must be sure to keep the sticks from the same broom handle as a pair. The wood in broom handles is often more resonant than that of doweling.

Poinciana seed pod shakers

The ripened seed pods from the Poinciana (Flame Tree) make very interesting shakers. The large seeds in the pods rattle like the rain or swish like the wind. The Poinciana tree grows abundantly in southern Florida. These pods are also available from musical instrument companies listed at the end of this chapter.

Coconut shells

Coconut shells sawed into two equal parts make a unique sound when beaten on the floor, open side down.

Sandblocks

These can be made with two blocks of wood the same size. 2" × 4" × 4" is a size the child can easily handle. Coarse sandpaper should cover one side, with the sandpaper folded up on the sides enough to allow tacking it securely. Rubbing the blocks together makes a swishing sound.

Rattlers

These may be made by filling containers with various amounts of materials such as old buttons, rice, dried beans, acorns, or bottle caps. Any kind of container that can have the lid or top secured in place will do—for example, metal band-aid boxes, plastic boxes, etc. Contact paper in colorful designs adds to the attractiveness of these shakers.

Wrist bells and ankle bells

These may be made by sewing jingle bells on one-inch elastic made into loops which are large enough to slip over the child's hands and shoes. Black elastic is most practical for this.

Horseshoe bells

New horseshoes of different sizes may be played with a ten-penny nail. This gives a sound effect similar to a triangle. And just as the triangle must be held by a small loop of elastic or plastic-covered wire, so must the horseshoe, or much of the resonance is lost. Different sizes of horseshoes may be collected and played like the flowerpots.

Scraps of nickel-coated pipe

Scrap pipe and nickel-coated or steel fittings found at a plumbing company add all kinds of delightful sounds. Holes should be drilled in the varying lengths of pipe so that each piece may have a wire loop attached for easy handling.

Cowbells

A collection of cowbells of different sizes and tone quality will provide the children with another interesting musical resource for the exploration of sound and melody. They may be played as individual bells or, with the clappers removed, they may be hung up like the flower-pots and played with a metal striker.

MUSIC AND MOVEMENT

A child's world is a world of movement—
 he moves to investigate
 he moves to learn
 he moves to express himself
 he moves because he can no longer sit
  still.
A child's musical world also is a world of movement—
 through movement he discovers the
  feeling of musical rhythms
 through movement he expresses what
  he perceives in music
 through movement he expresses the
  meaning of a song.

This is how the child discovers the magic of music through music from tip to toe.[5]

Movement is a universal medium of expression for the child. Teachers need to make use of the child's natural urge to move by providing adequate space and freedom for him to explore creatively the many ways he can move in space.

Achieving body awareness and identification of feelings are paramount learnings for the young child. These then are constant objectives in rhythmic movement activities.

The teacher may say, "Can you make your hands move like happy hands? sad hands? angry hands? tired hands?" The children will suggest other feelings their hands can express.

This may also be done with the face and with the feet. Using pictures of children showing some mood or emotion, the teacher may suggest that a small group of the children move the way the child in the picture seems to feel.

A child may move across the room expressing an emotion or mood while the rest of the group tries to identify how the child is pretending to feel.

It is interesting to observe the varied reactions young children give to such suggestions as these:

"Move as if you had just come into the
 room and you saw something new."

"Move as though you were very tired."
"Move as if something has just frightened
 you."
"Move as if you were lost."

Non-Locomotor Movement

Movement can be non-locomotor, that is, take place in a given space with feet firmly on the floor. Such movements might include:

pushing	swaying
pulling	bending
clapping	stretching
punching	twisting
stamping	shaking.

Suggestions such as these stimulate interesting bodily reactions while the children stand in one place:

"Push down toward the floor."
"Push out toward the walls."
"Punch with your fists up toward the sky."
"Move like a washing machine cleaning a
 load of clothes."
"Move like a tree during a wind storm."
"Make yourself as small as you can."
"Stretch up and become as tall as you can."

The teacher may give such directions as (sing or play quickly on resonator bells):

Locomotor Movement

Locomotor movement takes the child from one place to another. He may walk, skip, hop, jump, run, roll, crawl, etc. He can move *slowly* or *fast, lightly* or *heavily*.

As the children explore movement in the group, there is no attempt to keep them in a circle. Rather, the teacher suggests that each child find a space in which to move. He can stretch his arms out and turn around and around, moving so that he does not touch another child. Then, as he moves about on the floor, he is cautioned to watch where he goes so that he does not "bump fenders."

Different parts of the child's body may lead him about—his head, one hand, one foot, one shoulder, an elbow, his chin, etc.

---

[5]Lorraine Watters *et al., The Magic of Music* (New York: Ginn & Co.), p. 125. Used by permission.

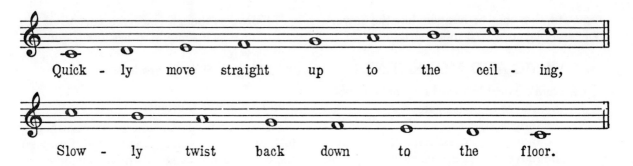

Quick - ly move straight up to the ceil - ing,

Slow - ly twist back down to the floor.

The teacher makes different suggestions and then allows the children to "think up" other ways of following some part of their bodies.

To help the children learn to distinguish the qualities of lightness or heaviness in movements, the teacher will give them many kinds of movement experiences that will help them feel the difference in the amount of tension used in their muscles.

The following are examples:

"Move about like a feather floating around in the air."
"You are wearing heavy moon-walking boots. How are you going to move?"
"The sidewalk is very hot and you are barefooted. Show us how you are going to get to your friend's house up the street."
"You have your skates on. How will you move on the sidewalk?"

"There is ice all over everything. How will you walk to keep from falling?"
"Someone spilled glue on the floor, and you have to walk through it. How will you get where you are going?"
"Pretend you are inside a big, big ball and you are trying to get out."

Singing directions adds interest to the movement.

Young children can become aware that movement includes *direction*. By moving about on command, they soon learn the concept of forward, backward, sideways, around, over, under.

"Skip all over the floor lightly."
"Walk backwards, looking back over your shoulder."
"Now walk sideways and back again."
"Run forward very heavily."

Slow - ly, soft - ly creep a - bout,

Quiet - ly mov - ing in and out.

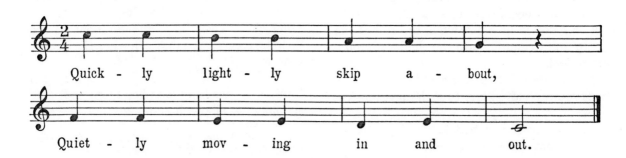

Quick - ly light - ly skip a - bout,

Quiet - ly mov - ing in and out.

"Step carefully over the tacks that were spilled."

"Move quickly around and around and in and out without bumping fenders."

"Twist yourself up in a ball on the floor."

"Now unravel yourself up tall and straight."

To add interest to some of these directions, use an appropriate musical instrument to pick up the children's rhythmic movement.

Poems such as the one which follows give the children opportunties for dramatic movement.

WHEN I WAS A LITTLE BABY
(A Dance-Poem of Growing Up)

When I was a little baby
   I was very small,
When I was a little baby
   I couldn't walk at all.

I lay on my side with my head to my knees,
   I was just as round as a ball,
Then I'd stretch and turn to the other side,
   And be round again and small.

Then I'd lie on my tummy and raise my head,
   And like daddy, I wanted to swim,
So I kicked my feet and moved my arms,
   Cause I wanted to be like him.

Then I'd lie on my back and clap my hands
   And kick my little feet,
I was very, very happy because
   I knew I was going to eat.

When I grew a little bigger
   I still couldn't walk at all,
But guess what I did all by myself—
   I began to crawl.

First, very, very slowly,
   Looking from side to side,
Then faster and faster and faster,
   Like going for a ride.

Then I grew a little older,
   And I tried to stand up tall,
I wobbled and wobbled from side to side
   And often I would fall.

Sometimes I'd hurt myself, a-huh,
   And sometimes I would cry,
But I'd get up, then fall again,
   I'd try and try and try.

I had to grow stronger every day
   And my mommie showed me how.
You want to know just what I did?
   I will tell you now:

I drank lots and lots and lots of milk,
   Ate everything on my plate,
And when I got up, I didn't fall
   'Cause I could stand up straight.

I stand like a real big person now,
   I hold my head up high,
I don't wobble and I don't fall
   Even looking at the sky.

Walking now is easy for me
   My steps are very long,
I lift my legs and take big strides
   Because I'm very strong.

I can raise my knees so very high,
   They say Hello to my chest:
Hello, hello, hello, hello,
   That's what I love best.

I can stretch my arms above my head,
   Like reaching for the sun,
I can bend way down and touch my toes,
   Then up, and down, what fun.

I can walk on the very tips of my toes,
   When someone's sleeping, I do—
'Cause I don't want to wake them up,
   I wouldn't be noisy, would you?

I can stretch my arms like the wings of a bird
   And fly so very fast,
When I was a baby I couldn't do that
   But now I'm grown up at last.

I can fly and fly and sometimes turn,
   Faster and faster I go,
My wings spread wide and my head up high,
   That's really fun, you know.

It's good to be a baby,
  But growing up is best,
And even big folks when they're tired
  Must always take a rest.

So now I'll lie down quietly,
  I won't even take a peep,
I'll close my eyes for a little while
  And I'll go fast asleep.[6]

—*Edith Segal*

The following poem is also good for directing the child's movement. It helps the child learn to relax and loosen his muscles.

RAGGEDY DOLL[7]

The raggedy doll said, "I don't mind
If my pants are held with a pin behind,
Or that the sawdust is out of my toe—
'Cause I'm just a raggedy doll, you know.

My arms are so floppy, they fling and flap
And my head rests all the way down in my lap.
The rest of me goes to and fro—
'Cause I'm just a raggedy doll, you know.

If somebody pulled me up by a string,
I'd stand so straight I'd certainly sing.
But my legs are so wobbly they just let go—
'Cause I'm just a raggedy doll, you know.

I can't move a muscle—I can just smile,
But I can stay here for a long, long while.
I feel so soft from my head to my toe—
'Cause I'm just a raggedy doll, you know."

—*Author unknown*

Recorded Music for Rhythmic Movement

Although much emphasis is placed on movement without using musical selections, good instrumental music adds another dimension to the child's creative experiences with rhythmic movement. The "activity-type" records with directions for movement in the re-

cording should be used sparingly with young children. They need more opportunity to work out their own spontaneous interpretations of the music. (See bibliography at the end of the chapter for a listing of records which have proved helpful for use with young children.)

Body Extenders

Kindergarten children often feel freer in exploring movement when they are holding something in their hands. The prop appears to extend their potential for body movement. "Relating to a prop [body extender] helps the child to make more varied use of space."[8]

Body extenders stimulate improvisation and "dramatic imagery."

The following is a list of typical props:

Small hoops—The child may hold a hoop with one hand and move it about as he feels the music; he may swing it about, holding it with both hands; or two children may hold the same hoop together and move with the music as partners.

Silk scarves—As the child moves about, his scarf will flutter behind him or beside him, depending on the way he is holding it. He may choose to stand still and wave it in front of him or from side to side.

Large nylon scarves—Large pieces of parachutes make excellent scarves for a number of children to hold at the corners and lift up and fill with air, then allow to float down. While a group is "floating" the scarf, other children may dance under it. (If an old parachute is not attainable, a long length of nylon cloth may be used. Remnants can frequently be obtained from local mill end stores.)

Puff balls—Large puff balls may be made of colored nylon net. Long strips 6" wide may be cut and stitched by hand down the center of each strip. When the thread is drawn up, the nylon makes a ball. It takes several lengths for each ball. A loop of ribbon on each ball makes it easy for the children to hold while dancing. The children will think of many ways of using them with the music.

Turkey feathers—With a feather in each hand, a child will often respond much more creatively to music—or he will do his own dance without an accompaniment. Teachers

---

[6]From *Be My Friend and Other Poems for Boys and Girls* (New York: The Citadel Press, 1952), p. 41. Used by permission of the author.

[7]Reprinted from *Rhythmic Activities for the Classroom*, copyright © 1969, Instructor Publications, Inc., Dansville, N.Y. 14437. Used by permission.

[8]Miriam B. Stecher et al., *Music and Movement Improvisations*, Vol. 4, Threshold Early Learning Library, New York, 1972, p. 95.

who are fortunate enough to have peacock feathers will find that they add even more to the child's sense of accomplishment in his rhythmic movement or dance.

Cloth streamers—Pieces of thin material cut in streamers about 3″ × 40″ become "the wind" or "sunbeams" or what have you as the children dramatize an incident or a musical story. Or they may just thrill at the trail of rippling cloth behind them indoors or out as they dart about. Crepe paper streamers serve as well but are less permanent.

Large seed pods—Poinciana seed pods, referred to earlier in this chapter, are good for "rain" sounds as the children shake them in different ways, or they may be used much as maracas to shake as the children dance to Spanish music.

Elastic loops—Elastic, one and one-half to two yards in length, may be sewed together to make large loops. Different widths of elastic, from one-half to one inch, may be used. The child may hold this in his hands and stretch and let it contract to electronic music which ascends and descends. He may hold the loop by his feet and hands and pull his body up and down as the elastic gives with the pressure. Or he may lie on the floor, hold his feet up, hook the elastic over his feet, and hold the other part of the loop with his hands. Pushing his feet away from his body stretches the elastic and helps him control his movement. This activity helps the child get the feel of tension and relaxation as he moves in space.

Balloons—As several children relate, each to a fairly large balloon, the teacher might comment:

"Throw and catch with the music. Bounce it up again with your head way up high."

"Follow the upness and downness of the balloon with your voice."[9]

TEACHER PARTICIPATION

Aware that music and young children belong together, the teacher nurtures this relationship by providing an environment that is warm and accepting and allows the children freedom, within limits, to express their thoughts and feelings

—in free, spontaneous, happy singing,

—in expressive bodily movements and in dramatization,

—in discovering the joy of listening,

—in making music with instruments,

—in creating original songs and dances...[10]

In order that the children may enjoy these activities in music, rhythm, and movement, the teacher must provide adequate room indoors and out, a relaxed atmosphere, and rich, firsthand experiences out of which the children can create song and dance.

The teacher provides a variety of equipment and encourages the children to experiment with sound and movement in ways that give them personal satisfaction. She will allow for creativity to flow through every type of musical activity.

The teacher keeps in mind the fact that she is not trying to make musicians of the children. She is concerned not so much with what they can accomplish musically as with how the musical experiences meet the needs of the children and contribute to the growth and development of the individual children.

The teacher must never allow herself to be held back by lack of formal music training. Her attitude is more important than her skill. Actually, the opportunity for the resourceful teacher to join with the children on their level, unhampered by rigid traditions or preconceived methods, might prove to the youngsters that music is a dynamic experience in which one can explore and experiment, *ad infinitum*. Enthusiasm is contagious. Children will quickly sense the genuine interest of their teacher and share it.[11]

BIBLIOGRAPHY

Andrews, Gladys. *Creative Rhythmic Movement for Children*. Englewood Cliffs, N.J.: Prentice-Hall, 1954.

---

[9]*Ibid.*, p. 96.

[10]Erluth Epting, "The Place of Music in Our Lives," in *Music for Children's Living*, A.C.E.I. Bulletin No. 96 (1955), p. 5.

[11]Beatrice Landeck, "Music with the Twos to Nines," p. 12. Reprinted by permission of the Association for Childhood Education International, 3615 Wisconsin Ave., N.W., Washington, D.C. 10016. From *Children and Music*, 1948.

Cherry, Clare. *Creative Movement for the Developing Child*, 2nd ed. Palo Alto, Calif.: Fearon Publishers, 1971.

Clark, Carol E. *Rhythmic Activities for the Classroom.* Instructor Handbook Series: Dansville, N.Y., 1969.

Gray, Vera, and Percival, Rachel. *Music, Movement, and Mime for Children.* New York: Oxford University Press, 1962.

Rowen, Betty. *Learning Through Movement.* New York: Teachers College Press, 1963.

Sheehy, Emma D. *Children Discover Music and Dance.* New York: Teachers College Press, 1968.

Stecher, Miriam, *et al. Music and Movement Improvisation.* Threshold Early Learning Library, Vol. 4. New York: The Macmillan Co., 1972.

Taylor, Margaret Fisk. *Time for Wonder.* Philadelphia: The Christian Education Press, 1961.

Thompson, Peggy. *Come, Let's Dance.* New York: Herder & Herder, 1969.

Songbooks for Kindergarten

Ginglend, David R., and Stiles, Winifred E. *Music Activities for Retarded Children.* Nashville: Abingdon Press, 1965.

Hilyard, Imogene. *Making Music Your Own—K.* Morristown, N.J.: Silver Burdett Co., 1966. (Album of six 12-inch records accompanies this book.)

Landeck, Beatrice. *Songs to Grow On.* New York: William Sloane Associates, 1954.

McCall, Adeline. *This Is Music: for Kindergarten and Nursery School.* Boston: Allyn & Bacon, 1966. Records available.

McNeil, Margaret C. *Come Sing with Me.* Valley Forge, Pa.: Judson Press, 1972. Record of songs available.

Songs for Early Childhood. Philadelphia: The Westminster Press, 1958.

Watters, Lorrain E., *et al. The Magic of Music.* Atlanta: Ginn & Co., 1965. Records available.

RESOURCES

Records
Available from:
Educational Activities, Inc.
P.O. Box 392
Freeport, L.I., N.Y. 11520
Learning As We Play
Honor Your Partner—Album No. 7

Basic Concepts Through Dance—Body Image
Learning Basic Skills Through Music, Vol. 1, Hap Palmer
Learning Basic Skills Through Music, Vol. 2, Hap Palmer
Learning Basic Skills Through Music—Building Vocabulary, Hap Palmer

Available from:
Children's Record Center, Inc.
5373 W. Pico Blvd.
Los Angeles, Calif. 90019
Come See the Peppermint Tree, by Evelyn Lohoefer and Donald McKayle
Visit to My Little Friend
Creepy Crawly Caterpillar
Merry Toy Shop
(All three on 12″ long play records.)
Dance—A Story—Little Duck
(Storybook included.)

Available from:
Educational Record Sales
157 Chambers St.
New York, N.Y. 10007
Adventures in Resting, Vol. 1
Adventures in Resting, Vol. 2
Lullabies for Sleepyheads, by Dorothy Olson
Peter and the Wolf (Prokofiev)
The Nutcracker Suite (Tchaikovsky)
Columbia ML 5593, New York Philharmonic, Leonard Bernstein

Available from:
Lyons
Division of Magnavox Co.
430 Wrightwood Ave.
Elmhurst, Ill. 60126
Listen, Move and Dance, Vol. 1 by Vera Gray
Listen, Move and Dance, Vol. 2 by Vera Gray
Dance, Sing, and Listen

Musical and Rhythmic Instruments
Available from:
Lyons
430 Wrightwood Ave.
Elmhurst, Ill. 60126
and
Peripole, Inc.
P.O. Box 146
Lewistown Rd.
Browns Mills, N.J. 08015

6
Play as Education:
Games and Finger Plays

"Play is a child's way to work. Play is a child's way of life."[1]

"Play is the most complete of all educational processes, for it influences the intellect, the emotions and the body of the child."[2] Through play activities the child clarifies his understandings and enriches his vocabulary; he relives experiences and satisfies his need for feeling important and enjoying success.

"A child's play is his way of exploring and experimenting while he builds up relations with the world and with himself."[3]

Hemphill says that "play is essentially research, motivated by curiosity to find out how to live and to be."[4]

Lawrence Frank adds that "play offers the child the major opportunities for self-learning,

---

[1]Jeff Callard, "A Declaration of Faith in Play," *Offspring* (Fall–Winter 1969), p. 34.
[2]N. V. Scarf, "Play Is Education," in *Early Childhood Education—Crucial Years of Learning* (Washington, D.C.: Association for Childhood Education International, 1966), p. 72.
[3]*Ibid.*, p. 72.
[4]Martha Locke Hemphill, *Partners in Teaching Young Children* (Valley Forge, Pa.: Judson Press, 1972), p. 55.

for 'learning by discovery' and for cultivating his creative abilities."[5]

Appropriate play activities help to promote the child's power of concentration, spark his imagination, and develop his initiative and his ability in problem solving.

Play can also serve as a safety valve for the child as he gives vent to pent-up feelings or reenacts a situation about which he was overly fearful.

The child begins to form important moral and spiritual values through his play experiences with his peers. He begins to understand what it is like to be in another's position. He begins to appreciate the good feeling tones in the group as he and his friends learn to respect one another and learn to share, take turns, and discover more acceptable means of solving their relational problems. In all this growing he comes to better understand himself and his peers.

An important observation that Lawrence Frank has made is that "in play the child learns what no one can teach him."[6]

"Piaget's experimental work has underlined the importance of the early play experiences of young children. There are elements of this exploratory play experience that are seen to be vital to later periods of mathematical and scientific explorations."[7]

Play takes many forms in day-by-day living in the kindergarten: dramatic play, outdoor physical activities, rhythms and creative movement, and games of many kinds.

DRAMATIC PLAY

Dramatic play is the simplest form of play. It is the spontaneous reliving of some experience, real or imaginary, in which the child identifies himself with his environment. He *is* whoever or whatever he *plays* he is. One minute he can be deeply engrossed in "driving a jet plane thirty miles an hour," then with no difficulty at all he can become a bus driver or the mailman delivering letters and magazines to the "family" living in the home center. With the same ease he can become a watchdog, a cat, or a wild animal of his choosing.

"Through this play children give voice to and enact their feelings, their wishes, their understandings. Through this re-enactment children learn and gain security and confidence in the world."[8]

It is through this type of play that the young child handles his problem of being "little." In this play he is a *big* person, an important person, in control of the situation as he plays out episodes and relationships that seem significant to him.

Lawrence Frank describes the child's dramatic play by saying that he "continually rehearses, practices, and endlessly explores and manipulates whatever he can manage to transform imaginatively into equivalents of the adult world."[9]

Another type of dramatic play which young children enjoy is play-acting very familiar stories. The children will invent their own costumes from the dress-up clothes in the home center. However, with neither costumes nor "props" a short story can come to life almost like magic. This play-acting in no way implies a performance. Yet a group, during free play, may present a "play," arranging chairs for the audience, "selling tickets," and giving the performance. This activity would be carried on while other children, not involved in it, are engaged in other learning centers in the kindergarten room.

Young children derive great satisfaction from dramatic play experiences of all kinds if they are in control of the situation. They are learning the rudiments of the democratic way of life in their firsthand, real-life situations in the group.

There are several basic elements essential to the child's enjoying good dramatic play experiences.

1. The teacher must provide an atmosphere of "freedom within limits" in which the child can play. (The "limits" would deal primarily with a consideration of the rights and property of others and the safety of the individual and the group.)

[5]Lawrence K. Frank, "Play and Child Development," in *Play—Children's Business* (Washington, D.C.: Association for Childhood Education International, 1963), p. 5.
[6]*Ibid.*
[7]Leonard Marsh, *Alongside the Child—Experiences in the English Primary School* (New York: Harper & Row, 1972), p. 48.
[8]Esther B. Starks, "Dramatic Play," *Childhood Education* (Dec. 1960), p. 164.
[9]Frank, "Play and Child Development," p. 4.

2. The teacher should provide adequate "play tools" that would stimulate creative, imaginative play. By "play tools" are meant such equipment as: building blocks of assorted sizes and shapes; accessory block play equipment such as toy cars, airplanes, trucks and boats; "dress up" clothes; child-size playhouse furnishings including dolls, doll clothes, toy telephones, cooking utensils and dishes, and doctor and nurse play accessories; scrap materials such as cartons and wooden boxes of all sizes, key carrier and old keys, rope, old canteen, flashlight, old camera, empty shampoo bottles (plastic), worn out wrist watch, etc.; wheel toys, barrels, wooden crates, saw horses, walking boards, etc. for outdoor play.

3. The children should have adequate time to enjoy a satisfying experience in their dramatic play, but not long enough for them to become over-stimulated and fatigued.

4. There must be adequate space for the children to play comfortably without getting in the way of other small groups of children engaged in other creative play activities.

5. The children need rich firsthand and vicarious experiences to reenact. They must have had experiences with many different adults before they can "try on" the roles of those adults.

OUTDOOR PHYSICAL ACTIVITIES

Fresh air and sunshine, adequate play space, suitable play equipment, and exuberant joy are all conducive to the physical growth, health, and happiness of young children.

Outdoor space needs to be organized so that there is adequate room for safe use of wheel toys in a designated area and plenty of space for large-muscle play that would in no way interfere with the riding activities.

The outdoor equipment need be neither expensive nor elaborate. One large piece of climbing apparatus is sufficient. The "climb around," a modified type of jungle gym, permits the child to climb upward at a slant, and after reaching the top he may slide down one of four poles in the center. Sand, sawdust, or pine bark mulch should cover the ground under and around such equipment.

The best outdoor equipment for the all-around development of the children is that which can be used creatively by them in a variety of ways. In other words, it is unstructured—it can be moved about easily and can be used as the child's imagination dictates. Such equipment includes sawhorses of various heights (two of each height, preferably), walking and jumping boards of different lengths, ladders, hollow blocks, smooth crates and packing boxes, corrugated boxes, barrels, wagon, wheelbarrows, tricycles of different sizes, and an Irish mail; large bean bags, long lengths of cotton rope, playground balls, and an old parachute.

A large sandbox which can be covered at night and sunned during the day offers quiet play for an individual or a small group. Sand tools such as the following are needed: wooden or rubber shovels, small plastic buckets, wooden spoons, sifters, old colander and pans, small plastic or wooden boats and cars, plastic funnels and measuring cups.

A space at the edge of the yard should be provided for digging activities. In the springtime the digging may evolve into gardening experiences.

RHYTHMS AND CREATIVE MOVEMENT

For a detailed treatment of rhythms and creative movement, refer to the chapter on "Experiencing Music and Movement with Young Children" in this text.

GAMES

Games afford fun and relaxation for the young child. They provide a variety of opportunities for growth and development in motor and language skills; in social habits of taking turns, fair play, and cooperation; and in building meaningful concepts. Game activities are effective means of developing self-control and self-assurance and give the child opportunities to explore the roles of winner and loser, of leader and follower.

The games in which kindergarten children function most easily are those which are loosely organized with only a few simple rules. Competition in game activities should be kept at a minimum. Games that require the elimination of players who fail to meet the game task or are last to perform *should not be used with young children*. It usually follows that the children who need most to have supporting, positive experiences are the very ones eliminated first.

Games for young children need to be active, with most of the group kept moving or otherwise involved. Little children find it hard to wait for their turn to participate.

The following are representative of different types of games within the ability level and interests of kindergarten children:

Singing Games

(For music and directions, see chapter on "Songs" in this text.)
"Looby Loo"
"Punchinello"
"Ring-a-Jig-Jig"
"The Farmer in the Dell"
"Round the Village"
"Five Little Chickadees"
"Pop Goes the Weasel"
"Susan Is Hiding"

Outdoor Circle Games

BUSHY TAIL AND SHINY EYES

The children sit in a circle. Two children are chosen for the little squirrels Bushy Tail and Shiny Eyes. They get down on all fours, facing each other in the center of the circle. They act out the poem which the children chant together:

> Bushy Tail and Shiny Eyes
> sat in a hole in a tree.
> Said Bushy Tail to Shiny Eyes,
> "You can't catch me."

Hopping and running, Shiny Eyes tries to catch Bushy Tail. When Bushy Tail is caught, the two squirrels choose two more children to take their places, and they return to the circle.
—Source unknown

SHADOW TAG

(On a bright sunny day the children will enjoy stepping on each others' shadows.) The children form a circle. One child is chosen as the runner. He runs around outside the circle, touching another child who must run after him. If the second child can step on the runner's shadow, he "catches" him. If the runner returns to the chaser's place in the circle, he is safe and the other child then becomes the runner.

DUCK, DUCK, GOOSE

The children sit in a circle on the grass. One child is chosen "It." He runs around outside the circle saying, "Duck, Duck, Duck," tapping a different child lightly on the head each time he says "Duck." When he says "Goose," the person he taps jumps up and chases him around the circle. If he can get to the vacant spot in the circle without being caught, he is safe, and the child who chased him becomes "It."

TOSS BALL

The children form a circle with not more than ten children to a circle. The teacher stands in the center of the circle and tosses the ball underhand to a child, calling his name as he or she throws the ball. It is more fun for the children and keeps them more involved if the teacher turns quickly back and forth around in the circle and doesn't just throw the ball to the children in order.

ROLL THE BALL UNDER THE BRIDGE

Children stand with feet apart in a circle formation. Each child's feet touch the feet of the children on either side of him. Each child pretends to be a bridge. One child in the center of the circle tries to *roll* a basketball-size ball under a bridge. A child may try to keep the ball from rolling between his legs by blocking it with his hands. He may not kick ball. If the ball goes between a child's legs and out of the circle, that child becomes "It" and the child who rolled the ball becomes a bridge.

PARACHUTE PLAY

You will need a small-size parachute which should be spread out on the ground in an open space in the play area. The children spread themselves around the parachute and take hold of the edges. Each child pulls on the parachute to stretch it out. Then the circle of children begins walking around, keeping the parachute stretched tightly. Someone may use a drum to set the pace for the walking. A faster tempo on the drum will indicate that the children should quicken their pace. This can be increased to running.

On a windy day the children will enjoy letting the parachute billow upward. This is done by having the children and adults all hold on to the edge of the parachute. At a given signal, everyone runs in toward the center of the circle, tossing the parachute up without letting go of it. The wind will catch the chute, and it will balloon upward. Then everyone steps backward. This is fun to repeat as the group becomes skilled in tossing upward together.

It adds to the fun to designate one child to let go of the chute and run under it to the opposite side of the circle while the chute is up in the air.

Bright colored chutes add to the glamour of the play. It is fun to play the game of "Duck, Duck, Goose" while the parachute is spread out on the grass. The children will enjoy sitting around the edge of the chute.

As the children become more familiar with the parachute, they will think of more ways to play with it.

BALLOON TOSS

You will need an inflated balloon (preferably round). It is well to have a spare or two in case one bursts.

Children form a circle, standing close together. Two children are chosen to stand inside the circle. A balloon is tossed up in the air, and the two children inside the circle try to keep it up in the air. If they let it fall to the ground, they must each choose a child to enter the circle, and they return to join the other children.

The teacher and children will think of variations which the group will enjoy.

Active Indoor Games

BEANBAG GAMES

Small groups will enjoy developing skill in tossing a beanbag at a target. The target may be a hula hoop on the floor; the children try to toss the beanbag into the hoop. Or the hoop may be tied to a broom handle that is suspended between the backs of two chairs. The children will enjoy trying to toss the beanbag through the hoop.

Masking tape may be put down on the floor in various shapes into which the children try to toss the beanbag. The shapes may be geometric shapes. Beanbags may be made in the shape of a triangle, square, circle, and a rectangle. The children will enjoy tossing the bags, trying to match the shapes—the triangle-shaped beanbag into the triangle outline on the floor, etc.

LEADER GAME[10]

Henry, show us what to do,
We will do the same as you.
This way, that way, we will do
Just the same as you.

DO THIS—DO THAT

The leader explains that when he says "Do this," the group is to do what he does. When the leader says "Do that," the group will not move.

SIMON SAYS

The leader gives directions for the children to follow *when* the direction is prefaced by "Simon says." When the direction is given without the preface "Simon says," the children are not supposed to move.

This game is a good one for helping children identify body parts, as many of the directions will have to do with touching different parts of the body.

Start out giving the directions slowly, and as the children gain skill in following, quicken the pace.

LOOKING FOR A FRIEND[11]

(This is an appropriate game song for the beginning of school.)

Children may sit or stand in a circle while one child walks around the inside of the circle and the leader sings to any tune ("Farmer in the Dell" fits):

> I'm looking for a friend,
> To take a walk with me,
> So will you be my friend
> And take a walk with me?

---

[10]Reprinted from *Pre-Kindergarten Curriculum Guide*, Curriculum Bulletin No. 11, 1965–1966 Series, with permission of the Board of Education of the City of New York.

[11]From *Children's Leader*, Nursery-Kindergarten, January–March 1964, The Evangelical United Brethren Church. Used by permission of The United Methodist Publishing House.

At the end of the stanza, the child who has been walking around looking at the others chooses a friend, takes him by the hand, and they walk together as the second stanza is sung:

> I'm glad I found a friend
>   To take a walk with me.
> We like to be together,
>   We're happy you can see!

The game may continue as the child who was chosen becomes the "chooser," and the first child returns to his place, or as the leader chooses a child from the circle to take a turn to look for a friend.

—Author unknown

INDOOR TAG

Children stand in a circle. One child is chosen to be "It." He moves around in the circle in any way he chooses. He may skip, hop, march, trot, crawl, tiptoe, etc. The children in the circle hold out their hands, palms up. "It" taps a child on his hands. The child tapped must turn and move around the circle, just as the child who tapped him. When they meet they may take hands and swing around. Then "It" returns to the circle and the other child becomes "It," moving around in the circle in a different way.

SOMETIMES I'M TALL

One child is chosen to guess. He stands with his back to the group and closes his eyes. The group repeats and acts out the following jingle:

> Sometimes I am very, very small,
> Sometimes I am very, very tall.
> Sometimes small,
> Sometimes tall.
> Guess what I am now!

On the last line the group either stays tall or becomes small. If the child guesses correctly, he may then choose another child to take his place.

The game should be played only three or four times. Its chief values are in relaxing the group and in giving the children experience in concentrating on following directions in the poem.

Guessing Games

BUTTON, BUTTON, WHO HAS THE BUTTON?

The children sit on the floor in a circle. It is best to keep the group to less than twelve. (This means that in most kindergartens two circles would be needed.) A child is chosen to sit in the center of the circle and hide his eyes. Another child is chosen to hide the button. Everyone in the circle holds his hands together out in front of him. The leader with the button keeps his hands tightly together and moves around the circle pretending to put the button in all the children's hands. When he has placed it in one child's hands, he calls "Ready!" All the children sit quietly with their hands folded so that the person who is guessing will have no clues.

The person guessing may hide the button the next time.

Seasonal variations add interest to such a game. See suggestions under "Seasonal Games."

WHO HAS THE SPOOL?

Spools or small wooden beads (3 or 4 in number) may be threaded on a long length of strong cotton cord. The cord should be long enough, when tied together, to reach around the circle of children.

The children may stand or sit in a circle with both hands on the cord. (The beads or spools should be small enough for the children to put their hands over and conceal them from sight. Small plastic rings may also be used, if spools or beads are too large.)

One or two children sit in the center of the circle and try to see the object move from one hand to another as it is passed around on the string.

When one child finds the object, those in the center go back to the circle and new children are chosen. It is wise to let the "leaders" choose the persons to take their places.

ONE POTATO, TWO POTATO

A small group of no more than eight stands in a circle with their hands out in front of them made into fists.

The leader walks around tapping the hands of each child as the group chants:

One potato, two potato, three potato, four,
Five potato, six potato, seven potato, more.

The leader taps a fist each time the group says the name of a number or the word "more." The child whose hand is touched on the word "more" must put that fist behind his back.

The last player to have both his fists behind him becomes the leader, and the game starts over again.

GUESS WHAT?

Materials needed: Pictures of animals and objects such as *dog, elephant, chair, squirrel, car, boy, shoe,* etc.

Paste one picture on the outside of each 7″ × 10″ manila envelope. In each envelope place six or eight cards on which are printed statements that either describe the pictures or are false statements. For example, in the envelope marked *dog,* with *a picture of a dog on it,* such statements as these might be included:

It has four legs.
It can fly.
It has two ears.
It barks.
It likes to climb trees.
It makes a good pet.
Its babies are called kittens.

Rules for playing: The teacher reaches into the envelope and pulls out a card and reads it to the group. If the statement is true about the picture, the child names the object pictured. If the statement is false, the child may respond by saying "It is *not* a _____."

Children can take the lead in the game by making up the descriptive statements themselves. The cards would be eliminated and only the pictures would be used.

NAMING OBJECTS

Place four or five familiar objects on a tray. Keep them covered with a cloth. Remove the cloth and let the children look for several seconds, then cover the tray and let a child name as many objects as he can recall.

Change the objects in arrangement without the children observing, and repeat the procedure. Replace the items with new ones.

As the children gain skill in remembering the objects, increase the number.

GUESS WHAT IS MISSING

A variation of the game "Naming Objects" is "Guess What Is Missing." Use the same equipment. Let the children look at the items for several seconds and then close their eyes. The leader removes one item and asks the group "What is missing?" The one guessing correctly becomes the leader.

To add challenge to the game, rearrange the items while the children have their eyes closed, but don't remove an item. At another time remove two items at once.

GUESS WHAT'S IN THE BAG

Materials needed: A cloth bag about eight inches square with a drawstring in it to facilitate opening and closing; a variety of objects that will fit into the bag (one at a time) such as a pair of kindergarten scissors (blunt ended), a crayon, a small ball, a small car, a spool, etc.

Rules of the game: The children sit in a circle on the floor with hands behind them. One object is put into the bag so that the children do not know what it is.

The bag is passed around the circle behind each child's back as the group sings the following words to the tune of "Here We Go Round the Mulberry Bush":

We are passing the bag around,
   the bag around,
   the bag around.
We are passing the bag around
Guess what's in it now.

The child holding the bag as the song ends feels the object in the bag behind his back and tries to determine what it is. He has three guesses. He may open the bag to confirm his guess.

A different article is then placed in the bag and the game starts over again.

WHAT IS IT?

Equipment: Pictures of well-known objects mounted on cards. (These could be the same cards used for recognizing initial sounds.)

Place the cards in a paper bag. One child draws a card and describes the picture of the object. The children try to guess the object from the description.

This game promotes vocabulary usage and focuses the child's attention on details.

WHOSE NAME IS IT?

(After the children have become familiar with their names in print, they will enjoy a game which uses their printed names.)

Equipment: The teacher manuscripts the names of all the children in the class on separate cards.

These cards are placed in a pile, printed side down. A child is chosen to select a card and look at the name without revealing it to the class. He then begins describing the child. Example: "This child has on sneakers, jeans, and a red and white shirt. This child has brown hair. Whose name do I have?"

The child whose name is correctly guessed becomes the next person to draw a name and describe the child. In this way a child will not draw his own name.

Games of Touch

IDENTIFYING OBJECTS

Unknown to the children, the teacher has placed 3 to 6 small objects (ball, toy car, toy airplane, pencil, key, penny, or other objects) in a cloth bag which is large enough to allow the objects to lie loosely in it. One at a time the children try to guess what the objects are by their sense of touch.

GUESS WHAT YOU HAVE

Children sit in a circle with their hands behind them. The teacher has a number of small objects familiar to the children. She moves around the circle and puts something in a child's hands. He must guess what it is by feeling it only. If he guesses correctly he becomes the person to give another child an object.

The children will enjoy the secrecy involved in not letting anyone see the object he puts in another child's hands.

Games Involving Hearing

RING THE BELL

One child in the group is chosen to hold a small bell. Another child is chosen to close his eyes. The child with the bell slips quietly to another part of the room. When he is ready, the group calls out "Ready." The child who has closed his eyes calls "Ring the bell." He listens as the other child rings the bell, then points in the direction from which he thinks the sound is coming. If he is not correct, he must choose someone to take his place, and the bell ringer has another time to play. If he *is* correct, he becomes the bell ringer and another child is chosen to guess.

SOUND PATTERN GAME

The teacher uses rhythm sticks or drum, or she may clap out sound patterns, and lets the children clap back the pattern. It is better for the teacher to give the pattern each time, for she will be more distinct and vary the patterns according to the ability of the children in the group. The following suggest a variety of patterns: __.__; .__.__.; .__; ..__.; .....; (. means a short clap; __ means a long clap).

DOG AND BONE

One child is selected to sit on a chair with his back to the group. He is the dog. A small object is placed under his chair. The object represents a bone. He closes his eyes and listens for someone to come up and try to get his bone without being heard. If the dog hears a noise, he barks and points in the direction of the noise. If he is correct he may choose another dog to take his place, and the game starts over. The entire group must learn that everyone must be very still to give the person who is trying to get the bone a fair chance to do so.

HUCKLE-BUCKLE BEANSTALK

One child is chosen to step outside the room while another child hides a small object in the room and then slips quietly back to his place. The children begin clapping as a signal for the child who is outside to come into the room. As he searches for the object, the group claps. They clap softly when he is far away from the object and louder as he comes nearer to it. When he spies the object, he calls "Huckle-Buckle Beanstalk" and goes to his place in the group. Two more children are then chosen, one to go out of the room and the other to hide the object. To vary the game and include more children, the teacher may select four or five to go out and hide. This would mean that the group would not clap as the children search.

LISTEN, LISTEN

The teacher makes a familiar noise behind a room divider and repeats this verse:

Listen, listen	Listen, Listen
With each ear;	With your ears;
Tell me what it	Let's ask *Mary*
Is you hear.	What *she* hears.

Suggested sounds: dropping a book, pouring water, ringing a bell, crumpling paper, whistling, and many others.

WHICH BELL RANG?

Equipment: Several bells of different sizes and tone qualities.

Line these bells up and ring each one for the children so that they can hear the different tones and associate them with the proper bell.

The children turn around and close their eyes while the leader rings one of the bells. The children turn around and guess which bell was rung.

The game is excellent for helping the child develop auditory discrimination, particularly if the bells are selected so that some have wide differences in tone and volume, while others have less distinct differences.

Visual Discrimination Games

FINDING MISSING PARTS

Each child has one of two parts of a picture. The pictures should be mounted on cardboard and cut in such a way that something is missing. For example, a picture of a barn might be lacking the roof, or a cat might be minus a tail. The children move about and try to find the child who has the other part of the picture. When the children are introduced to this game, the teacher might start with two or three pictures.

WHAT IS MISSING?

Four or five objects are placed on the floor in the center of the circle. One child is chosen to close his eyes while another child removes one object from the group. The child who was hiding his eyes tries to guess which object is missing. To make it a little more difficult, the objects may be moved around on the floor and more than one object may be removed at a time.

WHO IS MISSING?

One child looks over the group and then hides his eyes. A child slips out of the room. The one chosen opens his eyes and tries to decide who left the room. The game may be made more difficult by letting two or three leave the room at a time.

FIND THE TWIN

Equipment: Paper shapes with two of each should be prepared. One set of shapes might be geometric shapes, one might be colored leaves, one might be Halloween objects such as pumpkin, jack-o'-lantern, black cat, owl, witch, or ghost.

The teacher places one set of the shapes about in the room in plain view.

Then she holds up one of the duplicate set at a time and says:

> Look around the room.
> What do you see?
> If you can find a twin to this,
> Bring it here to me.

Two children may be chosen to look for the "twin." The one finding it may choose the next shape to hold up. After several times the children will learn the jingle and be able to say it with the teacher.

(The word "twin" may be new to the children. The teacher will help the children discover its meaning.)

Team Games

"GRAB BAG"

Materials needed: Four red triangles, circles, and squares; four blue triangles, circles, and squares the same size as the red shapes; a large paper bag

Number of children: Five on each team lined up, seated, facing each other about ten feet apart. The leader places the bag at a point midway between the two teams. One team is designated the red team, the other the blue team.

Rules for the game: One child from the red

team reaches into the bag without looking and draws out one paper shape. If it is red, he places it on the floor before his group. If he drew a blue figure, he has to put it back in the bag.

One child from the blue team draws a shape, and if it is blue he places it before his team. If not, he puts it back in the bag.

The leader shakes the bag up after each drawing to insure that the shapes stay well mixed.

The object of the game is to see which team can draw all twelve of its colored shapes first.

To make the game a bit more interesting, the teams may be required to keep all of the triangles together, all of the circles together, and all of the squares together. The children will soon observe how many of each shape they need to draw.

Variations: This game may be played at special seasons of the year. Examples:

Red leaves, yellow leaves

Paper jack-o'-lanterns: 12 with smiling faces, 12 with very sad faces

12 paper Christmas trees undecorated, 12 paper Christmas trees with decorations

Games for Special Days

GUESS WHO HAS THE JACK-O'-LANTERN?
(recommended for older five's)

Formation: Children seated on the floor in a circle with their hands behind them.

Equipment: Small yellow paper or plastic jack-o'-lantern.

Action: One child is chosen to sit in the center of the circle with his eyes closed. While the pianist plays a simple melody, the children pass the jack-o'-lantern around the circle behind their backs. When the music stops, the child in the circle opens his eyes and tries to guess who has the jack-o'-lantern. If he guesses correctly, the child who was holding the jack-o'-lantern gets to hide his eyes, and the game starts all over.

GUESS WHAT IS MISSING?

Formation: Children informally grouped on the floor.

Equipment: Long, heavy string, five small metal clamps or clamp clothespins, and a picture of a witch, a black cat, a pumpkin, a jack-o'-lantern, and a ghost. These may be cut out of colored paper so that they can be more uniform in size.

Action: The clothesline may be strung up between two small chairs. The five pictures are clamped onto the clothesline. Everyone gets a good look at the arrangement. Then one child is chosen to be "It." He turns with his back to the clothesline and hides his eyes. Another child is chosen to remove one picture from the line. Then the child who is "It" tries to guess which picture is missing. The game may be played several times. Changing the position of the various pictures makes the game a little more challenging.

One group of children changed the words to a simple singing game which they enjoyed and created another Halloween game. It is a variation of "Punchinello."

PUMPKIN YELLOW
(See page 110 for melody, "Punchinello")

Formation: Children stand in a circle facing the child who is chosen to be Pumpkin Yellow.

Action: Children join hands and walk around the circle as they sing the first stanza:

What can you do, Pumpkin Yellow, funny fellow?
What can you do, Pumpkin Yellow, funny you?

Child in center begins some action such as jumping up and down, twirling around, tapping his feet, etc., while the group claps and sings:

That's very fine, Pumpkin Yellow, funny fellow.
That's very fine, Pumpkin Yellow, funny you.

As the children sing the next stanza, they imitate the child in the center of the circle:

We'll do it too, Pumpkin Yellow, funny fellow.
We'll do it too, Pumpkin Yellow, funny you.

As the group sings the last stanza, the child in the center of the circle chooses another child to take his place:

Whom do you choose, Pumpkin Yellow, funny fellow?
Whom do you choose, Pumpkin Yellow, funny you?

FIVE LITTLE JACK-O'-LANTERNS
(Adaptation of "Five Little Chickadees")

Formation: Five small chairs placed in a row facing the children as they sit informally on the floor.

Action: Five children are chosen to be jack-o'-lanterns and sit on the chairs. They act out the song the group sings:

Five little jack-o'-lanterns looking at the door,
One ran away and then there were four.

Refrain:
Jack-o'-lantern, jack-o'-lantern happy and gay,
Jack-o'-lantern, jack-o'-lantern, run away.

Four little jack-o'-lanterns sitting by a tree,
One ran away and then there were three.
Refrain.

Three little jack-o'-lanterns looking at you,
One ran away and then there were two.
Refrain.

Two little jack-o'-lanterns sitting in the sun,
One ran away and then there was one.
Refrain.

One little jack-o'-lantern left all alone,
He ran away and then there was none.
Refrain.

Christmas Games

SNOWMAN AND HIS SNOWBALL
(Variation of Dog and Bone)

Formation: Children seated informally on the floor with a small chair out in front of the group.

Equipment: A snowball made of a large piece of cotton rolled into a ball and tied securely with white string.

Action: The snowman sits on the little chair with his back to the group and his eyes closed. His snowball is placed on the floor under his chair. A child is chosen from the group to try to retrieve the snowball without the snowman hearing him. If he is successful in getting back to his place with the snowball without the snowman hearing him, he becomes the next snowman. If not, he places the snowball back under the snowman's chair and another child is chosen to try to get it. The group may decide on a signal for the snowman to use if he hears the child getting away with his snowball. The child who returns to the group successfully will also need an appropriate signal.

PASSING THE CHRISTMAS BELL

Formation: Children seated on the floor in a circle.

Equipment: Red paper bell.

Action: One child is chosen to be "It" and sit in the center of the circle with his hands over his eyes. As the children sing the song "We Are Passing the Christmas Bell," they pass the paper bell around the circle behind their backs. When the song ends, they all keep their hands behind them and the child in the center opens his eyes and tries to guess who has the bell.

Song: "We Are Passing the Christmas Bell"
Tune: "Here We Go Round the Mulberry Bush."

We are passing a Christmas bell,
    A Christmas bell, a Christmas bell,
We are passing a Christmas bell,
    Guess who has it now.

HUNT THE CHRISTMAS BELL

Formation: Children seated informally on the floor.

Equipment: A small jingle bell fastened to a red paper bell.

Action: One child is chosen to hide with the bell while another child in the group is chosen to hide his eyes. When the child with the bell has found a place to hide, he rings the little bell. This is the signal for the other child to "wake up" and follow the sound of the tinkling bell until he finds where the child is hiding. When he discovers the child with the bell, two more children are chosen to take their places and the game starts over again.

BIBLIOGRAPHY ON PLAY

Almy, Millie, ed. *Early Childhood Play.* New York: Selected Academic Readings, 1968.

Herron, Robin, and Sutton-Smith, Brian, eds. *Child's Play.* New York: John Wiley & Sons, 1971.

Piaget, Jean. *Play, Dreams, and Imitation in Childhood.* New York: W. W. Norton & Co., 1962.

Piers, Maria W., ed. *Play and Development.* New York: W. W. Norton & Co., 1972.

Pamphlets

Play—Children's Business. Washington, D.C.: Association for Childhood Education International, 3615 Wisconsin Ave., N.W. 20016.

Play—the Child Strives Toward Self-Realization. Washington, D.C.: National Association for the Education of Young Children, 1834 Connecticut Ave., N.W. 20009.

FINGER PLAYS

Finger plays should not take the place of children's poetry, for they are just interesting, rhyming jingles accompanied by finger or hand movements. Their place is to:

> help young children enlarge their vocabularies,
>
> encourage attentiveness and alertness,
>
> help develop muscular control of the fingers,
>
> create fun and help the children to relax,
>
> help to build math concepts, and
>
> serve as a type of quiet transition for the group from one activity to another.

HERE'S A BALL

Here's a ball
  (make small circle, thumb and first finger of one hand).
And here's a middle-sized ball
  (make large circle, thumb and first finger of both hands),
And a great big ball I see
  (make large circle, joining both arms).
Shall we count them?
Are you ready?
One, two, three
  (repeat all three motions).
                    —Author unknown

Adaptations of this may be made, using seasonal materials of the three sizes:

colored leaves	Christmas bells
paper jack-o'-lanterns	Valentine hearts
turkeys	flowers
pumpkins	

The children will make up their own versions as they become more aware of the comparative sizes.

---

[12]From *From One Generation to Another,* by Pauline Palmer Meek, p. 74, revised edition, © John Knox Press 1972.
    [13]*Ibid.,* p. 73.

JACK-IN-THE-BOX

Jack-in-the-box, all shut up tight
  (make a fist with thumb tucked in),
Not a breath of air, not a ray of light.
How dark it must be!
He cannot see.
But open the lid
And up jumps he
  (pull thumb up quickly).
                    —Author unknown

This can be a relaxation activity. Have the children squat down low and jump up to the words of the last line of the poem.

DRESSING [12]

(Imitate suggested motions.)

I comb my hair
I wash my face
I put my arm in the sleeve-hole place;
I snap my belt,
Put on my shoe.
Now I'm all dressed, so what shall we do?

MY TURTLE [13]

I have a little turtle
  (hand makes a fist),
His house is on his back,
Whenever he wants to look around,
His head comes out a crack
  (poke thumb out between third and fourth finger).
Whenever he wants to move around,
He runs with all his might
  (index and little fingers climb up other arm);
But when you try to catch him,
He locks his house up tight
  (make fist).

FIVE LITTLE KITTENS

Five little kittens
Sleeping on a chair;
One rolled off,
Leaving four there.

Four little kittens—
One climbed a tree
To look into a bird's nest,
Then there were three.

Three little kittens
Wondered what to do;
One saw a mouse,
Then there were two.

Two little kittens
Playing near a wall;
One little kitten
Chased a red ball.

One little kitten
With fur as soft as silk,
Left all alone
To drink a dish of milk.

—*Source unknown*

FIVE LITTLE LEAVES[14]

(Adaptation of "Five Little Chickadees,"
page 110.)

Five little leaves, lying by the door,
One blew away, and then there were four.

Refrain:
Red leaf, brown leaf, happy and gay,
Red leaf, brown leaf, blow away.

Four little leaves, lying by a tree,
One blew away, and then there were three.
Refrain.

Three little leaves that blew and blew,
One blew away, and then there were two.
Two little leaves, lying in the sun,
One blew away, and then there was one.
Refrain.

One little leaf left all alone
It blew away, and then there was none.
Refrain.

—*Judith Gabel Lutz*

TWO HALLOWEEN OWLS

Two Halloween owls sitting on a limb,
One named Jack and the other named Jim.
Fly away Jack and fly away Jim.
Come back Jack and come back Jim.
Two Halloween owls sitting on a limb,
One named Jack and the other named Jim.

This is a variation of "Two Little Blackbirds Sitting on a Hill."
Tune: "Twinkle, Twinkle, Little Star."
Motion: With the first stanza hold up index finger on each hand with the words "Two Halloween owls sitting on a limb." Indicate which finger is Jack and which is Jim. Then when they "fly away," move hands behind back, one at a time. On "Come back Jack and come back Jim," bring the fingers back to original position.

The second stanza begins "Four Halloween owls sitting on a limb." Hold up two fingers on each hand.

Continue the finger play, adding one finger on each hand until there are ten Halloween owls.

This finger play helps the child with the number concept of adding 1 and 1, 2 and 2, etc. It also introduces him incidentally to counting by 2's.

To add interest to the finger play, the teacher can cut out ten little paper owls and attach them with tape to her fingers.

—*Josephine Newbury*

JACK-O'-LANTERNS[15]

(*Use finger puppets made of little paper jack-o'-lanterns stuck to a ring of masking tape, sticky side out, the size to fit over the ends of the fingers.*)

Five little jack-o'-lanterns sitting on a gate,
The first one said, "My, it's getting late!"
The second one said, "There's a breeze in the air."
The third one said, "But we don't care."
The fourth one said, "Let's run, let's run!"
The fifth one said, "Isn't Halloween fun?"
"Woo-oo-oo!" went the wind, out went the light,
Away ran those jack'-o-lanterns on Halloween night.

FIVE LITTLE VALENTINES[16]

Five little Valentines were having a race,
The first little Valentine was frilly with lace;
The second little Valentine had a funny face;

[14]From *Behold God's Glory!* by Judith Gabel Lutz, p. 29, revised edition, © John Knox Press 1973.
[15]Adapted from *Finger Plays for Young Children,* Leaflet No. 11 (Minneapolis: University of Minnesota Press), p. 22. Used by permission.
[16]*Ibid.,* p. 24. Used by permission.

The third little Valentine said, "I love you."
The fourth little Valentine said, "I do, too."
The fifth little Valentine was sly as a fox,
He ran the fastest to your Valentine Box!

(Small paper Valentines may be attached to the inside of the teacher's fingers on one hand. As she mentions each one, she holds up that finger.)

MR. JUMPING JACK[17]

(May be sung to the tune of "Turkey in the Straw")

Mr. Jumping Jack is a funny old man,
And he jumps and he jumps as fast as he can.
His arms fly out and his feet fly too.
Mr. Jumping Jack, how do you do?

WHERE IS THUMB MAN?[18]

(May be sung to the tune of "Are You Sleeping?")

Where is thumb man (*hands behind back)*?
Where is thumb man?
Here I am *(one fist forward with thumb standing).*
Here I am *(other fist forward, thumb standing).*
How do you do this morning *(wriggle one thumb in direction of other)*?
Very well, I thank you *(wriggle other thumb).*
Run away, run away *(hands behind back again).*

This finger play may include all fingers:
Where is pointer?
Where is tall man?
Where is ring man?
Where is small man?

HERE'S A BUNNY[19]

Here's a bunny
(hold up arm, clasp fingers over thumb to make a fist)

With ears so funny
(raise index and middle finger up, tips curved down).
And here is his hole in the ground
(with left arm form circle against your side).
When a noise he hears, he pricks up his ears
(point index and middle finger up),
And jumps into his hole in the ground
(put right arm, which is rabbit, into hole made with left arm).

FIVE LITTLE ROBINS[20]

Five little robins, happy as can be,
The mother, the father,
And their babies three.
The mother caught a worm
The father caught a bug,
And all the little robins
Began to tug.
This one got the bug,
This one got the worm,
And the littlest baby robin said,
"Next time's my turn."

TOUCH YOUR NOSE[21]

Touch your chin;
That's the way this game begins.
Touch your eyes,
Touch your knees;
Now pretend you're going to sneeze
(finger under nose).
Touch your hair,
Touch one ear;
Touch two red lips right here.
Touch your elbows
Where they bend;
That's the way this touch game ends.

ENUMERATION[22]

I have five fingers on each hand
(hold up both hands, with fingers outspread),
Ten toes on both feet
(point to feet).
Two ears, two eyes, one nose, one mouth
With which to gently speak
(point to ears, eyes, nose, mouth in turn).
My hands can clap
(clap hands).
My feet can tap
(tap feet).

[17] *Ibid.*, p. 15. Used by permission.
[18] *Ibid.*, p. 4. Used by permission.
[19] *Ibid.*, p. 7. Used by permission.
[20] *Ibid.*, p. 8. Used by permission.
[21] Reprinted from *Rhymes for Fingers and Flannelboards* by L. B. Scott and J. J. Thompson © 1960 with permission of McGraw-Hill, Inc.
[22] From *Fingers and Action Rhymes*, by Mabelle McGuire. Reprinted with permission of the publisher, The Instructor Publications, Inc., Dansville, N.Y.

My eyes can brightly shine
  (point to eyes with both index fingers).
My ears can hear
  (cup hands to ears).
  My nose can smell
  (point to nose and sniff).
My mouth can speak a rhyme
  (point to mouth).

TURTLE[23]

This is my turtle
  (make fist; extend thumb);
He lives in a shell
  (hide thumb in fist).
  He likes his home very well.
He pokes his head out when he wants to eat
  (extend thumb).
And pulls it back when he wants to sleep
  (pull thumb back in fist).

TWO LITTLE EYES[24]

Two little eyes that open and close.
Two little ears and one little nose.
Two little cheeks and one little chin.
Two little lips with the teeth closed in.

OUR TURKEY[25]

Our turkey is a big fat bird
  (spread arms and hands in a big circle in
front of you)
Who gobbles when he talks.
His red chin's always drooping down;
  (dangle both hands under chin, the fingers
of one touching the wrist of the other);
He waddles when he walks
  (hands on hips and shift weight from one
foot to the other for "waddle").
His tail is like a spreading fan
  (link thumbs together and spread fingers
wide for large fan),
And on Thanksgiving Day
  (hold same position),
He sticks his tail high in the air
  (keep same position and move far over
head)
And whoosh he flies away
  (unlock thumbs and bring arms in wide,
fast arc to sides)!

—Thea Cannon

A WONDERFUL WINTER SURPRISE[26]

Five little snowflakes, high, high, high,
Started down to earth from a cloud in the sky.
The first little snowflake said, "What fun!"
The second one whispered, "I see the sun!"
The third one said, "Let's all stay together!
We might melt in warm sunny weather."
The fourth one sighed, "Are we going far?"
And here is the fifth one—a beautiful star!
  (Have a small snowflake cut from thin
white paper attached to little finger.)

STRETCHING ACTIVITIES

HANDS ON SHOULDERS, HANDS ON KNEES

Hands on shoulders, hands on knees,
Hands behind you, if you please.
Touch your shoulders, now your nose,
Now your hair and now your toes.

—Source unknown

"I'M ALL FULL OF HINGES"

I'm all full of hinges and everything bends (do
  so),
From the top of my head way down to my ends.
I'm hinges in front (bend forward from the
  waist),
I'm hinges in back (bend backward);
If I didn't have hinges (bend all ways)
I think I would crack (fall slowly).

—Source unknown

HANDS ON YOUR HIPS

Hands on your hips,
Hands on your knees,
Put them behind you, if you please.
Touch your shoulders,
Touch your nose,
Touch your knees,
Touch your toes.

---

[23]Reprinted from *Pre-Kindergarten Curriculum Guide*, Curriculum Bulletin No. 11, 1965–1966 series, with permission of the Board of Education of the City of New York.
  [24]*Ibid.*
  [25]From *Finger Plays and How to Use Them*, edited by Tessa Colina, © 1952, Standard Publishing Co., Cincinnati, Ohio. Used by permission.
  [26]From *Ten Busy Fingers*, by Elsie S. Lindgren. Fortress Press. Copyright 1955. Used by permission.

Raise your hands high in the air,
Now at your sides,
Now on your hair.
Raise your hands up as before
While we clap one, two, three, four.

—Source unknown

HEADS AND SHOULDERS

(Tune: "Here We Go Round the Mulberry Bush")

Our heads, our shoulders, our knees, our toes;
Our heads, our shoulders, our knees, our toes;
Our heads, our shoulders, our knees, our toes;
We'll all *(any movement)* together.

(Movements may be "turn around," "clap hands," "stamp feet," "bend over," "wave arms," "sit down.")

To vary this action game, reverse the order, beginning with toes and moving up to the head.

CLAP, CLAP, CLAP[27]

Clap, clap, clap!
  One, two, three.
Who will clap
  His hands with me?
Clap, clap, clap!
  Clap, clap, clap!
Fold your hands
  Upon your lap!

Roll, Roll, roll,
  One, two, three.
Who will roll
  His hands with me?

Roll, roll, roll,
  Round and round.
Roll your hands
  Without a sound!

Shake, shake, shake!
  One, two, three.
Who will shake
  His hands with me?
Shake, shake, shake!
  With all your might,
Shake your left; then
  Shake your right!

Clap, clap, clap!
  One, two, three.
Who will clap
  His hands with me?
Clap, clap, clap!
  Clap, clap, clap!
Fold your hands
  Upon your lap.

—Nona Keen Duffy

BIBLIOGRAPHY OF FINGER PLAYS

Institute of Child Welfare, University of Minnesota. *Finger Plays for Young Children*, No. 11.

Jacobs, Frances E. *Finger Plays and Action Rhymes.* New York: Lothrop, Lee & Shepard Co., 1941.

McGuire, Mabelle. *Finger and Action Rhymes.* The Instructor Handbook Series. Dansville, N.Y.: Instructor Publications.

Miller, Mary, and Zojan, Paula. *Finger Play.* New York: G. Schirmer, Inc., 1955.

Pierce, June. *The Wonder Book of Finger Plays and Action Rhymes.* New York: Wonder Books, Inc., 1955.

Scott, Louise Binder, and Thompson, Jesse J. *Rhymes for Fingers and Flannelboards.* New York: McGraw-Hill, 1960.

7
Songs

GOOD MORNING

Good morn - ing, good morn - ing, Good morn - ing to you!

Good morn - ing, good morn - ing! Oh, how do you do?

From *The American Singer, Book I*, by John W. Beattie *et al.* Used by permission of American Book Co.

HOW ARE YOU?
(¿Cómo está usted?)

Juan García

"¿Có - mo es - tá us - ted?" means "How are you?"
(¿Koh´ - moh ehs - tah oos - ted´?)*

If you are well, you say, "*Muy bi - en, muy bi - en.*"
(*Mwee bee - ehn,´ mwee bee - ehn.´*)

TEACHER   CHILD

"¿Có - mo es - tá us - ted?" "*Muy bi - en, muy bi - en.*"

*Pronunciation

From *The Magic of Music—Kindergarten*, © Copyright, 1970, 1965, by Ginn and Company. Used with permission.

ROUND OF THANKS

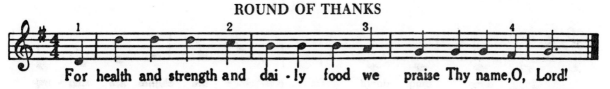

For health and strength and dai - ly food we   praise Thy name, O, Lord!

Reprinted with the permission of the Association for Childhood Education International, Washington, D.C. Copyright © 1954 and 1958 by the Association.

"M" IS FOR MARY

D. R. G.   D. R. G.

"M" is for Mary, It's eas - y you see.

"M" is for Mary, Now show it to me.

From *Music Activities for Retarded Children* by David Ginglend and Winifred Stiles. Words and music copyright © 1965 by Abingdon Press. Used by permission.

"M" is for Mary, I found it, you see,
"M" is for Mary, It's easy for me.

Chanted or sung, this little song can help vary the ways in which letters are presented and can help teach recognition of common objects and the development of a "sight" vocabulary.

1. Children's names on cards may be placed on a blackboard ledge. A duplicate card is shown to the child as the song is sung. The card is given to the child, and he finds the matching card. Later only the first letter of his name is on the card he receives. Still later, no card is given to use as a clue. The second verse is sung when the child brings back the right card.

2. The alphabet may be taught in this manner beginning with pictures of familiar objects. The initial letter or the complete object name may be on the picture card. Related groups of things may be used: fruits, vegetables, furniture, animals, et cetera.

3. The color names, number names, days, et cetera, may be presented in a similar manner.

4. Use pictures of objects needed for speech practice.

BELLS

Ding, dong, ding, dong! Four o'-clock the chimes are ring-ing;

Back and forth the bells are swing-ing, Ding, dong, ding, dong!

From *The American Singer, Book I*, by John W. Beattie *et al.* Used by permission of American Book Co.

ALL BY MYSELF

M. D.   Miriam Drury

1. There are man-y things that I can do, All by my-self;
2. I can wash my hands and wash my face, All by my-self;

I can comb my hair and lace my shoe, All by my-self.
I can put my toys and blocks in place, All by my-self.

Words and music copyright 1935 by Presbyterian Board of Christian Education, renewed 1963; from *When the Little Child Wants to Sing*; used by permission of The Westminster Press.

Other phrases may be substituted for the above, as suggested by the conversation or experience in connection with which the song is sung. Some possible phrases are: "hook my dress," "close the door," "feed my dog," "count my blocks," "sing a song," "go to church," "go to school."

WE HAVE A GOOD FRIEND

J. N.   J. N.

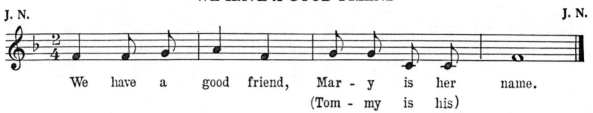

We have a good friend, Mar-y is her name.
(Tom - my is his)

SEA SHELL

Esther S. Duncan

1. Sea shell, sea shell, Sing a song for me,
2. Sea shell, sea shell, When I hold you near,

Sing a-bout the o - cean, Tell me a-bout the sea.___
I can hear the o - cean Whis-per-ing in my ear.___

From *The Magic of Music—Kindergarten*, © Copyright, 1970, 1965, by Ginn and Company.
Used with permission.

ALL OF ME

Sadie K. Knight
Evelyn M. Andre

Mary Lou Moody
Harmonized by V. Earle Copes

1. Hands to help with, eyes to see;
2. Ears to hear with, feet so free;
3. Nose to smell with, legs to climb a tree;
4. I am grow - ing, big as can be;

I'M VE-RY HAP-PY WITH ALL OF ME.
I'M VE-RY HAP-PY WITH ALL OF ME.
I'M VE-RY HAP-PY WITH ALL OF ME.
I'M VE-RY HAP-PY WITH ALL OF ME.

From *The Methodist Teacher—Nursery*, Summer 1967. © Graded Press. Used by permission.

THE WEATHERMAN

Agnes Bell

What is the weath-er, weath-er, weath-er?

What does the weath-er-man say to-day?

I say it's sun-ny,* sun-ny, sun-ny,

"Sun-ny," says the weath-er-man to-day.

° Windy, cloudy, rainy, snowy, may be substituted.

From *The Magic of Music—Kindergarten*, © Copyright, 1970, 1965, by Ginn and Company. Used with permission.

Children will thoroughly enjoy dramatizing this song. Remember that girls make good "weathermen" too.

A few moments of extra practice on the tone call "sun-ny" may help uncertain singers to use higher and more accurate singing voices.

WHAT DO YOU DO?

Mary Jaye, Old Game Song

Arranged by Darrell Peter

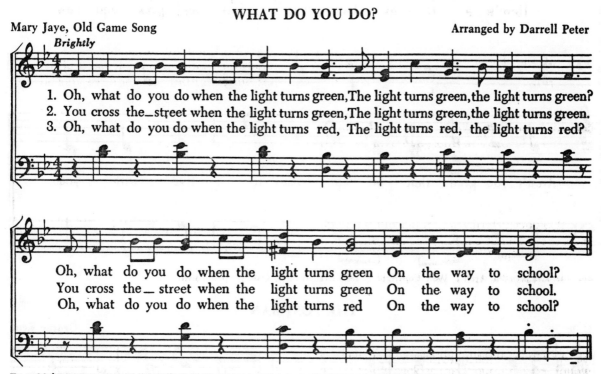

1. Oh, what do you do when the light turns green, The light turns green, the light turns green?
2. You cross the_street when the light turns green, The light turns green, the light turns green.
3. Oh, what do you do when the light turns red, The light turns red, the light turns red?

Oh, what do you do when the light turns green On the way to school?
You cross the_ street when the light turns green On the way to school.
Oh, what do you do when the light turns red On the way to school?

4. You stop and wait when the light turns red . . .
5. Oh, what do you do when the light turns yellow . . .
6. You do not cross when the light turns yellow . . .

SOMETIMES I'M HAPPY

Harriet Cramton

Lee Duckworth
Arr. V. E. Copes

Some - times I'm hap - py; some - times I'm sad. Some - times I'm
sor - ry; some - times I'm glad. But most im - por - tant of
all, you see, I know what it means for me to be me.

TINY BABY

E. M. A.

Evelyn M. Andre
Harmonized by V. Earle Copes

From *The Kindergarten*, April 2, 1967. Copyright © 1960 Graded Press. Used by permission.

THE POSTMAN

G. K.

George Kent

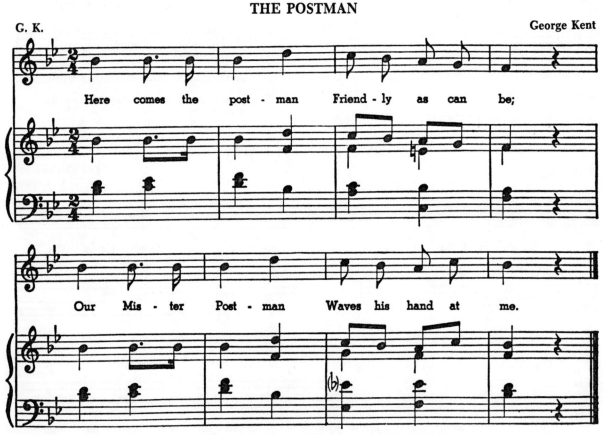

From *The American Singer, Book I*, by John W. Beattie *et al.* Used by permission of American Book Co.

FRIENDS

E. McE. S.

Elizabeth McE. Shields

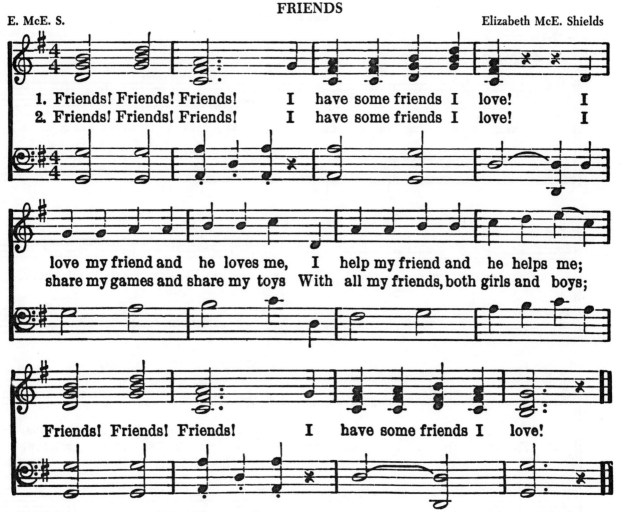

1. Friends! Friends! Friends!   I have some friends I love!   I
2. Friends! Friends! Friends!   I have some friends I love!   I

love my friend and he loves me,   I help my friend and he helps me;
share my games and share my toys With all my friends, both girls and boys;

Friends! Friends! Friends!   I have some friends I love!

From *Happy Times in Our Church*, by Elizabeth McE. Shields (Richmond: John Knox Press, 1940). Used by permission of Mrs. Harold V. Bird.

LEAVES

A. C. H.

Alicia C. Hardin

Leaves of yel-low, red, and brown, Fall-ing, fall-ing, fall-ing down.

Used by permission of the author.

FALLING LEAVES

1. Leaves are fall-ing all a-round, All a-round, all a-round.
2. See them ly-ing on the ground, On the ground, on the ground.

From *Music Course* (First year music), by Hollis Dann. Used by permission of American Book Co.

OUR HELPERS

L. W.

Lucille Wood

Who is com-ing to our door? Knock-i-ty, knock-i-ty, knock, knock, knock.

Run and see who it can be. Knock-i-ty, knock-i-ty, knock, knock, knock.

1. It's the gro-cer-man at our door, Bring-ing gro-c'ries from his store.
2. It's the milk-man at our door, Leav-ing milk, a quart or more.
3. It's the mail-man at our door, Bring-ing let-ters, three or four.

Knock-i-ty, knock-i-ty, knock, knock, knock, Knock-i-ty, knock-i-ty, knock, knock, knock.

From *Sing a Song of Holidays and Seasons, Home, Neighborhood and Community*, by Roberta McLaughlin and Lucille Wood. Used by permission of Bowmar. Copyright 1960.

The wood block will make a good knocking sound.
Perhaps you can play the knockity tune on the
song bells or xylophone.

HALLOWEEN

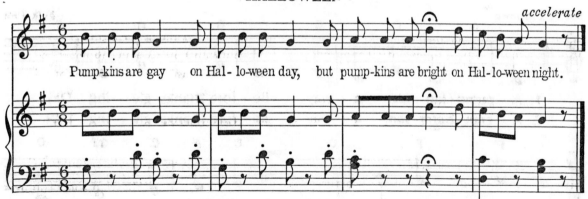

Pump-kins are gay on Hal-lo-ween day, but pump-kins are bright on Hal-lo-ween night.

Copyright © 1929 by Satis N. Coleman and Alice G. Thorn. Reprinted from *Singing Time* by Satis N. Coleman and Alice G. Thorn, by permission of The John Day Company, Inc., publisher.

HALLOWE'EN'S HERE

Composed by third-grade group.

Hal-lo-we'en has come at last, Witch-es, gob-lins, big black cats,

Fun-ny fac-es round a-bout, Peo-ple laugh and peo-ple shout.

BOO!

Reprinted with the permission of the Association for Childhood Education International, Washington, D.C. Copyright © 1954 and 1958 by the Association.

HALLOWEEN IS COMING

Children's Song

Oh, Hal-low-een is com-ing, Hal-low-een is com-ing, Oh,

Hal-low-een is com-ing, Oh, what fun.

From *The Kindergarten Book* of *Our Singing World* series, Copyright, 1959, 1957, 1949, by Ginn and Company. Used with permission.

Adaptations which the children will enjoy might be: "Thanksgiving Day Is Coming"
"Christmas Day Is Coming"
"Valentine's Day Is Coming"

PUMPKIN SONG

1. A pump-kin ran a-way Be-fore Thanks-giv-ing Day.
2. A cran-berry ran a-way Be-fore Thanks-giv-ing Day.

Said he, "They'll make a pie out of me if I should stay."
Said he, "They'll make some sauce out of me if I should stay."

From *Come Sing With Me*, by Margaret Crain McNeil. Judson Press, copyright 1972. Used by permission.

The children will enjoy playing this one. It is easy to be a cranberry or a pumpkin.

I'M GLAD IT'S SNOWING

1. I'm glad it's snow-ing, snow-ing, snow-ing. I'm glad it's snow-ing, snow-ing snow.
2. I can throw snow-balls, snow-balls, snow-balls. I can throw snow-balls in the snow.
3. I can go crunch-ing, crunch-ing, crunch-ing. I can go crunch-ing in the snow.

From *The Kindergarten Book* of *Our Singing World* series, ©Copyright, 1959, 1957, 1949, by Ginn and Company. Used with permission.

THE JOLLY SNOWMAN

I made a jol-ly snow-man. I set him in the sun.

Next day I went to find him. Guess what! My snow-man was gone!

From *Kindergarten Songs and Rhythms*, Margaret L. Crain, ed. Copyright 1954, Judson Press. Used by permission.

The children will enjoy "melting" in the sun.

"THUMBS IN THE THUMB-PLACE"

Marie Louise Allen

English Nursery Song
Arr. by Edith Lovell Thomas

"Thumbs in the thumb-place, Fin-gers all to-geth-er!"
This is the song We sing in mit-ten weath-er:

This is the song We sing in mit-ten weath-er.
"Thumbs in the thumb-place, Fin-gers all to-geth-er."

When it is cold, It does-n't mat-ter wheth-er

Mit-tens are wool Or made of fin-est leath-er.

O HEAR THE BELLS THAT RING AND RING

Miriam Drury
Arr. by W. Lawrence Curry

Traditional Carol; alt.

O hear the bells that ring and ring On Christ-mas Day, on Christ-mas Day! O hear the bells that ring and ring On Christ - mas Day in the morn - ing!

Words and music copyright 1935 by Presbyterian Board of Christian Education, renewed 1963; arrangement of music copyright 1958 by W. L. Jenkins; from *Songs for Early Childhood*; used by permission of The Westminster Press.

Play the chime music before and after the song is
sung. Use both hands, and hold the sustaining
pedal down for the entire line.

AWAY IN A MANGER

Traditional

1. A - way in a man - ger, no crib for His bed,
2. The cat - tle are low - ing, the Ba - by a - wakes,

The lit - tle Lord Je - sus laid down His sweet head.
But lit - tle Lord Je - sus, no cry - ing He makes.

The stars in the sky looked down where He lay,
I love Thee, Lord Je - sus, Look down from the sky,

The lit - tle Lord Je - sus, a - sleep in the hay.
And stay by my cra - dle till morn - ing is nigh.

LISTEN! LISTEN!

T. B.

Talmadge Butler

HAPPY BIRTHDAY

German Folk Tune

Hap-py Birth-day, Hap-py Birth-day, Hap-py Birth-day to you. Hap-py
(Bill Simms.)

Birth-day, Hap-py Birth-day, Hap-py Birth-day to you. Hap-py

Birth-day, Hap-py Birth-day, Hap-py Birth-day to you.

A VALENTINE

W. E. G.

Wanda Estes Guokas

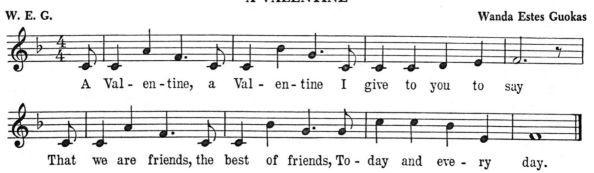

A Val - en -tine, a Val - en -tine I give to you to say

That we are friends, the best of friends, To - day and eve - ry day.

Used by permission of Mrs. Wanda Estes Guokas.

CAN YOU GUESS WHO?

Second-Grade Class
Second-Grade Class

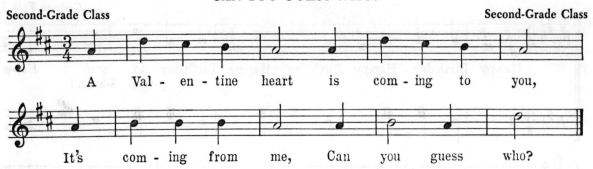

A Val - en - tine heart is com - ing to you,

It's com - ing from me, Can you guess who?

Used by permission of the teacher, Center Hill Elementary School, Atlanta, Georgia.

SING O SING

Brightly

Sing, O,— sing for it is Spring. Flow - ers bloom and rob - ins sing.

Copyright © 1929 by Satis N. Coleman and Alice G. Thorn. Reprinted from *Singing Time* by Satis N. Coleman and Alice G. Thorn, by permission of The John Day Company, Inc., publisher.

A RAINY DAY

Second-Grade Class
Second-Grade Class

Pit - ter, pat - ter all a - round,
Splish - ing, splash - ing see the rain
Drip - ping drop - ping soon 'twill stop

Dance the rain - drops on the ground.
As it hits our win - dow - pane.
Now we hear just drip, drip, drop.

Used by permission of the teacher, Josephine Newbury.

THE ROBIN

A lit-tle rob-in red breast was sit-ting in a

tree Cheer-up, Cheer-up, Cheer-up he sang, as hap-py as could be

RAIN

Kindergarten, 1958

P.S.C.E. Kindergarten, 1958

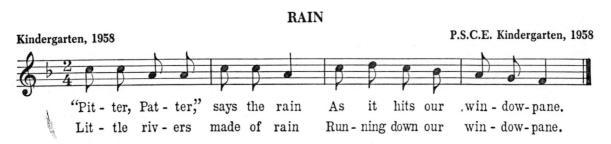

"Pit - ter, Pat - ter," says the rain   As   it   hits our   win - dow-pane.
Lit - tle riv - ers   made of rain   Run - ning down our   win - dow-pane.

Used by permission of the teacher, Josephine Newbury.

DANDELIONS

Harvey Worthington Loomis   Arthur Edward Johnstone

All a-round the lawn you pass; See the but-tons made of brass! The pret - ty yel - low dan - de - li - ons but - ton down the grass.

From *Music Course* (First year music), by Hollis Dann. Used by permission of American Book Co.

GOD HAS MADE EVERYTHING BEAUTIFUL

Ecclesiastes 3:11

Gladys Reeves Finklea
Arranged by V. Earle Copes

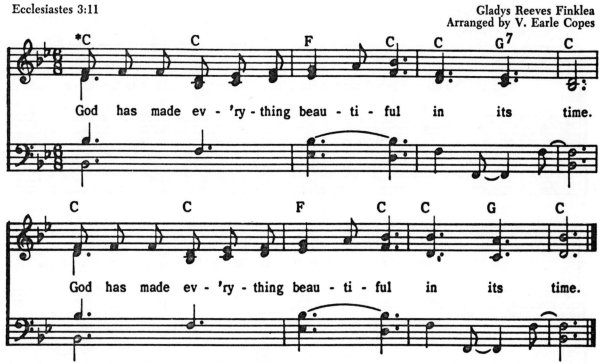

°Autoharp in Key of C.

Copyright, 1960, Graded Press. Used by permission of Graded Press

WHERE IS THUMBKIN?

Finger Game

French

From *The Kindergarten Book* of *Our Singing World* series, Copyright, 1959, 1957, 1949, by Ginn and Company. Used with permission.

OLD MISTER ELEPHANT

J. W.   J. Wolverton

From *The American Singer, Book I*, by John W. Beattie *et al*. Used by permission of American Book Co.

This is a good activity song. Children walk bent
over with arms swinging back and forth, hands
clasped together making a trunk.

OLD MR. SCARECROW

(Adaptation of "Old Mr. Elephant")

Old Mr. Scarecrow, happy and gay.
Old Mr. Scarecrow, nodding all day,
  Waving his arms
  And scaring the crows,
  Standing all day in his old ragged clothes.
Old Mr. Scarecrow, happy and gay,
Old Mr. Scarecrow stands all day.

—*Josephine Newbury*

OUR MR. SNOWMAN

(Adaptation of "Old Mr. Elephant")

Our Mr. Snowman, frosty and cold.
Our Mr. Snowman, not very old.
Standing alone
In the wind while it snows,
Wearing a hat and a carrot nose.
Our Mr. Snowman, frosty and cold
Our Mr. Snowman won't grow old.

—*Josephine Newbury*

HEY JIM ALONG, JIM ALONG JOSIE

American Folk Song

From *The American Singer, Book I*, by John W. Beattie *et al.* Used by permission of American Book Co.

    3. Hop Jim along, etc.

    4. Tiptoe along, etc.

SUSAN IS HIDING

M. D.   Miriam Drury

Words and music copyright 1958 by W. L. Jenkins; from *Songs for Early Childhood*; used by permission of The Westminster Press.

2. Who'll try to find her? She's not far away.
3. I'll try to find her. O where can she be?
4. Johnny has found her; Now he can be IT.

You may substitute another child's name or the name of an object ("Scissors are hidden. O where can they be?"). The lower notes in the chords may be played with the left hand.

The children close their eyes. One child is sent to hide. The children open their eyes and one child is chosen to find "Susan" (insert children's names in the song).

The game may be varied by giving the child who is hiding a tiny bell to ring when he is hidden. The person looking for him will listen for the bell.

Adaptations for seasonal activities may be made. For example: "The pumpkin is hiding. O where can he be?" or "The turkey is hiding. O where can he be?"

WALKING SONG

Adapted   German Folk Song
Lively

Keep step with me, I'll   step with you,   Two   by   two.

Oh,   don't you hear the   mu - sic play,   On   our   way?

From *The American Singer, Book I*, by John W. Beattie *et al.* Used by permission of American Book Co.

ISN'T IT FUN?

W. E. S.   Traditional Melody

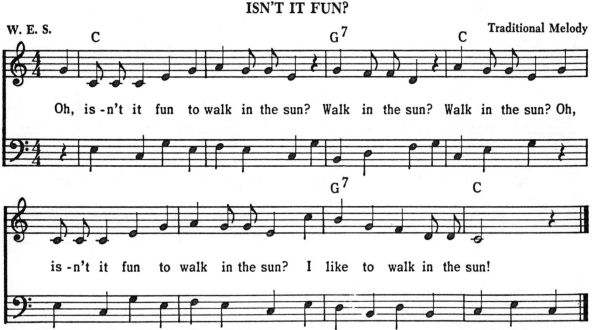

Oh, is -n't it fun to walk in the sun? Walk in the sun? Walk in the sun? Oh,

is -n't it fun   to walk in the sun?   I like to   walk in the sun!

From *Music Activities for Retarded Children* by David Ginglend and Winifred Stiles. Copyright © 1965 by Abingdon Press. Used by permission.

Isn't it fun to walk in the rain?
Isn't it fun to walk in the snow?
Isn't it fun to walk in the leaves?

1. Dramatize the song by walking in various ways. Then add other kinds of walk such as:

Isn't it fun to walk like a clown, cat, bear, duck, ghost.
Isn't it fun to walk to the store, to school, to church.

2. Encourage the children to suggest something that is fun to do. The group can sing as one child does the action. The teacher or leader may help the child by suggesting something that is fun such as:

Isn't it fun to tap on the floor, knock on the door, slide on the ice, play in the snow, dig in the sand, et cetera.

I TAKE MY LITTLE HANDS

As sung by B. Kuscin

From *Music Activities for Retarded Children* by David Ginglend and Winifred Stiles. Copyright © 1965 by Abingdon Press. Used by permission.

1. Dramatize: "I take my little hands and go clap, clap, clap." Add other actions such as feet, stamp; fingers, snap; toes, tap; eyes, wink; head, shake; finger, point.

2. Using rhythm instruments, sing "I take my little sticks and go click-click-click." Only the children with sticks will play for that verse. Continue using other instruments.

IF YOU'RE HAPPY

Traditional Melody

1. Suggest actions that may be done sitting down such as tap your head, tap your feet, shake your hands, wink your eye, wave good-bye. Wait for the right time to make the motions.

2. Add actions that dramatize daily happenings—wash your hands, shine your shoes, comb your hair, say your prayers, dust the chair, iron your clothes, et cetera.

3. For an active game children stand in a circle and perform the action you suggest—touch your toes, take a bow, turn around, jump up high, step so high, touch the sky, that's enough, et cetera.

FIVE LITTLE CHICKADEES

Singing Game

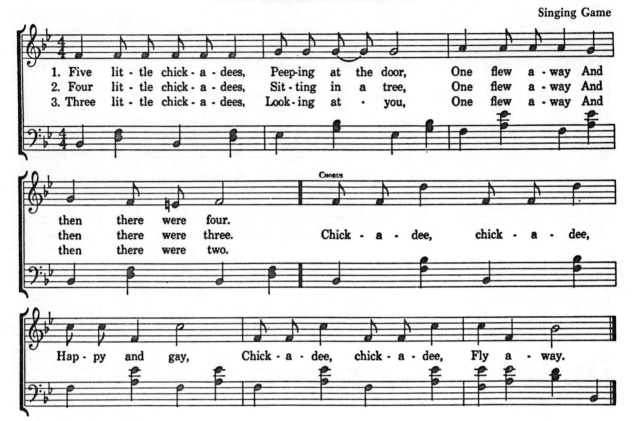

1. Five lit-tle chick-a-dees, Peep-ing at the door, One flew a-way And
2. Four lit-tle chick-a-dees, Sit-ting in a tree, One flew a-way And
3. Three lit-tle chick-a-dees, Look-ing at you, One flew a-way And

then there were four.
then there were three.   **CHORUS**   Chick-a-dee, chick-a-dee,
then there were two.

Hap-py and gay, Chick-a-dee, chick-a-dee, Fly a-way.

4. Two little chickadees,
   Sitting in the sun,
   One flew away
   And then there was one.

5. One little chickadee,
   Left all alone,
   It flew away
   And then there was none.

Directions:

Five children may sit on the floor or on chairs in a row facing the group. As each stanza is sung a chickadee gets up and "flies" about, returning to the singing group.

PUNCHINELLO

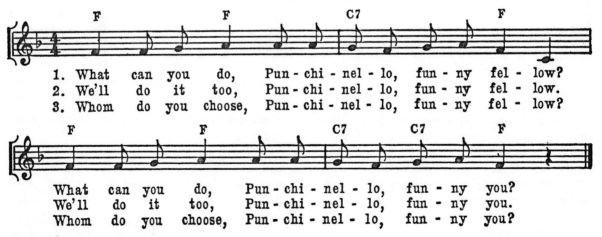

1. What can you do, Pun-chi-nel-lo, fun-ny fel-low?
2. We'll do it too, Pun-chi-nel-lo, fun-ny fel-low.
3. Whom do you choose, Pun-chi-nel-lo, fun-ny fel-low?

What can you do, Pun-chi-nel-lo, fun-ny you?
We'll do it too, Pun-chi-nel-lo, fun-ny you.
Whom do you choose, Pun-chi-nel-lo, fun-ny you?

Source unknown.

Directions:

Children form a circle. One child is chosen to stand in the middle of the circle and be Punchinello (the clown). As the children sing the first stanza, Punchinello does something to be a "funny fellow," such as hopping on one foot, swinging his arms up and down, or any movement he chooses. The group then sings:

We'll do it, too, Punchinello, funny fellow.
We'll do it, too, Punchinello, funny you.

As the children sing this stanza, they imitate Punchinello's movement. As they sing the last stanza they join hands and move around the circle:

Whom do you choose, Punchinello, funny fellow?
Whom do you choose, Punchinello, funny you?

Punchinello chooses someone to replace him and he returns to the circle. The game begins all over again.

ROUND AND ROUND WE GO

A. E. McM.

Anne E. McMichael

Round and round we go, Twirl-ing to and fro, Whirl-ing like a top, Then all at once we stop.

Used by permission of Miss Anne E. McMichael.

Possible Uses:

Singing, with or without accompaniment.
Rhythm, with piano, using full accompaniment; with flute or recorder, using melody only.
Instruments could be added to the singing.
Creating new verses.

LOOBY LOO

English Game Song

From *The American Singer, Book I*, by John W. Beattie *et al.* Used by permission of American Book Co.

3. I put my right foot in, etc.
4. I put my left foot in, etc.
5. I put my whole self in, etc.

(For some groups it might be better to change the words "right" and "left" to "one" and "other." It is confusing to use right and left hands and feet in a circle formation even when children know left from right.)

Directions:

Holding hands, children move around in a circle as they sing the refrain. As they begin the stanza, they drop hands, face the center of the circle, and act out the words.

DRAMATIC SINGING GAMES

ROUND THE VILLAGE

English Game Song

1. Round and round the vil-lage, Round and round the vil-lage,
2. In and out the win-dows, In and out the win-dows,

Round and round the vil-lage, As we have done be-fore.—
In and out the win-dows, As we have done be-fore.—

From *The American Singer, Book I*, by John W. Beattie *et al.* Used by permission of American Book Co.

3. Stand and face your partner, etc.
4. Follow him (her) to London, etc.
5. Shake your hand and leave him (her), etc.

Directions:

Children stand in a circle. They are the houses in the village. One child is chosen to be "It." As the children sing the first stanza, "It" skips around the outside of the circle.

On the second stanza the children in the circle join hands and hold them up high, pretending the space between each child is a window. As the children sing the second stanza, "It" weaves in and out of the circle, going through the windows.

On stanza three "It" chooses a partner and stands facing the child.

As the children sing stanza four, "It" again weaves in and out the windows with the partner following. At the end of this stanza, the two children go to the center of the circle.

On stanza five they shake hands and bow. A new "It" is selected, and the game begins again.

STRETCHING

K. S. J. Slow, sustained

Katherine Scott Jones

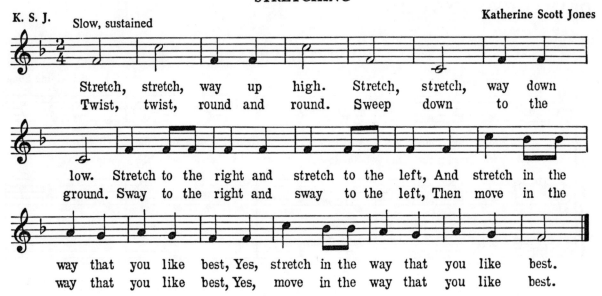

Stretch, stretch, way up high. Stretch, stretch, way down
Twist, twist, round and round. Sweep down to the

low. Stretch to the right and stretch to the left, And stretch in the
ground. Sway to the right and sway to the left, Then move in the

way that you like best, Yes, stretch in the way that you like best.
way that you like best, Yes, move in the way that you like best.

Used by permission of Mrs. Katherine Jones Gilliam.

POP! GOES THE WEASEL

American Folk Song

Fast

1. A pen - ny for a spool of thread, A pen - ny for a nee - dle,
2. — All a - round the chick - en coop The mon - key chased the wea - sel,

That's the way the mon - ey goes, Pop! goes the wea - sel.

From *The American Singer, Book I*, by John W. Beattie *et al.* Used by permission of American Book Co.

Directions:

The children form a circle. One child skips around inside the circle. On the word "pop" the children give one big clap and the child in the circle stops and takes the hand of the child directly in front of him. The song is begun again and these two children skip around in the circle until the word "pop." They must stop and each take the hand of the child they are facing. These new partners skip around and stop on the word "pop," and each has a new partner. When eight children are skipping, the game may be started over, with everyone in the center of the circle moving back into the circle. A new leader is chosen to start the game again.

**Traditional American Song
Arranged by Cameron McGraw**

THE OLD GRAY CAT

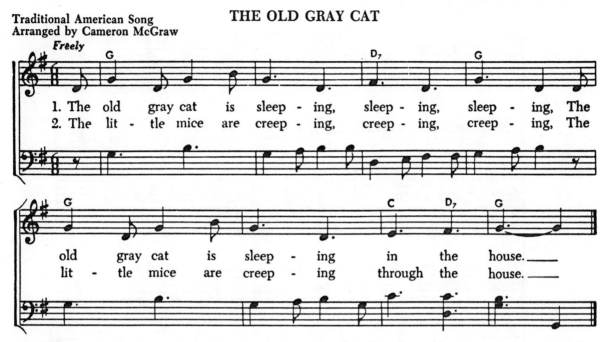

1. The old gray cat is sleep - ing, sleep - ing, sleep - ing, The old gray cat is sleep - ing in the house.____
2. The lit - tle mice are creep - ing, creep - ing, creep - ing, The lit - tle mice are creep - ing through the house.____

3. The little mice are nibbling . . . in the house.
4. The little mice are sleeping . . . in the house.
5. The old gray cat comes creeping . . . through the house.
6. The little mice all scamper . . . through the house.

One child can be the cat. The other children can be mice. As the mice scamper through the house, the cat tries to catch a mouse. The child who is caught becomes the cat. Repeat as many times as desired.

For an additional dramatic effect, play verses 1, 3, 4, and 6 in the key of G major (as written). Play verses 2 and 5 in the key of G minor (ignore the key signature and play the note B as B-flat whenever it occurs in the song). Play verse 6 at a faster tempo.

WE STEP, STEP, STEP

A. E. W.   Alice E. Workman

We step, step, step, and tap, tap, tap, And then we turn a-round.   We step, step, step, and tap, tap, tap, And

bow with-out a sound.   We clap down low, we

clap up high, We clap the ground, we clap the sky. We

step, step, step, and tap, tap, tap, And then we sit right down.

From *Experiences in Music for First Grade Children*, copyright 1949 by Silver Burdett Company. Reprinted by permission.

Children may follow suggested actions in the song. It will be a good singing game.

RIG-A-JIG-JIG

English Folk Song Arranged by Darrell Peter

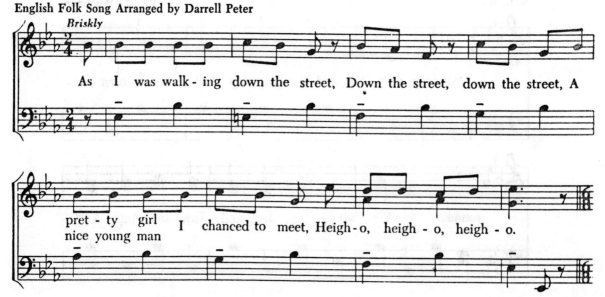

As I was walk-ing down the street, Down the street, down the street, A

pret-ty girl I chanced to meet, Heigh-o, heigh-o, heigh-o.
nice young man

Rig - a - jig - jig, and a - way we go, A - way we go, a - way we go;

Rig - a - jig - jig, and a - way we go, Heigh - o, heigh - o, heigh - o.

Children may be seated or standing in a circle. One child walks around inside the circle as the group sings the first part of the song. He chooses a friend as a partner, and they skip around while the group sings "Rig-a-jig-jig." The child who was chosen then walks alone as the song is sung again. His partner returns to the group.

The children may choose to go down the street in different ways such as on tiptoe, skating, hopping, trotting, etc. The chorus indicates skipping as the appropriate movement.

To make the game more personal, the child's name may be substituted: "As Ted was walking down the street, . . . A friend of *his* he chanced to meet."

ELEPHANTS

Words and Music by Lillian Wiedman

Heavily

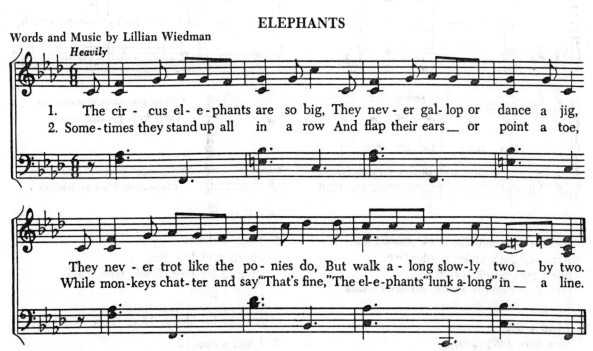

1. The cir - cus el - e - phants are so big, They nev - er gal - lop or dance a jig,
2. Some - times they stand up all in a row And flap their ears __ or point a toe,

They nev - er trot like the po - nies do, But walk a - long slow - ly two __ by two.
While mon - keys chat - ter and say "That's fine," The el - e - phants "lunk a - long" in __ a line.

BARNYARD SONG

A cumulative song that may be learned in short sections.

Lively

1. I had a cat, and the cat pleased me, I fed my cat un-der yon-der tree; Cat goes fid-dle dee dee.

2. I had a hen, and the hen pleased me, I fed my hen un-der yon-der tree; Hen goes chim-my chuck, chim-my chuck,

Cat goes fid-dle dee dee.

*These measures repeated an extra time for each verse.

© Copyright Edward B. Marks Music Corporation. Used by permission.

Back to 𝄋

3. I had a duck and the duck pleased me,
   I fed my duck under yonder tree;
   Duck goes quack, quack,
   Hen goes chimmy chuck, chimmy chuck,
   Cat goes fiddle dee dee.

4. I had a hog,
   Hog goes griffy, gruffy,
   (Repeat for Duck, Hen, Cat)

5. I had a sheep,
   Sheep goes baa, baa,
   (Repeat for Hog, Duck, Hen, Cat)

6. I had a goose,
   Goose goes swishy, swashy,
   (Repeat for Sheep, Hog, Duck, Hen, Cat)

7. I had a cow,
   Cow goes moo, moo,

(Repeat for Goose, Sheep, Hog, Duck, Hen, Cat)

8. I had a dog,
   Dog goes bow-wow, bow-wow,
   (Repeat for Cow, Goose, Sheep, Hog, Duck, Hen, Cat)

9. I had a horse,
   Horse goes neigh, neigh,
   (Repeat for Dog, Cow, Goose, Sheep, Hog, Duck, Hen, Cat)

To add to the interest of this song and to help the children recall the correct order in the song, collect and mount on pieces of cardboard pictures of each of the animals. Line the pictures up in the order in which the animals appear in the song and turn them as the song progresses—each time a new animal is added.

THREE LITTLE KITTENS

Mother Goose

Arthur Edward Johnstone

Three lit-tle kit-tens, they lost their mit-tens, And they be-gan to cry:____ "O moth-er dear, We ve-ry much fear That we have lost our mit-tens." "What! lost your mit-tens, You

naugh-ty kit-tens! Then you shall have no pie." _____ "Mee-

ow, mee-ow, mee-ow, mee-ow! And we can have no pie." _____

From *Music Course* (First year music), by Hollis Dann. Used by permission of American Book Co.

THE ELEPHANT

Author Unknown

Josephine Newbury

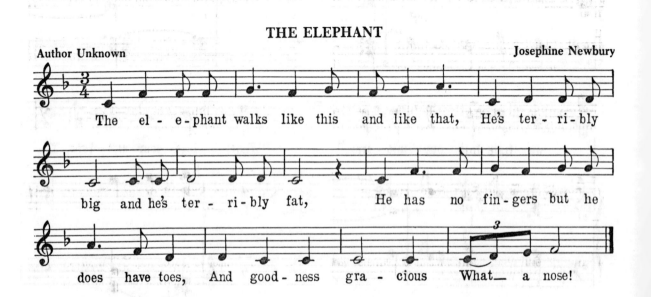

The el-e-phant walks like this and like that, He's ter-ri-bly

big and he's ter-ri-bly fat, He has no fin-gers but he

does have toes, And good-ness gra-cious What a nose!

SIX LITTLE DUCKS

Gaily

Folk Song

1. Six lit-tle ducks that I once knew, Fat ones, skin-ny ones, fair ones, too.

CHORUS

But the one lit-tle duck with a feath-er in his back,

He led the oth-ers with a quack, quack, quack,

Quack, quack, quack, quack, quack, quack,

He led the oth-ers with a quack, quack, quack.

2. Down to the river they would go,
   Wibble, wobble, wibble, wobble, to and fro.

3. Home from the river they would come,
   Wibble, wobble, wibble, wobble, ho hum hum

THE BOY AND THE BILLY GOATS THREE
A Folk Story Based Upon Folk Music

Once upon a time there was a boy who had three billy goats. Every morning he would take them up the hill to eat grass.

COME WITH ME, MY BILLY GOATS THREE

(Repeat the music for climbing. The knees should be lifted high in climbing.)

One morning he was very tired and sleepy. He sat down under a tree.

I'LL REST AND SLEEP

way from me.   Ho hum,   Ho hum,   Ho hum.   (yawns)

And soon he was fast asleep. But the billy goats three were not tired and sleepy.
They were very hungry.

THEY RAN ALL ABOUT

Folk Tune

They ran and they ran and they ran all a-bout,

Ran all a - bout, ran all a-bout; They came to a field where the

corn was tall, They jumped, jumped o - ver the wall.

(The movement is in galloping rhythm.)

After a while the boy woke up and rubbed his eyes.
"Where am I? And where are my billy goats three?"

YOO HOO!

Boy: Come here, come here, billy goats three!
Goats: Baa baa! We like this corn to eat.
　　　We're going to stay here all day and eat and eat.
Boy: Then I will drive you out!

THEY RAN ALL ABOUT

Folk Tune

The boy sat down under the tree and cried and cried.

RABBIT CAME A-HOPPING

Folk Tune

Rab - bit came a - hop - ping, a - hop - ping, a - hop - ping;

Rab - bit came a - hop - ping And stopped be - neath the tree.

Rabbit:

"Why are you cry - ing?"

Boy (mournfully):

"I have been try - ing to

drive my goats a - way from there." "Then leave the job to me!"

Rabbit (boastfully):

Rabbit: Come here, come here, billy goats three!
Goats: Baa! We like this corn to eat. We're going to stay here all day and eat and eat.
Rabbit: Then I will drive you out!

THEY RAN ALL ABOUT

(Repeat music. See page 124.)

So Mister Rabbit sat down under the tree beside the boy and cried and cried.

FOX CAME A-LOPING

Folk Tune

Mis - ter Fox came lop - ing, a - lop - ing, a - lop - ing,

Mis - ter Fox came lop - ing and stopped be - neath the tree.

Fox: Rabbit (mournfully):

"Why   are   you   cry - ing?"   "I   have   been   try - ing   to

Fox (boastfully):

drive the goats a - way from there." "Then leave the job to me!"

Fox: Come here, come here, billy goats three!

Goats: Baa baa! We like this corn to eat. We're going to stay here all day and eat and eat.

Fox: Then I will drive you out!

Song: They ran and they ran and they ran all about,

    Ran all about, ran all about.

    (Fox) "I can't drive them out, oh, what shall I do?

    Boo hoo! What shall I do?"

So Mister Fox sat down under the tree beside the boy and Mister Rabbit and cried and cried

HONEYBEE CAME BUZZING

Folk Tune

Fast

Zz ——— zz ——— zz ——— zz ——— Zz ———

zz ——— zz ——— zz ——— Hon - ey - bee came buzz - ing, a-

hold pedal down

(A buzzing chorus of voices throughout)

Boy ⎫
Rabbit ⎬ : You are too small. You cannot drive the goats out of the field of corn.
Fox ⎭

Bee: Then I will show you how! Come here, come here, billy goats three!

Goats: Baa baa! We like this corn to eat. We're going to stay here all day and eat and eat.

Bee: Then I will drive you out!

Song: The bee flew in and they ran all about,
Ran all about, ran all about.
He flew in their hair and stung them all,
They jumped back over the wall.

Boy ⎫
Fox ⎬ : Oh, thank you, honeybee, for driving the goats out of the field of corn.
Rabbit ⎭

Song: Come with me, my billy goats three,
Up on the hillside,
Where the grass is fresh and green,
Oh, come with me up the hillside.

THE END

From *The American Singer, Book I*, by John W. Beattie *et al.* Used by permission of American Book Co.

This is a story that young children enjoy dramatizing. The teacher may sing it rather than telling it, and let the children "play it." They will soon be able to sing the repetitive parts of the song-story.

8
Art for
the Artist's Sake

The child lives in a world rich with emotion and ideas which cry for expression. This sympathetic statement brings us closer to an understanding of inner forces which discourage or encourage growth.

THE LITTLE BOY[1]

Once a little boy went to school.
He was quite a little boy.
And it was quite a big school.
But when the little boy
Found that he could go to his room
By walking right in from the door outside,
He was happy.
And the school did not seem
Quite so big anymore.
One morning,

---
[1]From *School Arts Magazine*, October 1961. Used by permission.

When the little boy had been in school awhile,
The teacher said:
"Today we are going to make a picture."
"Good!" thought the little boy.
He *liked* to make pictures.
He could make all kinds:
Lions and tigers,
Chickens and cows,
Trains and boats—
And he took out his box of crayons
And began to draw.

But the teacher said: "Wait!
It is not time to begin!"
And she waited until everyone looked ready.

"Now," said the teacher,
"We are going to make flowers."
"Good!" thought the little boy,

He *liked* to make flowers,
And he began to make beautiful ones
With his pink and orange and blue crayons.

But the teacher said, "Wait!
And I will show you how."
And she drew a flower on the blackboard.
It was red, with a green stem.
"There," said the teacher,
"Now you may begin."

The little boy looked at the teacher's flower.
Then he looked at his own flower.
He liked *his* flower better than the teacher's.
But he did not say this,
He just turned his paper over
And made a flower like the teacher's.
It was red, with a green stem.

On another day,
When the little boy had opened
The door from the outside all by himself,
The teacher said:
"Today we are going to make something with
    clay."
"Good!" thought the little boy,
He *liked* clay.

He could make all kinds of things with clay:
Snakes and snowmen,
Elephants and mice,
Cars and trucks—
And he began to pull and pinch
His ball of clay.

But the teacher said:
"Wait! It is not time to begin!"
And she waited until everyone looked ready.

"Now," said the teacher,
"We are going to make a dish."
"Good!" thought the little boy,
He *liked* to make dishes,
And he began to make some
That were all shapes and sizes.

But the teacher said, "Wait!
And I will show you how."
And she showed everyone how to make
One deep dish.
"There," said the teacher,
"Now you may begin."

The little boy looked at the teacher's dish.
Then he looked at his own.
He *liked his* dishes better than the teacher's.
But he did not say this.
He just rolled his clay into a big ball again,
And made a dish like the teacher's.
It was a deep dish.

And pretty soon
The little boy learned to wait,
And to watch,
And to make things just like the teacher.
And pretty soon
He didn't make things of his own anymore.

Then it happened
That the little boy and his family
Moved to another house,
In another city,
And the little boy
Had to go to another school.

This school was even Bigger
Than this other one,
And there was no door from the outside
Into his room.
He had to go up some big steps,
And walk down a long hall
To get to his room.

And the very first day
He was there,
The teacher said:
"Today we are going to make a picture."
"Good!" thought the little boy,
And he waited for the teacher
To tell him what to do.
But the teacher didn't say anything.
She just walked around the room.

When she came to the little boy
She said, "Don't you want to make a picture?"
"Yes," said the little boy,
"What are we going to make?"
"I don't know until you make it," said the
    teacher.
"How shall I make it?" asked the little boy.
"Why, any way you like," said the teacher.

"And any color?" asked the little boy.
"Any color," said the teacher,
"If everyone made the same picture,

And used the same colors,
How would I know who made what,
And which was which?"
"I don't know," said the little boy.
And he began to make pink and orange and
blue flowers.

He liked his new school . . .
Even if it didn't have a door
Right in from the outside!
—Helen E. Buckley

Art to the child is more than a matter of painting pictures or making objects. It is a means by which he expresses his individuality and communicates his ideas about himself and his world.[2]

One of the important daily responsibilities of the teacher is to provide for the children an environment conducive to enjoyable, satisfying art experiences. This will mean providing the right kinds of art equipment and supplies and having them ready for the children's use when they need them. When the materials are prepared and arranged in the art area of the room each morning, one can almost hear the paints, clay, finger paint, chalk, crayons, scrap materials, paste, and paper calling out to the children as they enter the room, "Come try me and see what you can do and say with me."

The young child's beginning interest in art is sensory. It is muscular and it is exploratory. He likes the feel of clay as he squeezes it in his fists, pinches it with his fingers, or rolls it between his hands into little balls or long wriggly snakes. He finds satisfaction in moving a big easel brush over a large sheet of paper and watching the colors move about and change before his eyes. Most young children thoroughly delight in squishing and squashing finger paint about with the palms of their hands, their fingers, fists, arms, and even their elbows. They are intrigued with the way the patterns appear and change as if by magic.

Almost all kindergarten children have had experiences with crayons before they come to school. This, then, is an art medium with which the child feels quite comfortable. He finds colored chalk and pastels even more gratifying because he can make bolder, more vivid marks on the paper.

The young child delights in trying to cut and paste pictures. In all his early art experiences he finds deep satisfaction in making discoveries about the properties of the various media and what he can do with them.

Charles and Margaret Gaitskell remind teachers that "the period of manipulation is a happy and educative one for children."[3]

During this exploratory, manipulative stage, the young child tests his ideas with the art media. His actions have meaning for him but are usually unrecognizable to adults.

What started out as a large sheet of newsprint only partially covered by a few blobs of paint of a single color later evolves into a pattern of a number of colors painted with real purpose but still non-objective in form.

Victor Lowenfeld suggests that

To look for reality in our children's drawings is one of the most common mistakes. "It does not look real" is the worst thing you can say to a child about his art. That Mary's art does not look real to the adult eye . . . by no means indicates that it is not real to her. However, the kind of reality is quite different. Reality in appearance does not make things real to your feelings and emotions.[4]

As the young child becomes more aware of his environment and his relationship to it, he begins to paint symbols. One of the first of these symbols which is recognizable is the circle which very soon becomes the sun with all its radiating rays.

As the child continues to experiment with the materials with which he is working, he begins to paint the human figure—a big circle with eyes, nose, and mouth and a straight line out from either side as the arms with radiating fingers on the ends. If legs appear, they are attached to the bottom of the "head." Sometimes his man will have only the legs extending from the head.

---

[2]Jane Cooper Bland, *Art of the Young Child* (New York: The Museum of Modern Art, 1957), p. 3.
[3]Charles and Margaret Gaitskell, *Art Education in the Kindergarten* (Peoria, Ill.: Charles A. Bennett Co., 1952), p. 5.
[4]Viktor Lowenfeld, *Your Child and His Art* (New York: The Macmillan Co., 1954), p. 21.

The young child paints only what is important to him at the time.

Again Lowenfeld explains that

The child expresses in his art *his* level of growth, which cannot be changed or "corrected" through superficial criticism. Growth is a continuous process, and we cannot force the child into it. Since Johnny is not ready to relate his painting to reality, a criticism which forces him to compare it with reality would only be discouraging. For him it is much more important to establish a relationship between his own *experience* and his creative expression.[5]

Later the child will begin painting and drawing identifiable gabled houses with the chimney going off to the side and a tree with big red apples growing on it in the yard.

Further in his development he will add a base line—perhaps a strip of green across the bottom of the page to represent grass. About the same time he will add a strip of blue across the top for the sky. Rarely does the young child paint the sky so that it touches the grass. The teacher accepts this, for this is "the way it is" for the child. One teacher whom the author knew was determined to "correct" this art form. She even took the kindergarten children outdoors and had them look at the sky, saying, "Now you see the sky comes right down to the ground."

A very self-assured five-year-old challenged the teacher, however. "No it doesn't," he explained, " 'cause I've been up there. We went in a plane to New York one time."

Jane Cooper Bland says of the young child that "he lives through a series of experiences as he paints or models and his final creation might be compared to a motion picture of which we see only the last frame."[6]

An example of this was observed as a five-year-old painted a most interesting picture which grew and changed moment by moment. The observer thought the child had finished, and she was delighted with the child's satisfaction throughout the painting experience. She was also pleased with the finished product: the picture showed a little boy and girl playing in the yard beside their red (brick) home. There was a big bright yellow sun up in the left-hand corner.

Instead of removing his picture from the easel to put it on the drying rack, the child picked up the container of black paint and proceeded to cover the picture from top to bottom with big bold black strokes. The observer couldn't understand the child's "apparent dislike for his painting, causing him to destroy it."

Removing the picture from the easel, the child turned to a teacher nearby and said, "See my picture. It's night now. First it was day and then it got all dark with nighttime."

"In all creative activity it is the process of creating—of remembering, organizing, imagining and expressing—that is important to the child."[7] The teacher's concern with regard to the kindergarten child and his art experiences is in what happens to the child as a result of the experience and not in the finished product. In other words, the teacher's purpose can be stated simply as "art for the artist's sake, not for art's sake."

The young child paints and draws according to the way he feels. "His proportion of one object to another is not based on what he sees but on what importance it has for him."[8] A kindergarten child painted "his birthday," including cake with candles and birthday gifts, all of which he painted much larger than anything else—even himself. Another child painted a picture of himself walking his new brown puppy. In his painting the puppy filled most of the page. He himself was represented by a very small figure of a child holding a rope tied around the puppy's neck. These two pictures were out of proportion realistically, but *in proportion* to the emotional attachment the children had for the subjects of their paintings.

TEACHER INVOLVEMENT

In order to provide adequately for the child's art experiences, the teacher must understand the child's needs and plan for him accordingly.

First of all, the young child needs a class-

[5]*Ibid.*
[6]Bland, *Art of the Young Child*, p. 7.
[7]Elementary Education Service, *A Guide for Kindergarten* (Richmond: State Department of Education, 1968).
[8]*Art Guide: Let's Make a Picture* (Washington, D.C.: Association for Childhood Education International, 1969), p. 24.

room environment that is free from adults who are overly zealous about his progress and about his creative productions. He needs an environment that has a warm, friendly, accepting climate.

He needs to feel free enough with the teachers and the materials to express his feelings and thoughts, whatever they may be. He needs to feel comfortable about making a mess —even with paint spills—knowing that there is clean-up equipment easily accessible to him.

He needs to have adequate space that is convenient to the materials he wishes to use. To have the most satisfying art experiences, the child needs to have an attractive classroom in which to work and play—a room where there is beauty here and there, with interesting color combinations which are changed frequently— flowers, mobiles, picture books, a beautiful picture, a scarf of unusual design, an attractive wall display, and lovely music. (A kindergarten child, while listening to a recording of the *Nutcracker Suite,* said "Hey, I think I'll go and *paint* some pretty music." And she did!)

The kindergarten child also needs ample time to experiment with and explore the potentialities of the medium with which he is working at a given time.

He needs to have a wealth of rich, firsthand and vicarious experiences out of which to create with paint and clay and other materials.

The child needs to feel he has made his creation himself. The adult never takes the brush or crayon to "show the child how to make it" or to "touch up" the child's work. Neither does he or she give the child pictures or patterns to copy to make his art work more realistic. This means that there should be no photograph materials or coloring books used in the kindergarten. These materials do not train the child to stay within the lines, as is sometimes suggested reasoning for using them. Observations of children's own creative drawing and painting indicate that they are far more concerned with filling in carefully the lines of figures of their own creations than with the adult-prescribed "fill-in pictures."

The fill-in pictures stifle the child's imagination and creativity and make it impossible for

him to be able to express his own feelings.

The young child needs to have a wide variety of art materials with which to experiment and work during the year. He also needs a variety of types of art activities in which to try out his abilities, extend his interests, and develop his skills.

There are occasions when the kindergarten child needs to work with an art medium to help him drain off his bad feelings. He may find easel painting helpful, or he may need to beat and pound and punch and pull a chunk of clay or push finger paint around for a while. Having experienced release through such activities, the child himself may begin to recognize times when he needs to "work out" his feelings, just as one very frustrated child did when he announced to his teacher, "I think I *need* to finger paint right now."

The child needs to enjoy creating with art media without having to feel that whatever he draws or paints or makes has *to tell a story or be something.* And he should be free from having to explain "what it is" to adults unless he volunteers the information. On occasion a teacher, desiring to understand more about a particular art experience a child has had, might comment casually to him, "That is so interesting. Could you tell me what you were thinking about as you made it?"

THE PAINTING [9]

Once a little boy was going to paint a picture.
He put the paper on the easel,
And he looked at all the jars of color
In front of him.
"What are you going to paint?" asked the
    teacher.
"The sky," said the little boy,
"I'm going to paint the sky."
"Good," said the teacher,
"Do you have enough blue paint?"
"Yes," said the little boy,
And he took up the blue brush
And made a wide band across the top of his
    paper.
"There," he said, "There is the blue sky,"
And he looked around for the teacher,
But she had gone.

Then the little boy looked out of the window
To see if his sky looked like the real one.

---

[9]Used by permission of the author and the Association for Childhood Education International.

And it did.
But was the sky *always* blue?
The little boy put down the blue brush
And thought about the sky.
"Sometimes," he thought, "Just before night,
The sky is pink—and a little purple."
So he took up the pink brush
And then the purple,
And pretty soon there was a sunset on his paper.

Then the little boy remembered winter,
And how the sky looks when the snow comes
    down.
So he took up the white brush
And made soft snowflakes over all
The blue and the pink and the purple sky.
And some of the snowflakes melted
To make more colors, and the little boy felt
    happy
Like he always did when the snow came down
In the wintertime.

And just as he was about to put down his brush
And he finished, he remembered a day in sum-
    mer
When the sky grew dark.
And he remembered that he had been a little
    scared,
And he had run to tell his mother about it.
So now he took up the black brush
And painted great storm clouds
With flashes of red and orange lightning
Streaking through them.
"It's thundering, too," said the little boy softly
    to himself,
"Boom! Boom! Boom! And the wind is blowing!"
And he made the rain come down—hard rain—
In long green lines across the sky,
And all the colors ran together in rainbows
At the bottom of his paper.

"Now I will make the sun shine,"
Said the little boy to himself,
And he made a big, round sun in the middle of
    his paper.
But the painting was so wet,
And there were so many colors in it,
That the yellow sun turned brown in the sky.
But the little boy didn't care—
His picture was finished
And it was just the way he wanted it.

He looked around for the teacher,
And pretty soon she was there—
Standing by the easel and looking at all the col-
    ors:
All the blue and the pink and the purple;
All the white and the black;
All the red and orange and green;
And the yellow that had turned brown.
The teacher looked at all the wet and dripping
    colors
Which had run together
In the snow and the wind and the rain
Of the little boy's painting.

And she said, "My goodness!"
"I thought you were going to make the sky!"
"I did," said the little boy,
"I made all the skies I know about."
And he took his picture off the easel
And put it carefully away to dry.
                                        —*Helen E. Buckley*

The young child needs encouragement and commendation, when deserved, for his artistic efforts. He needs to enjoy respect for himself and his work, both from his teachers and his peers. The teacher should refrain from negative criticism and comparison of children's art work. The only comparisons that should be made are with the individual child's own work, to show him and his parents how he has grown during the year.

The kindergarten child needs to experience from his parents the same understanding, acceptance, and respect for his art work that he receives at school. This may not always be true unless the parents have some awareness of the expectancies of a five-year-old and his creative work.

In order that the children's parents may have a better understanding of the kindergarten's philosophy of art education, the teacher should interpret to them very early in the year the art program.

One of the most effective ways of doing this is to have an "art workshop" parents' meeting at a time when both parents are free to attend. The teacher would have the kindergarten room set up with art centers in which the mothers and fathers may experiment and work with all the different art media the children will be using during the year. The teacher will help the parents to learn on their own some of the values conserved for the individual through his involvement in different art activities.

At the close of an exciting evening of discovery for the parents, the teacher should let the group deal with questions that they may have about the child and his art experiences. He or she might want to have some duplicated materials for the parents to take home with them, including perhaps some of the needs of the child in his art experiences and how parents and teachers can best respond to them. The teacher might want to include also recipes for finger paint and homemade play dough.

An inexpensive publication which might be made available for the parents is the pamphlet *Color Book Craze*, published by the Association for Childhood Education International, 3615 Wisconsin Ave., N.W., Washington, D.C. 20016. An excellent movie which might be used with the parents is *The Purple Turtle*. It is in color, 16 mm, and runs fourteen minutes. It may be ordered on free loan from:

The American Crayon Company
P.O. Box 2067
Sandusky, Ohio 44870

This film shows young children in their classroom enjoying a variety of art activities. The audience hears the imaginative chatter of the children as the film focuses in on their free, productive hands. It is hard not to get caught up in the joy and exuberance of the "embryonic artists" shown in the movie.

ART ACTIVITIES

Easel Painting

To allow for the daily demand of this activity, the class needs two double easels. If space is at a premium, several easels that are hinged to the wall may be constructed. This type can be folded back against the wall when not in use, thereby conserving space.

Some children prefer to paint on a table or counter top, and some like to paint on the floor. When the child stands at a table or counter top he can make large, free-swinging strokes on the paper. He is also able to paint without having the experience of paint running down his picture "in drip-drops," as one child expressed it.

Whether the tempera paint used is liquid or powder, the teacher will be sure that the colors are strong and bright. (Instructions for mixing tempera paint are found on page 142.) At first only the primary colors of red, yellow, and blue should be available for the children. They will enjoy mixing these and discovering new colors for themselves. Later other colors may be added for their use.

Newsprint 18″ × 24″ is the least expensive paper. It is available in several pastel colors as well as in the usual neutral shade. Sheets from the classified ad section of the daily newspaper can be used very effectively, particularly if the paint is mixed to a consistency which covers the print.

A folding wooden drying rack for laundry is quite adequate for drying the children's paintings.

Finger Painting

As an art activity, finger painting, or hand painting, as it might be called, is always popular with the young child. He can achieve a variety of effects with the paint as he tries the palm of his hand, his knuckles, the side of his hand, his fist, and his fingernails. Discovering these effects and the effects of mixing colors and exploring different techniques in controlling the paint are a part of the pleasure and satisfaction the child derives from finger painting.

Finger paint paper may be used for the finger painting, but because of the cost involved, many schools have turned to a less expensive paper. Roll shelf paper which is glazed or plastic-covered serves quite well. The widest roll, preferably 18″, should be used. Pieces can be cut 24″ long. The 18″ × 24″ size will allow the child opportunity for large sweeping movements over the paper.

(Note: If shelf paper is used the teacher should check to be sure it is not treated with chemicals to kill insects.)

A large sponge may be used to thoroughly wet the glazed side of the paper. The child is then ready to spread two tablespoonfuls of the paint all over the paper with the palm of his hand. (If the dry tempera is to be added, the mixture is now ready.) What happens next on the paper is a surprise to everyone as the child moves his hands, fingers, fingernails, and fists or arms about through the paint. The child's "picture" may be saved by lifting it carefully by the bottom corners and laying it out on newspaper to dry. The newspaper absorbs the moisture from the paper, aiding in the drying of the paint. If the paper curls on the edges when dry, it may be pressed on the unpainted side with a warm iron.

Finger painting done right on a formica-top table *without* paper, however, gives the child complete freedom and lessens attempts at trying to "draw a picture" with the use of his index finger. The younger child has a much better experience if he uses the finger paint without the paper. He will experiment with the medium more readily and use more freely his whole hands, his arms, and even his elbows. Every movement the child makes in the paint is a creation of design and rhythm. The child's "creation" may be preserved for him by placing a sheet of newsprint (12″ × 18″) on top of his finger painting and smoothing it down carefully. When lifted, this paper will have a print of the finger painting. This is called a monoprint.

Sponge Painting

Pieces of cellulose sponge cut small enough for the children to handle make good applicators of paint. Paint pads, each of a different color, are needed for this activity. The child presses his piece of sponge on a stamp pad, then on his paper. (See directions for making stamp pad in the section of this chapter entitled "Recipes and Helpful Hints.")

There are different techniques which may be used with different effects:

1. Stippling is done by lightly pressing the sponge on the pad and then lightly touching it to the paper. The print shows the irregular holes in the sponge. Designs may be made and color combinations appear as the child overlaps the prints with the sponge. Winter pictures may be made by using white paint stippled on black or dark blue construction paper.

2. Stippling around a cardboard figure makes an interesting silhouette—a leaf, geometric shapes, or shapes related to seasonal activities: pumpkins, bells, Christmas trees, hearts, etc. (The children can cut these from folded paper and then stipple around them.)

3. Cut the sponge into geometric shapes: circle, square, triangle, and rectangle, and let the children stipple with them, making all kinds of designs or objects by their creative arrangement of the shapes.

4. Some children will enjoy just painting a picture with the sponges, much as they use an easel brush. As they wipe the sponge on the paper, they realize an entirely different effect.

Gadget or "Junk" Printing

All that is needed for this activity is several of the stamp pads, each for a different color paint, and a tray of junk objects such as thread spools, large screws, plastic bottle tops, discarded hair curlers, flat potato masher, plastic forks, small plastic bottles, small scraps of wood, plastic pot scraper, a small roll of corrugated cardboard, and any other small object that will print.

Paper 12″ × 18″ gives the child ample space to work freely but does not give him too much space to cover. This is a good activity for using scrap paper which may be in odd sizes.

To add interest and variety, the paper may be cut in geometric shapes.

This is an art activity in which any child can realize accomplishment. It is highly manipulative and brings thrills as designs emerge and interesting color combinations appear.

String Painting

The same stamp pads are needed for this activity as for junk printing and sponge painting. Sixteen-inch lengths of heavy soft cotton string are needed.

The child folds his paper in half to begin with and then opens it out flat. (Manila paper is best for this.) He drops the string onto a pad and with a plastic fork presses it on the pad until it is covered with paint. The pad should not be too heavily saturated with paint or the string will absorb too much and will be too wet. Experimenting with this will be necessary to discover the right amount of paint to use.

The child lays the string down on one side of the fold, arranging it in any way he chooses. He then folds the other side of the paper over the string and presses gently. Opening up the paper, he removes the string, replacing it on the stamp pad. He repeats the process with strings of other colors. His finished product will be symmetrical and beautiful.

Another technique in string painting gives an entirely different result. Instead of leaving the string within the folded paper, the child leaves a short end hanging off the edge. He folds the other side of the paper over the string and holds it securely with one hand. With the other hand he pulls the string, moving it gently from side to side until it comes all the way out. Some of the prints that appear will be thrilling surprises for the child.

Blotto Painting

Tempera paint is available in small containers with a medicine dropper in each. Primary colors and black are needed.

A heavier, less absorbent paper than newsprint is needed for this activity. Manila paper does nicely, as does any paper that has a tough, semi-slick finish.

The child folds the paper in the middle, then opens it out. With medicine droppers he drops paint along the center fold.

When the child has dropped different colors along the fold and perhaps several drops to the side of the fold, he then folds one side of the paper over and with the palm of his hand rubs the paper from the fold outward. This mixes and spreads the paint across the paper.

When he opens the paper out flat, he has a wonder "picture" that is the same on both sides. He will delight in seeing what happened to the yellow and blue colors that ran together—or the red and yellow. No two pictures ever turn out the same.

The secret of success is in putting just the right amount of paint on the paper and in rubbing it in a way that pushes the paint outward from the fold of the paper.

Blow Painting

The materials needed for this activity are: soda straws; tempera paint in small containers; medicine droppers; and non-absorbant, semi-slick paper, 9" × 12" in size.

The child puts a drop or two of one color paint on the paper, then immediately begins blowing through a soda straw to make the drops of paint run around. When he has exhausted those drops, he uses two or three more drops of a different color. If he drops these near the first ones, he can blow the paint into the other "little rivers" and mix the colors.

The colors used will depend on the season of the year. In the fall orange, yellow, brown, and black may be used. In the spring pastel shades may be mixed for the children to use, or they may mix them.

The secret of success in this activity is to have the paint mixed to a consistency which allows it to be blown over the paper easily. This will mean that the teacher will need to experiment beforehand with the paint and the type of paper the children will use.

Painting with Felt Markers

Bright shades in water color are available commercially in felt-tip markers. These should be nontoxic and washable. Kindergarten children enjoy this medium for drawing, especially those who enjoy crayon drawing. The children's drawings are bolder in color and sharper in form. This is a pleasing addition to the children's experiences with art media.

Crayon Drawing

Large kindergarten crayons and large pieces of newsprint give children another means of telling what they are thinking and how they feel about it. (Small crayons cramp young children's hands.) Soft wax crayons of a good quality give the best satisfaction. Because of the influence of coloring books in their homes since their "scribbling days," children at first may be lost without a picture to color. But with proper motivation they will soon find much greater satisfaction in "saying their story their own way" or in just making a pretty picture with their crayons and paper.

Another technique which has fascination for the child is called "crayon rubbing." Anything he may wish to transfer on his paper may be used. Different textures are good to use—sandpaper, screen wire, plastic net, or corrugated cardboard. In the fall, colored leaves which have been pressed and dried make beautiful rubbings. The leaf is placed on the table, vein side up. A little rubber cement will hold it in place while the child rubs over it. Any type of paper will do. Crayons need to have their paper covering peeled off and be in short lengths.

With the side of the crayon the child rubs back and forth over the leaf until a crayon copy of it appears. Several colors of crayons may be used and mixed over the leaves to represent the fall colors seen in them.

Note: When the activity is over and the children are cleaning up, have them just lift up the leaves and with their fingers rub the rubber cement off the table. It will roll right up and brush off. Do not try to wash the table until all the rubber cement is off. Water makes it very difficult to remove this type of glue.

Cutting and Pasting

Materials for this activity are always available for the children. For most pasting of paper, regular white library paste works well. Small plastic jars with airtight lids make good containers for the paste. Paste brushes cut down on the child's eating the paste, which he would lick from his fingers. Little plastic butter spreaders for corn on the cob are light and easy for the children to handle. They are also *very* durable and much less expensive than the commercial paste brushes sold in art supply stores. The stiff nylon bristles wash easily in cold water.

Collages

Given a piece of cardboard, glue, and a box of scrap materials, the young child will enjoy creating the interesting "bumpy pictures" which adults call collages.

Ordinary library paste is not always satisfactory for this activity, because when it dries the heavy objects drop off. There is a commercial glue which is white, very adhesive, nontoxic, and washable. It comes in small squeeze bottles, or small amounts may be squeezed out into a small container and brushes used.

There is no end to the kinds of materials which may be used: bits of yarn, lace, rickrack, colored string; cloth of all textures; seeds and small sticks; artificial flowers; feathers; short lengths of colored soda straws; colored toothpicks; short lengths of colored paper folded into cat stairs or pulled across the edge of a pair of scissors to curl them; scraps of colored corrugated cardboard, etc.

This activity stimulates the child's imagination and sets his creative powers to work. The result: "beautiful nothings."

Torn Paper Pictures

Children enjoy tearing scraps of colored paper into odd shapes. They can then arrange the colors and shapes and paste them on 9" × 12" colored paper.

For the most part, the children will make a random arrangement. Some, however, will see objects in the shapes as they put them together with real purpose.

Coffee Grounds Pictures

Save coffee grounds, and after drying them store them in a tight container.

The children can make coffee pictures by spreading glue (nontoxic school glue) about on cardboard and sprinkling the grounds on the glue. This can be an added touch of interest to a "collage" picture after it is finished. The "coffee pictures" are not only fun to make; they smell good too!

Tissue Paper Cutting

Ten-inch squares of colored tissue paper may be used for cutting "colored lace." The easiest method for the young child is for him to fold the paper in half, making a rectangle, then in half once more, making a square. One more fold is needed to make a triangle of the folded paper. The child holds with one hand the point that is closed and cuts in and out along both folded edges. He may also serrate the open edges. When the paper is opened, he has a lacy design.

After the children learn how to cut these designs, they may be ready to cut snowflakes from white tissue paper. The folding of the paper is more complex. The first fold is to make a triangle by bringing the bottom point to touch the top point and creasing the base line. (See page 140.)

The next fold is from left to right or side to side, making figure 2.

The third step is to open back out to figure 1 with the folded side down. Using the vertical crease as a guide for the center, bring one side up as in figure 3. Then fold the other side over as in figure 4.

Following the middle crease, fold points over to touch, as in figure 5. Holding the folded point in one hand, cut in and out on both sides, being careful not to cut entirely across the paper.

When opened out, the paper is a six-pointed snowflake.

These may be used for decorations in the

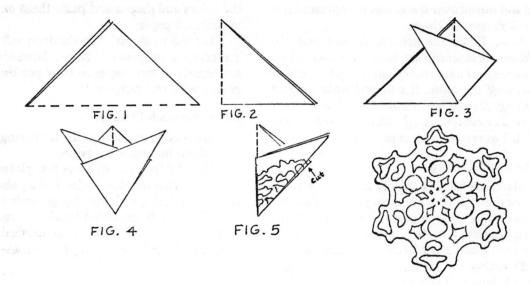

FIG. 1   FIG. 2   FIG. 3

FIG. 4   FIG. 5

room or pasted on dark blue or black construction paper.

This, like *all* art activities, is not to be used as a total group activity. A teacher or an aide or a parent may work with one or two children at a time. Only those who can and wish to will engage in this activity.

This is certainly appropriate to use during or after a big snow when the children have actually looked at snow crystals under a strong magnifying glass.

Chalk

Colored chalk (the large sticks—one inch in diameter) is available from educational or art supply houses. It is a freer medium than crayons and produces vivid color effects. Because of its size, chalk covers more quickly.

While chalk may be used on wet or dry paper, teachers find that young children use the medium with more ease if they draw on wet paper. When buttermilk is used to moisten the paper, there is no need to use a fixative to prevent the chalk from smearing and rubbing off. The child may apply the buttermilk to his paper with a large easel brush. Manila drawing paper has a texture which makes interesting pictures, and it is more durable than newsprint.

Pastels come either with a plain or an oil base. These can be used for making overall chalk pictures to which the child later adds finger paint.

If the pastel colors used on the paper are dark ones, then white or yellow finger paint may be used. If the colors are lighter, black finger paint makes a more attractive picture.

To get the best effect, the child covers an entire piece of manila paper, 9" × 12" with the pastels or dry chalk. He should use a number of colors in little patches, covering the paper completely. Then he makes a finger paint design on a formica shelf or table. He then places his chalk drawing, chalk side down, over the finger paint and blots it up. The colors show through in the thin spots of the finger paint.

When dry, these pictures may be mounted on colored construction paper that makes a complementary matting. If they are to be mounted, they will look better if pressed on the back with a warm iron. This makes the "painting" look as if it was done in oils—a very welcome gift to parents for some special occasion.

Note: Be sure children wash their hands well after working with chalk.

Soap Painting

Experimenting with this medium can bring some very different effects. For example, the mixture may be left white for making snow paintings, or food coloring may be added to give individual desired effects.

The children have as much fun mixing the medium as they do painting with it. It takes 2 cups of soap flakes (*not detergent*) and 3/4 cup of cold water. The children may measure these ingredients into a large bowl. They can mix it with a rotary beater until it becomes thick and has a creamy consistency.

If color is desired, food coloring may be added. Easel brushes may be used for painting with the soap mixture. For fine lines, the children may use Q-Tips. These pictures will take time to dry and should not be moved until they are dry.

Clay Modeling

Moist potter's clay is preferable for use by young children. If it is not available locally as a natural resource, powdered clay may be purchased from an art or school supply house. Directions for mixing are given on the package. Ready-mixed clay is also available in five-pound packages but is more expensive.

A ten-gallon galvanized garbage pail with a tightly fitting lid can be used for storing the clay to keep it moist and in good condition for modeling. A damp cloth kept over the clay will also help, especially if the clay is kept in large balls ready for the children to use. The clay may be kept in plastic bags and then stored in the galvanized can. Each time the clay is put away it should be rolled into balls the size of a baseball. A hole should be punched in each ball, and the hole filled with water. The clay should be squeezed together over the hole before being stored. Hardened clay which has not been baked may be reclaimed for use by breaking it up and pouring water over it slowly until all the water is absorbed. It is usually necessary to let this clay stand for several days. When it can be worked into smooth modeling consistency, it is ready for use and can be stored with the rest of the clay.

A special table, perhaps with a formica top, may be used for clay activities, or clay boards, preferably small breadboards which have had a coat of lacquer or pieces cf masonite may be used on other tables. As in all art activities, it is a part of good housekeeping to use newspapers to cover and protect equipment. The children will be more at ease in their work and can do a better job of cleaning up after their activities if plenty of newspapers are used.

Young children need to work with large chunks of clay. The only guidance necessary for them as they experiment with this medium is to explain that wetting the ends of the pieces of clay which they want to put together will help to hold them in place. Small jar lids with a little water in them may be placed on the table so that the children may share them as they work and have need of the water.

Other Modeling Activities

There are other commercial modeling materials on the market that have a different feel and consistency from the natural potter's clay. There is the non-hardening plastic dough and the popular Play Doh, with which most young children are familiar.

Then there are the cooked and uncooked doughs which the teacher and children can make. These can be used with rolling pin and cookie cutters for home play activities.

Each of these types of modeling materials has a somewhat different contribution to make to the young child's modeling experience.

Cardboard Box Construction

The teacher should keep a continuing collection of small cardboard boxes of varying shapes and sizes. Cardboard tubes and box partitions add to the versatility of the construction. School glue that is white, nontoxic, and washable is needed for this activity. Masking tape and a stapler are also often needed. Such materials, along with tempera paint, are enough to spark the child's imagination for creating fascinating pieces of sculpture.

Construction Work

Equipment needed for woodworking activities are: a worktable or bench; 3 hammers; 2 saws; 1 screwdriver; 1 plane; 2 brace and bits; sandpaper of varying degrees of coarseness; nails (3/4", 1", 1 1/2"); plywood tool board with painted outlines of tools and with hooks for hanging in place; box of scrap wood of varying sizes—soft wood, free from splinters; wooden wheels; dowel sticks. Tools should be of good quality—not cheap toys, but of a size and weight which young children are able to handle easily.

If the woodworking activities can be carried on in an alcove of the room away from other activities, there is less danger of accidents, and the necessary noise is not disturbing. This is also a good outdoor activity, but *wherever it is carried on, there should be close supervision by an adult.*

Block Construction

Unit blocks are conducive to a variety of self-expressional activities. Hollow blocks stimulate large muscular activities and dramatic play as the children create boats, jet planes, trains, buses, grocery stores, or farms. Low, open shelves for storage of blocks place the responsibility on the children for the housekeeping activities involved with this equipment.

In all the activities herein mentioned, the emphasis is intended to be primarily on the child's creative response to the medium. The important aspect of any art activity is what it does for the child as he works in the process, rather than the finished product he creates.

RECIPES AND HELPFUL HINTS

Finger Paint

> 5/8 cup dry laundry starch
> 1 pint water
> 3/4 cup soap flakes
> 1/4 cup talcum powder
> 1 teaspoon artificial oil of sassafras as a preservative

Mix the starch with a little cold water to make a creamy paste. Add to pint of water and cook slowly until mixture becomes "clear," or glossy. Stir constantly. Let the mixture cool a bit, then add soap flakes and powder, stirring until evenly distributed. Add oil of sassafras. *(Note: If the starch mixture becomes too stiff as it cooks, thin it with a little water. Avoid letting it become lumpy.)* Color may be added in the jar, mixing in the dry tempera. However, children enjoy adding the color themselves. This can be done if the powdered tempera is put into salt shakers. After the child has spread the clear starch mixture all over the surface he is to paint, he may sprinkle on the desired color and work it about through the finger paint until it is thoroughly mixed.

Modeling Dough

Uncooked dough. Mix thoroughly one cup of flour and one cup of salt. Slowly add food coloring and enough water to make this mixture pliable. One tablespoon of salad oil added will keep the mixture from hardening. (If Christmas tree ornaments are to be made of this dough, the salad oil should be omitted.)

Cooked dough. Mix one cup flour and 1/2 cup cornstarch into one cup cold water in a large bowl. Boil one cup salt and four cups water in a large pan. When boiling, pour salt water slowly into mixture in the bowl. Then return this milky-looking fluid to the pan and cook on low heat until thickened, stirring constantly (3–5 minutes). When cool, stir in 4–5 cups of flour. (If tempera paint is to be added for color, it should be added as the flour is added. If food coloring is to be used, it should be added before the flour is added. The colors should be bright and strong.) Then knead in more flour until the dough is soft and pliable but not sticky.

If this dough draws moisture due to weather changes while stored, more flour may be kneaded into it. If it becomes too thick, more water may be worked into it.

Preparing Tempera Paint

Liquid tempera comes in a concentrated form. All that is needed is to thin it with water to the correct consistency.

Powdered tempera requires more care in mixing. The best results in preparing this opaque paint for use may be obtained in the following way:

1. Pour into a small container the amount of water desired.

2. Pour the powdered paint into the water slowly, mixing thoroughly to a thin, creamy consistency. When the paint will cover the print of newspaper, it is thick enough for use.

Paint Extender

Liquid starch may be added to tempera paint to improve the texture and eliminate some of the dripping—about two tablespoons of starch to each small container of paint. Another mixture may be made and used in the same amounts as a paint extender by cooking cornstarch to the consistency of gravy.

Stamp Pads

Stamp pads for use in string painting, sponge painting, stippling, and gadget printing may be prepared as follows:

Small aluminum frozen pie containers should be fitted with two thicknesses of pieces of scrap felt. Saturate the felt with a thicker than usual mixture of tempera paint. Test it with the object for printing to determine the right amount of moisture. More paint may be added to the pad with a paint brush as needed. The pads should be washed out and dried after each session in which the stamp pads are used.

Thin pieces of cellulose sponge cut to fit the bottom of the pans also make effective pads and are more durable than the felt.

Painting Smocks

These can be very easily made from men's discarded sport shirts. Buttoned down the back, the shirt covers the child well and at the same time allows freedom of movement. Smocks are necessary equipment for most art activities. If the shirts are too large for the children, they may be made to fit by taking a tuck over each shoulder until the sleeve is raised to a place comfortable for the child. The smock can be made "paint proof" by sewing a piece of plastic on the inside of the back of the shirt, up around the neck and armholes and down the side seams.

Scissors Holder

Molded egg cartons taped shut make very useful scissors holders when turned upside down with small slits pierced in each egg container. The kindergarten, blunt-end scissors fit perfectly. With the handles erect in the carton, they are easy for the children to grasp when needed.

MATERIALS AND EQUIPMENT

2 double easels
Paint—powdered and/or liquid tempera, all colors and black and white
Paint extender—liquid starch
Easel brushes—long-handled, black-bristle, flat, in sizes 1/2", 3/4", and 1" (several 1/4" brushes may be needed at times)
Plastic or metal containers for easel paints
1/2 gallon plastic bucket for washing brushes
Felt (watercolor) markers (assorted sizes)
Paper:
   Newsprint—plain and colored, 12" × 18" and 18" × 24"

Manila paper, 12" × 18"
Bogus paper in rolls (especially good for painting winter pictures)
Colored tissue paper
Wallpaper (scrap rolls or sample books)
Colored construction paper—9" × 12" and 12" × 18", assorted colors
Colored corrugated paper for collages and for bordering pictures for display
Cardboard—tagboard and poster board
Wrapping paper—large widths for making self-portraits
Gift wrap paper
Newspaper (classified ad section)
Scissors—blunt-end, several pairs of "lefties"
Colored chalk—large, 1" sticks, pastels (regular and oil base)
Crayons—large, round, and of good quality wax
Paste—library paste and white school glue (nontoxic and washable type)
Paper bags
Clay boards—formica or bread boards, 10" × 14"
Modeling materials—commercial types and homemade dough
Tape—masking, cellophane
Stapler
Cellulose sponges
Woodworking equipment—workbench and tools: hammers, saw, plane, brace and bit, sandpaper, nails
Laundry drying rack
Scrap materials: cloth scraps, lace, yarn, rickrack, ribbon, cardboard, feathers, artificial flowers, wood, small boxes of all sizes, thread spools, bottle tops, plastic forks, clothespins, plastic hair curlers, cardboard cylinders, dried coffee grounds, wallpaper (rolls or sample books), gift wrap paper, styrofoam meat trays, molded egg cartons, cardboard dividers from wholesale egg boxes, newspaper, any small object suitable for gadget printing, ad infinitum.

BIBLIOGRAPHY

Art Guide: Let's Make a Picture. Washington, D.C.: Association for Childhood Education International, 1969.

Bland, Jane Cooper. *Art of the Young Child.* Rev. ed. New York: Museum of Modern Art, 1968.

Cole, Natalie R. *Children's Arts from Deep Down Inside.* New York: The John Day Co., 1966.

Di Leo, Joseph H. *Young Children and Their Drawings.* New York: Brunner/Mazel, 1970.

Gaitskell, Charles D. and Margaret R. *Art Education in the Kindergarten.* Peoria, Ill.: Charles A. Bennett Co., 1952.

Kellog, Rhoda, and O'Dell, Scott. *The Psychology of Children's Art.* Del Mar, Calif.: CRM Books, 1967.

Lowenfeld, Viktor. *Your Child and His Art.* New York: The Macmillan Co., 1954.

Merritt, Helen. *Guiding Free Expression in Children's Art.* New York: Holt, Rinehart & Winston, 1964.

Ota, Koshi. *Printing for Fun.* New York: Ivan Obolensky, 1960.

Pile, M. *Art Experiences for Young Children.* Threshold Early Learning Library. New York: The Macmillan Co. School Division, 1972.

Whitman Creative Art Books:
Painting, First Book
Painting, Second Book
Print Art, First Book
Racine, Wisconsin: Whitman Publishing Co., 1966.

AUDIO-VISUALS

Movies

Early Expressionists. 16 mm, color, 15 minutes. A recording of four-year-olds' spontaneous and rhythmic movements with various art media.

Available from:
Modern Talking Pictures Services, Inc.
2323 New Hyde Park Road
New Hyde Park, N.Y. 11040
(or the nearest regional office).

Learning Through the Arts. 16 mm, color, 22 minutes. Shows the natural reactions of kindergarten children as they explore the arts.

Available from:
Audio-Visual Services
Kent State University
Kent, Ohio 44240

The Purple Turtle. 16 mm, color, 14 minutes. Kindergarten children are photographed as they work creatively with a variety of art media.

Available from:
The American Crayon Company
P.O. Box 2067
Sandusky, Ohio 44870

Filmstrips

Painting I. 46 frames, color, captions. Techniques demonstrated include brush painting, cord painting, sponge painting, roller painting, straw painting, finger painting, monoprinting, and blot painting.

Print Art. 62 frames, color, captions. The printing process with all kinds of scrap materials.

Both of these filmstrips demonstrate art activities in which kindergarten children can participate.

These filmstrips are available from:
Western Publishing Co., Inc.
Education Division
150 Parish Drive
Wayne, N.J. 07470

Art and the Growing Child. Color, sound.
This filmstrip shows illustrations of children's art work as they mature.

Available from:
McGraw Hill Book Co.
Text Films Department
330 W. 42nd Street
New York, N.Y. 10036

9
Poems

Someone has very aptly said that the mind of the teacher of young children should be lined with poetry. The teacher should be familiar with a variety of poetry for young children and also have several collections of poems to which she can turn to have the appropriate "word treasures" to fit almost any occasion. She will be able then to share with an individual or group a poetic expression which will highlight an experience or add a touch of humor to an incident. The teacher's love for and appreciation of poetry is certain to "rub off" on the children.

In a happy, relaxed classroom where children are exposed to good poetry, creative poetry is always close at hand. Poetry, like music, flows in and out of the young child's work and play, emerging from some rich sensory experience to add beauty and sparkle to his activity.

A bibliography at the end of this chapter gives several collections of poetry for young children. Other well-selected poems relating to many interests of young children and supplementing the poems which follow in this text may be found in chapter 7, "Poems," in the *Church Kindergarten Resource Book* by Josephine Newbury (pages 178–210).

AUTUMN

AUTUMN LEAVES

Whirling, swirling
   all around,
Leaves come twirling
   to the ground.

—Josephine Newbury

AUTUMN RIDDLE

First they dress in green,
   Then they change to brown;
And some will even wear
   A red or golden gown!
    (Leaves)

—Author unknown

WHIRL AND TWIRL

Like a leaf or a feather,
In the windy, windy weather,
We will whirl around
And twirl around
And all sink down together.

—Author unknown

DANCE OF THE LEAVES

The autumn leaves are dancing down.
   Dance, leaves, dance!
Leaves of crimson, gold, and brown.
   Dance, leaves, dance!
Let the wind whirl you around,
Make a carpet for the ground,
Soon you'll sleep without a sound.
   Dance, leaves, dance!

—Author unknown

BABY SEEDS

In a milkweed cradle
   Snug and warm,
Baby seeds are hiding
   Safe from harm.

Open wide the cradle,
   Hold it high!
Come, Mr. Wind,
   Help them fly.

—Author unknown

JACK O'LANTERN[1]

I made a jack-o'-lantern
His smile was big and wide
I put him in the window
So he could look outside.

And people smiled to see him
So I learned this from my Jack
If you just smile at people
People smile right back!

—*Gina-Bell-Zano*

FUNNY PUMPKIN FACE

Funny, funny pumpkin face,
    You're laughing, please tell me why.
"I'm glad that I'm a jack-o'-lantern
    Instead of a pumpkin pie."

—*Josephine Newbury*

HALLOWE'EN

Tonight's the night of Hallowe'en
    When spooky things I'll see
And Jack-O-Lantern's grinning
    From ear to ear at me.

—*Josephine Newbury*

JACK-O'-LANTERN

Our pumpkin's now a jack-o'-lantern
    Who grins and winks his eye,
Today he's a funny pumpkin face
    But tomorrow he'll be a pie.

—*Josephine Newbury*

THANKSGIVING TIME

When all the leaves are off the boughs,
    And nuts and apples gathered in,
And cornstalks waiting for the cows,
    And pumpkins safe in barn and bin;
Then mother says, "My children dear,
    The fields are brown and autumn flies;
Thanksgiving Day is very near,
    And we must make Thanksgiving pies."

—*Author unknown*

TURKEY GOBBLER

Run, Mr. Turkey,
    As fast as you can,
Before you are caught
    And popped into a pan.

—*Josephine Newbury*

WINTER

THE COMING OF WINTER[2]

Leaves are falling,
      falling,
          falling.
Wind is calling, calling, calling
For the birds to hurry, hurry, hurry,
For the squirrels to scurry, scurry, scurry.
Wind is blowing, blowing, blowing.
Now it's snowing, snowing, snowing.
North Wind grows bolder, bolder, bolder.
The days get colder, colder, colder.

Streams flow slower, slower, slower.
Temperatures fall lower,
      lower,
        lower.

Ice and snow bring fun, fun, fun
Till the season's done, done, done.

—*Nancy Bartram*

WINTER WHERE IT'S COLD[3]

Snowflakes swirl about me;
Cold wind bites my nose.
Crisp air makes my cheeks red,
And Jack Frost nips my toes.
Smoke curls from the chimney,
And blankets I unfold.
Oh! My favorite weather
Is winter where it's cold.

—*Jean Harris*

WINTER WHERE IT'S WARM[4]

My winter home is warm all year
With trees so green and tall.
I wear no mittens and no hat
And need no shoes at all.
I play outdoors and often swim
And walk my doggie too.
I think it's fun to feel the sun
All year round—don't you?

—*Jean Harris*

[1]From *The Kindergartner*, October 26, 1969. Copyright © 1969 by Graded Press. Used by permission.
[2]From *We Do It Together*, November 17, 1963. Copyright 1963 by Graded Press. Used by permission.
[3]From *The Kindergartner*, February 16, 1969. Copyright © 1968 by Graded Press. Used by permission.
[4]*Ibid.* Used by permission.

WINTER CLOTHES[5]

Can you guess what I wore
On my feet to the store?

My big boots!

What covered my head
When I slid on my sled?

My fuzzy cap!

What made my hands warm
In the swirly snowstorm?

My red mittens!

What kept me all snug
Like a tight, loving hug?

My snowsuit!

Even in the wind and snow,
I am warm from head to toe!

—*Jean Myrick*

TREES IN WINTER[6]

Trees, trees, where are your leaves?
Your branches look bare and cold.
Autumn, you say, took them away,
Now only the snowflakes you hold.

—*Judith Hynd Bowling*

BOOT-PRINTS IN THE SNOW

Up and down the yard we go,
Making boot-prints in the snow.
    Big steps,
    Little steps,
    Around and around,
    Oh, what fun
    With snow on the ground!

    Black boots,
    White boots,
    Red boots bright.
    Isn't it strange
    Our boot-prints are white?

—*Josephine Newbury*

ICICLES[7]

An icicle hung on a red brick wall,
And it said to the sun,
    "I don't like you at all!"

Drip, drip, drip.
But the sun said,
    "Dear, you've a saucy tongue,
    And you should remember
    I'm old and you're young."
Drip, drip, drip.
But the icicle only cried the more,
Though the good sun smiled on it just as before,
Until at the end of the winter day,
It had cried its poor little self away!
Drip, drip, drip.

—*Author unknown*

SPRING

AN OPEN SECRET[8]

Pussy Willow had a secret
That the snowdrops whispered her,
And she purred it to the south wind
While it stroked her velvet fur;
And the south wind hummed it softly
To the busy honey-bees,
And they buzzed it to the blossoms
On the scarlet maple trees.
And these dropped it to the wood brooks
Brimming full of melted snow,
And the brooks told Robin Redbreast
As he flitted to and fro;
Little Robin could not keep it,
So he sang it loud and clear
To the sleepy hills and meadows:
"Wake up! Cheer up! Spring is here!"

—*Anonymous*

SPRING CHORUS[9]

The frogs know it's spring
And that's why they sing,
"We like it, we like it, we like it!"

The blackbirds and thrushes
Sing in the rushes,
"We like it, we like it, we like it!"

The blossoms so gay
Seem to smilingly say,
"We like it, we like it, we like it!"

The spring rain on the back
Of each duck makes him quack,
"I like it, I like it, I like it!"

[5]From *Nursery Days*, January 12, 1969. Copyright © 1968 by Graded Press. Used by permission.
[6]Used by permission of the author.
[7]From *Together We Speak*, by Helen Kitchell Evans. Reprinted with permission of the publisher, The Instructor Publications, Inc., Dansville, N.Y.
[8]*Ibid.* Used by permission.
[9]From *Ranger Rick's Nature Magazine*, May–June 1971. Copyright 1971. Used by permission of National Wildlife Federation.

The tadpoles all swim ,
With vigor and vim
'Cause they like it, they like it, they like it!

And down on the ground
A bug chorus is found,
"We like it, we like it, we like it!"

So with spring all about,
I, too, have to shout,
"I like it, I like it, I like it!"
            —*Solveig Paulson Russell*

ROLY-POLY CATERPILLAR

Roly-poly caterpillar
Into a corner crept,
Spun around himself a blanket,
Then for a long time slept.
Roly-poly caterpillar,
Wakening by and by—
Found himself with beautiful wings
Changed to a butterfly.
            —*Author unknown*

FROM CATERPILLAR TO BUTTERFLY

One day a big black caterpillar
    crawled out upon a twig.
And there he spun a gray cocoon
    that wasn't very big.
And there he slept all snug and warm,
    until one summer's day
The small cocoon just opened up,
    and there so bright and gay
A beautiful orange butterfly
    flew merrily away.
            —*Author unknown*

CATKIN

I have a little pussy,
    Her coat is soft and gray;
She lives down in the meadow
    And she never runs away.
Although she is a pussy
    She'll never be a cat
For she's a pussy willow!
    Now what do you think of that?
            —*Author unknown*

WHO KNOWS?

Good morning, pussy willow!
    Although you cannot sing,
I wonder if you're purring
    A song about the spring.

I hold you close to listen
    And stroke your silver fur.
Was that the March wind blowing,
    Or do I hear you purr?
            —*Elizabeth Cushing Taylor*

DANDELIONS[10]

Dandelions yellow, hiding in the grass,
Dandelions pretty, nodding as I pass;
Dandelions silver, dandelions gray,
Dandelions pretty, I'll blow your hair away!

THE DANDELION

O dandelion, yellow as gold,
    What do you do all day?
I just wait here in the tall grass
    'Till the children come out to play.

O dandelion, yellow as gold,
    What do you do all night?
I wait and wait till the cool dew falls
    And my hair grows long and white.

And what do you do when your hair is white
    And the children come out to play?
They take me up in their dimpled hands
    And blow my hair away.
            —*Anonymous*

DAFFODIL

A little yellow cup,
    A little yellow frill,
A little yellow star,
    And that's a daffodil.
            —*Author unknown*

SPRINGTIME

In the heart of a seed
Buried deep, so deep,
A dear little plant
Lay fast asleep.

"Wake!" said the sunshine,
"And creep to the light."
"Wake!" said the voice
Of the raindrops bright.

---

[10]From "Finger Plays for Young Children," Leaflet No. 11, reprinted by permission of the Institute of Child Development, University of Minnesota.

The little plant heard
And it rose to see
What the wonderful
Outside world might be.
— *Kate Louise Brown*

RAIN[11]

What fun it is to have it rain
And beat against my windowpane,
I walk outside that I may see
And feel cool dampness over me.

I hear its music on the street
As falling rain and pavement meet,
It wets my tongue, my eyes, my face,
As it splashes every place.

I taste the water fresh and pure,
And then with pattering rhythm sure,
I smell the earth washed bright and clean,
With whiffs of lilac in between.

I like the rain, it helps things grow,
It bathes the grass, makes rivers flow.
How good it is to have it rain—
Perhaps it soon will come again.
— *Mary Jackson Cathey*

UMBRELLAS

One umbrella,
Two umbrellas,
Three umbrellas gay!

Down the street
They go like flowers
On a rainy day.
— *Author unknown*

RAIN

The rain is raining all around,
It falls on field and tree,
It rains on the umbrellas here,
And on the ships at sea.
— *Robert Louis Stevenson*

RAIN[12]

The rain comes down
And looks so sharp

As it spatters on the street
Like needles falling
All around
And sewing up my feet.

But when I feel rain
On my cheek
It's not like that at all.
Soft like a kiss
Against my face
The raindrops fall!
— *Marguerite Marks*

UNDERNEATH THINGS[13]

Under the sky is a cloud
Under the cloud is a tree
Under the tree's an umbrella,
Under the umbrella's me!
— *Georgia Deal*

SPRING RIDDLE

There's a flower in the garden,
    It's just like a cup;
It's yellow, as yellow as butter,
    And they call it _____
                    (buttercup)
                    — *Author unknown*

ROBIN'S SECRET

We have a secret, just we three,
    The robin and I and the green apple tree;
The robin told the tree, and tree told me,
    And nobody knows it—just we three.

But of course the robin knows it best,
    Because he built the ___, I shan't tell the
        rest;
And laid the four little ___ somethings in the
    ___.
    I'm afraid I shall tell it every minute.

But if the tree and the robins don t peep,
    I'll try my best the secret to keep;
But I know when the little birds fly about,
    Then the whole secret will be out.
    — *Anonymous*

WHO HAS SEEN THE WIND?

Who has seen the wind?
Neither I nor you;
But when the leaves hang trembling
The wind is passing through.

---

[11]Used by permission of the author.
[12]From *We Do It Together*, July 28, 1963. Copyright by Graded Press. Used by permission.
[13]*Ibid.* Used by permission.

Who has seen the wind?
Neither you nor I;
But when the trees bow down their heads
The wind is passing by.
—*Christina Rossetti*

HOORAY FOR MAY[14]

No more clumsy winter boots,
No more zipping up snowsuits,
Mittens have been put away,
Don't need caps or muffs today.
I like spring when I can wear
My head and knees and elbows bare.
—*Merial B. Olsson*

ANIMALS

A HAPPY PET[15]

My pussy cat
Is soft and fat
   And gently do I pet her.
I give her milk
To drink. I think
   It makes her purr much better!

She need not fear
For I'll take care
   Of her—and not forget her.
—*Elsie S. Lindgren*

WOULDN'T IT BE FUNNY?

Wouldn't it be funny,
Wouldn't it now,
If the dog said, "Moo,"
And the cow said, "Bow-wow,"
And the cat sang and whistled,
And the bird said, "Meow"?
Wouldn't it be funny?
Wouldn't it now?
—*Author unknown*

THE SQUIRREL

Whisky, frisky,
Hippity hop,
Up he goes
To the treetops!

Whirly, twirly,
Round and round,
Down he scampers
To the ground.

Furly, curly,
What a tail!
Tall as a feather,
Broad as a sail!

Where's his supper?
In the shell.
Snappity, crackity,
Out it fell.
—*Author unknown*

CHICKADEE[16]

"Chickadee, Chickadee,"
Look at him sing in the evergreen tree;
   Cold it is blowing,
   Fast it is snowing,
But for cold weather, oh, little cares he!
   "Chickadee, Chickadee,"
Listen to him singing his song full of glee;
   Telling his name,
   Always the same,
"Chickadee, Chickadee, Chickadeedee!"
—*Virginia Baker*

DUCKS[17]

"Let's go for a walk
And quack and talk."
"And talk and quack
And then come back."
—*Miriam Clark Potter*

HOW CREATURES MOVE

The lion walks on padded paws,
The squirrel leaps from limb to limb,
While flies can crawl straight up a wall,
And seals can dive and swim.
The worm, he wiggles all around,
The monkey swings by his tail,
And birds may hop upon the ground,
Or spread their wings and sail.
But boys and girls have much more fun;
They leap and dance
And walk and run.
—*Author unknown*

---

[14]From *We Do It Together,* May 14, 1961. Copyright 1961 by Graded Press. Used by permission.
[15]From *Ten Busy Fingers,* by Elsie S. Lindgren. Copyright 1955 by Fortress Press. Used by permission.
[16]From *Together We Speak,* by Helen Kitchell Evans. Reprinted with permission of the publisher, The Instructor Publications, Inc., Dansville, N.Y.
[17]From *The Golden Book of Little Verses.* Copyright © 1953 by Western Publishing Company, Inc. Used by permission.

THE FROG ON THE LOG[18]

There once
Was a green
Little frog, frog, frog—

Who played
In the wood
On a log, log, log!

A screech owl
Sitting
In a tree, tree, tree—

Came after
The frog
With a scree, scree, scree!

When the frog
Heard the owl—
In a flash, flash, flash!

He leaped
In the pond
With a splash, splash, splash!
                        —*Ilo Orleans*

THE ELEPHANT

The elephant walks like this and like that.
He's terribly big, and he's terribly fat!
He has no fingers, but he does have toes.
And goodness gracious!
        Wh-a-t a nose!
                        —*Author unknown*

HOMES

HOMES[19]

Fish live in the water;
Chipmunks under the ground;
Squirrels live in hollow trees;
Birds nest all around.

Bees live in hives;
Beavers under the lake.
I live with Mother and Father
In the happy home they make.
                        —*Jean Brabham McKinney*

THE WOODPECKER'S HOME

A redheaded woodpecker up in a tree
Pecked out a hole in the trunk, you see.
"Rappity-tap, tappity-tap-tap," said he.
"I'm doing my best to build my nest
In a hole high up in a tree.
Rappity-tap, tappity-tap-tap," said he.
                        —*Josephine Newbury*

HOMES

Birds build a home in a bush or a tree,
And toads live under a stone,
But a spider weaves a beautiful web,
And ants make a hill all of their own.
The turtle carries a house made of a shell;
The squirrel's home is a hole in a tree,
And fish dart about in water deep.
Each likes his own home, you see.
Homes for everyone—and my home for me.
                        —*Author unknown*

SOMEONE I KNOW[20]

I know a girl with rosy cheeks,
And tiny, bouncing feet.
Her blue eyes shine like morning dew,
Her smile is dimply-sweet.

Today she held her hands to me,
And when I bent and kissed her,
She didn't mind a single bit,
'Cause she's my baby sister!
                        —*Florence A. Renner*

TINY BABY BROTHER[21]

I have a baby brother
With a tiny little nose.
His fingers are all tiny,
And so are all ten toes.

With everything so tiny,
I can't help wonder why
My tiny baby brother
Has such a great, big cry.
                        —*Goldie J. Christenson*

---

[18]From *The Zoo That Grew* by Ilo Orleans. Henry Z. Walck, publisher. Used by permission of Friede Orleans Joffe.

[19]From *Nursery Days*, May 14, 1967. Copyright © 1967 by Graded Press. Used by permission.

[20]From *We Do It Together*, October 22, 1961. Copyright 1961 by Graded Press. Used by permission.

[21]From *Nursery Days*, January 28, 1968. Copyright © 1967 by Graded Press. Used by permission.

GROWING

SOMETHING SPECIAL [22]

I know something happy,
Exciting as can be,
Something very special
And beautiful to see.

It's not a real live thing.
It's something mothers bake
And light with little candles—
It's a BIRTHDAY CAKE!
—*Solveig Paulson Russell*

GROWING UP

My birthday is coming tomorrow
And I won't be four any more,
I'm getting so big that already
I can open the kitchen door;
I'm very much taller than Baby,
Though today I am still only four,
And I'm bigger than Bob-tail the puppy,
I'm growing more and more.
—*Adapted; source unknown.*

CAKE [23]

Four bright candles
And one to grow on,
Five bright candles
All to blow on.

I make my mouth
Round like an O.
I wait and think,
Then wish—and blow!
—*Miriam Clark Potter*

Note: The number may be changed to suit the age of the child.

IT'S EASY! [24]

I am growing, I can tell!
My shoes don't fit me very well;
My last year's dress is much too small;
My coat grows short, while I grow tall!

In other ways I'm growing too.
Things that once seemed hard to do,
Now seem easy, on most days;
I'm growing up in *friendly* ways.

It's easier to take my turn;
It's easier for me to learn
To share, to help friends large and small.
Why! Growing up's not hard at all!
—*Dorothy Webber Caton*

COMMUNITY WORKERS

CHILDREN'S DOCTOR [25]

I'd like to be a doctor,
With a waiting room that's wide,
For lots of little children
To come and wait inside.

With a parrot and some gold fish,
Pretty pictures on the wall,
And some nurses nice and smiling
Coming when they hear me call.

I'd have some pills and medicines,
Like a tasty chocolate treat,
For boys and girls to take each day
Just before they eat.
—*Jean Brabham McKinney*

I'D LIKE TO BE A SPACEMAN [26]

I'd like to be a spaceman
With some fine spacemen suits,
With helmets and with gloves
And high stepping boots.

I'd like to ride a rocket ship
And blast off to the sky,
Around the earth up to the moon
As far as I could fly.

Then I would float back down again
And parachute to the sea
Where a green helicopter
Would come whirring by for me.
—*Jean Brabham McKinney*

[22]From *The Kindergartner*, March 23, 1969. Copyright © 1969 by Graded Press. Used by permission.

[23]From *The Golden Book of Little Verses*. Copyright © 1953 by Western Publishing Company, Inc. Used by permission.

[24]From *We Do It Together*, November 10, 1963. Copyright © 1963 by Graded Press. Used by permission.

[25]From *Nursery Days*, June 1, 1969. Copyright © 1969 by Graded Press. Used by permission.

[26]From *Nursery Days*, May 18, 1969. Copyright © 1969 by Graded Press. Used by permission.

I WANT TO BE AN ARTIST[27]

I want to be an artist
When I am grown up big;
I want to draw all sorts of things—
A cow, a duck, a pig.

I want to paint a sunset,
A sky with stars so bright,
The things I see outdoors by day,
And from my bed by night.

I want to hang my paintings
On the wall—all in a row,
With lots of people coming
To see my picture show.
              —*Jean Brabham McKinney*

TRAINED NURSE[28]

I'd like to be a trained nurse
In a uniform of white,
Working in a doctor's office,
Or a hospital at night.

Looking after little children
Who are sick—with fever too . . .
Helping them to feel much better
By the nice things I would do.

Bringing trays with bowls of ice cream—
Rubbing aching little heads—
Seeing that the sheets are smooth and cool
On tumbled little beds.
              —*Jean Brabham McKinney*

I'D LIKE TO BE A MINISTER[29]

I'd like to be a minister
Helping lots of people,
Giving sermons in a church
With a towering steeple.

I'd have a room just like mine,
A choir to softly sing,
Pretty flowers, rows of pews,
And bells to gaily ring.

I'd have a Bible of my own
To read from loud and clear,
To all the listening people
Who came to worship here.
              —*Jean Brabham McKinney*

FIREMAN[30]

I'd like to be a fireman
With a ladder and a hose,
With a fire truck and a siren
Shrieking everywhere it goes.

I'd like to use my ladder
To rescue lots of people,
And the long black hose to put out fires
On rooftop or on steeple.

I'd wear some big black rubber boots
A hat and raincoat too,
And I'd be ready night or day
My fireman's job to do.
              —*Jean Brabham McKinney*

ZOO KEEPER[31]

I'd like to be a zoo keeper
And keep the city zoo,
And see the stately penguins
And the strutting that they do.

I'd have a big zoo kitchen
With lots of things to eat;
Fresh fruit for the parrots
And for the lions, meat.

Honey for the bears
And fishes for the seals
And big loads of hay
For the elephants' main meals.
              —*Jean Brabham McKinney*

ZOO DOCTOR[32]

I'd like to be a doctor
For animals at the zoo;
For patients I'd have an elephant,
A camel, and a kangaroo.

Or frisky little monkeys
And funny chimpanzees,
Or green and yellow parrots
From towering jungle trees.

[27]From *Nursery Days*, June 29, 1969. Copyright © 1969 by Graded Press. Used by permission.
[28]From *Nursery Days*, June 1, 1969. Copyright © 1969 by Graded Press. Used by permission.
[29]From *Nursery Days*, March 30, 1969. Copyright © 1969 by Graded Press. Used by permission.
[30]From *Nursery Days*, June 15, 1969. Copyright © 1969 by Graded Press. Used by permission.
[31]From *Nursery Days*, May 11, 1969. Copyright © 1969 by Graded Press. Used by permission.
[32]*Ibid.* Used by permission.

With a big zoo hospital
Where the animals could stày,
Until I made them well again
And sent them back to play.
—*Jean Brabham McKinney*

BAKER [33]

I'd like to be a baker
With a white cap on my head,
And a big, shiny oven
Full of loaves of fragrant bread.

I'd make delicious cup cakes—
Coconut or chocolate drop.
Lemon pies I'd learn to bake
With meringue spread on top.

Best of all I'd bake some cookies—
Those that children like to eat,
And all my friends could come and munch
Each crunchy, tasty treat.
—*Jean Brabham McKinney*

MISCELLANEOUS

QUESTIONS

Do you ever lie in your bed and grin
Because a new day is about to begin?
Are you eager to see what lies ahead,
Or would you rather stay in bed?

How do you feel when it rains all day—
Are you sorry you can't go outside to play?
Or do you think, "What a wonderful chance
To stay indoors and paint or dance!"

When you sit down to eat, do you like to explore
Things that you've never tasted before?
Or do you think it would be a thrill
To eat the same food at every meal?

Have you ever had money that you didn't
    spend,
Or a broken toy that you couldn't mend?
Have you ever lost something you couldn't
    find?
Can you always say what's on your mind?

Does someone lift you to the shelf
That you can't reach all by yourself?

Do you have a pet of your very own,
Or a song that you sing when you're alone?

Do you ever notice things at night
That you didn't see in bright daylight?
Can you whistle songs the night birds make?
Does the darkness smell like chocolate cake?

Do you believe it's strange but true
That the seasons change, and so do you;
That people have smiles—
    even when they don't show them,
And questions have answers—
    even if we don't know them.
—*Moffett D. Swaim*

MY FRIENDS [34]

My friends are of different sizes.
Some short, while some others are tall;
    But whatever their size,
    When I look in their eyes,
I am sure that I do love them all!

Some friends that I have can run quickly,
While other friends always are slow;
    But however they move,
    All these people I love,
They are wonderful people to know!

My friends sometimes make me feel angry
When they won't let me do things my way;
    But then after I'm mad
    I begin feeling glad,
And I love all my friends anyway!

LOVE IS . . . [35]

Love is a special feeling;
A feeling that never ends,
A feeling of very good wishes
For strangers and for friends.

Love is a way of doing;
Doing things each day
That bring happiness to others
In a thoughtful, helping way.

---

[33]From *Nursery Days,* June 15, 1969. Copyright © 1969 by Graded Press. Used by permission.
[34]From *From One Generation to Another,* by Pauline Palmer Meek, p. 74, revised edition, © John Knox Press 1972.
[35]From *The Kindergartner,* October 5, 1969. Copyright © 1969 by Graded Press. Used by permission.

Love is a way of thinking;
Thinking kind thoughts of all,
Thinking good things about them,
Forgiving mistakes large and small.

Yes, love is a way of feeling,
Of thinking and doing, too;
And love, when you show it to others,
Brings happiness back to you!
—*Dorothy Webber Caton*

I WONDER [36]

I wonder at the honeybees;
They work and work all day
Making yellow honey,
Which they store away
In the comb, all sticky sweet,
For boys and girls like us to eat.

I wonder at the farmer's cows,
Which feed on grass all day,
And then when nighttime comes around,
Always know the way
Back to the barn so they may give
Rich milk so you and I can live.

I wonder at the speckled hens,
Who always in the day
Stop to lay their daily eggs
Upon their nests of hay,
So that you and I may eat
A delicious breakfast treat.

I wonder, do you think they know
God, in his wondrous way,
Planned for them to help provide
Our food for us each day?
—*Mabel Niedermeyer McCaw*

LIGHTS [37]

Red light says, "STOP";
Green light says, "GO";
Yellow says, "Wait,
Watch well, move slow."

It's nice we have
These lights to say,

"It's safe to go";
"It's wise to stay."
—*Jean Brabham McKinney*

RESTING AND GROWING [38]

Resting and growing are part of God's plan
For flowers and trees and even for man.
For every small creature God knows what is best,
And each in its time will grow and will rest.

The seeds in the winter lie quiet and still,
And not a thing happens to change them until
The earth says it's spring and it's time now to grow;
Then seeds start to swell and a sprout they soon show.

A tiny green sprout pops right through the ground,
And everyone knows something new has been found.
By seedtime and harvest we always will know
That God plans for all things to rest and to grow.
—*Jean S. Parkinson*

THE AIRPLANE

The airplane taxies down the field
And heads into the breeze,
It lifts its wheels above the ground,
It skims above the trees,
It rises high and higher
Away up toward the sun,
It's just a speck against the sky
—And now it's gone!
—*Author unknown*

Three funny men from our town
Went out for a walk one day;
The wind blew so hard
That it turned them around,
And they walked the other way,
Yes, they walked the other way.
—*Nursery rhyme*

MY SHADOW FRIEND

I have a funny shadow friend
    who romps and plays with me.
He's different from my other friends
    as you can surely see.
Sometimes he's like our baby,

---

who is so very small;
Sometimes he's like my father,
    who is very, very tall.
Sometimes small,
    Sometimes tall,
But sometimes—would you believe it,
He isn't there at all!

I wonder why?

—*Josephine Newbury*

MY SHADOW

I have a little shadow that goes in and out
    with me,
And what can be the use of him is more than
    I can see.
He is very, very like me from the heels up
    to the head;
And I see him jump before me, when I jump
    into my bed.

The funniest thing about him is the way he
    likes to grow—
Not at all like proper children, which is
    always very slow;
For he sometimes shoots up taller like an
    india-rubber ball,
And sometimes gets so little that there's none of
    him at all.

He hasn't got a notion of how children
    ought to play,
And can only make a fool of me in every
    sort of way.
He stays so close beside me, he's a coward
    you can see;
I'd think shame to stick to nursie as that
    shadow sticks to me!

One morning very early, before the sun was up,
I rose and found the shining dew on every
    buttercup;
But my lazy little shadow, like an arrant
    sleepy-head,
Had stayed at home behind me and was fast
    asleep in bed.

—*Robert Louis Stevenson*

BUBBLES

A little bubble,
A middle-sized bubble,
    And a big, big, bubble I see.

Up, up, up they float in the air.
    Pop!
        Pop!!
            Pop!!!
And they are not there.

—*Josephine Newbury*

BUBBLES, BUBBLES, BUBBLES

I blew some pretty bubbles,
    They danced in the air.
I watched them floating higher
    'Til POOF! they were not there.
Where did my bubbles go, oh where?

—*Josephine Newbury*

BUBBLES [39]

They sailed like moons
Up toward the sky
To show the birds
That balls could fly.

Some blew
To the ground
One lit on a rose,
And a big one burst
On the kitten's nose.

—*Miriam Clark Potter*

COLORS [40]

I watch for colors wherever I go!
How many colors do I know?

Red is the fire truck that zooms right by;
Red are the cherries in my favorite pie.

Green is the color of our Christmas tree
And the soft new grass that tickles me.

Blue is the sky on a summer day,
And the bird in my yard is a bright blue jay!

Yellow are the pears and bananas I eat
And the big school bus that goes down my
    street.

Brown is the color of a robin's nest
And the chocolate bars that I like best!

The world is full of colors I know.
I watch for colors wherever I go!
—*Jo Hershberger*

WHAT IS YELLOW?[41]

Yellow is the happiest
Color that I know.
Yellow is the sunlight
And the candle's glow.

Yellow are the buttercups,
Dotting springtime hills;
Yellow is the crocus
And the daffodil.

Yellow is the color too
Of a juicy pear;
Sometimes leaves are yellow,
Just like my own hair!
—*Jean Brabham McKinney*

I'M GLAD

I'm glad the sky is painted blue,
And earth is painted green,
With such a lot of nice fresh air
All sandwiched in between.
—*Mother Goose*

I BRUSH MY TEETH[42]

I brush my teeth,
For it's fun to do—
My nice, white teeth
That help me chew.

After each meal
And in-between,
I brush my teeth
To keep them clean.
—*Jean Brabham McKinney*

THE ZIGZAG BOY AND GIRL

I know a little zigzag boy,
    Who goes this way and that;
He never knows just where he puts
    His coat or shoes or hat.

I know a little zigzag girl,
    Who flutters here and there;
She never knows just where to find
    Her brush to fix her hair.

If you are not a zigzag child,
    You'll have no cause to say
That you forgot, for you will know
    Where things are put away.
—*Author unknown*

UP AND DOWN THE BEACH[43]

All up and down the beach
Happy families play.
Some are picnicking,
All are feeling gay.

Children with small shovels
Dig holes in the sand,
Fill them up with water,
Cover up their hands.

Babies watch from playpens,
Grandmothers sit and sun.
There are happy things to do
For me and everyone.
—*Georgia Deal*

AT THE SEASIDE

When I was down beside the sea
A wooden spade they gave to me
    To dig the sandy shore.
My holes were empty like a cup,
In every hole the sea came up,
    Till it could come no more.
—*Robert Louis Stevenson*

THE CONCH SHELL[44]

Conch shell, conch shell from the sea,
Conch shell, conch shell speak to me,
    As I hold you to my ear
    Whisper secrets I may hear,
    Let me hear the ocean roar,
    Sounds of waves that tumble o'er,
Conch shell, conch shell from the sea,
You are such a mystery.
—*Mary Jackson Cathey*

TEDDY BEAR[45]

I have this shaggy teddy bear;
I talk to him at night.
No matter what I say to him

---

[41]From *Nursery Days*, March 23, 1969. Copyright © 1969 by Graded Press. Used by permission.
[42]From *Nursery Days*, January 12, 1969. Copyright © 1968 by Graded Press. Used by permission.
[43]From *Nursery Days*, August 6, 1967. Copyright © 1967 by Graded Press. Used by permission.
[44]Used by permission of the author.
[45]From *We Do It Together*, November 10, 1963. Copyright 1963 by Graded Press. Used by permission.

He always thinks I'm right.
He never, never answers back;
He's quiet as can be.
I tell him all my secrets
And he keeps them safe for me.
—*Gina-Bell-Zano*

The following three poems are examples of haiku—Japanese-born, unrhymed poetry of three lines of five syllables, seven syllables, and five syllables respectively.

LONELY[46]

Quiet, upset, sad
By yourself, being alone
No one to talk to.
—*Vay Saurs*

FLOWERS[47]

Blooming in the spring
In them are pretty colors
Everyone likes them.

—*Vay Saurs*

ORANGES[48]

Sweet, juicy, tasty
Sparkly and deliciously
Cool and refreshing.
—*Vay Saurs*

TABLE GRACE

We give thanks for all things good,
For home and love and for our food,
For school and friends and things we share.
We thank you, God, for your love and care.
—*Josephine Newbury*

GOD IS NEAR[49]

I'm looking out my window
And I know that God is near,
For He made the lovely things I see,
The birdsongs that I hear.

The shadows of the big old elms
Make patterns on the ground,
And, hurrying through the young green leaves,
Wind makes a swishing sound.

The sunlight pours through dogwoods
With each blossom looking up;
It spills on purple lilacs—

Fills a tulip's yellow cup.

I thank you, God, I thank you
For these things I see and hear!
They make me know, deep down inside
That you are always near.
—*Margaret Newell*

GOD IS NEAR[50]

Sometimes when morning lights the sky
    And gladness fills the air,
I feel like telling things to God,
    He seems so very near.

Sometimes when flowers are in bloom
    And birds are singing clear,
I feel like singing things to God,
    He must be very near.

Sometimes when trees are standing tall
    With branches in the air,
I feel like saying things to God,
    I know He must be near.

Sometimes when work and play are done
    And evening stars appear,
I feel like whisp'ring things to God,
    He is so very near.
—*Elizabeth McE. Shields*

BIBLIOGRAPHY

Allen, Marie Louise. *A Pocketful of Poems.* New York: Harper & Row, 1957.

Geismer, Barbara Peck, and Suter, Antoinette Brown. *Very Young Verses.* Boston: Houghton Mifflin Co., 1945.

Hymes, Lucia and James L., Jr. *Hooray for Chocolate.* New York: William R. Scott, 1960.

Frank, Josette, ed. *Poems to Read to the Very Young.* New York: Random House, 1961.

Potter, Miriam Clark. *The Golden Book of Little Verses.* New York: Simon & Schuster, 1955.

---

[46]Used by permission of the author and her parents, Mr. and Mrs. Mark Saurs.
[47]*Ibid.*
[48]*Ibid.*
[49]Used by permission of the author.
[50]From *Happy Times in Our Church*, by Elizabeth McE. Shields (Richmond: John Knox Press, 1940), p. 130. Used by permission of Mrs. Harold V. Bird.

10
Stories

Through experiences with good literature for young children, the kindergarten child sees life about him in word pictures which bring new and satisfying interpretations to him. His aesthetic sense is quickened, his intellectual growth is stimulated, and his knowledge is extended beyond his present environment as he enjoys treasured times with an adult who shares with him a variety of stories.

The child comes to understand himself better as he identifies with the experiences of the children and adults in a good story. It is frequently quite a revelation to him to discover that other children have problems and joys, surprises and disappointments which are not unlike his own.

Experiencing a good story with the young child can introduce him to a whole new realm of good humor, beauty, and imagination, and can bring immeasurable pleasure and strengthen the bonds of friendship in the teacher-pupil relationship in a way unsurpassed by any other activity.

The stories which follow in this chapter are meant to be told to the children. Some will be more effective if a few props such as pictures or puppets are used, but for the most part they are to be told just as they are. Just as an artist creates on his canvas a scene of beauty with brushes and color, the teacher, with his or her voice and facial expression, takes the "narrative imprisoned on the printed page and sets it free to wing its way"[1] into the hearts and minds of the young child.

For additional stories of seasonal interest, conflict situations, and natural phenomena, refer to chapter 6 of the *Church Kindergarten Resource Book* by Josephine Newbury. For Bible stories refer to chapter 3 of the same text.

HOW WONDERFUL IS JOHNNY![2]

"Mo-o-ther," asked Johnny, "what is the best thing God ever made?"

"I hardly know, Johnny." Mother stopped to think. "Why do you ask that?"

"Wel-l-l, the wind was making my pin wheel go. And I think my pin wheel is the best thing I ever made—so I was just thinking . . ."

"That's hard to decide, Johnny. While I think about it, suppose you run out to the barn and tell Daddy that supper will be ready soon."

Johnny hurried off to the barn, where he found his father mending harness.

"Daddy, supper is almost ready and what was the best thing God ever made?" gasped Johnny, all in one breath.

"Right now I'd settle for you, son. But I didn't think so last week, when you let the pigs out of the pen," he said.

"Did God make *me*, Daddy?"

"He surely did, Johnny. God planned the way of it, the way everyone is born. Mother and I were part of his plan for you. People are very wonderful, son."

"Better than horses, Daddy? Better than automobiles?"

"Much better, Johnny. Let's play a little game and find out just how wonderful you really are."

Daddy looked all around. At last he picked up something from his worktable.

"Close your eyes, Johnny, and keep them closed. Now, take this in your hand and tell me what it is."

Johnny's hand opened and closed.

"It's a nail, Daddy," he shouted as his eyes flew open.

"That's right," said Daddy, smiling. "How did you know it was a nail?"

"I could *feel* it," said Johnny.

"And you remembered what a nail feels like. Automobiles can't feel or remember. Close your eyes again. Now, can you tell what I am holding near you?"

"Hay," said Johnny. "I can *smell* it."

"What color is my sweater?" asked Daddy.

"Blue," said Johnny. His eyes popped open. "I can *see* it."

"Turn around," was Daddy's next order. "Now what am I doing, Johnny?"

Johnny listened.

"Sawing—sawing a board," he cried. "I can *hear* you."

"This is the best of all," laughed Daddy. "Close your eyes and open your mouth. Now, what have you in your mouth?"

"A peppermint!" Johnny could hardly talk because he was laughing and chewing at the same time. "O Daddy, I like this new game!"

"It's called 'How Wonderful Is Johnny!'" said Daddy. "God made you to feel, and smell, and see and hear and taste. Automobiles cannot do any of these things, son. Dogs and horses *can*. But you have an *extra* gift from God, Johnny, which he gives only to people."

"What is it, Daddy?"

"You can *choose*, son. You can say yes or no. You can do bad things or good things. You can decide what is best."

"Like letting the pigs run away?" Johnny was really sorry about that. It had taken Daddy all afternoon to catch them.

"Yes, Johnny. And good things like sending your top to Billy when he had the measles, and you knew it couldn't come back to you."

"Is it very special to be people, Daddy?"

"It is the most important thing in the world to be *good people*," said Daddy seriously, "the kind God wants us to be." Daddy put away the harness tools.

"Come on, son—the best thing for us right now is to be on time for supper."

KEVIN LOSES A TOOTH[3]

"Mother!" Kevin called excitedly, running into the kitchen. "Something's wrong with my front tooth, look!" He put his tongue behind it and pushed until it stuck straight out.

Mother turned to look, then she smiled. "There is nothing wrong," she said. "Your tooth is just getting ready to come out."

---

[1]Claudia Royal, *Story-Telling* (Nashville: Broadman Press, 1955).

[2]From *God's World and Johnny*, by Dorothy Westlake Andrews. Copyright, MCMXLVIII, W. L. Jenkins, The Westminster Press. Used by permission.

[3]From *The Kindergartner*, May 25, 1969. Copyright © by Graded Press. Used by permission of Graded Press.

"But, why?" asked Kevin.

"Because it is time," said Mother. "You see, it is part of God's plan for growth. Just as the leaves fall off the trees in autumn to make room for the new green leaves in spring, when boys and girls begin to grow up, their baby teeth come out so that their grown-up teeth will have room to come in."

"Then will I get new teeth every spring?" asked Kevin, looking somewhat surprised.

"No," said Mother. "People only get one set of grown-up teeth. That is why we must take good care of them by keeping them clean and not eating too many sweets."

"I brushed my teeth after breakfast," said Kevin, "and you didn't even tell me."

"You really are growing," said Mother. "Learning to take care of yourself and doing it without being told are sure signs."

Kevin grinned and stuck his tongue behind the loose tooth and pushed again. Suddenly out it popped right on the kitchen table. Kevin looked so surprised that Mother laughed, then Kevin laughed too.

"I'm going to show Joey," he said and hurried outside. But in a few minutes, he was back. "Who's the Tooth Fairy?" he asked.

"Why do you ask?" Mother wanted to know.

"Joey says he lost a tooth last week and he put it under his pillow. While he was asleep, the Tooth Fairy came and took it and left something for him."

"This is a sort of game some parents play with their boys and girls when they lose their first tooth to show that they are proud and happy that they are growing in so many ways," Mother explained, "and just for fun, they call themselves Tooth Fairies."

"Could we play it tonight?" asked Kevin.

"I think that would be fun," said Mother.

That night, Kevin tucked his tooth under his pillow. The next morning the tooth was gone, but nothing was in its place. Then he looked on the table beside his bed and there, with a message written on it in chalk, was Father's little slate, the one he had used in school when he was a little boy. Many times Kevin had

asked if he might have it and Mother had always said, "Yes, when you are big enough to take good care of it."

Kevin took the slate and hurried downstairs.

"Look," said Kevin, "what does it say?"

Father took Kevin on his lap and read, "To our big boy with love, from Mother and Father."

Kevin stuck his tongue in the empty tooth space and grinned, "Thank you," he said.

—*Linda Alexander*

BINGS GROWS ON THE INSIDE[4]

(The purpose of this story is to help kindergarten children begin to know that growing has more aspects than physical change.)

Bings was the tallest boy in the kindergarten.

When people came to his house, they always said, "My goodness! Is this Bings? How he has grown!"

Sometimes they pretended they didn't believe he was Bings at all, but some other boy.

Then his mother always said, "Yes, this is our very own Bings. He's growing every day."

Sometimes they would take people into the kitchen to show them marks on the wall that showed how big he was when he was one year old, two years old, three years old, and four years old.

And now there was the five-year mark. Just last week he had a birthday. He had stood with his back against the wall, had taken a deep breath, and stretched his head up as far as it would go. Daddy had marked the place.

But do you know what? That five-year mark wasn't much higher than the four-year one. Daddy didn't notice this, but Bings did. He went back to look at it again when nobody else was in the kitchen. Yes, he was right. Between the four-year mark and the new one there was just a tiny space, and he could put his whole hand between the others. Bings put his finger on the new mark and stood under it to see if Daddy had made a mistake. No. The mark was in the right place. He just wasn't growing as fast as he used to.

He looked at the marks next to his that showed how much his little brother Charlie had grown. He had grown much more than a hand's

[4]Reprinted with permission from *Growing in the Fellowship* by Florence Schulz. Copyright ©, 1960, by the United Church Press, pp. 50–51.

worth between his last two birthdays. Charlie was growing just the way Bings *used* to grow. But now all Bings had grown he could measure with his thumb. He was sure something must be the matter.

But Daddy wasn't worried. Neither was Mother. They said, "Oh, that's all right. You have to grow on the inside for a little while. Then you'll grow on the outside again."

Bings didn't know what that meant. He wanted to keep growing on the outside so people could see the marks go higher on the wall. In kindergarten sometimes they took giant steps. How could he take giant steps if he didn't grow on the outside? His legs weren't inside, were they? How could you grow on the inside? That's what he wanted to know.

One day as he was coming up the walk after school, he could hear his baby sister Lolly on the sun porch babbling, "Ga-ga-ga-ga." That's what she called her doll. She couldn't say many words at all. Hardly anybody could understand her but Bings.

As he opened the door of the porch, he saw Charlie getting ready to mark up the wall again with a crayon.

"No, no, Charlie," Bings said.

He saw a big piece of brown paper on the table. "Write here, Charlie," he said and spread the paper on the floor.

Charlie looked at him, but didn't write on the paper. You could never tell what Charlie would do. Even when you told him what to do, sometimes he just looked at you. Somebody had to be with him practically all the time or he'd spill things, or break things, or burn and hurt himself.

"Even if you do grow faster than I do, you're not learning very much," Bings said. Charlie began to scribble on the paper. That's all he could do, just scribble.

Bings showed him the picture he had made in kindergarten. "See, Charlie?" he said. Bings could really draw now.

"Well, here's my kindergarten boy," said Mother. "Right on time too! I can trust you to get home from school the minute I have lunch ready. You're certainly growing dependable."

Bings wondered if that was growing on the inside. Lunch smelled so good he didn't say a word, but took giant steps to the bathroom to wash his hands. He was dependable. That's

what Dad said last night when he washed his hands before dinner without being reminded.

Bings knew what he was supposed to do. He wasn't a baby like Lolly or someone to be watched every minute like Charlie. Inside Bings knew what to do without being told, without having someone with him all the time. He was growing on the inside. He took giant steps to the lunch table.

Neither a four- nor five-year old—in fact no one—can see himself growing. Yet how natural is the question: How can you tell I'm growing? (As the child identifies with the experiences in this story he might begin to find some answers to this puzzling question about growth.)

FEELING GRUMPY [5]

(The story is more effective if the storyteller uses the tune for the Mother's song as printed at the end of the story.)

"What cheer! What cheer!" called a cardinal outside Paul's window. Paul got out of bed to watch the bird with a bright red coat. But Paul did not smile.

"Breakfast is ready!" called Mother from the kitchen. But Paul did not hurry, although he *could* dress himself very well.

When Paul had buttoned the last button and tied his shoes, he came downstairs. Daddy was almost through eating.

Paul was too late to eat breakfast with Daddy. Paul was too late to run and bring in Daddy's newspaper from the front steps. There was the newspaper folded neatly, right by Daddy's hat, ready to be picked up when Daddy went to work.

Paul sat down at the table. But it was not so pleasant to eat breakfast without Mother and Daddy.

Daddy blew Paul a kiss, put on his hat, picked up his newspaper, and was out of the front door on his way to work.

Mother was in the kitchen. She sang as she worked:

"Sing when you work,
Smile when you play,
Everybody helping
Makes a happy day."

---

[5]From *We Grow and Learn*, Part 3. Copyright, 1958, by Graded Press. Used by permission.

But Paul did not sing with her. Paul did not smile.

Soon Paul could hear Mother going upstairs. *Click, click* went her heels as she stepped about in the bedroom. She was still singing:

"Sing when you work,
Smile when you play,
Everybody helping
Makes a happy day."

"Paul!" Mother was calling. "Where is my helper? Come and make the beds with me."

Paul was quiet a minute. Then he called out with a cross voice, "I don't want to!"

Then the back door closed with a bang and Paul was out in the yard. What a long morning it seemed. Peggy did not come out to play. Paul's kitten was asleep on the back porch and would not run after the ball. There was not even a robin on the lawn to watch.

Slowly Paul opened the kitchen door and went into the house. Nothing seemed right. Perhaps he was hungry. Mother was sitting by the window writing.

"Mother," began Paul. "Will you make a sandwich for me—bread and jelly?"

Mother did not look up. She went on with her writing. Then she said, "I don't want to!"

Paul was surprised. Mother never spoke like that. He crouched down on the floor to look up into Mother's face.

There was a twinkle in her eyes. Paul looked at her in wonder. "That's what you said to me!" Mother answered.

Paul's arms went around Mother's neck. "I'll help you make the beds!" said Paul.

"And I'll make a bread and jelly sandwich for you," said Mother getting up and laying aside her pencil and paper. "After you have eaten your sandwich I am going to the store," Mother finished.

"May I go with you?" asked Paul. "I'll carry the basket."

When they were walking down the street, Paul carrying the basket, Mother said, "What an unpleasant world this would be if everyone said, 'I don't want to.'"

Mother and Paul began to sing:

"Sing when you work,
Smile when you play,
Everybody helping
Makes a happy day."

—*Jessie Eleanor Moore*

WHEN ANDY MISSED A TRIP TO THE FARM

"This surely is an extra good breakfast this morning," commented Father as he finished his last waffle.

"Sure is, Mom," added Andy.

"Well, I'm glad you both enjoyed it. I thought you would need a little bigger breakfast if you were going on a trip to the farm today."

"What?" asked Andy.

"That's right, son," explained his father. "I have to drive down to Rockville to plan with Mr. Barton for the new barn we want to build, and I thought if it were a sunny day you would enjoy going along. I hadn't mentioned it before because I didn't want to disappoint you if my plans changed and we couldn't go."

"Yippee!" exclaimed Andy. "When do we go?"

"In just a little while, but you'll have time to change into your jeans."

Andy went dashing into his room and was dressed in a jiffy.

"How do I look, Mom?" he asked as he buttoned the last button on his shirt.

"Just fine, but I believe I would take a sweater along if I were you," answered his mother.

"Sure, Mom." And with that Andy was ready to go.

"I'll wait out in front till Daddy is ready. All right, Mom?" he asked as he skipped toward the front door.

"Don't leave the yard, dear, for your father will be ready in just a few minutes, and he can't wait for you."

"I won't, Mom. I promise," called Andy, running out into the yard.

Just about that time Mike came riding up on his two-wheeler. "Hi!" he called to Andy. "You want to see my new puppies? They're in a box on our back porch."

"I can't. I'm going to Rockville with my daddy in just a few minutes," Andy explained.

"Oh, it won't take three minutes. Come on. I may even let you have one of the puppies when they get old enough," coaxed Mike.

"Well, I guess it won't take long, and I can be back in time to go," Andy thought to himself.

So off he ran down the sidewalk, following after Mike on his two-wheeler.

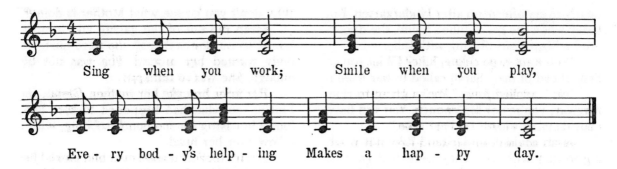

Sing when you work; Smile when you play,

Eve - ry bod - y's help - ing Makes a hap - py day.

What cute little puppies! Andy wanted to play with them, but Mike's mother told the boys that the mother dog didn't like for anyone to bother her babies. Andy and Mike watched the puppies getting their breakfast.

Andy was so busy watching the puppies that he forgot about going to the farm with his father. He didn't hear his mother calling him.

Andy's father waited a few minutes; then he had to drive away without him.

All of a sudden Andy remembered his promise. He remembered the trip to the farm. He ran all the way home and into the front door, calling "Let's go, Daddy. I'm ready."

But his father didn't answer. His mother called to him from the kitchen, "Your father has already left. He waited as long as he could. We called you and called you. He blew the car horn. You didn't answer. So you've missed your trip. I'm sorry!"

Andy couldn't quite believe it. "Why did he leave me?" he asked, half crying.

"You promised you would stay in the front yard to wait on Daddy. You didn't keep your promise," his mother explained.

Then Andy began getting mad. "I hate Mike. Why did he have to come over here and take me to his house? It's all his fault. He made me miss my trip!" Andy exclaimed, kicking at the door.

"Now Andy," began his mother, "I know you are terribly disappointed, and right now you are very angry. You are trying to blame Mike for it all. I suggest you go in your room and think it over. We can talk later when you are feeling better."

Andy did a lot of thinking that morning, but very little playing with his toys.

He didn't want much lunch, either. Somehow he wasn't very hungry. After lunch he curled up on the floor and went fast asleep. He didn't even know when his mother picked him up and put him on his bed. He slept most of the afternoon.

When Andy finally woke up he felt better. He thought he heard his father talking in the kitchen. He scrambled off the bed and down the hall toward the kitchen.

Then he heard his father asking, "I wonder who that is coming down the hall? Could it . . . ?"

But before his father said more, he knew, of course, that it was his little boy. Andy grabbed his father and hugged him and said, "I'm sorry for what I did, Daddy. I forgot my promise. I won't do it again. I missed you today."

Andy's father picked him up and said, "I'm glad to know you are sorry. I missed you, too, and you missed a good time. Mr. Barton's oldest son was planning to take you fishing down at the pond. Mrs. Barton made strawberry ice cream for us for lunch. She couldn't send you any, but she did send Mother a big box of fresh strawberries for our supper. And here is what Mrs. Barton sent you."

Andy knew what was in the box before he looked into it, for he heard a little "mew, mew" sound, and he felt something move.

"For me?" Andy asked, looking in the box. "A kitten for me?"

"A kitten for you, Andy," his father explained. "And I suspect he's hungry right about now."

Andy thought he was too.

—*J. Newbury*

NOT BIG ENOUGH

Sarah rode her new two-wheeler down the street to ask Julie to ride around the block with her. This was something they did together nearly every afternoon after kindergarten. But today when she got to Julie's house, she discovered a bigger girl playing with Julie.

"You want to go riding, Julie? I'll let you go first, ahead of me," Sarah called to her friend.

"No," replied Julie. "We're going to ride. Anyway, you're not big enough. You still have your training wheels on your bike."

Sarah couldn't understand Julie not wanting to play with her. They were *best friends.* She turned around slowly and rode back home. It was hard to keep the tears back. "I'll go see what Mother is doing," she thought to herself.

She tried to tell her mother about Julie, but this time Mother seemed too busy to really listen. She was sewing on a new dress she was making for a neighbor.

Sarah picked up some scraps of the cloth and started to cut with her mother's electric scissors.

"No, Sarah, put those scissors down," her mother scolded. "You're not big enough to cut with them. Why don't you go see what Glenn is doing?"

The words "not big enough" kept ringing in Sarah's ears as she went out to find Glenn.

She found him working on a new model airplane, and he didn't want to play with her.

"Can I help you make it?" she asked. "I'll be careful."

"No, not this one," her brother replied. "You're not big enough to work on this kind of model plane. You have to be able to read and all that stuff. Why don't you go see what Phil is doing?"

There were those words again, "not big enough." And no one would play with her. Sarah was really feeling sorry for herself now. But maybe it would be different with Phil.

She found him out in the garage. He had rows of bottles and jars on the work bench, and he was pouring something green from one to another.

"What are you doing, Phil? Can I do it too?" Sarah asked.

"No," replied Phil. "Keep back, Sarah. This is my science project for school. Don't touch that bottle, do you hear?"

"Why not?" Sarah questioned. "What's it for, anyway?"

"Oh, you're not big enough to understand," he answered. "And you're in my way.

Why don't you go see what Mother is doing?"

Sarah ran out of the garage and into the house, screaming as though she were hurt. Nobody wanted her around. She was not big enough. She was so unhappy.

Her cries brought her mother, Glenn, and Phil to see what had happened to her. They found her lying on the couch sobbing, with a pillow over her head.

Sarah's mother leaned over and picked her up. Sarah hid her face in her arms, still sobbing. Her mother sat down in her big rocker and stroked Sarah's hair gently while she rocked.

"What's the matter, Sarah?" Glenn asked.

"I think I know," replied her mother with a nod to the boys.

"Well, I guess I do, too," said Phil.

"Me too," added Glenn.

The boys went on back to their work, leaving Sarah and their mother to rock and talk alone.

Finally Sarah wiped her eyes, sat up, and smiled. Her mother smiled back and said, "Sarah, suppose you and I go into the kitchen and you can make a surprise dessert for supper —one that you are big enough to make all by yourself."

"Chocolate pudding?" asked Sarah.

"Yes, if you like," her mother answered.

And do you know, that is just what Sarah did. And she *was* big enough.

(This story was inspired by an incident recounted by the mother of a five-year-old girl who met rejection repeatedly one lonely afternoon.)

—J. Newbury

THE BROKEN LAMP

It was a warm sunny Saturday in early spring. Everything had gone well all day for Robby until he discovered that his older brother Jim was leaving to play baseball. He begged to go along, but his father reminded him that Jim's team was practicing and he could not go with him this time.

Robby was angry. He didn't see why he couldn't go with Jim. He stomped into the basement, slammed the door behind him, and went straight into his father's workshop. He knew he was not allowed in there unless his father was with him. But he didn't care. He was mad at his father—real mad. And he felt like doing something he knew was wrong.

Just then his father walked into the workshop. In a loud cross voice he asked, "What are you doing in here, Robby?" Robby didn't really know why he was in the workshop, but he did know that he was mad—too mad to talk. He picked up a scrap of lumber from the workbench and, quick as a flash, hit the lamp his father was making for his mother's birthday. The lamp fell with a hard thud on the floor and broke into several pieces.

Now Robby's father was mad. "You knocked that lamp off the workbench on purpose, young man," his father said in a loud cross voice.

Robby still didn't say anything. He knew that it was true. He had meant to knock the lamp off the workbench. And right then he was glad to see it broken.

When Robby saw the look on his father's face, he was *almost* sorry, but not really. His father didn't say another word, but he turned and walked heavily up the stairs. Robby knew by the way his father looked and walked that he was mad, very mad.

Robby went out in the backyard, still pouting and very mad. His frisky little puppy, Scamper, came running up to him to romp and play. But Robby kicked at Scamper and shouted, "Go away. Leave me alone, you old pup."

Scamper didn't understand, but he turned and walked to the far end of the yard, whining all the way.

How alone Robby felt! His brother was gone. His father was gone. And now his dog was gone too. He sat down in the shade of the old apple tree and pulled at the grass around him—whole handfuls at a time. Finally he stretched out on the grass. It felt cool, and before he knew it he was asleep.

Robby's father had been watching him from the kitchen window. He left Robby alone for a while. Then he went quietly and very carefully lifted him in his arms and carried him into the house. He laid him on the sofa and placed Robby's favorite little soft pillow under his head.

Robby was so tired that he kept right on sleeping and sleeping. When he did wake up, the first thing he saw was his father sitting in his big easy chair reading the evening paper.

Robby didn't ask how he got on the sofa. He was sure he knew. He walked slowly over to where his father was sitting. He stood by the arm of the big chair until his father noticed him and laid down his newspaper. He had a big smile for Robby on his face.

Robby climbed into his lap and whispered, "I'm sorry I broke the lamp. Really I am."

Hugging him tightly his father said, "That's my big boy, Robby. We'll make another lamp for Mother—you and I together."

Just then Scamper came bounding into the room. He ran straight to Robby, wagging his tail and yipping friendly little barks. Robby reached down and lifted Scamper into his lap and stroked his soft head. Scamper wriggled and wagged his tail and licked Robby on the cheek.

Everything seemed to be better now. No one felt alone any more.

(The above story line was taken from *The Broken Vase*, by Pauline Palmer Meek, published by John Knox Press.)

—*J. Newbury*

TAKE HER BACK!

George waited impatiently on the front steps of his home, carefully watching for the sight of his father's car. This was the day he had been looking forward to for so long. Father was bringing Mother home from the hospital with his new baby sister, Mary Beth. Just think—someone of his very own to play with!

George had moved into the big room with a big bed months ago and had helped his parents fix up his old room for the baby. Now everything was ready and waiting.

"If they would only hurry and get here," thought George.

Just then he saw his father's car turn the corner.

"Grandmother," he called, "they are here! They are here!" He ran out to the driveway to meet them.

He was so glad to see his mother. He had missed her so much, he thought, as he gave her a big hug and kiss. He loved his grandmother too, but he had still missed his mother.

"Come and see your sister, George," said his father.

Mother carefully pulled back the blanket as George eagerly looked inside.

"She sure is little and squirming," said George. "Will she always be that red?"

Mary Beth sucked hungrily on her tiny clenched fists. Before anyone could answer George, Grandmother came rushing out and eagerly took Mary Beth into the house.

Then things really became hectic. It was time for Mary Beth to be fed. Bottles of formula had to be fixed and diapers had to be changed. Father scurried about trying to be helpful by fixing lunch for the rest of the family. Mother looked tired, and George stood around feeling troubled and left out.

After Mary Beth finished her bottle, she went to sleep immediately. Grandmother explained that babies slept a great deal of the time. Mother took a nap, and Father went back to work.

As George played quietly in his room he couldn't help thinking, "So this is the new baby!" Things hadn't turned out at all the way he had thought they would.

George heard a call from the front door. "How's your baby sister today?" It was his favorite Aunt Sue with a beautifully wrapped gift in her hand.

"O.K. I think she just woke up," said George. "I can hear her crying again."

"Well, maybe this present will cheer her up," said Aunt Sue as she hurried past George and walked back to the baby's room.

George felt very left out as he walked into the yard and sat gloomily in his swing.

Neighbors came and visited. All asked George where his beautiful baby sister was. George found it easier to go to his room and stay out of the way.

"Will Mother love Mary Beth more than me?" he wondered.

Occasionally he would go in and look at Mary Beth. "She doesn't even seem to know me," thought George. "She is so little. It will be a long time before she can play."

The next few days were very much the same—fixing formula, changing diapers, giving baths, and feeding Mary Beth. Mother and Father were tired because Mary Beth had cried during the night. George heard his Grandmother say something about "colic." It seemed to George that Mary Beth did nothing but sleep, eat, and cry.

During dinner one evening things were calm and pleasant. Mary Beth was asleep. Mother looked rested and pretty in her new dress. It seemed almost like old times.

George looked up at his parents and blurted out, "Take her back to the hospital!" Mother and Father looked at him as if they were shocked. "Take her back," cried George. They both looked at him and then at each other as if they understood.

Mother came around the table, took George in her arms, and gave him a big hug. "I know how you feel, George. You wish there weren't any baby around here for Mother to take care of, but don't you ever worry; Mother loves you just the same and always will."

Father reached over and patted George's head. "We both love you very much, and you just remember that. Mary Beth takes a lot of our time right now. Mother and I did the exact same things for you when you were her age."

A cry was heard from Mary Beth's room. "May I get her bottle from the refrigerator for you?" asked George.

"Maybe you would like to hold her while she drinks it," said Mother.

"That will be fine," said Father, "if it doesn't take too long. I have a good bedtime story for George tonight."

As George held Mary Beth and watched her gulp her milk, he looked up at his mother and father and flashed his big contagious smile. "I believe I've changed my mind," he said. "Let's keep her!"

—*Rosetta Saurs*

JULIE'S NOSE

Julie was having such a good time roller skating. The skates had been her very favorite birthday present. Though she had received them only a week ago, she was beginning to skate very well.

At first she was able only to slowly slide first one foot and then the other, not daring to lift either off the sidewalk. She also had to hold on to the fence or her mother or father. Now she could manage alone, even lifting one foot and then the other. It wasn't easy to keep her balance when her feet kept rolling, but Julie had worked hard at learning.

As she skated toward the corner she heard her father call, "Julie, it is time for dinner."

"Coming," called Julie. "Just watch how fast I can skate now!"

She turned and started back to the house, so very proud of her new skill. Looking up at her father and laughing, she failed to see a big crack in the sidewalk. Her skate hit the crack and Julie fell forward on the sidewalk, skinning her nose and both hands.

Oh, how it hurt! Her father came and gathered her into his arms. Julie couldn't hold back the tears.

As Julie tried to wipe away the tears she noticed blood. Her poor nose! It was bleeding!

Her mother and father quickly cared for Julie's nose and hands. They cleaned the scrapes and gently applied some medicine. Her hands didn't hurt very much, but her nose surely did.

"Look," said her father, holding Julie up to the mirror. "Your nose is all fixed."

It wasn't until Julie saw herself that she remembered kindergarten. She would have to go to school the next morning. The thought was too much.

"The children will laugh at my nose," cried Julie, and the tears began to flow again.

She had a hard time going to sleep, for she imagined all the things her friends would say when they saw her the next morning. She was so tired, however, that she finally dropped off to sleep.

The first thing Julie did the next morning when she waked up was to run to the mirror. She hoped her nose would be well, but of course it wasn't.

"Do I have to go to school?" Julie asked her mother.

"You only have a skinned nose," answered her mother. "You wouldn't want to miss a whole day from school because of that, would you?"

Julie wasn't sure, but she went to her room and dressed slowly.

"Hurry, or I'll be late," called her father, who always took her to school on his way to work.

The closer they came to her kindergarten, the worse Julie felt. When they parked the car and began walking down the walk, Julie took very short steps. She finally stopped and said, "I just can't go in. They will laugh at me. I just know they will!"

Mrs. Barton, Julie's teacher, had been watching Julie's hesitating steps and her father's coaxing. Mrs. Barton went to the door and there she immediately saw what was causing the problem—Julie's nose!

"Why Julie," she said, "you have a skinned nose just like one I had when I was your age. I'll bet you fell on your new skates!"

"You had a skinned nose too?" asked Julie.

"I surely did. I fell in the gravel and really scratched up my face."

Julie listened very carefully as she hung up her sweater.

Just then Beth came running in the door and saw Julie.

"What happened to your nose? Does it hurt much?" she asked.

Several other children gathered around to look.

"Since Julie had an accident, let's let her be hostess today," suggested George. All the children agreed.

"You can sit by me during together time," said Charlotte, as she put her arm around Julie's shoulders. Julie began to feel much better.

It was then that Billy came running in the door. He took one look at Julie and blurted out, "Gee, Julie, you sure do look funny. Your nose looks just like a clown!"

Julie's face fell. She looked into the mirror on the kindergarten wall. First came a weak little smile. Then the little smile turned into a great big smile, and then that smile turned into a giggle.

"You know something? I do look kind of funny!" Then everyone had a good laugh with Julie.

"Come on, let's go play," chuckled Julie.

—*Rosetta Saurs*

OPEN-ENDED STORIES

PAM'S DECISION

Terry had just had a birthday. She was five years old and old enough now to learn to skate, her father had said. How she had wished for skates so that she could skate with the other children in her neighborhood!

Being five years old was wonderful, Terry thought, but the best part of it was having a pair of skates of her very own. Pam, Terry's best friend, had let Terry wear her skates once, but they were a little large for Terry. Pam would soon be six, and she was bigger than Terry.

Now that Terry had her own skates, she couldn't wait to put them on and go whizzing along on the sidewalk like the other children.

It seemed that Pam and the others in the neighborhood had the same idea—skating. There were Todd and Jan, Pam, Max, and Julie, all coming up the street trying to see who could get to the corner first.

Terry had her skates on before the other children had reached the corner. By the time they were back in front of her house she was ready to join them.

The race was on again. Pam stopped for Terry when she saw that Terry needed some help. They skated out of the yard onto the sidewalk together. They were holding hands. This made it easier for Terry to keep her balance. But even then Terry would fall. Skating wasn't as easy as she thought it was going to be.

The rest of the children had already gone to the corner and were coming back. Terry tried to join them, but she fell again and caused Pam to fall. Max and Todd, Julie and Jan skated on. They had to stop until Terry and Pam could get up. This spoiled the race.

Terry kept trying. She wanted to learn to skate like the others, but she kept falling and getting in their way.

Finally Todd said, "Come on, let's go around the corner to the playground and skate there. We can't have any fun with this baby who can't skate. She messes up our races. You coming too, Pam?"

Pam looked at Terry, who was having trouble keeping back the tears.

What do you think Pam did?

(Allow for discussion of the children's answers.)

—*Josephine Newbury*

THE BROKEN COOKIE-JAR LID

Judy was helping her mother make cookies —sugar cookies, her favorite kind.

Judy helped stir up the cookie dough. She helped to roll it out. That was fun, but she thought that sprinkling sugar on the cookies was the best part of all. She and her mother watched and waited as each pan of cookies baked.

Judy could hardly wait for the first panful to cool enough to taste them. Her mother poured two glasses of milk and put two cookies on a little plate for Judy and two on a plate for herself. "I think we deserve a treat," she said. "Smelling these cookies baking made me hungry. How about you, Judy?"

"Yum, yum," answered Judy. "And tasting them is making me hungrier."

When all the cookies were baked and cooled, Judy's mother stored them in the big cookie jar she kept on the counter in the kitchen.

She fixed a little plate of cookies and wrapped them in a napkin to take to the grandmother living next door.

This made Judy want to eat another cookie. "Please, Mother," she teased, "just one more, please!"

"Not now, Judy. It's too near lunchtime," her mother replied. And with that she left with the cookies for the neighbor.

Judy was alone in the kitchen. Her mother would be gone several minutes. "Now I can have another cookie and Mother won't know about it," Judy thought to herself.

She pulled a chair over to the counter and climbed up on it so that she could reach the cookie jar. She remembered that her mother had told her never to climb on a chair and try to reach things on the kitchen counter. But she was growing; she was five years old now, and she didn't see why she couldn't climb up and help herself.

She also remembered that her mother had just said she could not have any more cookies to eat now. But she was on the counter, and she could reach the cookie jar. "I'll take just one cookie," Judy said to herself. And so she did.

Just then she heard her mother coming back home. In her hurry to put the lid on the cookie jar, she let it slip. It rolled right off the counter onto the floor and broke.

Judy jumped down from the chair and ran to her room. Just as she closed the door to her room, she heard her mother open the kitchen door.

What do you think Judy did then?

(Allow for discussion of how Judy and her mother felt and what they did about this situation.)

—Josephine Newbury

THE LITTLE FIRE TRUCK

Paul and Joey had been playing with Joey's little cars in his big sandbox most of the afternoon. They had had such a good time making roads for the cars to run on. They had even made a mountain of sand with a road winding around it.

They were just beginning to make a tunnel for another road when Joey's mother came out to remind the boys that it was five o'clock—the time Paul's mother had said he must come home.

The boys didn't want to stop their play. They were having so much fun! Paul had pretended he was a fireman as he pushed Joey's new little red fire truck around on the roads in the sandbox. He liked the little fire truck better than any little car he had ever seen. How he wished he had a little red fire truck!

As Joey's mother started back into the house, she reminded the boys again, "It's time for Paul to go home. Joey, you'd better bring your little cars in for the night. It might rain. Come back again to play, Paul," she added.

Joey brushed the sand off his little cars, one at a time, and dropped them into the box he called his garage. Paul still had the little fire truck in his hand. Quickly he slipped it into the pocket of his jeans.

Joey didn't notice what had happened, and he didn't miss the fire truck. Paul helped Joey shake the sand off two of the match-box cars, then he decided he must go home.

Running out of the yard he called, "Bye, Joey. See ya'."

But as Paul came nearer his house, he began walking slower and slower. Every few steps he would stop to feel the little red fire truck in his pocket. He was thinking . . .

What do you think happened after that?

(Give the group time to work through this conflict situation.)

—Josephine Newbury

THE SMALL ONE
(A Halloween story to finish)

Once upon a time there was a very small pumpkin growing in Farmer Bill's pumpkin patch. It was round and smooth, but it just hadn't grown as fast as all the other pumpkins in the field.

One day in October two men came to Farmer Bill's farm in a big truck. They wanted to buy pumpkins to take into the city to sell for Halloween.

The little pumpkin became excited over the thought of getting to go to the city—of being taken to a store and of having someone want him for a jack-o'-lantern. He could hear the men talking as they walked around through the vines selecting the pumpkins and loading them into the truck.

He kept waiting for one of the men to come over to his vine and pick him. How he wanted to go with the other pumpkins in the truck to the city! If only he could be a jack-o'-lantern for Halloween and make the children laugh and shout! But the big truck drove away without him.

The little pumpkin was very sad, but not for long, because . . .

—Josephine Newbury

SEASONAL STORIES

THE SMILING PUMPKIN[6]

Peter sat by the window in the big bus and looked out. He and Mother were going to visit Uncle John and Aunt Susan while Father was away. It seemed to Peter that the houses and trees and people were flying past the window. Soon the big bus stopped. "Arlington!" called the driver. And there was Uncle John standing beside the big bus and looking in at the window.

Peter and Mother were soon in Uncle John's car. Aunt Susan was waiting for them at home.

"Peter! Peter! are you a pumpkin eater?" asked Uncle John as he drove the car along the road.

"I hope that Aunt Susan has some of her delicious pie for us!" said Mother.

---

[6]From *The Kindergartner*, October 25, 1964. Used by permission of the Graded Press.

"Look! Look!" cried Peter. There were piles of big yellow pumpkins at a vegetable stand that they were passing.

"How many pies those pumpkins would make!" said Peter.

"I couldn't even guess!" said Uncle John.

The next morning Peter was in a hurry to go outdoors to play. He had his own wagon at Uncle John's. He must go and see if it was in the shed where he had left it. Yes, there it was waiting for Peter.

Uncle John was in the garden. He was covering the strawberry bed with straw to keep it warm when the snow and ice should come.

Peter pulled his cart up and down the garden paths. Over by the fence he saw something bright yellow. When he pushed the brown leaves aside there was a little pumpkin.

"Uncle John! Uncle John!" called Peter. "See what I found!"

Uncle John came to look. "This pumpkin is yours," said Uncle John.

"Will Aunt Susan make a pie out of it?" asked Peter.

"No, indeed!" answered Uncle John. "This pumpkin is yours. You found it!"

Peter proudly pulled his cart back to the house.

After dinner Uncle John asked, "Peter, would you like to make your pumpkin smile?"

Peter was always ready for something new, so he carried his pumpkin out to the shed. Uncle John used the knife. Peter watched, but his part was to take all the seeds out of the inside of the pumpkin. Soon the pumpkin had two eyes, a funny nose, and a smiling mouth cut in his jolly face. Peter laughed.

"That's what this funny pumpkin is supposed to do," said Uncle John, "make people laugh. And tonight is a special time for making people laugh. It is Halloween."

Soon the pumpkin had a flashlight hidden inside his round head. When the light was turned on his eyes shone and his smile seemed big and broad. Peter laughed and laughed.

"May we put him on the supper table?" asked Peter.

"That's a good idea!" answered Uncle John.

When supper was ready and everyone was

at the table the pumpkin was smiling in the center of the table and everyone laughed.

After supper Uncle John said, "Tonight I must go and see Mr. Jones. He has a sore foot and cannot walk. He gets very lonely."

"Would he laugh if he saw my smiling pumpkin?" asked Peter.

"It might help," answered Uncle John.

Aunt Susan said, "Peter, you may go with Uncle John. I'll dress you up."

Soon Peter and Uncle John were outside in the darkness. Peter was wearing Uncle John's big straw garden hat. Only his nose showed under it. He had on a red flannel shirt of Uncle John's and a pair of overalls, with the legs turned up to make them fit. He was carrying his smiling pumpkin.

When Mr. Jones saw Peter he laughed. And when the light was turned on inside the pumpkin Mr. Jones laughed.

"This has been the happiest Halloween I have ever had," he said.

—*Jessie Eleanor Moore*

THEODORE'S SURPRISE[7]

Theodore Duff was visiting Uncle John on the farm. His friend, G. Edgar Price, was visiting Uncle John's farm, too.

"Uncle John is my favorite relative," said Theodore. "You know why? 'Cause he has red hair just like mine. And he likes doughnuts and I do, too."

Theodore said this to G. Edgar because he wanted him to like Uncle John. He also wanted G. Edgar to like Uncle John's farm.

"This is the best farm in the whole country," said Theodore. "Uncle John showed me all over the place the last time I was here. This time I'll show you around."

"I wish I had an uncle who had a farm," said G. Edgar.

Uncle John wanted G. Edgar to see the fields and all the animals. But first he wanted to find out how much Theodore remembered about his last visit.

"What will you show G. Edgar?" Uncle John asked Theodore. "First we'll walk in the cornfield," said Theodore. "It's scary because you can't see over the top and the corn rustles.

"Then we'll climb the apple trees and see the apples growing on the branches.

"We'll go see the little calves. We can

[7]Adapted from *Five-Year-Olds in the Church.* Copyright © 1956 and 1960 by The Seabury Press, Inc. Used by permission.

scratch their heads, just the way you showed me," said Theodore to Uncle John.

"We'll pick up the fuzzy baby chicks, too. Then we'll look for Matilda and her kittens in the barn. G. Edgar will like the kittens. We'll play with them," Theodore said.

Uncle John pushed back his hat and scratched his head.

"Aren't you forgetting something important?" Uncle John asked.

"No, what?" Theodore asked.

"Something has been happening ever since your last visit."

Theodore looked surprised. He and G. Edgar and Uncle John all looked at each other.

Finally Uncle John said, "Go see what the farm looks like now, but stay out of the pasture. Maybe you'll find out for yourselves what has happened."

Theodore and G. Edgar went first to the tall green cornfield. It didn't look like the same field. There was no tall green corn. The field was empty except for some stacks of yellow cornstalks.

"What happened?" asked Theodore, looking all around. "Where's the corn?"

Next they went to the apple orchard and climbed a tree. "That's funny, there aren't any apples," said Theodore, looking through the leaves.

"I guess somebody picked all the apples," said G. Edgar.

They walked to the pasture and looked through the fence. The calves were no longer little. Some were halfway grown up.

So were the chickens. The chickens looked especially funny. Their necks were long, and their feathers didn't fit them very well.

G. Edgar was interested in everything he saw, but Theodore didn't understand. They hurried to the barn and found Matilda and her family. But even Matilda's kittens were different. They were almost as big as Matilda herself.

"I wanted you to play with the kittens," said Theodore. "Now they are just cats."

Now Theodore and G. Edgar understood what Uncle John was talking about. Everything on the farm had been growing.

"You saw the farm in summer," said Uncle John to Theodore. "Then everything was still growing. All summer long everything was busy growing and some things grew up more than others."

Uncle John took them over to the corncrib. It was full of corn for the animals' winter food. Some chipmunks were busy getting their share for winter, too.

Then Uncle John took them down into a cool dark cellar.

"Why, here are all the apples!" said Theodore. They were heaped in big baskets. Large yellow pumpkins leaned against each other.

"These are some of the things that grew up all the way," said Uncle John. "This is the farm's harvest."

He filled two boxes of apples and picked out two pumpkins. "These are for you to take home," he said to Theodore and G. Edgar, "so you won't forget how the farm looks in fall at harvest time."

"Thank you," said G. Edgar, who liked Uncle John and his farm very much.

"Thank you," said Theodore to his favorite uncle.

—*Elsie B. Eagles*

JOHNNY AND BILLY MAPLE LEAF[8]

(This story will be more effective if the teacher collects maple leaves to illustrate Johnny and Billy. If maple trees are not available, the teacher can change the story to fit the fall leaves of a local tree.)

Johnny Maple and Billy Maple were two leaves that lived at the top of a tall maple tree. They could look down and see everything that was happening.

When the fire bell rang, Johnny and Billy watched the engine pull out of the firehouse. They would shout to the other leaves just where the fire was.

When Mr. Pickard, the policeman, blew his whistle at the corner of Main and High Streets, they could see the cars stopping.

One morning Billy called to Johnny. He said, "Your shirt is turning yellow."

Johnny laughed. "Your shirt is turning red," he told Billy.

"Mother Tree said this would happen," Billy remembered, "but I wonder why."

"She told me it's because it is autumn,"

[8]Reprinted from *Instructor*, © September 1960, the Instructor Publications, Inc. Used by permission.

Johnny replied. "Soon we will go on a trip, too."

"A trip?" asked Billy in surprise.

"Yes," said Johnny. "Look down on the ground. Already some leaves have left us."

The next morning when Billy woke up Johnny had gone.

"Where are you, Johnny?" cried Billy.

But Johnny didn't answer.

"Oh, well," said Billy, "soon it will be my turn to leave Mother Tree. Then I will hunt for Johnny."

Sure enough! That's just what happened. Along came a big gust of wind. Billy Maple waved good-bye to Mother Tree and went sailing through the air. Down, down, down he went, till he reached the ground.

"Hi, boys!" shouted Billy, as he saw old friends. "Where's Johnny Maple?"

"You'll have to hunt for him," shouted the other leaves. "Every time Mr. Wind blows we travel round and round trying to find our old friends."

"What's it like down here?" asked Billy.

"Oh, it's fun," said the other leaves.

Billy was in a hurry to find Johnny. "Hello! Hello!" he called to all the other leaves. "Have you seen Johnny?"

"I saw him yesterday," said Betty Birch.

"I think he is on the other side of the park," said Dinah Elm.

"Come, Mr. Wind," called Billy, "please blow me to the other side of the park."

"All right," said Mr. Wind, and he blew so hard that three people lost their hats and the water in the pond splashed up on the lily leaves.

"Johnny!" called Billy Maple. But he didn't find him.

Soon Billy got tired. He went to sleep. In the morning he heard a voice he knew.

"Billy Maple!" Johnny was calling. "Here I am."

"Where?" asked Billy, rubbing his eyes.

"Here," said Johnny.

"But, but, but—" said Billy, "You've lost your red shirt. You have a brown shirt now. And it is all stiff and starched."

"Look at yourself," laughed Johnny. "*You* have a brown shirt. And it is stiff and starched too. If it weren't, Mr. Wind couldn't blow you across the park."

Billy jumped up. "This is fun," he said as he felt the wind against his stiff shirt. "Can we play like this all winter?"

"Oh, no," said Johnny. "You get tired of playing all the time. Polly Poplar says the gardener will gather us up. He has an important job for us to do."

Billy Maple puffed out his new stiff brown shirt. "I like that," he said. "Is it *very* important?"

"Yes, indeed!" said Johnny. "The gardener needs us to keep the roots of the plants warm during the winter."

"I'll do my part," said Billy proudly.

"When the frost comes and the snow comes, we will snuggle closer and closer to the roots," Johnny said.

And that's what Billy and Johnny did.

BUTTONS AND THE MAGIC APPLES [9]

Buttons was the best finder in his family.

He found Daddy's cuff link when it rolled under the bed.

He found Mother's earring when it rolled under the seat of the car.

He found Grandmother's glasses when they were lost on the top of her head.

He even found Pop-pop's magnifying glass so he could read the evening paper.

But he could *not* find the magic apple his Aunt Joan had told him about.

Aunt Joan lived on a farm, and her orchard was full of red, rosy apples, hundreds and hundreds of them. But when he asked her for one, she said, "Yes, you may have an apple if first you find me a magic one."

"What's a magic apple?" Buttons asked.

"It's one with a star in it," answered Aunt Joan.

Buttons looked and looked at all the apple trees. There were apples with shiny green leaves, apples with bright red spots, green apples, apples even with worm holes—but none with stars!

Buttons walked back to the house, very disappointed, and very, very hungry.

"Aunt Joan," he said, "I've looked everywhere, but I can't find an apple with a star."

She laughed and said, "Here, sit down beside me, and we'll both not only find an apple with a star, but we'll eat one."

She chose the biggest, reddest, shiniest ap-

⁹From *Growing*, April–June 1960. Copyright © 1960, W. L. Jenkins. Used by permission.

ple from the bowl. *(take an apple from the container on the table)* on the table. Then she took her paring knife and cut the apple carefully *(do this as you talk)* across the middle.

Inside was the most perfect star Buttons had ever seen *(show the apple; point out the star)*.

"It is magic, it is magic!" Buttons shouted happily. "I'm going to look for a star every time I eat an apple." He looked again at the star. It was *almost* too pretty to eat, but not quite. Buttons bit into the apple and said contentedly, "Thank you, God, for starry apples."

THE LITTLE ACORN[10]

(This story-poem may help to develop the child's sense of security in God's plan for growth and may encourage a trustful acceptance of inevitable changes that come in the process.)

High in a treetop, up near the sky
A new little acorn began to cry:
"I'm so very tiny! I'm so very small!
Why can't I be big? I don't like this at all!"

"Hush," said the oak tree, "don't cry, little seed;
I'll give you some sap and whatever you need.
Hold on to my branch there with all of your
    might.
I'll take care of you. You'll grow all right."

He felt the spring sun shining right through his
    cap;
He sipped through his stem the sweet-tasting
    sap.
He knew he was growing, and, oh, it was fun
To swing back and forth in the wind and the
    sun!

A summer breeze gave him a twist and a twirl
"Hello!" said a bluebird. "Hello!" said a squirrel.
"Look at me," said the acorn, "up here in the
    tree!
This is a *wonderful* place to be.

And that's where he stayed the whole summer
    long.
He drank the sweet sap, and he grew big and
    strong.
When thunderstorms thundered and winds
    blew at night,

That acorn could hold on tighter than tight!

When summer was over and autumn winds
    blew,
The mother tree told him some things he must
    do:
"Let go, little acorn, let go and fall down
See the leaves falling down to the ground?"

"When you are with them snuggled below,
Winter will come with a blanket of snow.
There you can sleep the whole winter through.
When springtime comes, you'll know what to
    do."

The acorn looked down, and he said, "No! No!
Why can't I stay here? I don't want to go."
And he hung on and hung on till the branches
    were bare.
He felt very lonesome, but still he stayed there.

"Let go!" roared the north wind. "Let go now!
    Let go!
You must not stay up there if you want to
    grow."
"I'm grown," said the acorn, "I'm fat as can be.
I've *done* all the growing there *is* in me."

"Oh, no!" said the north wind, "there's more;
    you will see.
Some day you'll grow up to be a big tree!"
"Yes, little acorn," the mother oak said,
"Now you get right down there into your bed."

Well . . . it was cold . . . and lonesome . . . and
    so
The acorn decided he'd better let go.
"Whoosh!" went the north wind—a blustery
    blast!
Down went the acorn at last, at last!

The leaves made him cozy; he rested down
    there,
And soon there was ice and snow everywhere.
All winter long you could see nothing of him,
But when springtime came the sun shone on
    him.

---

[10]Reprinted with permission from *Growing in the Fellowship* by Florence Schulz. Copyright ©, 1960, by the United Church Press.

It melted the snow, warmed him right through
his cap;
It made him wake up from his long winter nap.
His shell cracked and opened and out came a
stem!
Warm raindrops fell on it again and again.

It stretched toward the sunshine; it grew very
high.
It grew leafy branches that reached toward the
sky.
"Hello!" said a squirrel. "Hello!" said a bird.
And—deep in the trunk of the tree could be
heard

A voice like the acorn's! It said, "Look at me!
Oh, *this* is a *wonderful* thing to be!"

MISCELLANEOUS STORIES

THE FEEL OF THINGS [11]

One sunshiny day in summer Frank was
ready to play out-of-doors. "Mother," he said,
"it is so hot. I should like to take off my shoes
and socks."

"Very well," Mother replied, "you may
take them off."

Quickly Frank sat on the floor and untied
the lace of one shoe. He loosened it—there, and
there, and there. Then he took hold of the heel
of the shoe and pulled and pulled. Off came one
shoe! Then Frank untied the lace of the other
shoe. He loosened the lace carefully—there,
and there, and there. Then he took hold of the
heel and pulled and pulled. Off came that shoe!

> Off came one shoe,
> Off came two!
> Frank loosened it,
> Frank pulled it,
> He knew what to do.

Next Frank took hold of the top of one sock.
He pushed it down over the heel and over the
toe and one sock was off. He wiggled his toes
and stretched them. Then Frank took hold of
the top of the other sock. He pushed it down
over the heel and over the toe and another sock
was off. He wiggled those toes and stretched
them. How comfortable it was to have shoes off

[11] Reprinted by permission of the Association for Childhood Education International from *Told Under the Blue
Umbrella*.

and socks off this warm, moist day. Frank stood
up.

> Sock off the heel,
> Sock off the toe,
> Frank is ready,
> Off he'll go.

First Frank stepped on the mat before the
door. The mat was rough. It scratched his toes.
It pricked his feet. So Frank sang,

> "Rough mat,
> Prickly mat,
> Scratchy mat there;
> I feel you, mat,
> I like you, mat,
> Because my feet are bare."

Next Frank stepped on the porch and
down the steps. The wooden steps were warm,
for the sun had been shining on them all the
long morning. So Frank sang,

> "Wooden steps,
> Warm steps,
> Sunny steps there;
> I feel you, steps,
> I like you, steps,
> Because my feet are bare."

"And now I'll go a little farther," said
Frank. Then he walked on the gray stone path.
The path was shady. It felt cool. His feet made
a little sound "pat, pat, pat, pat" as he walked.
So Frank sang,

> "Pat, pat,
> Cool path,
> Smooth path there;
> I feel you, path,
> I like you, path,
> Because my feet are bare."

"And now I'll go a little farther," said
Frank. Then he walked on the soft, green grass.
The grass was cool. It tickled his toes. His feet
made no sound. Then Frank sang,

> "Cool grass,
> Soft grass,
> Tickly grass there;
> I feel you, grass,
> I like you, grass,
> Because my feet are bare."

"What fun it is to be barefoot," said Frank,
as he walked back over the cool, shady path and
up the warm, sunny steps and on the rough mat
into the house. There stood his shoes. They
could not take a walk without Frank's feet in
them. There lay Frank's socks. They could not

take a walk without Frank's feet in them. So Frank sang them a little song and here it is:

"I like to feel the mat,
Rough mat,
Scratchy mat,
With my feet,
My bare feet,
My bare, bare, bare feet.

"I like to feel the steps,
Warm steps,
Sunny steps,
With my feet,
My bare feet,
My bare, bare, bare feet.

"I like to feel the path,
Smooth path,
Cool path,
With my feet,
My bare feet,
My bare, bare, bare feet.

"I like to feel the grass,
Soft grass,
Tickly grass,
With my feet,
My bare feet,
My bare, bare, bare feet.

"Bare feet, bare feet,
Bare, bare, bare feet;
I stretch my toes,
I wiggle my toes,
I feel with the toes
Of my bare, bare feet."
—*Mary G. Phillips*

THE FARMER[12]

Farmer Bill lived on a small farm with his wife, his little daughter Susie, a dog named Muffy, and a cat named Tiger.

Farmer Bill hoped that some day he would have *many* farm animals. Right now he had just twelve: two quacking ducks, two clucking hens, two noisy pigs, two quiet sheep, two chewing goats, a horse for Susie to ride, and a cow that gave rich milk.

Yes, Farmer Bill had *exactly* twelve animals on his farm—and twelve makes a dozen, you know.

It was springtime—the time of year when many farm animals are born. Farmer Bill knew that it wouldn't be long until there would be some new animal babies on *his* farm. He could hardly wait to find out how many there would be.

Springtime was a busy time for Farmer Bill. Each morning he fastened a plow to his tractor and plowed his fields. Then he used a harrow to break up the lumps of earth and smooth out the land so that he could plant his corn.

But even with all this work to do, Farmer Bill remembered to take very good care of his farm animals. And each day he looked to see if any of the baby animals had been born.

Susie found the first babies. One morning she looked out her bedroom window.

"Baby birds!" she shouted.

Then she watched as Mother Robin fed the baby birds a fat, juicy worm.

Of course, Farmer Bill thought birds were pretty, and they *did* help him by eating bugs. But baby birds weren't the animal babies that Farmer Bill was hoping to see. He started for the barn but stopped when he heard Susie calling.

"Kittens!" she cried.

There, under the porch, was Tiger with her four new kittens. Like the baby birds, the kittens were enjoying their breakfast—but not a breakfast of worms. No sirree! They were having their mother's warm milk.

Now Farmer Bill liked kittens because kittens grow to be cats—and cats keep rats and mice away from the barn. But kittens aren't *farm* animals! They weren't the kind of animal babies that Farmer Bill was hoping to see.

Farmer Bill hurried back to the barn. He was just starting up his tractor when Susie called again. She sounded so excited that Farmer Bill jumped off the tractor and ran to the house.

"Puppies!" Susie announced.

Muffy had just given birth to five fat puppies. Susie started to pick up one of the puppies, but she pulled back her hand when Muffy growled.

Of course, Farmer Bill liked puppies, but he didn't *need* puppies. He needed *farm* animals. Susie kept finding animals, but she just didn't find the right kind!

---

[12]Used by permission of the author.

It was lunchtime when Farmer Bill drove his tractor in from the field. As he came up the road, he saw Susie standing beside the barn. She was wildly waving her arms and calling something to him.

Farmer Bill made his tractor go as fast as it would go. He gave the ducks and chickens a *terrible* scare when he roared in at the barnyard gate. In less than a minute he was running toward the barn.

You'll never guess what Farmer Bill saw when he looked in that barn!

Susie had put some little toy cars all around a big toy car. She was pretending that the big car was the mother and that the little cars were babies!

"A joke," said Farmer Bill, and he began to laugh.

Just then Mother started ringing the big bell. She always rang it when she needed Farmer Bill in a hurry.

Farmer Bill ran to the house with Susie close behind him. He rushed into the kitchen. There stood Mother, grinning from ear to ear. On the table was a big chocolate cake with six cupcakes around it—a mother cake and six baby cakes.

"A trick," grumbled Farmer Bill, and he scowled at the cakes.

Mother thought that this was the best trick of the whole year, but Farmer Bill didn't think so. He was grumpy all through lunch.

As soon as he had finished eating, he took a cupcake in each hand and went back to the barn.

A few days later Mother and Susie were washing the dishes when they heard Farmer Bill calling from the barn. Mother winked at Susie. She thought that Farmer Bill was planning to get even. This time he would play a trick on *her*.

Farmer Bill called again and again, but Mother and Susie didn't hurry.

Later they strolled down to the barn. And when they got there, Susie squealed with delight.

"A calf!" she said, and she jumped up and down.

A wobbly little calf was standing beside its mother. Susie patted the calf. It felt all soft and warm.

About a week later Farmer Bill told Mother and Susie that there was something in the pasture they might like to see.

You can be very sure that this time Susie didn't dilly-dally one little bit. She ran all the way.

"A colt!" she squealed.

There stood a little colt with spindly legs. It was only three hours old.

The very next day Farmer Bill heard some grunting and squealing coming from behind the barn. He ran quickly to see what was going on.

"Baby pigs!" he called at the top of his voice.

Susie and her daddy counted nine new pigs. Wasn't that a large family for a mother pig to feed?

Later that spring a little lamb was born, and a mother goat had two kids. Some ducks and chickens hatched out, too.

Farmer Bill was happy now. He had started out with an even dozen farm animals—just exactly twelve. Now he had thirty-seven, not counting the baby birds, the kittens, the puppies, the "baby" cars, OR the "baby" cupcakes.

—*James L. Hymes, Jr.*

A VISIT TO THE FARM[13]

(Dots in this story indicate a pause while listeners think of and supply the word.)

Look at the turkey gobbler.
    Oh, see him strut along,
His tail spread out into a fan.
    Just listen to his song:
        "Gobble, gobble, gobble,
        Gobble, gobble, gob."

Look at the geese a-waddling,
    A-waddling as they walk,
Their necks stretched forward as they go.
    And this is how they talk:
        "Honk-honk-honk,
        Honk-honk, honk-honk."

Look at the rooster stretching up.
    He stands so proudly tall.
His wings they flap, his comb shows red.

[13]From *In and Out with Betty Anne,* by Dorothy Baruch. Used by permission.

Now, listen to his call:
    "Cockadoodle, cockadoodle,
    Cockadoodle-doo."

Look at the ducks go gliding
    Into the water clear.
As they swim out across the pond
    Their language you can hear:
    "Quack, quack, quack,
    Quack-quack, quack-quack."

And so, you see, each feathered friend
    Speaks in a different way.
"Gobble, cockadoodle-doo,
    Honk-honk, and quack," they say.

Once a little girl went to spend a day at a farm in the country. The farm belonged to Uncle Ned. The little girl's name was Betty Anne. Uncle Ned offered to take Betty Anne around the farm to see all the animals.

In one field were some cows—some black and white cows. They were chewing hay and looking lazily around. One black and white cow had a tiny baby black and white . . . calf. As Betty Anne stood there watching, the cows began to moo. They lifted their heads. It seemed to Betty Anne that they were saying:
    "Moo, moo, moo,
    We give our milk to you."

In the next field were some horses. There was a chestnut-brown horse, there was a snow-white horse, there was a dapple-gray horse, and there was a black horse with a tiny baby . . . colt. And there was a black and white pony, too. When the pony saw Betty Anne, he ran over to the fence whinnying. It seemed to Betty Anne that he was saying:
    "Wheeee, wheeee,
    Come ride on me."

Next door in another field were some sheep, with woolly fur all over them. There was a mother sheep with a little tiny baby . . . lamb. The mother said, "Bah, ha, ha," and the baby answered, "Maa-aa-aa."

There were some pigs, too. They were big and grunty. There was one enormous fat pig with three baby piggiewigs. She kept saying, "Wunk, wunk, wunk," to them in a low gruff voice, and they kept squealing back at her in tiny weeny voices. It seemed to Betty Anne that they were saying:

    "Ooee, ooee, ooee, say we,
    Little baby piggies three."

Betty Anne and Uncle Ned came to some bunnies next. They were soft and cuddly looking and had long, long ears, and they didn't say anything at all. They just went hop, hop, hop, and jump, jump, jump, and then sat still and wiggled their noses, and ate carrots and lettuce and cabbage.

The chicken yard was away at the far end of the farm. Uncle Ned showed Betty Anne how the pigeons flew about in a pen covered with wire meshing. The pigeons looked at Betty Anne with unblinky eyes. They seemed to be saying:
    "Coo, coorooroo,
    And how are you?"
Uncle Ned showed Betty Anne the chickens, too. He showed her how the nests in which the hens laid their eggs were arranged like little boxes in the wall. The hens would fly up into the nests, which had straw in the bottom. Whenever one of the hens laid an egg she would get very excited. Then she would sound as if she were calling out:
    "Cuck-cuck-cuck-cuck-caw-awk,
    I've laid an egg for you,
    Cuck-cawk and now I'm through."
Uncle Ned showed Betty Anne a mother hen with some little yellow baby chicks. The mother hen kept calling, "Cluck, cluck, cluck," to the baby chicks, and they kept answering, "Eep, eep, eep," as if they were asking:
    "Tweet, weet, weet,
    Aren't we sweet?"
And the big rooster, who didn't want to be forgotten, crowed as loudly as he could, as if he were saying:
    "Cock-a-doodle-doo,
    Look at me, too."
Then what do you think Betty Anne saw standing way over in the corner with a tail spread out behind like a fan? A turkey gobbler, a real live Thanksgiving turkey. He just stood there without saying anything at all.

"Doesn't he talk?" asked Betty Anne.

"Oh yes, he does," answered Uncle Ned. "He says, 'Gobble, gobble, gobble.' I imagine when he says 'Gobble-gobble' that he's trying to sing

    " 'On Thanksgiving day you'll see
    You will want to gobble me.' "

And Uncle Ned grinned.

"It's starting to grow dark, Betty," he continued, "so I guess we had better be getting back to the house."

On the way back they called good-by to the turkey, who said . . . "Gobble-gobble"; and to the rooster, who said . . . "Cock-a-doodle-doo"; and to the hen, who said . . . "Cuck-cuck, cuck-cuck-cawk"; and to the baby chicks, who said . . . "Eep, eep, eep"; and to the pigeons, who said . . . "Cooroo, cooroo"; and to the piggies, who said . . . "Ooee, ooee, ooee"; and to the pony that called . . . "Whee-ee-ee"; and to the cow who said . . . "Moo, moo, moo"; and to the lamb, who said . . . "Maa-aa-aa"; and to the bunnies that didn't say anything at all but just went hop, hop, hop, and jump, jump, jump.

So many animals we've seen,
    It's been a lovely day!
And each and every one of them
    Had something else to say,
And each and every one of them
    Spoke in a different way.

—*Dorothy Baruch*

BIG TREE[14]

Big Tree stood in Marc's back yard. Big Tree had been there a long time, longer than Marc could remember.

No one knew how old Big Tree was, not Marc's father, not Marc's mother.

Everyone knew how old Marc was. He was three.

Marc liked Big Tree.

Big Tree was very high. The highest branches stretched way, way high into the sky.

Big Tree was big around: so big that Marc could not reach around him, not at all; so big that Marc could hide behind him without one bit of Marc showing.

Big Tree was strong. When the wind blew, and the lightning flashed, and the thunder crashed, Big Tree's branches tossed and creaked. But his branches did not break, and his roots stayed tight and deep in the ground.

In spring, the grass turned green. The tulips bloomed. It was Marc's birthday. Big Tree

stretched out his branches and showed some new little leaves to the sun.

Blossoms came, and seeds. They dropped all over the ground. They even dropped on Marc.

"Stop dropping on me, Big Tree," said Marc. But Big Tree did not stop until all the blossoms were dropped.

In summer, Big Tree held his leafy green branches close to the hot sun. Marc and his mother had a picnic in the cool shade. The ants built little hills at Big Tree's roots. Daddy long-legs climbed up and down Big Tree's cool black trunk.

In fall, Big Tree slowly let go his leaves. Yellow and brown, down they came, with hundreds of little twigs. Marc raked the leaves into big piles.

Winter came. It began to snow. Marc made a snowman and stood it beside Big Tree. The ants were gone, the daddy longlegs were gone. The outside was cold, very cold.

One day the snowman melted. The sun began to feel warm. Marc changed into his spring jacket. The grass turned green again, and the tulips bloomed.

Big Tree stretched out his branches and showed some new little leaves to the sun.

It was spring again, Marc knew it was his birthday time again. Both Marc and Big Tree were one year older.

Still no one knew how old Big Tree was.
BUT
Everyone knew how old Marc was. Do you?

—*Phoebe M. Anderson*

LITTLE DUCKLING TRIES HIS VOICE[15]

Once upon a time fat Little Duckling went on a journey into the Wide World. He wandered along the Barnyard Road, and presently he saw the Kitty Cat.

"Me-ow!" said the Kitty Cat.

"O-o-oh!" cried Little Duckling. "Isn't that a pretty sound! I think I'll talk that way!"

But do you suppose Little Duckling could say "Me-ow"?

No indeed!

He tried, but the best he could do was: "Me-e-ack! Me-e-ack!"

And that wasn't pretty at all!

So Little Duckling waddled on and on. After a while he saw Puppy Dog.

[14]Reprinted with permission from *Big Tree* by Phoebe M. Anderson. Copyright ©, 1960, United Church Press.

[15]From *Child Life Magazine*, copyright 1923, 1951 by Rand McNally & Company. Used by permission of Mrs. Paul Ihrig.

"Bow-wow," said Puppy Dog.

"O-o-oh!" cried Little Duckling. "Isn't that a lovely noise! I think I'll talk that way!"

But do you suppose Little Duckling could say "Bow-wow"?

No indeed!

He tried, but this is the way he sounded: "B-ack! B-ack!" And that wasn't lovely at all!

Then Little Duckling waddled on and on. Soon he saw a Yellow Bird in a tree.

"Tweet-tweet-tweet-tweet-tweet!" said Yellow Bird.

"Oh, oh, oh!" sighed Little Duckling. "Isn't that a sweet song! I think I'll sing that way!"

But do you suppose Little Duckling could sing "Tweet-tweet"?

No indeed! He tried his very best, but all he could say was : "Twack! Twack!"

And that wasn't sweet at all!

So Little Duckling waddled on and on. After a while he met Big Cow.

"Moo-o-o!" said Big Cow.

"O-o-oh!" thought Little Duckling. "Isn't that a beautiful roar! I think I'll roar that way!"

But do you suppose Little Duckling could say "Moo-o-o"?

He tried, but all he could manage to say was: "M-ack! M-ack!"

And that wasn't beautiful at all!

Little Duckling was very sad. He could not say "Me-ow" like Kitty Cat. He could not say "Bow-wow" like Puppy Dog. He could not say "Tweet-tweet" like Yellow Bird. He could not say "Moo-o-o" like Big Cow.

He waddled slowly on and on. All at once he saw his own Mother Duck coming toward him along the Barnyard Road.

"Quack! Quack!" cried Mother Duck.

"O-o-oh!" whispered happy Little Duckling to himself. "That is the prettiest sound in the whole Wide World! I think I'll talk that way!"

And he found he could say "Quack! Quack!" very nicely.

—*Marjorie M. LaFleur*

THE BOY AND HIS GOATS

Once there was a little boy who had three billy goats. Each morning he would take his goats out to the hillside to eat the green grass.

One morning as the boy climbed the hillside with his goats he became tired and sleepy.

He sat down under a tree to rest while his billy goats ate the fresh green grass.

Soon the boy was fast asleep, but the goats were not tired and sleepy. They were still hungry.

On the other side of the fence nearby was a field of corn. The billy goats thought that the corn would make a better dinner, so they jumped over the fence and began to eat.

By and by the little boy woke up from his nap. He looked around for his goats, but he could not see them anywhere.

He began calling for them, "Yoo-hoo, yoo-hoo. Oh, billy goats, where are you?"

The three goats answered,
"Baa, baa, baa,
We're eating the corn.
We're here to stay.
We won't come out
Till the end of day."

The little boy started to run after the goats with a stick to chase them out of the cornfield. But the goats would not leave. So the little boy sat down under the tree and began to cry.

About that time a little rabbit came hop, hop, hopping along.

"Good morning," he said cheerfully. "Why do you cry?"

"I am crying because I can't drive my goats out of the cornfield," explained the little boy.

"Just leave the job to me," boasted the little rabbit.

"Come here, goats, come here," he called as he hopped toward the goats.

But the goats answered,
"Baa, baa, baa,
We're eating the corn.
We're here to stay.
We won't come out
Till the end of day."

"Then I'll drive you out," shouted the rabbit. But the goats wouldn't leave, so the rabbit hopped back over and sat down beside the boy. He began to cry too. The two cried and cried and cried.

Soon an old fox came trotting along. When he met the little boy and the little rabbit, he stopped and asked, "Why do you cry?"

The rabbit answered, "I cry because the little boy cries. The boy cries because his goats are in the cornfield and he can't drive them out."

"Well," said the fox, "just leave that job to me. I'll drive them out for you, little boy."

The old fox ran toward the goats calling,

"Goats, goats,
Now listen to me,
You must leave this field
Right away, don't you see?"

But the goats only answered,

"Baa, baa, baa,
We're eating the corn.
We're here to stay.
We won't come out
Till the end of the day."

"Then I'll drive you out," shouted the fox as he began chasing the goats. But the goats wouldn't leave, so the fox went back over and sat down beside the boy and the rabbit and began to cry and cry.

"Buzz, buzz, buzz" sang a little honeybee flying through the air. As he came near the boy, the rabbit, and the fox sitting under the tree crying, he called, "Good morning. Why do you cry?"

"I cry," replied the fox, "because the rabbit cries. The rabbit cries because the boy cries. The boy cries because his goats are in the cornfield and he can't drive them out."

"Just leave the job to me," said the honeybee as he buzzed away toward the goats.

With that the little boy, the rabbit, and the fox stopped crying. They started laughing.

"A little bee," said the fox. "Who does he think he is? If I couldn't drive the goats out, how does he think he can? Ha, ha, ha."

"Then I'll drive you out," shouted the bee. He flew in and out among the goats, singing "Buz-z-z, buz-z-z."

Then the goats knew that the little honeybee would sting them if they didn't run. So they turned and jumped over the fence, scampering back to the little boy.

The little boy was so happy to have his goats back with him on the green, grassy hillside!

"Thank you, honeybee," he said. "Thank you for driving my goats out of the cornfield."
—*Rewritten by Josephine Newbury*

THE GINGERBREAD MAN

Once upon a time there was a little old woman and a little old man who lived all alone in a little old house at the edge of town.

One day the little old woman said to the little old man, "Because we have no children, I am going to bake a gingerbread man to live with us."

So she rolled out some gingerbread on her kitchen table and cut out a nice fat gingerbread man. She added two raisins for eyes, a bean for a nose, and a cherry for his mouth. Then she dressed him in a suit of chocolate icing and put him in the oven to bake.

When the clock struck one, she opened the oven door to see if he was done. But before she knew what had happened, the shiny brown gingerbread man jumped out of the oven and ran across the floor to the open door singing:

Run, run, as fast as you can. You can't catch me, I'm the gin-ger bread man.

As the honeybee flew closer to the goats, he buzzed louder and louder,

"Listen to me,
You billy goats three,
You're leaving this field,
Do you hear me?"

Again the goats answered,

"Baa, baa, baa,
We're eating the corn.
We're here to stay.
We won't come out
Till the end of the day."

The little old lady ran after him, waving her broom in the air. But the gingerbread man wouldn't stop. He ran right on out of the yard and past the little old man, who was hoeing in his garden. The gingerbread man waved to the little old man and sang:

(Refrain)

The little old woman and the little old man kept running, but they couldn't catch him.

The gingerbread man kept on running. He soon passed some men who were plowing in a field. He waved to them and called:

(Refrain)

The workmen left their plows and started down the road after the gingerbread man, but they couldn't catch him. So they went back to work.

Soon the gingerbread man passed an old black and white spotted cow standing under a tree by the road. He waved to her and sang:

(Refrain)

The cow joined the little old woman and the little old man as they ran down the road after the gingerbread man. But they couldn't catch him. After a while the cow gave up and went back to the shade of the tree to chew her cud.

The gingerbread man ran on and on. Soon he met a pig that was squeezing under the fence to cross the road. He waved to the pig, singing again:

(Refrain)

The pig wriggled out from under the fence and started down the road after the gingerbread man. But his legs were so short that he couldn't run fast enough to catch the gingerbread man either. So he went back to find the other pigs he had left in the field.

By this time the gingerbread man had come to the woods. He kept right on running. Soon he saw a sly old fox coming out of his den.

The gingerbread man stopped running. He didn't know where he was, so very politely he asked, "Please, Mr. Fox, can you tell me which path leads out of the woods?"

The fox replied, "I'm a little deaf. Come closer."

The gingerbread man came closer and closer and closer. Just then the little old woman called out, "Oh, gingerbread man, where are you?"

"Don't answer her, gingerbread man," said the fox.

"Oh, ho! You *can* hear, you sly old fox!" said the gingerbread man as he turned and started running back the way he had come. And as he ran on out of the woods, the old fox could hear the gingerbread man singing:

(Refrain)

—*Rewritten by Josephine Newbury*

THE LITTLE OLD HEN

There was once a little old hen who was always busy scratching about for food. One day she found some grains of wheat, but she did not eat them.

She called her friends, the duck, the goose, and the pig, to come and see what she had gathered.

"I am going to plant these wheat seeds in my garden," she said. "Who will help me?"

"I will," said the duck.

"I will," said the goose.

"I will," said the pig.

So they all went out together to plant the grains of wheat.

Soon the seeds began to grow. They grew and grew and grew. Finally the wheat was ready to cut.

The little old hen again called her friends, the duck, the goose, and the pig. She said to them, "The wheat is ready to be cut. Who will help me?"

"I will," said the duck.

"I will," said the goose.

"I will," said the pig.

So the little old hen and her three friends worked together to cut the wheat. What fun they had!

Then one day when the wheat was ready to grind, the little old hen said to her friends, the duck, the goose, and the pig, "The wheat is just ready to grind into flour. Who will help me?"

"I will," said the duck.

"I will," said the goose.

"I will," said the pig.

And they each took turns grinding the wheat on the millstone.

"What nice flour this is!" exclaimed the little old hen. "Now who will help me make it into dough for a loaf of bread?"

"I will," said the duck.

"I will," said the goose.

"I will," said the pig.

Each one helped mix up the dough. They worked it and worked it until it made a big loaf of bread.

When the dough was ready to be baked, the little old hen asked of her three friends, "Who will help me bake the bread?"

"I will," said the duck.

"I will," said the goose.

"I will," said the pig.

And they did. And my, how good the bread smelled while it was baking! Finally it was baked—brown and crusty all over.

The little old hen turned the bread out of the pan to cool. It would be ready to eat very soon.

While the bread was cooling, the little old hen made a pot of tea and opened a fresh jar of her special strawberry jam. She was thinking of something nice to do for her three friends.

When the bread was ready to cut, she called the duck, the goose, and the pig once more.

"The loaf of bread we baked is cool enough to cut now," she explained. "Who will help me cut it?"

"I will," said the duck.

"I will," said the goose.

"I will," said the pig.

And they did. Each took turns cutting the bread and stacking it on the bread tray.

While her friends were busy cutting the bread, the little old hen was busy pouring four cups of tea. "Now," she said, "I'm not going to ask who will help me eat the bread. Here is a place at the table for each of you. Please do sit down and let me serve you some of the best home-baked bread you have ever tasted. And help yourself to the strawberry jam; I made it myself."

"Um-m, um-m," said the duck.

"Um-m, um-m," said the goose.

"Um-m, um-m," said the pig.

Everyone had a good time at the little old hen's tea party. As they left she said to them, "Now do come back again sometime."

"Thank you, I will," said the duck.

"Thank you, I will," said the goose.

"Thank you, I will," said the pig.

And they did.

—*Rewritten by Josephine Newbury*

THE ONE STORY OF THE BIBLE

(The numbers are used to suggest pages for an illustrated scrapbook of the story.)

1. Our Bible is a wonderful book which tells us of God's great love for all people and the ways in which he has shown us this love.

2. We read our Bible with our families; mothers and fathers read it and think about what it says. We see and hear it read in our churches and right here in our kindergarten. Someday you will be able to read for yourself the wonderful story of God's love.

3. The Bible tells us that long, long ago God called a man named Abraham. To help all God's people know that he loves us, God promised that through Abraham all the people on earth would be blessed.

4. Abraham obeyed God. We know that God loved him and all people. And so Abraham did as he felt God wanted him to do.

5. Because of God's love for him, Abraham worshiped God wherever he went. He talked to God and tried hard to do the things God wanted him to do.

6. Many, many years later, the people of Abraham's families found themselves in a strange land where people did not know God. But God's people did not forget him, and they kept telling the wonderful stories of God's love. Later, when they came away from the strange land, they continued to tell the story around their campfires at night so that everyone would know of God and his love for them.

7. When they came to the new land, they remembered God and his love and continued to thank him and to seek to obey him.

8. But down through the years, there were those people who forgot God and turned away from him and his ways. They lived in ways that did not please God. They did many things that made God very sad—but he still kept right on loving people. He loved them in spite of their selfishness and disobedience. There were times when God had to punish them to try to help them understand what was right and what was wrong.

9. As the years passed, although there were those people who completely turned their backs on God, there were always some who remembered God and tried to show their love for him by doing what they believed he wanted them to do. Some of these cared for others who needed food, clothes, and help.

10. God's people gave their money gifts so that the poor and sick might have care. In these ways, they showed that they knew God's love.

11. There were those people who wanted to help other people to turn to God and live as children of God. These men were called prophets. They were chosen by God to speak to the people of his great love for them. These prophets reminded the people of God's promise that, when it was the right time, he would send one who would show them what God is like and

what they ought to be like. Those people who listened to the prophets waited anxiously for the coming of this Savior.

12. They heard Isaiah, one of the prophets, as he spoke to them:

"For to us a child is born, to us a son is given; and his name will be called 'Wonderful Counselor, Mighty God, Everlasting Father, Prince of Peace,' Prepare (make ready) the way of the Lord."

13. Through many ages they had heard from their Scriptures that this promised one would come from God.

14. People had sung great songs of praise to God in the temple as they thought of his love and goodness and how the Savior would come. And then one day, in the fullness of time, just as God had promised, he sent Jesus his Son to live on earth among his people and to be their Lord and Savior. This was God's very best way of showing how much he loved his people. And this is how it happened.

15. God sent an angel to a young Jewish girl named Mary and said to her, "Do not be afraid, Mary, for you have found favor with God. You will have a little son whose name is to be Jesus. He will be great, and he will be called the Son of the Most High." Mary was overjoyed with this wonderful news, and she sang praises to God for it.

16. Now in those days the ruler of the land wanted to know how many people lived in that country. He commanded that everyone should go to his hometown to have his name placed on the rolls.

17. So it was for this reason that Joseph and Mary had to go to Bethlehem, the town where Joseph's family lived.

18. The town was very crowded with people, and Joseph had a hard time finding a place for them to stay, but finally he did find room in a rough stable, and while they were there God's Son Jesus was born to Mary, just as the angel had said. We read about this wonderful event here in this part of the Bible—here we can know how much God loved his people then and that he is loving us today—each of us—and wanting us to love him.

19. "And in that region . . . (Luke 2:8–14)

20. "When the angels went away from them into heaven, the shepherds said to one another, 'Let us go over to Bethlehem and see this thing that has happened, which the Lord has made known to us.' " (Luke 2:15)

21. "And they went with haste, and found Mary and Joseph, and the babe lying in a manger." (Luke 2:16)

(Sing "Away in a Manger.")

22. And the shepherds fell on their knees and gave thanks for the wonderful Baby. We also read in our Bible where it says, "God so loved the world that he gave his only Son, that whoever believes in him should not perish but have eternal life." (John 3:16)

23. This baby grew as you are growing until he became the man Jesus who went about showing God's love by his teachings and the stories he told, and by the wonderful things he did. He even suffered in his body and died, but because God's love is stronger than death, Jesus arose from the dead and is living today, our friend and our Savior. Because of God's love for us, he sent his Son Jesus to help us to know what he is like and that he loves each one of us and wants us to love him and his way of life.

—*Josephine Newbury*

WHAT IS CHRISTMAS?

It was just a few days before Christmas. Benny was watching some men who were decorating an outdoor Christmas tree.

As he saw the men hang a big star on the top branch, Benny kept wondering, "Why do people put stars on the tops of Christmas trees? And what is Christmas?"

"I'll go ask Grandpa Ross," thought Benny. "He knows about everything."

Grandpa Ross always had time for Benny and his questions, and he seemed to know how to help Benny with the answers.

"Grandpa," began Benny, "what is Christmas?"

"Well now," said Grandpa slowly, "suppose we just think about it together. First you tell me what you believe Christmas is."

"It's Christmas trees," began Benny, "with colored balls and lights on them."

"Yes, but it's more than that. Think again," Grandpa replied.

"Oh, I know," exclaimed Benny. "Christmas is hanging up our stockings on Christmas Eve for Santa Claus to fill."

"Not exactly, Benny. Christmas is better than that."

Before Grandpa could say more, Benny exclaimed, "I know, Grandpa, I know! It's Santa Claus coming down the chimney to bring us toys."

"No, my boy. You must think harder. Christmas is more than that, much more."

"Well then, it's the toys Santa brings us—the things we ask him for. Isn't that Christmas, Grandpa?" asked Benny.

"Christmas is more wonderful and more beautiful than anything, Benny. Just keep thinking," urged Grandpa Ross.

Benny thought about all the beautiful things he had seen at Christmas time. Could it be the pretty wreathes that people hang on their front doors, the bright red Christmas flowers they have in their homes, or the lovely candles they burn in their windows at night?

Grandpa didn't say anything. He just looked at Benny. Benny decided himself that Christmas was more than wreathes and flowers and candles.

"Well, then, it must be the stores in the city. They are wonderful and beautiful, and they have lots and lots of pretty things in them. Mother took me with her to see the toys one day. I saw Santa Claus and talked to him, too."

Again Grandpa Ross didn't answer. He just sat thinking. Benny wondered if he would ever discover what Christmas really is.

Grandpa sat back and puffed on his pipe and said, "Christmas is bigger and more wonderful than anything you have thought of, Benny. Let's go into the house and perhaps we can find the answer there."

Benny was glad to go back into Grandpa's warm, cozy home, but he really wondered where he would find the answer there.

Grandpa walked over to the table and picked up his big Bible. "Come here, Benny," he called. "This is where we find out what Christmas is."

Opening the Bible, Grandpa began to read:

"And in that region there were shepherds out in the field, keeping watch over their flock by night. And an angel of the Lord appeared to them, and the glory of the Lord shone around them, and they were filled with fear. And the angel said to them, 'Be not afraid; for behold, I bring you good news of a great joy which will come to all the people; for to you is born this day in the city of David a Savior, who is Christ the Lord. And this will be a sign for you: you will find a babe wrapped in swaddling clothes and lying in a manger.' And suddenly there was with the angel a multitude of the heavenly host praising God and saying, 'Glory to God in the highest, and on earth peace among men with whom he is pleased!'

"When the angels went away from them into heaven, the shepherds said to one another, 'Let us go over to Bethlehem and see this thing that has happened, which the Lord has made known to us.' And they went with haste, and found Mary and Joseph, and the babe lying in a manger. And when they saw it they made known the saying which had been told them concerning this child; and all who heard it wondered at what the shepherds told them." (Luke 2:8–18)

Then Grandpa stopped to explain, "Wise men from countries far away saw the bright star in the sky. They traveled a long, long time until they came to the little town of Bethlehem where Jesus was born. They had brought gifts for the young child. The Bible tells us about it."

"Lo, the star which they had seen in the East went before them, till it came to rest over the place where the child was. When they saw the star, they rejoiced exceedingly with great joy; and going into the house they saw the child with Mary his mother, and they fell down and worshiped him. Then, opening their treasures, they offered him gifts, gold and frankincense and myrrh." (Matthew 2:9b–11)

"This, Benny, is what Christmas is," explained Grandpa Ross. "It's a time that we remember about Jesus' coming into the world to show God's love for us and to show us what God is like. It is the time we celebrate Jesus' birth. And because of our love for Jesus, we want to do loving things for others at Christmas time and all through the year."

"Christmas time is a *giving time*, Benny. Making gifts for others is one way of showing love."

"Christmas time is a *sharing time*. Your grandmother is planning to let you and Sallie and Jim make cookies to have to share when your friends come in to play on Christmas."

"Oh, goody, that will be fun!" broke in Benny.

"And Christmas time is a *singing time,*" continued Grandpa. "People remember the song the angels sang the night Jesus was born. We, too, sing songs about his birth, the shepherds, and the Wise Men who came to worship him."

"I can sing 'Away in a Manger' and 'Silent Night,' too," interrupted Benny.

"That's fine, Benny. I am sure we shall sing those carols on Christmas Eve at our church service."

"Will I go, too?" asked Benny.

"Yes indeed! We all go to the church for the Christmas Eve service. Our minister reads from the Bible, and we sing Christmas hymns and carols and thank God for sending his Son, Jesus, to show his love for all people."

"And then, Benny, we always take gifts to help some people in need. We want them to know more of God's love for them, too."

"Well, I think I know what Christmas is now, Grandpa, and it's better than I thought it was. God loves us a lot, doesn't he?"

"He surely does, Benny. He surely does."

That night before Benny went to bed, he climbed up by the window where he could look out at the Christmas tree in the yard. There was the big, bright, shining star on the very top branch, lighting up the whole tree.

Benny thought of all the things he and Grandpa Ross had talked about that afternoon. Then he remembered the words of Grandpa's prayer at the supper table. And they became Benny's prayer:

Dear God,
> Thank you for Christmas.
> As we look at the star on the top
> of the Christmas tree,
> we think of the star that shown
> over Bethlehem
> when Jesus was born.
> Help us to show our love for him
> whose birth we celebrate. Amen.
> —*Josephine Newbury*

CHRISTMAS BELLS

High up in the steeple hung the Christmas bells. They had hung there many, many years. On each Christmas Day they always had rung beautiful music. One day one of the little bells cracked and could ring no more. A new little bell was hung in its place. Christmas was coming very soon.

"What shall I do? I do not know how to ring," said the little bell.

"Never mind," said the other bells. "You will know when the time comes. Just wait and listen, and you will know."

So the little bell waited and listened. The street far below was full of people, some coming this way and some going that. At nighttime the street was full of lights: some were in store windows, some were in the trolley cars, and some were on the automobiles.

But the little bell liked best to watch the people passing and to hear what they said, for he was waiting to hear what to ring on Christmas Day.

An old man came by. He was somebody's grandfather. His arms were full of bundles. The little bell could hear him saying, "Now I have something for little John and for the baby, and won't they be surprised?" and he laughed. Then came some boys and girls hurrying home from school, talking and laughing together.

"Oh, I have something to give to Mother and Father," said one.

"And I have something for Grandmother," said another.

The little bell could hear each one telling of what he was going to give.

Soon came a mother walking past with such a happy face and more packages than you could count. There was something for everyone at home—father, brothers, sisters, baby. The little bell watched them all and listened and thought.

At last Christmas Day came, and the Christmas bells began to ring. All the people stopped to listen to the beautiful music of their ringing. Then the little bell knew what to say, and it rang out: "Loving—giving—loving—giving." And all the other bells sang the same song: "Loving—giving—loving—giving."

—*Author unknown*

TEDDY'S CHRISTMAS STOCKING

It was Christmas Eve, and what do you think Teddy was going to do before going to bed? He was going to hang up his Christmas stocking by the fireplace in the living room.

Teddy had been playing with his pretty red and white stocking all evening. He would put some of his old toys in it just to see how it would look on Christmas morning filled with new surprises. He even tried to guess what the surprises might be.

Finally Mother said, "Teddy, it's almost your bedtime. Let's hang up your stocking and get ready for bed."

Now some nights Teddy would beg to stay up just a little longer, but on this night it was different. He didn't mind going right to bed. He wanted to be sure and wake up early on Christmas morning to find out what was in his stocking and under the Christmas tree.

My, how flat and empty his stocking looked as he hung it by the fireplace!

"I'm going to hurry to sleep tonight," said Teddy, as he gave his mother and daddy goodnight hugs and kisses.

And do you know, that's just what happened! Who do you think was the first one awake on Christmas morning? Why, Teddy, of course!

"Merry Christmas," he called out to his mother and daddy. "Come and see our surprises!"

By the time his mother and daddy got into the living room, Teddy had taken his stocking down and was feeling all the funny bumps in it.

"I wonder what this is," he said as he felt something near the top. It was round and red and could bounce.

It was a . . . ball.

Next he felt something hard and round. It was shiny and would ring. It was a bell for his trike, to let his friends know when to get out of his way as he rode by.

Teddy kept feeling and guessing. There was something else hard, but it had wheels on it. He figured that one out in a hurry. It was a little car like the one he had seen in the toy store window just a few days before.

There was still another hump in the stocking. What could it be? It, too, was round. It smelled spicy. Teddy had to work to get it out. And do you know, it was a big juicy orange for his Christmas breakfast!

At first Teddy thought that he had discovered all the surprises in his stocking. But when he felt more carefully, he found that there was

[16]Reprinted by permission of the Association for Childhood Education International from *Told Under the Blue Umbrella.*

something down in the toe. It was small and round. It would buy a candy bar or a popsicle at the store. Yes, Teddy had a shiny new dime all his own.

"Happy Christmas, everybody," he said as he waved his red Christmas stocking that was again flat and empty.

—*Josephine Newbury*

THE LITTLE BLUE DISHES [16]

Once upon a time there was a poor woodcutter who lived with his wife and three children in a forest in Germany. There was a big boy called Hans and a little boy named Peterkin and a dear little sister named Gretchen, just five years old. Christmas came and the children went to the toy shop to look at all of the toys. [Enumerate toys].

"Gretchen," said Peterkin, "what do you like best?"

"Oh! that little box of blue dishes," said Gretchen. "That is the very best of all."

On Christmas Eve the children hung up their stockings, although their mother had said that they were so poor they could not have much this Christmas. Hans ran out after supper to play with the big boys. Gretchen and Peterkin sat talking before the fire about the Christmas toys and especially about the box of blue dishes. By and by Gretchen ran off to bed and was soon asleep. Peterkin ran to look in his bank. Only one penny, but he took it and ran quickly to the toy shop.

"What have you for a penny?" said he to the toy man.

"Only a small heart with a picture on it," said the man.

"But I want that set of blue dishes," said Peterkin.

"Oh, they cost ten cents," said the man.

So Peterkin bought the candy heart and put it in Gretchen's stocking and then Peterkin ran off to bed.

Pretty soon Hans came home. He was cold and hungry. When he saw Gretchen's stocking he peeked in, then put his hand in and drew out the candy heart. "Oh," said Hans, "how good this smells," and before you could say a word he had eaten the candy heart. "Oh dear," he said, "that was for Gretchen for Christmas. I'll run and buy something else for her," so he ran to his bank and he had ten pennies. [Count pennies.]

Quickly he ran to the toy store.

"What have you for ten pennies?" he asked the storekeeper.

"Well, I'm almost sold out," said the toyman, "but here in this little box is a set of blue dishes."

"I will take them," said Hans, and home he ran and dropped them in Gretchen's stocking. Then he went to bed.

Early in the morning the children came running downstairs.

"Oh!" said Gretchen, "look at my stocking," and when she saw the blue dishes she was as happy as could be, but Peterkin could never understand how his candy heart changed into a box of blue dishes. Can you?

—Author untraced

A JOKE ON SANTA[17]

Away up at the North Pole in the land of ice and snow, there is a big, big home that has on the mailbox the name "Santa Claus."

During the month of December, there is a lighted Christmas tree out on the front lawn and a beautiful one inside the house in the hall leading into Santa's workshop.

Santa has a number of funny little elves who work·with him in the toy shop.

There is Happy Jack, who is always laughing and singing as he works all year long, making toys for girls and boys. Happy Jack is always making the other elves laugh, so you see why Santa named him Happy Jack.

Then there is Jingle Bell. He is always trying to get out of work he is supposed to do, especially when it comes time to clean up the toy shop each night after the elves have finished their work. So, in order to keep up with him, Mrs. Santa sewed a jingle bell in his little pointed cap. Now Santa Claus can always know where he is, and naturally everyone calls him Jingle Bell.

There is another interesting little elf. His name is Cold Toes—well, not really, but that's what Mr. and Mrs. Santa call him, because he has always complained about his toes being cold. While he would be painting the faces on the baby dolls, he would keep saying, "My toes are cold; my toes are cold." Sometimes Santa would find him sitting in front of the fireplace with his toes toward the fire. And it was always the same thing. This little elf would complain that his toes were so cold he couldn't work on the toys. So you can see why everyone called him Cold Toes.

Mrs. Santa spends lots of her time in the candy kitchen, where she makes all kinds of Christmas candies—candy canes, lollipops, stick candy, and chocolates of all kinds. Santa is always dropping into the kitchen to sample the candies.

One morning in early December, Mr. and Mrs. Santa began whispering about how they would surprise the little elves for Christmas. They planned a happy secret for each one.

One cold, cold morning a few days later Santa sat down in his rocking chair to rest a few minutes and wait for the mailman. But he didn't have to wait long before he heard a shrill whistle. And looking out the window, he saw the mailman leaving letters in his mailbox.

Grabbing his warm cap, he ran out to the mailbox. "I wonder if those are more letters from boys and girls," he thought to himself as he reached into the mailbox for the letters the mailman had left. He didn't stop to look at the letters, for it was cold. He hurried back into his warm toy shop.

"Well, well," he began as he opened the first envelope, "here's a letter from Teddy in Richmond, Virginia." All the little elves stopped their work and gathered around Santa to listen as he read Teddy's letter.

Dear Santa,
How are you? I hope my letter will not be too late. My little sister is not big enough to write to you, so I am writing for her. She needs a new Poo Bear. Our puppy, Scuffy, took her Poo Bear outdoors and left him in the rain. Poo isn't any good any more. I would like a big ball—red and blue if you have one, and some skates.

Merry Christmas,
Teddy

"Here's one from Jimmy who lives in Chicago. Let's see what he says."

Dear Santa,
I am 5 years old. My mother is writing my

---

[17]Adapted from *Children's Activities*. By permission of Highlights for Children, Inc., Columbus, Ohio.

letter because I can't write yet. I would like a toy train that runs on a track and a book about fire trucks because my daddy is a fireman. I would like a new pair of fur-lined mittens to wear when I play in the snow. I am too big for my mittens I wore last year. Don't get lost on your trip from the North Pole.

Much love,
Jimmy T.

I signed my own name.

"Can we fill these orders?" Santa asked of the elves. Happy Jack spoke up, "I know we have some Poo Bears, for I've just now finished sewing vests on two bears."

Mr. Santa checked with Mrs. Santa about the mittens, because this is one of the things she always makes. Jingle Bell found several extra trains and pairs of skates that hadn't been spoken for. Santa was relieved that there were toys enough to go around.

After checking in the toy shop, Santa went into his office and sat down in his big chair at his desk to read his other mail.

He just happened to look over at his little calendar on his desk. For a moment he just couldn't believe his eyes. He jumped up from his desk and ran out of the room calling, "Mrs. Santa, come in here, quick!"

"What in the world is the matter, Santa? What is it? I've never heard you so excited before!" Mrs. Santa exclaimed.

Santa was pointing to his desk calendar, "Look at the date. Where has the time gone? Do you see that it is Christmas Eve morning and I should be on my way to deliver the toys for all the girls and boys? Oh, what can I do? What can I do?"

Mrs. Santa called Jingle Bell and Happy Jack. They came running to see what all the loud talk was about.

"Now listen, elves," she began. "Somehow we have let the date slip up on us. Today is Christmas Eve. Santa must start out immediately in order to deliver all the toys for the girls and boys before Christmas morning. We must load the big sleigh as fast as we can. Call all the helpers. Santa just must not be late. Everybody to work, and be in a hurry about it!"

Santa sent two of the elves out to round up the reindeer and hitch them up to the sleigh.

You should have seen how everyone helped—especially Jingle Bell. Cold Toes worked so fast and hard that he almost forgot about his toes being cold.

In no time at all the big sleigh was packed high with toys. The eight reindeer were hitched to the sleigh, and Santa was ready for his journey to deliver the toys. "Good-bye, Mrs. Santa," he called as he hurried out of the door.

"I'm coming," he called to the elves as he raced out to the sleigh.

It was a bright, beautiful day. The reindeer moved swiftly along the way. As Santa checked his watch, he realized that he was going to make it all right after all.

The elves in the toy shop had worked so hard and so fast to get Santa off that as soon as they had an early supper they were ready to go to bed.

Mrs. Santa waited until she was sure all the elves were sound asleep; then she slipped into their bedrooms and left the gifts that she and Santa Claus had for them.

She had made Jingle Bell a new little cap with a jingle bell on it. For Happy Jack she had knitted a pair of green mittens with fur cuffs. For Sam she had made a new red jacket, for Buster, a pair of woolen socks, and—would you believe it—for Cold Toes, Mrs. Santa had made a little pair of fur-lined boots. When she came to Cold Toes' bed, she put the new little boots under his bed and took his old shoes out of the room.

Looking at them she commented, "Well, no wonder he is always complaining of his toes being cold. The soles are so thin." Then, as she stuck her fingers into one of the little shoes, she felt something down in the very toe of the shoe.

"What's this, I wonder?" she asked herself as she pulled out a small piece of crumpled paper. Straightening it out, she read December 20. Taking another wad of paper from the shoe, she read December 21. Feeling in the other shoe she found a little piece of paper that read December 22, and—would you believe it—there was still another little paper which read December 23.

Mrs. Santa rushed into Santa's office to check his desk calendar, for she had guessed immediately what had happened. She had guessed right. The little pieces of paper Cold

Toes had stuck into the toes of his shoes were off of Santa's calendar.

Mrs. Santa ran back to Cold Toes' bed to wake him up. "Cold Toes, Cold Toes," she exclaimed. "Wake up, wake up!"

Cold Toes sat up in his little bed, rubbing his eyes. "What is the matter, Mrs. Santa? What do you want?"

Holding the little pieces of paper in her hands, she asked of Cold Toes, "Tell me, where did you get these papers you stuffed into the toes of your shoes?"

"Oh, those papers. Well, there was a little pad on Santa's desk that had lots more of the papers on it. I just took 4. I didn't think he would miss them; he had more of them. And they kept my toes from getting so cold. Did I do something wrong?"

"I should say you did," Mrs. Santa explained. "That is Santa's calendar. It tells him what day it is, and with these 4 pages torn off, the calendar reads wrong. Do you realize what a terrible mistake Santa has made—going to the homes of the boys and girls this evening—4 nights early? The children won't have their stockings hung up, and many homes will not have put up their Christmas trees. Oh, what shall we do? What shall we do?"

Mrs. Santa stopped talking and thought for a moment. She knew something must be done to stop Santa and she also knew that she would have to be the one to stop him. There was no time to be lost—not a minute. Mrs. Santa woke up Happy Jack and Sam, and together they hitched up the young reindeer to the small sleigh.

In a twinkling of an eye they were off, riding swiftly along in the early evening. The moon was full and shown brightly across the new-fallen snow. This helped light the way for Mrs. Santa and Happy Jack. As they rode past the moon, Mrs. Santa asked which way Santa had gone. The Man in the Moon replied, "South, around the North Star, but what is Mr. Santa doing going out tonight? This isn't Christmas Eve. No one will be looking for him."

Mrs. Santa couldn't take time to answer the Man in the Moon, but waved a thank-you to him as she rode by.

On and on they went, faster and faster. By now the north wind was blowing quite strong. This helped the sleigh go even faster.

Finally, would you believe it, Mrs. Santa and Happy Jack caught up with Mr. Santa. They arrived just as he parked his reindeer and sleigh on the rooftop of a large house.

Mrs. Santa began calling as loudly as she could, "Mr. Santa, wait. Don't go down that chimney. Wait for me."

Now Santa didn't know what the trouble could be, but he waited until Mrs. Santa caught up with him. He ran to meet her. Out of breath, she tried to explain just what had happened.

Santa listened. At first he didn't say anything; then he began to laugh and laugh. Mrs. Santa could laugh, too, now that she had caught up with Mr. Santa and had stopped him before he had made any deliveries of toys.

"Well," said Santa, "back to the toy shop we must go before we are discovered, and I'll speak to that chilly little elf."

Cold Toes hadn't gone back to sleep. He was too troubled over what he had done. He was watching when both sleighs returned to the yard outside the toy shop. Cold Toes was very sorry for what he had done, but he still thought he'd better hide from Santa Claus. He wasn't sure just what would happen, for he had almost caused Santa to make a terrible mistake.

About that time the door to the shop opened wide, and in came Mr. and Mrs. Santa and Happy Jack. In his biggest voice Santa called, "Cold Toes, come here this minute!"

Cold Toes crept out from under his bed and went slowly into Santa's office. He expected the worst.

Santa picked up Cold Toes and said, "Cold Toes, you almost caused me to deliver the children's toys four nights too early. Think how terrible that would have been. What am I going to do to you?" Santa sounded upset and a little cross.

Really Cold Toes didn't know, but he thought that almost anything would be fair enough for what he had done. Yet he hadn't meant to do anything wrong. He didn't know that the little pad of papers was Santa's desk calendar and that it was so important.

"I'll tell you what I'm going to do," Santa began slowly. "I'm going to give you a big thank-you hug, because now I shall have three full days to rest before I have to take the toys on Christmas Eve. Everything is ready and the sleigh is packed. Isn't that wonderful? And to show you how glad I am, I think I'll let you go with me on Christmas Eve and help drive the reindeer."

"Oh, would you Santa? Would you? I'll never bother your calendar again." And he never has.

And for three days Santa just sat in his rocking chair in front of his nice warm fire thinking about how he nearly made the terrible mistake of going out four days early to deliver the toys to the girls and boys.

—*Retold by Josephine Newbury*

THE HUNGRY BUNNY[18]

In a little hole under a big bush lived a little brown bunny. He had a funny little black nose that wriggled when he was happy. One morning the little bunny stirred in his small bed of tiny twigs and dry, brown grass. He thought to himself, "I am so hungry." So he hopped out from his little bed to find something to eat. He looked under a bunch of leaves and behind his bed, but he could find nothing. The hungry bunny knew he must go into the woods to find some tender green grass to eat. He went to the top of his hole and looked out. Everything around him was white. During the night the soft snow had silently covered the ground. The hungry bunny could not see any grass. So . . . *(Song)*

As he hopped through the woods, little brown bunny saw Mrs. Sparrow in a tree. He called, "Mrs. Sparrow, I am very hungry and I can find no food. Do you have anything that I can eat?"

Mrs. Sparrow flew down to the ground. "Yes, brown bunny. Here are some nice dry seeds for you to eat."

"Thank you," said the hungry bunny. But the seeds were too hard for the bunny to chew. So the hungry bunny thanked Mrs. Sparrow again and said, "Goodbye, Mrs. Sparrow. I must go on my way because I am very hungry." *(Song)*

Brown bunny stopped. There sitting on a tree stump he saw Mr. Squirrel. "Good morning, Mr. Squirrel. How are you today?" asked the little bunny, wiggling his nose.

"I am fine," said Mr. Squirrel, whose bushy

tail curled up his back to keep him warm. "But what brings you so far from your warm house in this cold weather?"

"I am so very hungry," said the little bunny. "I have no food in my house, and the snow has covered all the green grass."

Mr. Squirrel said, "I have some nuts that I buried last fall. You may have some of them."

The hungry bunny took the nuts and thanked Mr. Squirrel. He put a nut in his mouth, but he could not crack it. His teeth were not as sharp and strong as Mr. Squirrel's. So on through the woods hungry bunny went. *(Song)*

Brown bunny stopped to look for some berries, but he could find none. He did not wriggle his little black nose, because he was very cold and tired. And he wasn't very happy. It was getting late and he had not found any food—not anything a bunny could eat. So on he went. *(Song)*

Finally hungry bunny was about to give up. He turned to start back to his little home when he saw something big and white standing in the snow. It was round and fat and had a funny looking hat on the top of its head. It had a smile that reached almost from ear to ear, a long, orange nose, and two round black eyes.

"Good morning," said brown bunny very politely. There was no answer, so hungry bunny hopped a little closer. "Hello! I am so hungry. Can you help me?" called brown bunny. But still there was no answer.

When bunny hopped closer, he saw that the big funny thing was made of snow. It was a snowman! Brown bunny looked up at the round face. He saw that his mouth was a long curved twig; his big round eyes were two black buttons; and his orange nose was a long carrot! Brown bunny wriggled his little black nose and jumped up and down with delight.

"If Mr. Snowman would just give me his nose, I wouldn't be hungry any more," thought brown bunny.

About that time Mr. Blue Jay flew by. He saw brown bunny and he flew down to say hello. And do you know, he perched right on Mr. Snowman's long, orange, carrot nose. But Mr. Jay was too heavy. The carrot couldn't hold him up. With a big plop it fell into the snow right at brown bunny's feet.

---

[18]Used by permission of the author.

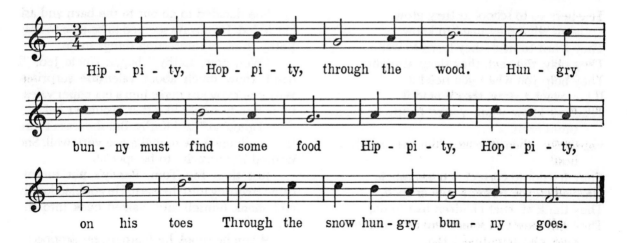

Hip - pi - ty, Hop - pi - ty, through the wood. Hun - gry
bun - ny must find some food Hip - pi - ty, Hop - pi - ty,
on his toes Through the snow hun - gry bun - ny goes.

Brown bunny wriggled his little black nose and jumped up and down with delight. "Thank you, Mr. Blue Jay. Thank you, Mr. Snowman," said brown bunny. "Now I will not be so hungry."

Mr. Snowman smiled as brown bunny sat and munched away on the crisp, crisp carrot. And when brown bunny had eaten the last bite of the carrot, he waved good-bye to the snowman and went hopping back to his home. *(Song —second stanza)*

Hippity, hoppity through the wood.
Happy bunny has found some food.
Hippity, hoppity on his toes
Back to his home happy bunny goes."
—*Wynn Horton McGregor*

A NONSENSE STORY[19]

Once upon a time there was a bi-i-i-g elephant. His name was Jumbo. He lived in a forest. Every day he went through the forest and down the hill (hand motions) to the river for a drink of water.

One day as he was going through the forest, he met a bi-i-i-g tree. "Get out of my way, you tree," said the elephant.

"Say please," said the tree.

"I won't say please," said the elephant.

"Then I won't get out of your way," said the tree.

"I will wrap my trunk around you and pull you up by the roots," said the elephant.

"Go ahead," said the tree. So the elephant wrapped his trunk around the tree. He pulled, and pulled and pulled (thumb is tree, other hand pulls) until he pulled the tree up by the roots. Then the elephant stepped right over it and walked down the hill to the river to get a drink of water.

The next day as he went through the forest he met another tree. "Get out of my way, you tree," said the elephant.

"Say please," said the tree.

"I won't say please," said the elephant.

"Then I won't get out of your way," said the tree.

"I will wrap my trunk around you and pull you up by the roots," said the elephant.

"Go ahead," said the tree. The elephant wrapped his trunk around the tree. He pulled and he pulled and he pulled, but he could not pull this tree up because it was too big.

He pulled and he pulled and he pulled. He pulled so hard that he fell over backwards and tumbled head over heels (fists going in circles around each other and down hill) down the hill to the river, where he fell in the water with a big SPLASH! (Make splash with both hands.)

After that, whenever he met a tree, he said, "Excuse me, please," and he walked around it.

TEACHERS AND WHAT THEY DO[20]

Do you know what teachers do
To be your teachers for you?

---

[19]Reprinted by permission of the United Church Press from Florence Schulz, *Summer with Nursery Children.* Copyright, 1958, by The Pilgrim Press.
[20]Used by permission of the author.

Teachers go to school as they grow,
To learn what they need to know.
They learn to read, they learn to write,
They play, they eat, they sleep at night.
They help you when you need it.
If you want a story, they'll read it.
Teachers know when you're happy or some-
    times cross,
Especially when it seems like they're always
    boss!
They try not to correct you too much,
Only when you forget a rule or such.
They think of what children like to do,
They will show you something new and join in
    your play sometimes, too.
Teachers comfort you when you're sad,
They understand when you are mad.
They are happy when you are glad.
Teachers are busy all day through—
Showing their love and care for you!
                    —*Mary Garland Cox Johnston*

KATHY'S VALENTINE SURPRISE

It was February thirteenth, the day before
Valentine's Day, and Randy was in bed with a
very sore throat.

"Keep him in bed two or three days," Dr.
Martin had said to Randy's mother.

What a disappointment this was! Randy
would miss the valentine party at school. But
that was not all he would miss. Randy would
miss his pets. You see, he lived on a big farm
where he had not just *one* pet like most boys; he
had five very special pets. There was his little
dog Flip; his duck he called Belinda; his turkey
gobbler, Big Tom; Pink Nose, his lamb; and Old
Ned, the horse.

Randy missed his pets very much when he
was sick, but they missed him too. He always
seemed to have a surprise tucked away in his
pockets for them. Sometimes it was a special
dog biscuit for Flip, then again it might be sun-
flower seeds for Big Tom, or a lump of sugar or
an apple for Old Ned.

Randy's little sister, Kathy, kept thinking
about his being sick and having to stay in bed on
Valentine's Day. She wondered what kind of
surprise she could make for him.

She knew Mother was baking some heart-
shaped cookies as her valentine surprise. But
what could Kathy do? She thought and thought.

She decided to go out to the barn and ask
Uncle Jed. He always seemed to be able to help
Kathy think of interesting things to do.

"Well now, Kathy," began Uncle Jed, "I
don't know much about valentine surprises.
Why don't you just make him a big paper valentine? Randy would like that, wouldn't he?"

"I guess so," said Kathy. But she wasn't sure
that she knew how to make one very well. She
wanted the surprise to be special.

Just then Big Tom, Randy's pet turkey,
came strutting into the barn. He gobbled loudly
and shook himself and walked back into the
yard.

When he shook his feathers, he dropped a
pretty one by Kathy's feet. She picked it up and
right then she had an idea.

She knew what she would do to surprise
Randy. She would go to each of his pets and ask
for something to put on a big valentine for
Randy. He would like that, she knew.

"Thank you," Kathy called to Uncle Jed as
she skipped out into the barnyard to find Randy's other pets.

She didn't have to look far. Old Ned was at
the watering trough getting a drink. Kathy
quickly explained to the horse what she wanted
to do and asked him for some hairs from his tail
to put on the big valentine.

Ned was glad to do something for Randy, so
he gave Kathy the hairs she wanted. And she
was off to look for another pet.

"Belinda, Belinda, where are you?" Kathy
called.

"Quack, quack," answered Belinda, wad-
dling up from the duck pond.

As she reached Kathy she shook herself
again and quacked louder. A feather from her
wing dropped to the ground before Kathy
could explain why she had called her.

"Oh thank you, Belinda! This is such a
pretty feather. I will put it on a big valentine
I'm making for Randy from all of us! It will
make him so happy."

"Quack, quack," said Belinda, as much as to
say, "I'm glad."

"Now I have a feather from Big Tom turkey and one from Belinda and some hairs from
Ned's tail," thought Kathy. "I'll have to find Flip
and Pink Nose so they can add something to our
valentine for Randy."

Kathy saw her father out by the pasture, so

she knew it would be all right for her to follow him. As she ran up to him, she tried to tell him all about her plan for Randy's surprise valentine.

"Hold on," broke in Father. "You have feathers from Tom and Belinda and hairs from Ned's tail. And you're doing what with them?"

But before Kathy could answer, she saw Randy's pet lamb, Pink Nose, rubbing up against the wire fence. She ran over to the lamb and was about to ask him for some wool to put on the valentine for Randy, when she saw a nice little patch of wool on the wire fence right where Pink Nose had been scratching his side.

"Oh thank you, Pink Nose," exclaimed Kathy. "This will make Randy so happy."

"Baa, baa," said the little lamb, as if he were saying, "I'm glad."

On her way back home Kathy stopped to show her father what she had. This time she explained her plan so that he understood. And Father was glad his little daughter was being so thoughtful of her big brother, Randy.

"Here, Flip. Here, Flip," Kathy kept calling as she walked along the path leading back to the house. Flip was Randy's other pet, and he would surely want to add something to Randy's valentine, she thought.

Just as Kathy climbed the back steps of the house and opened the kitchen door, Flip bounced into the kitchen ahead of her.

But oh my, you should have seen the kitchen floor! Flip made muddy footprints all around. When Mother came in, Flip hid under the table.

Kathy showed her mother what she had and told her of her plan. "But what can Flip give me for Randy's valentine?" she asked.

Looking down at the floor, Mother said, "It looks like Flip had an idea. Why not get his footprint?"

"But how?" asked Kathy.

"Here, hold this piece of paper from my note pad," began Mother. "Now come on out from under the table, you muddy-pawed dog. We want one more footprint, but not on my kitchen floor this time."

Flip crawled out slowly and put his front paw down on the paper, just as though he understood Kathy's plan.

"Thank you, Flip," she said. "Randy will be so happy."

"Bow-wow," barked Flip, just as if to say, "I'm glad."

After supper Kathy and her mother worked together on the valentine, whispering so that Randy would not hear about his surprise. Kathy cut out a large red heart. Then she cut out five small white hearts, one for each of Randy's pets. She pasted their gifts on the little hearts and then pasted them all around on the big heart.

Mother helped Kathy print a little verse on the valentine which read:

A Special valentine for you
From friends of yours,
Can you guess who?

"What a lovely surprise, Kathy," Mother said. "I know it will make Randy so happy."

"I'm glad," said Kathy. "I'm happy, too."

The next day was Valentine's Day. Kathy was up bright and early. She had a reason. She had something special to do. Knocking on Randy's door, she called, "Happy Valentine's Day—surprise, surprise!"

What a nice surprise Randy did have! And as Kathy had said, he was so happy!

—*Josephine Newbury*

THE TWINS' VALENTINE SURPRISES

Judy and Jody were twin sisters who had just had their fifth birthday. They were growing every day in so many ways. One way in which they were growing was in thinking up nice things to do for others. They would go to their room and talk and plan together. Then when Mother or Daddy least expected it, Judy and Jody would surprise them with something that they would enjoy. Sometimes they would paint a special picture or make up a little puppet play to entertain them after supper.

It was the morning before Valentine's Day, and Judy and Jody were wondering what kind of valentine they could give their parents. They wanted it to be a special kind of valentine that would show their mother and daddy how very much they loved them.

So they went to their room to think and plan. They didn't want their mother to know about their special surprise.

"I've got an idea," began Judy. "Let's you and me be valentines."

"Be valentines?" echoed Jody. "How can we be valentines?"

"Well, valentines say 'I love you,' don't they? And Mother said the best way to tell anyone you love them is to show them—right?"

"Yes, but how can we do that?"

"Well, we can help Mother tomorrow and do work in the house so she won't have to. That will show her how we love her, won't it?"

The twins finally agreed that this would be a good idea. They decided to make some small red hearts and leave them around in the house whenever they finished a job.

They asked their mother how to print "I love you." Then each twin made several little red hearts and printed the message "I love you" on each one. Judy printed her name at the bottom of the hearts she made, and Jody printed her name at the bottom of the hearts she made.

The girls could hardly wait until the next morning to begin being real valentines. It was hard for them to keep their secret, but they did.

In the morning when Mother came in to wake the twins, she found them already up and dressing. This was a surprise, for usually the twins were hard to get out of bed in the morning. But not this morning!

The girls squealed, "Surprise, surprise!" Judy hugged Mother and whispered, "Happy Valentine's Day. I love you."

Jody hugged Mother and whispered, "Happy Valentine's Day, Mommie. I love you."

Mother hugged both the girls together and said, "Happy Valentine's Day to my twins. Come on downstairs now and you can have breakfast with Daddy. He will be so glad you are up and dressed before he leaves for work."

The twins were glad they were up, too. They tiptoed down the stairs and out to the breakfast table. Then, quiet as two little mice, they put their arms around their daddy and said, "Surprise—happy Valentine's Day, Daddy!"

Daddy was surprised and very glad to have the twins eat breakfast with him. "This is almost the nicest Valentine surprise I've ever had," he said as he pulled the twins chairs out for them to sit down at the breakfast table.

After breakfast the twins went back to their room and decided on another surprise. As quietly as they could they made up their beds. They helped each other straighten the spreads so that their beds looked almost as good as when Mother made them. Then each took one of her little red paper hearts and with a piece of tape stuck it to the pillow on her bed.

About that time they heard their mother coming up the steps.

"Let's hide," Jody whispered, as she pulled Judy into their clothes closet. When Mother walked into the room the girls jumped out of their hiding place and squealed, "Surprise! Happy Valentine's Day!"

Again Mother hugged her twins and said, "Thank you, girls. What nice valentines you are. You did such a good job of making your beds."

Later in the morning the twins decided to carry out the trash for their mother. They put a little red heart on each trash can, just as they had done with their beds.

When their mother found the trash cans emptied and the little red hearts on them, she knew her valentine twins had been working again.

What a happy Valentine's Day this was for everyone!

Then Mother had an idea. She called Judy and Jody to the kitchen. "How would you girls like to make a valentine surprise for dinner tonight?" she asked.

"Oh, could we? What? How can we?" they asked. Mother opened a box she had kept hidden in the cabinet for days. "I found these little heart-shaped gelatin molds at the store the other day. I thought you might like to make some red gelatin shaped like hearts," she explained.

"O goody!" exclaimed Judy.

"Can we make it right now?" asked Jody.

The twins had made gelatin dessert before, but it was more fun today because they were making it into valentines.

That evening just before time for their father to come home from work, Judy and Jody had one more idea. They knew that when their father came in he liked to rest a few minutes in his big chair and read the evening paper. So they brought the newspaper in and laid it on his chair. Then they went to his room and brought his comfortable house slippers out and placed them in front of his chair. And they used the last of their little red paper hearts, taping one to the newspaper and one on the toe of each of his slippers.

How happy this made their father when he came home after a busy day at work!

Soon Mother called the family to the dinner table. The twins could hardly keep the secret of their special dessert. Judy said, "Daddy, you know what we did today? We made something good to eat." Then she put her hands over her mouth and giggled. But she didn't tell.

When it was time for dessert, the twins helped their mother remove the dishes from the table. Then they brought in their surprise valentine dessert.

This time Judy and Jody said, "Happy Valentine, everybody!"

"Thank you," said Father. "I know you girls must have made this pretty red dessert."

"They certainly did," explained Mother as she came in carrying a big heart-shaped cake. "And here is my valentine surprise to the family," she added, placing the cake on the table. "The twins have helped me so much today I had time to bake this special cake. Happy Valentine's Day to each of you."

"Thank you, Mommie," said the twins. "This has been the best Valentine's Day ever."

"I do believe it has," agreed Father. "And after we finish our dessert, I want to give you my valentine surprise."

And he did.

—*Josephine Newbury*

THE PICNIC BASKET[21]

(Note: This story will be much more interesting if a picnic basket is used as the story is told. Eyes, nose, and mouth cut out of colored paper may be taped to each side of the basket. One face should be sad and the other one should be happy.)

Jeanie, her mother, father, and little brother, Bobby, were sitting around the supper table talking about the kindergarten picnic they were all going to attend the next day.

As they were talking, the picnic basket down in a dark corner of the basement was wondering to himself: "When will I ever go on a picnic again? I am so lonesome and sad. I have been in this basement for such a long time."

Upstairs, Jeanie and her family were deciding what they wanted to take for their lunch. "Fried chicken," said Jeanie. "I'd like potato chips and peanut butter sandwiches," said Bobby. "And certainly I would like some of Mother's good potato salad," added Father. Mother thought a bit and then suggested that she might put in some carrot and celery sticks. Then she added, "Let's not forget the cookies that Grandmother sent us today. They will be our dessert."

After supper Daddy went to the basement to get the picnic basket. Oh, how dusty and sad it looked!

When Daddy brought the basket upstairs, he set it down by the table and joined the family. The picnic basket began to feel better. Mother picked it up, dusted it off, and set it up on the table. The basket began to feel even better.

The next morning Mother began to fix all the foods that the family had requested. As she finished part of the lunch, she would pack it in the basket. The picnic basket began to feel better and better. It began to feel full and so happy.

After the picnic basket was packed, the family went to meet Jeanie at her kindergarten for the picnic. On the way, the happy picnic basket was singing to himself *(Tune: "Did You Ever See a Lassie?")*:

We're going on a picnic, a picnic, a picnic,
We're going on a picnic, and I am not sad.
I'm filled full of sandwiches, and salad, and cookies,
We're going on a picnic, and I am so glad!

—*Judy Gable Lutz*

[21]Used by permission of the author.

11
Young Children and Science

Children are natural scientists. . . .
Their drives lead them
    to question—about their concerns and
        curiosities

to investigate—to see what happens if . . .
to manipulate—with fingers, arms, legs,
    and total body
to observe—with *all* their senses
to classify—by collecting, selecting,
    grouping and comparing
to report—by telling and "showing."[1]

---

[1]Board of Education of the City of New York, *Pre-Kindergarten Curriculum Guide.* Curriculum Bulletin, No. 11, 1965–1966, p. 105.

Science concerns itself with the physical world of forces and materials and the natural world of animals and plants.

Science experiences in the kindergarten should be an integral part of the child's total school experiences. It is in the kindergarten that a sound foundation is laid for later science learnings.

The aims of an effective kindergarten science program include:

> providing for the child experiences through which his understanding of the world will be expanded;
> giving him opportunities for growing in the scientific method of thinking; and
> helping him feel comfortable in his world.

In attempting to realize these purposes in the group's day-by-day living, the teacher will provide an environment which is rich in varied resources that stimulate curiosity and inquiry on the part of the child. Such an environment must also allow freedom for investigating, exploring, and experimenting.

Teachers will remember that science has been a part of the everyday experiences of the young children—almost since the day of their birth. They have accrued many accurate concepts, but they have also acquired many misconceptions, and they are unaware of many of the simple relationships found in the physical world. The following is an example of children's misinformation:

Playing out under a large oak tree, a group of five's were commenting on how big it was, how rough the bark was, and wondering what the acorns were good for. Finally, one child ventured the question "Where do oak trees come from, anyway?" To this an all-knowing peer replied, "Why okra, you dumb bunny. Anybody knows that."

That bit of conversation, overheard by the teacher, led to a number of science activities: collecting acorns and examining them, searching for sprouted acorns, examining the rings on a log which had recently been sawed in two, and planting acorns.

Many good science learnings will occur situationally, such as in the case just described, or when problems arise or from environmental changes. While the teacher is sensitive to all opportunities for situational teachings, he or she cannot rely on them for the science program. The teacher must have planned activities and make a real effort to acquaint the child with the world about him in ways that help him feel comfortable and at home in it.

A great deal of meaningful, firsthand experience is necessary for the child to develop appropriate understandings and to build basic science concepts.

Experimentation plays an important role in the child's learning through discovery. He begins most likely with the process of *observing*. This involves the child in discriminating by looking, by touching and smelling, and by listening. He compares and tests as he employs his senses.

The teacher is alert to the opportunities for extending the child's vocabulary, which symbolizes his sensory experiences in his observation. The teacher will help him to verbalize how an object or material seems to him—rough, soft, smooth, prickly, hard, heavy, light, sharp, etc. In this way the child's skill in describing develops in the process of observing.

As the child observes—comparing, contrasting, and examining—he gains information on which he can *predict*, or make hypotheses. This is the second process in discovery.

The teacher guides the child as he begins to *interpret* what he observes. Together they may ask, "What does this mean?" "Why do you think this happened?" "What do you suppose will happen now?"

Through careful observations the young child learns to compare and contrast, to identify likenesses and differences. From these data he begins to classify. Classification helps give meaning to materials and situations.

The kindergarten is not too early to begin encouraging the child to develop a scientific attitude. In order that this objective may be realized, teachers must understand what it means.

Glenn Blough describes a scientific-minded person as possessing these characteristics:

> He is open-minded—willing to change his mind in the face of reliable evidences—and he respects another's point of view.
>
> He looks at a matter from every side before he draws a conclusion. . . . .

He goes to reliable sources for his evidence. He challenges sources to make sure that they are reliable.

He is not superstitious; he realizes that nothing happens without some cause.

He is curious. He is careful and accurate in his observations. He plans his investigations carefully.[2]

Children discover science all through the day.

During block play—
Many science concepts are formed and put to use. Concepts of: space, shape, weight; balance and support; the use of levers, pulleys, ramps, bridges, wheels.

During art activities—
Jane adds blue paint to yellow. What happens?

"There's too much water in the clay today!"
"How much can I bend this wire?"
"Will this piece of wood bend?"
The free use of varied natural materials for pictures, sculpture, mobiles (e.g. clay, sand, seeds, twigs, etc.) give children a familiarity with their properties and possibilities.

Music—
The wonder of sounds and how they are made:

"Listen to that high note come out of my flute."
"What makes the music in the piano?"
"How will this jar sound when I tap it?"

Science in conjunction with water play—
Many chances for measuring, testing floatation, setting up currents, observing the characteristics of wetness vs. dryness, water vs. ice; the questioning of where the water comes from, where does it go, of absorption, of pressure, of bubbles. Use such materials as funnels, cones, strainers as part of water play. [Egg beaters, large paint-brushes, measuring cups, plastic squeeze bottles, small pitcher, materials that will float and materials that sink, rubber tubing for siphoning.]

And cooking experiences—
Observing the importance of chemical changes of such things as: wet dough to spongy cake, cream to butter, liquid to gelatin, sugar (a solid) dissolving in lemonade (a liquid).

Using the senses of smell, taste, touch, sight, hearing.

Mechanical experiences with beating, sifting, grating, cutting, stirring, kneading, etc.

And dramatic play—
It is possible that there is a future engineer building those bridges out of large hollow blocks and boards

And those . . . nurses in the make-believe hospital are wondering just what kind of care and medicine will help the patient.

The battery-connected bell tells the family in the housekeeping area that visitors are arriving.

And out of doors—
The outdoor area provides an actual science laboratory. There may be:

Insects and birds to watch, properly feed, identify.
Seasonal changes of weather, grass, of trees, earth.
Growing things to observe, collect, care for (weeds, grass, plants, trees).
Sand, earth, water, light and shadows, clouds, mist, rain, snow, sleet.

Indoors too—
Chances for sound making—the difference between bells, gongs, hitting a tire, or hitting a metal drum.

Equipment suggests experimentation with physical forces of rolling things down, pushing things up, balancing boards, using pumps, springs, wheels; of heavy vs. light weights.

---

[2]Glenn O. Bough and Albert J. Huggett, *Elementary-School Science* (New York: The Dryden Press, 1951), p. 17.

And into the community—
Trips around the neighborhood to see new things; to discuss familiar things; to collect; to hear the sounds of insects, birds, animals, cars, trucks, buses, machinery; to feed the pigeons.

A trip to a pond to feed ducks or watch for frogs or feel the icy spring water.
A visit to a farm to try a hand at milking a cow, to watch a sheep sheared, to hold a baby pig.
A trip to a nearby museum with displays of interest to young children.

Trips to note methods of transportation, communication, and community services (horse cart vs. cars vs. airplanes; telephone wires, electric signs, manholes and water pipes) (gasoline station). How do these things work? Children will ask. We must help them find the answers.

Trips to observe and identify service machinery—disposal trucks, snow removal machinery, bulldozers, tow trucks, garbage trucks.

Have you ever visited the office of a dentist, a doctor, a veterinarian?

Science is a more familiar part of our lives than we often believe. It is everywhere around us. All we need do is open our eyes and ears and accept its invitation to wonder at its beauty and its mystery.[3]

Numerous values are conserved for the child as he participates in science activities:

1. *Science experiences stimulate and satisfy curiosity.* The teacher keeps the science center up to date, putting out new materials which will spark the children's curiosity. She will also have resources available for the children, to aid them in discovering answers to their questions.

Young children will ask questions if the teacher encourages them to do so. They will ask questions if they observe their teacher expressing curiosity about things and events—if she gets excited and expresses wonder over a snow crystal, a bursting leaf bud, a little rock that has "a sparkle in it," a creepy, crawly caterpillar, or frost on a blade of grass.

Basic to all science experiences for young children is their questioning. Teachers must make the children feel comfortable in their questioning and must help them retain their sense of wonder.

2. *Science experiences help the child orient himself to space and time.* Concepts such as yesterday, tomorrow, and next week are difficult for the young child to grasp. The same is true of space—a block away, across the ocean, in outer space.

3. *Science experiences help develop basic concepts through varied firsthand contacts with the physical and natural world.* The child's general fund of knowledge is extended. Many learnings take place in the process of discovering the world in which he lives.

4. *One of the most important values conserved for young children through a good science program is that they gain skill in the ability to solve problems effectively and to use the scientific processes.*

5. *Science activities give young children experiences in the use of tools and equipment.* A tool chest filled with nuts and bolts, locks, pulleys, and rope inspires manipulation. An outdoor garden calls for the use of a variety of tools. Hand magnifying glasses, prisms, kaleidoscopes, periscopes, magnets of all kinds, materials for exploring sound, are but a few "science tools" which children need to learn to use.

6. *Science experiences contribute to social and emotional development of the young child.*
The child who feels himself inadequate—who has an unwholesome self-image—has difficulty with problem solving. He is fearful of making guesses or questioning.

The child can be helped in dealing with his fear through certain activities in the area of science. Shadows, particularly at night, are cause for fear in some young children. Play with light and shadow gives the child opportunities to create all kinds of grotesque patterns. Discovering how shadows are made may reduce his fear of shadow patterns at night.

[3]Maryland State Department of Health and Mental Hygiene, Division of Maternal and Child Health, *Child Care Guidelines*, No. 16 (December 1967) pp. 4–5. Used by permission.

7. *Through participation in science experiences appropriate to his maturity, the young child gains deeper appreciation for the world and feels more comfortable in his environment.*

Identifying relationships helps the young child feel more at home in the world. As he is helped to recognize the regular passing of the seasons in sequence, for example, he can recognize the orderliness, dependability, balance, and rhythm in nature.

A glass terrarium is an excellent illustration of the water cycle. The correct terminology, *evaporation* and *condensation,* should be used with the children as they observe these processes.

Watching and wondering about "miracles" around him are adventures which bring the young child exciting new discoveries of facts and relationships in the world.

PLANT LIFE

Discoveries About Plant Life:

1. *Different species of plants are capable of growing new plants in different ways.*

    a. *Many different kinds of plants reproduce their kind from seeds.*

Plant large butterbeans and corn seeds. Before planting the butterbeans, soak for about one hour. Be certain there are enough seeds for each child to have one or two to open up and discover the embryo plant inside. The beans for planting should not be soaked. Each child can plant three or four beans in a small paper cup. A small hole should be made in the bottom of the cup for drainage. A piece of masking tape with the child's name printed on it and taped to the cup will make it possible for him to watch his own "bean garden."

There are several ways that make it possible for the children to watch the process of germination of bean seeds so that they will understand what is happening to their own "bean gardens" underneath the soil. One effective way is to plant a bean seed in each compartment of an egg carton. The compartments may be numbered 1 through 12. Each day a bean may be dug up out of the soil, beginning with No. 1, to see what change has taken place.

Another way of showing the germination and growth of the young plant is to allow the seeds to sprout under glass.

Directions: Bind with adhesive tape the edges of two pieces of glass four or five inches square. Cut a number of pieces of colored blotting paper the same size. Dampen them, then place them on top of one piece of glass. Lay several bean seeds about on the blotting paper and cover with the second piece of glass. Secure these together with rubber bands and then stand the unit upright in a shallow pan of water. The blotting paper will continue to absorb enough water from the pan to keep the seeds moist. A small wooden block on either side of the "glass garden" will prop it upright for easy viewing.

The children will note that no matter which way the seed is turned under the glass, the roots grow down and the stem grows upward.

It will be interesting to plant corn seeds, too. They sprout rather quickly, but because corn is a monocotyledonous plant, the seed stays under the ground to nourish the plant. In contrast, the children will see the bean seed push up out of the soil. The two cotyledons separate above ground, turn green, and nourish the plant until the leaves are large enough to take over the job of manufacturing food for the plant. The bean seed will then shrivel up and drop off.

In the spring the children may take home a little bag of pumpkin seeds (saved from the Halloween jack-o'-lantern). Their parents may help them find a place to plant them. And, as frequently happens, the child may grow his own pumpkin for the following Halloween. There just might be one for a pumpkin pie, also!

During the year there will be other experiences of growing plants from seeds. (Young children need frequent reinforcement of learnings.)

A porous sponge resting in a dish of water makes an ideal "garden" for planting grass seed or bird seed. The latter will provide a variety of little plants.

In the spring the children will enjoy planting nasturtium seeds to take home and transplant in the family garden or window box.

b. *Some plants reproduce from leaves: African violet, air plant, begonia.*

African violets are easy to root from the leaves. Fill a small juice glass with water, and cover with a piece of waxed paper. Punch two holes in the paper and lower the stem of the leaf through one into the water. The other hole is used to pour water into the glass. The waxed paper keeps the leaf from getting wet. As soon as the roots are well formed, the leaf may be planted in a pot filled with soil prepared for African violets.

The *air plant* is fascinating for children to observe. A leaf may be broken off and laid aside where it gets sun occasionally. After some time tiny plants will be observed growing out of the edge of the leaf.

A leaf may be laid on a small pot of moist potting soil, and the same observation may be made. After the little plants with their leaves and roots appear, the leaf may be covered with soil. Be careful not to injure the new little plants.

The begonia (beefsteak) will produce new plants from the leaf, also. Place a leaf, vein side down, on a box of moist sand. Keep the sand moist but not too wet. In time new plants will begin growing from the leaf.

c. *Some plants reproduce from roots.*

The sweet potato is an interesting example of this type of plant reproduction.

Select a potato that has not been treated for commercial use. Be sure that it has one or two purple "eyes." Place in a glass jar with the pointed end down in the water. About one-half of the potato should be in the water. Roots will soon appear, and then the shoots. This plant makes a beautiful piece of winter greenery.

If the kindergarten is to have a spring garden, a potato may be sprouted as described above, but when the sprouts are about eight inches long they may be pulled off and, after a good rain, planted. (These sprouts are called potato slips.) From this planting, sweet potatoes may be gathered in the fall. The ground will crack open, showing that potatoes are under the vines.

d. *Some plants are reproduced from bulbs.*

Examples of this form of reproducing new plants include tulip, daffodil, narcissus, crocus, and hyacinth.

The children will enjoy planting *paper white narcissus* bulbs, watching them grow and bloom. Provide a shallow bowl. Put several small pieces of charcoal in the bottom of the bowl to keep the water fresh. Cover the bottom of the bowl with a layer of small pebbles or stones. Place the bulbs in the bowl and fill with pebbles so that just the tops of the bulbs are exposed. Fill the bowl with water up to the bottom of the bulb. Keep the water level at this height.

For best results the bowl should be placed in a dark place until the sprouts appear. The narcissus may then be brought out and placed in a sunny window.

Cut an extra bulb in half lengthwise so that the children can see the baby plant in the center. The layers of the bulb around the little plant contain the food for it.

Watching a hyacinth plant grow from a bulb in a special hyacinth bowl is an interesting experience and will be different from observing the narcissus bulbs grow.

The single species of hyacinths grow better than the double varieties. The special hyacinth bowl is made of smoked-colored glass with a cup-shaped top to hold the bulb.

Place a piece of charcoal in the bottom part of the bowl to keep the water sweet. The bowl is filled with water so that only the bottom of the bulb is in the water. Keep the bulb in a cool, dark place for about a month, or until the lower part of the bowl is filled with roots.

Another kind of flower bulb the children will enjoy planting is the *tulip*. Provide potting soil and a large flowerpot for planting the bulbs. Be certain that the children place a small porous stone or small piece of clay pot over the drainage hole in the bottom of the pot. They may then put in the soil and plant the bulbs according to the planting directions which come with the bulbs.

Bury the pot in the school garden. Then when the bulbs bloom in the spring, bring the pot indoors to enjoy. Foil paper may be wrapped around the flower pot, giving it a greenhouse look.

e. *Some plants multiply by runners.*

Strawberries produce new plants by sending out runners which take root. The children will enjoy making this discovery in their indoor garden. A flat box filled with rich dirt will allow space for the strawberry plants to multiply. It's possible to observe the flowers and developing strawberries before school is out.

f. Some plants multiply from tubers.

The *Irish potato* is a good example. Select a potato with a number of "eyes" that are just beginning to sprout. Cut the potato into pieces, being certain there is at least one eye to each piece. The children may plant these in a large pot for sprouting indoors. Or if the group will be in school during the summer, they may want to have a row of potatoes in their garden. There's nothing quite so exciting as digging potatoes from beneath the potato plants.

g. Some plants make new plants from stems.

Examples of this method of reproducing new plants are: coleus, geranium, wandering jew, and ivy.

Just before frost the children may bring to school slips from any of the above mentioned plants. They may put them, according to species, into jars of water so that they may watch them sprout roots.

When the root growth is substantial, the children may plant them in small pots. (Incidentally, these plants make nice Christmas gifts for the children's mothers.) One pound cottage cheese cartons make very practical pots.

The children might try another method of rooting coleus or geranium slips. Make a flat bed and fill with moist sand. Be sure it is well drained. Put the cuttings in the sand and cover each with a glass jar. Keep in the shade for about two weeks. Then bring this miniature greenhouse into the sunlight.

Pussy willows can be grown from branches of the pussy willow. Cut twigs (ten to fourteen inches long) from the ends of the branches of the mother plant. Peel a little of the bark off of the cut end and place in a jar of water. Roots will grow from the part of the twig under water. Leaves may appear along the twig. As soon as the roots are well developed, the twigs may be transplanted into pots of moist soil or in the ground outdoors.

2. Plants need food, water, light, and warmth.

The children can discover the differences in growth of plant life by setting up some experiments to test physical needs of plants.

a. Let the children put one plant in a pot of rich potting soil and another plant of the same species and size in a pot of sand. The two plants should receive the same amount of water at the same time, and they should be placed in a sunny window. It may take some time before the difference in growth becomes apparent. To make it more evident that plants require food for normal growth, a little plant food may be added to the water used on the plant in the pot of rich dirt.

Then later, after the difference in growth has been made evident, the children may transplant the plant growing in the sand into rich potting soil and note the changes that occur.

b. Two kinds of experiments may be undertaken to discover that plants depend on water for survival and growth.

One experiment will deal with seed germination. Let the children plant lima beans in two containers, being sure that the soil used is very dry. Mark the containers *water* and *no water*. Place the containers side by side so that everything in the environment is the same except that one plant is watered and the other is not. The children may guess what the outcome will be, and then after a week or ten days they can see whether or not they were correct. They should discover that seeds need water to sprout and grow new plants.

A second activity might be to take two equally healthy plants of the same size and place them in a warm, sunny place. These containers should be marked *water* and *no water*. The plant marked *water* should be watered regularly, as needed. The other plant should be given no water. The effects of drought will soon be noticeable.

c. To find out that plants need light to survive, the children may select and label two plants of equal size and of the same species— one *light* and the other *dark*. The container marked *dark* should be put into a closed closet, but should be given the same amount of water at the same time as the control plant.

Every few days the children may note the differences in the plants. Leave the plant in the dark long enough for it to lose its color and become a very unhealthy plant.

d. In the springtime the children can see the burst of growth in the plant world as soon as the days grow warm. They can note that all winter long the grass did not need mowing and the shrubs put out no new shoots.

If it is possible, they might experiment with two similar plants, placing one in the warm sunshine and keeping the other in a cold place. They should be watered at the same time. If the difference in temperature can be maintained, plants will show difference in rate of growth.

Perhaps an easier experiment to show that plants need warmth for normal growth would be in seed germination. Butterbeans are again a good kind of seed to use because they germinate so quickly. One container of seeds might be marked *warm* and kept at room temperature. The other container could be marked *cold* and placed in the refrigerator. They should be watered in equal amounts at the same time. Growth should be retarded in the cold environment.

Terrarium

Every kindergarten should prepare a terrarium for the science center. It could be called a glass-jar garden. All that is needed is a wide-mouthed gallon jar and small plants.

Turn the jar on its side, and spread about two cups of moist sand in the jar. Sprinkle bits of charcoal in the sand to retard souring of the soil. Spread leaf mold over this. Then place small plants in the jar in the leaf mold. Small ferns such as ebony spleenwort are interesting plants, as are pipsissewa, mosses, liverworts, and lichens. These small plants may be found on shady banks along a quiet little stream.

When the plants are arranged in the jar, they should be sprinkled lightly with a bulb spray, but not saturated with water.

Cover the jar with a lid. Set it on a shelf where it will be in the direct sun only a short time each day. Pieces of styrofoam may be cut and glued on the jar as a base to keep the jar from rolling.

If mold forms on the plants, it is an indication that there is too much moisture in the jar.

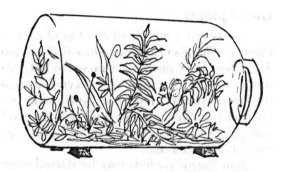

Leaving the lid off for a few hours will allow for the needed evaporation.

This type of terrarium may be used to help the children understand the water cycle. This is discussed under the section "Activities with Water."

Another type of terrarium may be made. A fish tank that will no longer hold water may be converted into a lovely indoor garden.

It may be made in the same way as the gallon-jar terrarium, with the exception of having screen wire cut and fitted over the top. This allows for sprinkling the plants as they need water. It also makes a convenient home for interesting insects such as crickets and praying mantis. Cocoons may be attached to the screen wire so that they will hang free in the terrarium.

Other Greenery

Avocado plant

An avocado seed is interesting to observe as it germinates and develops into a hardy plant. A special hyacinth bowl (dark glass with cup-shaped top) is excellent for sprouting the avocado. It is important to have the base of the seed just below the water line.

When the root system is sufficiently developed and the stalk and leaves are well started, the plant may be potted in rich potting soil.

Pineapple plant

Cut off the crown of leaves from the pineapple. Let the cut end dry thoroughly, then plant it in coarse builder's sand. As soon as the roots are formed, it may be transplanted to a large pot filled with potting soil. Growth of the leaves will be rather slow, but the pineapple plant will add variety to the indoor gardening activities.

Carrot garden

Cut about 2 inches off the top of carrots. Place a layer of small pebbles in a shallow dish. Add a few small pieces of charcoal to keep the water sweet. Place carrot tops, cut end down, in the water among the pebbles. Keep water at a level which covers the carrot pieces about halfway up. Feathery green leaves will sprout and live for several weeks.

New carrot gardens may be started every week or so to insure continual greenery.

Beet garden

Follow the instructions given for the carrot garden, using the tops of beets instead. The reddish, purplish leaves will be fascinating to the children.

Turnip tops will sprout in the same way. The children can observe the differences in the shape and color of the leaves of the dish garden plants.

Outdoor garden

Every kindergarten class needs an outdoor garden—a small plot of ground near the outdoor play area where the children can dig, plant seeds and bulbs, and care for growing flowers and vegetables.

In selecting seeds and bulbs, it is well to be certain that the plants will have time to mature before the school term is over. Having flowers to enjoy and to share and a "harvest" of vegetables to gather is a very important part of the gardening experience.

The children will enjoy planting pumpkin seeds from the Halloween jack-o'-lantern. They should know that it takes the pumpkins all summer to mature. They can have the satisfaction of knowing that they are helping next year's kindergarten class have a pumpkin to pick from the vine for their jack-o'-lantern.

BOOKS FOR CHILDREN ON PLANT LIFE

Bulla, Clyde R. *A Tree Is a Plant.* New York: Thomas Y. Crowell Co., 1960.

Jordan, Helene J. *How a Seed Grows.* New York: Thomas Y. Crowell Co., 1960.

Krauss, Ruth. *Carrot Seed.* New York: Harper & Row, 1945. (Record also available)

Podendorf, Illa. *Predicting with Plants.* Chicago: Childrens Press, 1971.

_____. *The True Book of Plant Experiments.* Chicago: Childrens Press, 1960.

Webber, Irma E. *Bits That Grow Big.* New York: William R. Scott, 1949.

_____. *Travelers All—The Story of How Plants Go Places.* New York: William R. Scott, 1944.

_____. *Up Above and Down Below.* New York: William R. Scott, 1943.

ANIMAL LIFE

Balanced Aquarium

A balanced aquarium is one stocked with

—fish,
—growing water plants to replenish the necessary supply of oxygen for the fish and to use up the excess carbon dioxide,
—snails or other scavengers to keep the aquarium clean, and
—aquarium gravel.

If the fish tank or aquarium is balanced and is kept out of direct sunlight, it will not need to be cleaned or to have the water changed more than once every few months. When water is added to the aquarium, it should first be allowed to stand in a bowl for a day. In order not to disturb the fish or stir up the gravel, lay a sheet of typing paper on top of the water and pour the fresh water in slowly.

Guppies are one of the hardiest species of fish—a good type to have in the kindergarten. Guppies will not overeat, as goldfish are prone to do. Guppies are also prolific live-bearers.

Box Turtles

During the spring months box turtles may be found in woods, fields, meadows, and on the open road. A box turtle makes an interesting pet for the group. He can be cared for indoors or out. A large wooden box makes an acceptable temporary home for the turtle. He likes dried grass or leaves to hide in and a shallow container for drinking water. The box turtle is a land turtle, so he does not need a swimming pool. He will enjoy an outdoor pen for exercise. His food can consist of raw apples, bananas, hard-boiled eggs, lettuce, ground beef, and food scraps. Uneaten food should be removed and replaced with fresh before it spoils. Children should not try to feed the turtle by hand, for it might bite their fingers.

Caring for Tadpoles

Frog eggs (a mass of eggs that looks like gelatin) may be found along the edges of quiet streams or ponds in the spring of the year. They may be taken to the classroom so the children can observe the eggs as they hatch. Pond water and a little mud from the bottom of the stream are needed. Stones, small sticks, and leaves from the stream should be added to the tadpole aquarium, since they contain tiny plants which the young tadpoles eat.

When the tadpoles hatch, they may be fed a little prepared goldfish food and a little yolk of a hard-boiled egg every few days. Food which isn't eaten in a couple of hours should be removed.

As the tadpoles begin to absorb their tails and get their hind legs, they should have a rock or stick on which to climb when they feel the need to get out of the water temporarily.

Watching the physical changes of the tadpole is fascinating to any observer, especially the young child. A hand lens aids in this observation.

Observing Insects

Insects such as grasshoppers, crickets, and praying mantis may be observed for short periods of time and then released to their native habitats.

Of these three insects, the praying mantis is probably the most unusual and interesting to observe. The female may build an egg sack. This is fascinating to watch. She requires several live crickets a day for her menu.

Crickets often entertain the children with their chirping music.

(Note: For directions on making cages, see Church Kindergarten Resource Book, *by Newbury, p. 218.)*

Ants

Commercial ant farms may be purchased, or an ant farm may be made. A widemouthed gallon jar serves well. Fill a quart jar with sand and place it in the center of the jar. Taking up space in the middle of the gallon jar forces the ants to make their tunnels near the outside so they may be viewed. Dig up an ant hill and dig into the colony with a trowel. Put a trowelful of soil with the ants into your ant house. Be sure to get ant eggs, and if possible get the queen ant. (She will be larger and will probably have wings.)

Be sure to get plenty of ants. Pack the soil gently around the inside jar. Leave about two inches clear at the top of the jar. Place a piece of sponge saturated with sugar water but not too wet on top of the soil. Cover the top with the lid. Be sure to have tiny holes punched in the lid—too small for the ants to slip through.

Because ants work better in the dark, wrap black paper around the jar and leave it for several days. When the paper is removed, the children will be surprised to see the little tunnels the ants have made.

Occasionally a little bit of food may be placed on top of the soil—bread crumbs, dead flies, a tiny piece of apple, or nutmeats.

Sprinkle the soil lightly with water once in a while so that the ants will have a drink.

Earthworms

Watching earthworms work through the soil is quite interesting to children. After a good rain, earthworms come to the surface of the ground.

Take a quart jar. Place about four or five inches of black dirt in the bottom. Put about an inch of sand on top of the dirt. Put five or six earthworms into the jar. Be sure to keep the jar in a cool place. Watch the earthworms tunnel through the soil as they mix and improve it.

Children should be helped to see how earthworms work for us in our gardens.

Wild Birds

Birds are a source of joy and wonder the year round. We enjoy listening to their songs, feeding them in winter, and putting out nesting materials in early spring.

During the winter months the children may put out wild bird seed, bread crumbs, apple wedges, suet, and peanut butter.

In early spring the children will enjoy collecting nesting materials for the birds: bits of string and ribbon, and cotton balls pulled apart. If there is a good place to hang it, a "bird nester" will be fun to fix and watch. Take a plastic berry basket or a mesh sack in which onions, potatoes, or oranges come from the grocery store. Insert a coat hanger and then have the children weave in bits of nesting materials. The supply of materials may have to be replenished once the birds discover the attractive building materials!

PHYSICAL WORLD

Activities with Water

1. *Water is wet, but you can make it wetter!* (Soap makes water wetter.) Experiment with small strips of newspaper dropped into two glasses of water—one plain, the other soapy. See which strips get wet first.

2. *Siphoning water—force of gravity.* Young children can easily learn to siphon water, and it is lots of fun to watch the water run by itself. The method of siphoning water can be introduced when there is a need for moving water and other ways are not possible.

A three- to four-foot length of ½" rubber tubing is easy for the children to manage. The tubing must be completely filled with water. Holding it tightly at each end, place one end under the water in the container that is to be emptied. The other end will convey the water into the bucket placed below the first container. If the tubing slips up out of the water which is being emptied, the flow of water is cut off. When this occurs, the tube must be filled again and the process begun all over.

3. *Water has a skin.* With a medicine dropper put drops of water onto waxed paper. Water drops stand up round because the water has a skin. Touch a drop with a piece of soap and the skin breaks, allowing the drop to spread out.

4. *Water is not always wet.* Prove this by touching a piece of paper to an ice cube in the freezer.

5. *Experiment with floating objects in water.* (Objects that are heavier than an equal volume of water will sink.)

6. *Water dissolves some materials (gelatin, sugar, salt) but not others (pencils, rocks, buttons, bottles).*

7. *Water freezes and takes the shape of its container.* Put water in differently shaped gelatin molds and place them in a freezing compartment. When solid, remove the ice from the mold.

8. *Ice is water in a solid state.* Put an icicle or an ice cube on a piece of blotting paper in a warm room. Watch what happens.

9. *Water goes into the air.* Water disappears into the air. This is called *evaporation*. Wherever there is water, evaporation is taking place—from wet sidewalks, dew on the grass, puddles in the yard, the bird bath, lakes, rivers, and the oceans. Evaporation takes place in our homes and in the kindergarten—from the fish bowl, the wet towel hanging in the bathroom, and from peoples' breath. Water evaporates from everything that is wet.

Try an experiment. Take two shallow containers and fill them with the same amount of water. Cover one tightly, but leave the other one open. Place them side by side on a shelf and see what happens.

10. *Evaporation is aided by the wind.* If you have a chalkboard in the class, try this experiment. Wet two sponges and squeeze most of the water out. Have two children make a wet mark the same size on the chalkboard, several feet apart. Then have another child fan one wet spot with a piece of a cardboard. Let the other spot dry as it will. See which wet spot evaporates first.

11. *Evaporation is aided by heat.* Cut a piece of cloth into two pieces about the size of a man's handkerchief. Wet them and squeeze as much water out of them as possible. Hang one near a radiator or register and hang the other in a cool place. See which one dries first.

12. *Spreading things out aids evaporation.* Take the same squares of cloth and wet them. Then squeeze as much water out of them as possible. Spread one out flat on a table and keep the other one wadded up. It would be interesting to time the evaporation to see the difference.

When water evaporates into the air, it is changed into something that isn't wet. It is called *water vapor*. We cannot see it, but there is always some water vapor in the air.

13. *Water comes out of the air.* When *water vapor* changes back to water, it is called *condensation*. When water vapor touches a cold surface, it condenses into water.

Dew on the grass and plants forms at night when the ground cools off, causing the water vapor in the warmer air around it to change into water droplets and cover the grass and other plants.

Frost is also water vapor that comes out of the air when the temperature of the objects on which condensation occurs is below the freezing point. Frost is not frozen dew, because the water vapor freezes directly into ice crystals on the cold objects.

Snow comes out of the air when the air is very cold.

Watch your breath on very cold mornings. Your breath is warm and filled with moisture. When you breathe, little "clouds" appear before you because the water vapor condenses when it comes into contact with the cold air.

Try an experiment. Fill a quart jar with ice cubes and screw the lid on tightly. Be sure the outside of the jar is dry to begin with. Very soon the outside of the jar will be moist. In a few minutes the drops of water will be larger, and soon they will become so heavy that they will begin making little rivers down the jar.

The jar was closed tightly. No moisture from inside the jar could escape. The children will see that the water has to come out of the air around the jar.

A terrarium that has an airtight glass lid is a perfect example of the *water cycle*—evaporation, water vapor, condensation. If the terrarium is in the direct sunlight during part of the day, it will work best. The sun draws the moisture out of the soil and plants. As the water vapor rises and touches the cold glass lid, it condenses. The water vapor forms tiny droplets on the inside of the glass lid. As these droplets are filled with more water, they form large drops of water which finally become too heavy to hang on any longer. They drop down on the plants and soil just as rain does. Because of the continual processes of evaporation and condensation, the terrarium stays balanced and never needs to have more water added.

This will help the children understand that rain is not the result of God's turning on a faucet and releasing the water. The sun draws water vapor out of water from everywhere. This is called *evaporation*. When the air becomes cool, the water vapor takes the form of tiny droplets. These make a cloud. As more tiny drops are formed, the cloud becomes larger, and as these tiny drops go together, they form larger and much heavier drops. Finally, when they are too heavy to remain up in the air, they fall to earth. This is rain.

Other Activities with Water

Young children need many experiences in water play. A water tub can provide many science and math opportunities. All kinds of objects are needed for the children to experiment with floating and sinking. Measuring equipment such as cup, pint, and quart containers give the children experiences in measuring and pouring. Each child should have a plastic rain coat, wearing it backwards so that it is fastened down the back.

Bubble blowing

Bubble blowing is a fun activity, both indoors and out. One-pound cottage cheese cartons make good containers for the soapy water. Plastic drinking straws make good "blowers." *Never use a detergent* in the bubble solution. Ivory soap chipped into small pieces is the safest to use, because children often forget and suck instead of blowing. Some young children may have to be taught to blow.

Outdoors the children will enjoy letting the wind blow the bubbles away. When bubbles are blown outdoors in weather just below freezing, it is an exciting surprise to see the bubbles freeze.

The easiest way to blow the bubbles outdoors is to use empty thread spools. Have the water very soapy, or have a cake of Ivory soap and a pan of water. Have the child dip the end of the spool in water, then touch it to the soap and blow gently through the opposite end of the spool. When a bubble is formed it may be gently tossed into the air. Or in very cold weather it will freeze. In order to hold the air in the bubble, the child must quickly put his finger over the hole in the spool.

Measuring rainfall

A commercial rain gauge may be set up according to the directions given with the gauge. However, a satisfactory gauge may be made using a quart bottle and a three-inch funnel.

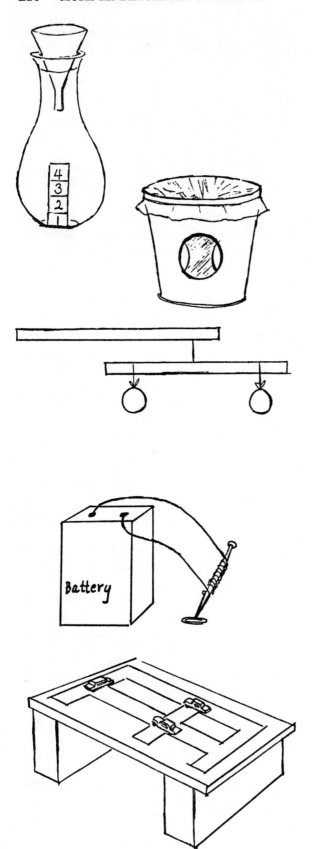

A piece of adhesive tape should be attached from the bottom edge of the bottle and up one side. It should be marked off in inches, using a ruler as a guide and India ink for the markings.

The bottle should be taped down to a box or table placed in the yard, where it will be completely exposed to the rain.

Measuring water content of snow

In geographical areas where snow occurs only several times during the winter, it will be interesting to measure the water content of the different snowstorms.

Plastic quart ice cream cartons make good containers. Let the children scoop up a container full of the snow and immediately snap the airtight lid on it. When the snow melts, they can examine the amount of water and mark and date the container.

This may be done with successive snowfalls. Comparing the amounts of water will be interesting. They may also be surprised at the little specks of dirt appearing in the water.

It must be remembered that snow is not rain that is frozen. It is frozen water vapor. Condensation occurs directly from the water vapor into snow (ice) crystals.

Water lens (a homemade magnifying glass)

Materials required:

—A soft plastic bucket or pail, between 5-pint and 5-quart capacity. (Most paint stores sell plastic paint-mixing pails in these sizes.)

—Clear plastic wrap (food wrap or dry cleaners' wrap; the latter works better because it tends to "give" more with the weight of the water).

¼-inch-wide elastic.

Directions:

1. Cut a piece of plastic wrap in a circle a few inches larger than the open end of the pail.
2. With a pen or a pencil draw three circles on the outer wall of the pail, each large enough for your childrens' hands to fit through. (Be sure to leave enough of a margin at the top, bottom, and sides of the circles to provide adequate supporting strength after the circles are cut out.)

3. With a sharp knife cut out the three circles.
4. Knot the elastic to make a big "rubber band" that will fit snugly around the top of the pail.
5. Lay the plastic wrap loosely across the top of the pail, fit the elastic around to hold the plastic in place *(see diagram on p. 210)*, and slowly pour water into the plastic until the weight of the water makes the plastic sag. Add as much water as you can without causing an overflow. Objects placed in the bucket will seem enlarged as the viewer looks through the plastic top.

—Adapted by courtesy of *Redbook Magazine*

Air

We cannot see air, but we can feel it. It has no shape or color, but it is all about us. We play with air, and it works for us.

1. Blow up a balloon, then release the air. The jet effect will be due to the air released from the balloon. Use a balloon on a medicine dropper in a small cardboard boat. It will move the boat as the air is released.
2. Wind helps to dry clothes. Take two handkerchiefs and wet them. Hang one in the wind and the other protected from wind. Which dries first?

Air is real. It can make things move. Wind is air in motion. Leaves move; sailboats move over the water. Fly a kite on a windy spring day.

Air takes up space. Crumple a piece of newspaper or paper towel and place in a plastic glass. Turn the glass upside down into a bowl of water. The water will not touch the paper because the air keeps the water out.

Air has weight. Blow up two balloons of the same size and hang them on a yardstick which is hung from its center to another yardstick so that the balloons balance. *(See diagram on p. 210.)* When one balloon is popped to let the air out, what happens to the balance rod? Why?

EXPERIENCES WITH MAGNETS

Experimenting with magnets offers young children opportunities to form many understandings on which scientific facts are based.

Some of the concepts which children may form through their play and experimentation with magnets are:

Magnets pull (attract) things made of iron and steel.
Magnets come in several different shapes and sizes.
Some magnets are stronger than others.
Magnets are stronger at their ends.
Magnets are used to help people in performing many kinds of work.
Magnets will pick up things made of iron or steel through such materials as cardboard, glass, plastic, paper, water, etc.

For a variety of experiences, magnets of differing shapes and strengths are needed:

horseshoe magnet
cylindrical magnet
bar magnet
U-magnet
ceramic magnet
electromagnet made with dry cell battery, plastic-covered copper wire, and large nail (See directions at the end of this section).

A few magnetic tools will be of interest to the children. Some of these might be:

magnetic screwdriver
magnetic pencil
magnetic key holder
magnetic hooks
magnetic memorandum boards
magnetic pot holders

Care of Magnets

Proper care of magnets is essential if they are to maintain their strength. When not in use, the "keeper" which comes with the magnet should be kept across the ends. The bar magnets should be stored together (opposite poles side by side). A wooden box makes the best storage container.

Making a Magnet

A paper clip, when straightened out, can be temporarily magnetized. Hold the paper clip firmly on the table and pull the magnet across it from left to right 20 to 25 times, being certain to pull the magnet in the same direction each time. This long, thin, magnetized paper clip will then be able to pick up other paper clips.

Activities Using Magnets

1. To determine which objects are of iron or steel, have the children collect and assemble such small items as:

pencil
eraser
bobby pin
rubber band
paper clips
small bits of cardboard
small plastic pill box
soft drink bottle cap
scrap of cloth
nickel
ping-pong ball
large nail
crayon
seashell
button
bottle cork
nut and bolt
piece of string
pair of blunt-end scissors
cotton ball
door key

Two shoe boxes are needed for sorting the objects. The boxes may be labeled in whatever way the children choose—one for objects which the magnet will pick up and the other for the objects which the magnet will not pick up. The boxes may say YES and NO or be identified by colors such as red and green.

2. To discover that some magnets are stronger than others, magnets of varying strengths may be given to the children for *experimentation*.

They will enjoy seeing which magnets can take an object from another magnet. They may also have some lightweight steel objects and some heavier ones, such as paper clips and a medium-size screwdriver.

3. To discover that magnets are stronger at the ends (poles), the children will need first of all to use bar magnets. If paper clips are placed

near a magnet lying flat on the table, they will "jump" to the ends of the bar.

When a horseshoe magnet is used, the children will find that it is the ends which pull and hold the objects.

The children can then experiment to see which magnet is the stronger, the bar or the horseshoe, and why. (The horseshoe magnet has both of its poles close enough together to work as a team in the "pulling" process.)

Warning: Iron filings should *never* be used in any science activity with young children, as they might get the filings in their eyes.

Making an Electromagnet

An electromagnet is one that is made with electricity. You will be able to have an "off-and-on magnet" when you follow these steps:

You will need a long, iron nail, a piece of plastic-covered copper wire (bell wire), and a 9-volt dry cell battery.

Begin by wrapping the wire around the nail about 25 times, leaving the ends of the wire equal lengths.

Scrape off the covering of both ends about an inch.

Connect one bare end of the wire to one of the screws on top of the battery. *(See diagram on p. 210.)*

Connect the other bare end to the other screw.

Now with the nail, pick up paper clips.

Loosen one screw on the battery to release the wire, and see what happens. The nail is no longer a magnet.

Reconnect the wire and you have a magnet again.

The electricity from the battery makes a circuit through the wire around the nail. This is what causes the nail to become a magnet. When one wire is disconnected, the electricity does not travel through the wire any longer. The nail is no longer a magnet.

By connecting and disconnecting the wire to the battery, one is able to have an "off-and-on magnet." This is a simple electromagnet.

4. To discover some of the ways magnets help people in performing work, the children will enjoy working with the magnetic tools given in a previous listing.

The electromagnet can be used to show

how the "magnetism" can be turned on and off by loosening one of the wires connected to the battery. Some of the children may have electric trains; many of their families have a washing machine and a vacuum cleaner. And most children have push-button doorbells. Although we cannot see the electromagnets in these machines, the electricity goes through the wires that are wrapped around the electromagnet.

5. To discover that magnets will attract iron or steel objects through such materials as cardboard, glass, plastic, paper, and water, here are some fun things to do:

a. Directing traffic with magnets

Materials needed: Strong horseshoe magnets, very small plastic cars into which paper clips have been glued, a sheet of cardboard on which streets have been drawn with a felt pen, and large blocks on which to elevate the cardboard of streets.

Activity: The small cars should be placed about on the cardboard ready for "operation" on the streets. *(See diagram on p. 210.)* Two children, one on each side, direct the cars in their movement by sliding the magnets along underneath the cars, on the underside of the cardboard.

b. Magnets working in water

Materials needed: Magnet on a string, nails, plastic tumbler of water.

Activity: Drop the nails in the water, then get them out without getting your hands wet. Let the child lower the magnet into the water and bring out the nails.

c. Magnet pulling through a plastic drinking glass

Materials needed: Magnet, clear plastic drinking glass, paper clip tied to a string.

Activity: Place the magnet in the plastic drinking glass and let the child hold the paper clip by the string near the glass and watch the magnet pull the clip to the side of the glass where the magnet touches.

d. Magnet pulling through the child's finger

Materials needed: Horseshoe magnet and paper clip.

Activity: Place index finger over paper clip. Hold the magnet against the finger on the top side and gently lift finger up. The paper clip will come up and stick to the finger as long as the magnet remains on the finger.

e. A fishing game

Materials needed: Fish cut out of plastic with a paper clip attached to the mouth, fishing pole made of a small piece of dowel with a small magnet attached to the line for bait, basin or plastic bucket of water. (A good outdoor activity.)

Activity: The children take turns fishing until all the fish are caught.

RESOURCES FOR ACTIVITIES WITH MAGNETS

Books

Ames, Gerald, and Wyler, Rose. *Prove It!* New York: Harper & Row, 1963, pp. 53–64.

Freeman, Mae. *The Real Magnet Book.* New York: Scholastic Book Services, 1970.

Parker, Bertha Morris, *et al. Magnets.* New York: Harper & Row.

Pine, Tillie S., and Levine, Joseph. *Magnets and How to Use Them.* New York: McGraw-Hill, 1958.

Filmstrip

Science Filmstrips—*Magnets.* Sets 1A and 2A. D. C. Heath Co.

Sources of Magnets

("Ten-cent store" magnets are ineffective for science experiments.)

Educational supply corporations usually handle magnets and magnet kits of good quality.

The following types of magnets are available from

Childcraft Education Corporation
964 Third Ave.
New York, N.Y. 10022:

    horseshoe magnet
    magnet laboratory kit
    giant horseshoe magnet
    ceramic magnets
    bar magnets

SOUND

Discoveries Children Can Make

Sound is made by people, animals, things, and physical elements.

Sounds may be loud or soft, high or low, quick or sustained.

Sounds are made when something vibrates.

Sound travels in all directions and through many kinds of materials.

Equipment Useful for Experimentation

tuning fork
brass bells of different sizes
stringed instrument
drum
rhythm instruments such as resonator bells, tone block, guiro, finger cymbals, triangle
autoharp
yardstick
stethoscope

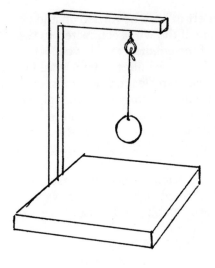

Materials for Demonstrating the Principles of Sound

small tin cans
cord (cotton, hard twist)
flower pots of different sizes
small wooden boxes
rubber bands of various sizes
mailing tubes
ticking clock
clear plastic bowls (small)
plastic funnels (small)
squares of felt, asbestos, masonite, carpet, etc.

Equipment for Use in Making Discoveries

Tin can telephones

Materials needed:
2 small tin cans
25' length of cotton cord (hard twist)

Punch a hole in the end of each can. Run the cord through the cans and secure with a large knot on the inside of each. Two children use the phone, one holding a can close around his mouth as he speaks, the other holding a can to his ear. The cord must be pulled taut between them. For answering, the children reverse the cans from mouth to ear and vice versa.

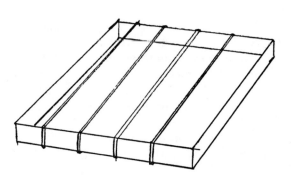

Stand for Observing Vibrations

Materials needed:
ping-pong ball
board 8″ × 8″ × 1″
wood strip 10″ × 1″ × 1″
wood strip 5″ × 1″ × 1″
small screw eye
tuning fork
Attach a ping-pong ball to a thread with

Let's Make Butter

Cream   Cup

Bowl   Butter Milk   Salt   Beater

Spoon   Butter

scotch tape and tie to the small screw eye on the arm of the stand. *(See diagram.)*

Strike the tuning fork and hold it close to the ping-pong ball and watch the ball bounce from the vibrations.

Rubber Band Instrument

Materials needed:

small wooden box without a top

several rubber bands of different lengths and widths

Slip the rubber bands over the box and pluck them. Pulling them more tightly over the edges of the box will change the pitches of the rubber bands. *(See diagram.)*

Experiences with Sound

1. Watching vibrations in water

Materials needed:

tuning fork

clear plastic drinking glass or small container filled with water

Directions: Strike tuning fork and immediately place the tines in the water. The water will be set in motion around the tuning fork as the vibrations move out from the fork.

2. Observing a simulated ear drum receiving sound

Materials needed:

small tin can with both ends cut out

large balloon

rubber band

a small amount of dry oatmeal or table salt

Directions: Cut the balloon so that it can be drawn tightly over one end of the tin can. Secure it tautly with the rubber band. Place a little of the oatmeal or salt on the top of the "drum." Turn on the record player, using a record with a very definite beat. Hold the drum with open end near the speaker until the oatmeal begins to jump around in time to the music. The child can understand that his eardrum vibrates when set in motion by sound waves, similarly to the head of this small drum.

3. Seeing how sound is transmitted or muted

Materials needed:

tuning fork

small wooden box with holes bored in one side

square of asbestos

Directions: Strike the tuning fork and hold it by its base and listen to the sound. Strike again and immediately hold the base on the table and note the difference. Repeat and hold the tuning fork on a piece of asbestos or the small wooden box. Note the distinct differences. Always be careful that the child does not touch the tines of the fork.

4. Observing how sound travels through material

Materials needed:

silver table fork

piece of string 30" long

Directions: Tie the handle of the fork securely in the center of the string. Wrap each end of string around each index finger several times and place one index finger in each ear. Gently strike the tines of the fork against the edge of a table and enjoy beautiful "Big Ben."

5. Tuned bottles or glasses

Materials needed:

8 glass bottles or 8 glasses of the same kind and size

water

Directions: Line up the glasses on the table. Tap each one gently with a silver spoon to see that the glasses full of air produce about the same tone when struck. Then let the children pour varying amounts of water into the glasses so that each glass produces a different tone. With careful discrimination in the use of the water, a musical scale may be produced. The children can play their own little tunes.

6. Listening to sound as it travels through materials

Materials needed:

ticking clock

yardstick

Directions: Hold the yardstick against the clock and stand at the other end with the yardstick to your ear. The sound will travel down the yardstick.

7. Discovering how sound is absorbed by some materials

Materials needed:

12" ruler

pencil

cotton

Directions: One child holds the ruler erect on a table and taps the end of the ruler. Across the table another child puts his ear to the table to hear the vibrations. Then the child holding the ruler places a thick piece of cotton under the ruler and taps it again. The child listening will detect that the sound is muffled. This is due to the fact that cotton contains many air spaces which are poor transmitters of vibrations.

8. Recording sounds for recognition

Young children are interested in all kinds of sounds, what makes them, and where they come from. With a small battery-operated tape recorder, a small group of children, with a parent or assistant teacher, might go for a listening walk and record the different sounds they hear (birds singing, cars passing, horns blowing, airplane overhead, ball bouncing, dog barking, etc.).

The group could return and play the tape for those who remained in the classroom and let them identify the outdoor sounds.

On another occasion a group, with an adult, could tape indoor sounds (water running, telephone ringing, toilet flushing, drum being played, someone whistling, child humming, a few notes played on the piano, etc.).

A recording which is excellent for sound recognition is "Muffin in the City—Muffin in the Country" (C114A). This 12″ long play record contains the stories of Margaret Wise Brown's books on sounds, *The Noisy Book* (city) and *The Country Noisy Book.* Books and recording are available from:

Children's Music Center
5373 W. Pico Blvd.
Los Angeles, Calif. 90019

9. Identifying objects by the sounds they make: bell, drum, scissors cutting, ball bouncing, baby doll crying, etc.

10. Identifying actions by the sounds they make: water running, door closing, clapping, etc.

11. Matching sounds using sound tubes
Materials needed:
10 tube-like containers with tops
(baking powder cans will be useful)

Directions: Place in five of the cans such items as ½ cup dry rice, 3 thumb tacks, 4 nails and a small jingle bell, a handful of acorns, and 3 marbles. Secure the tops on these. Mark the tops with a circle of red paper and glue securely. Then take the remaining cans and fill with the same items, matching each for the identical sound. Mark the tops of this set with circles of green paper.

Directions for use: The child lines up one set of the "tubes" and, shaking one at a time, listens for the matching tube of the other set.

PREPARING SIMPLE FOODS

Experiences in preparing a number of simple foods can result in numerous science learnings for young children.

Making Gelatin Dessert

A small group can work with a teacher making the gelatin dessert. The teacher may first read the directions to the children, then let one child open the box and pour the package into a mixing bowl, preferably clear pyrex so that the children can watch the change of the substance from a powder to a liquid when the boiling water is added.

Before adding the water to the gelatin, the children should have the opportunity of smelling, feeling, and tasting it. They could then guess what will happen to the gelatin powder when the hot water is added to it.

When the water is added and the powder is changed to a liquid, the children should talk about what has happened. After stirring in the correct amount of cold water, the children may be given a taste to see if it feels different in their mouths than it did as a powder.

The teacher may then pour this liquid into a small pitcher so that the children can pour it into little paper dessert dishes to have at their snack or party on the following day.

Again the children may speculate on what will happen to the gelatin when placed in the refrigerator. They can check their guesses the next morning.

In the conversation that takes place during the process, the teacher will acquaint the children with such words as *powder, liquid, dissolve, congeal,* and *solid.*

Several packages of fruit-flavored gelatin will be needed to serve the entire class, so every child can have this experience in a small group.

On the following day the children can recall the steps in the process of making the gelatin. When they eat the jello, they can check themselves on their prediction of what would happen to it when refrigerated.

Think of all the learnings taking place in this one simple experience. Besides the science understandings already pointed out, there is vocabulary development and such math concepts as measuring the water and counting the number of dessert dishes of jello that each box would fill. All the senses were involved except hearing.

Churning Butter

This activity is almost unheard of in the home life of the urban child. Making butter may also be a new experience to many kindergarten teachers.

The teacher can make a large chart which will help the children record what they do. The following are needed: one-half pint of whipping cream, tall glass bowl, dover beater, wooden spoon, salt shaker, small plate, glass measuring cup.

The chart might include:

Use colored tag board for the chart, or draw each symbol on a sheet of colored construction paper. *(See diagram on p. 214)*

The whipping cream should be left out of the refrigerator for several hours. Warm cream makes butter faster.

A child may open the cream carton and pour the cream into a clear measuring cup to determine how much cream the group will be working with. Another child may use white chalk to color in the picture of a cup to indicate the amount of cream there is to whip.

The cream is then poured into the glass bowl, and the children take turns whipping it. They will notice the changes through which the butter goes—bubbly at first, then increasing in volume and becoming thick. As they continue to whip the cream, they will notice little yellow "specks" appearing and the cream getting thinner.

Then the yellow "specks," which are bits of butter, suddenly begin sticking to each other and forming around the beater. The butter is churned, but it must be pulled together with a wooden spoon into a ball.

Pour the buttermilk into the measuring cup. Let the group see how much buttermilk they now have and have one child use white chalk to color in the amount on the other picture of the measuring cup.

Pour ice water into the bowl with the butter and let the children mash the butter pat around in the water with the *wooden* spoon. They will notice that the water begins to look milky. This is what is called "washing the butter."

Pour off the ice water and pour more ice water into the bowl and wash the butter again. Repeat this until the water does not look milky. You will then know that all the buttermilk is out of the butter.

Let a child press the butter out flat in the bowl and sprinkle it lightly with salt. Work the butter to mix in the salt, and make it into a pat.

Another child may color the picture of the pat of butter with yellow chalk.

The butter can then be refrigerated and will be ready to eat on crackers for snack the next day.

The group will want to recall the process of butter-making. If the pictures of the materials involved were drawn on separate sheets, they may be used to let the children arrange them in the order of the process.

Making Ice Cream

Making ice cream offers the children opportunities for math and science learnings, vocabulary enrichment, and delightful socializing inspired by delicious dishes of ice cream as a special snack-time treat.

The teacher may make a large rebus chart of the recipe for the group to follow as they mix the ingredients for the custard.

The following recipe for uncooked ice cream will serve 25:

    2 quarts sweet milk
    1 pint whipping cream
    4 cups sugar
    8 eggs
    4 teaspoonfuls vanilla

Beat the eggs until well mixed. Add the sugar and beat more. To this add the cream and mix well. Add the milk and vanilla and mix well. Pour into freezer container and put in place with the dasher inserted and connected to the top and handle of the freezer.

Use one part ice cream salt to four parts crushed ice. (Be sure to set the freezer in a plastic pan to catch the water that flows out.)

Turn the handle slowly until it becomes too hard to turn. The children will not need help turning until the very end of the process.

Making Peanut Butter

All that is needed is a manual food grinder, a dish, spoon, and roasted Spanish peanuts.

In order to avoid having peanut butter that is too salty, the peanuts should be rubbed in paper towels.

The peanuts should be ground and re-ground. Each time the ground peanuts are put back into the grinder, the more like peanut butter the substance will become. It will look and taste like commercial peanut butter, but the texture will be grainy.

Other Cooking Activities

If the kindergarten has access to a stove, the children will enjoy baking cookies and bread, making candy, or cooking fruit sauce.

THE SUN

The main concept we hope children will develop consists of understanding the following statements:

We get our daylight from the sun.
The sun warms the earth.
The sun is shining all the time—even on cloudy days.
On sunny days we see shadows.
On cloudy days there are no shadows.

Firsthand observations and frequent discussions will help the children develop meaningful concepts.

The children will enjoy watching the shadows of each other and of objects.

They will enjoy watching shadows change shape as the morning progresses and the sun is nearer overhead.

It will be interesting to record a child's shadow two or three times during one morning. To do this the teacher will need to tape a large sheet of brown wrapping paper on a walkway that is always in the sun. A child may stand with his back to the sun so that his shadow falls on the paper. The teacher may draw around the shadow with a felt pen and mark the time of day. A little before noon the same child may stand in the same place while the teacher draws around his shadow with a felt pen of another color and marks the time of day.

Some of the children would enjoy having their shadows drawn and then painting them dark gray or black.

Be sure to use the poem "My Shadow" by Robert Louis Stevenson, printed on page 157 in this book.

Shadows may be made indoors by shining a gooseneck desk lamp on a large piece of white poster board taped to the wall. The children may use their hands or objects. This is a good rainy day activity.

USING A PRISM

One way to produce a spectrum with a prism is to hold the prism with one edge toward a filmstrip projector and project this on a large piece of white poster board. You might compare the spectrum with a rainbow.

This same activity may be performed using the sunlight in the room rather than the projector.

This would be a good time to suggest to some of the children that they might want to try to make some colors they observed in the spectrum.

Using the primary colors—red, yellow, blue—allow the children to experiment with mixing colors and making new colors.

The picture book *Color Kittens*, by Margaret Wise Brown, would be appropriate to have for the children.

WEATHER

Young children are interested in the weather. They are beginning to understand how it affects their daily lives in different ways.

Taking special note of the weather at a regular time during the morning helps to make

January						
Sun.	Mon.	Tues.	Wed.	Thurs.	Fri.	Sat.
	O	☂	☃	☁	O	6
7	8	9	10	11	12	13
14	15	16	17	18	19	20
21	22	23	24	25	26	27
28	29	30	31			

O yellow Sun ☁ Gray Cloud ☂ colored Umbrella ☃ Snowman

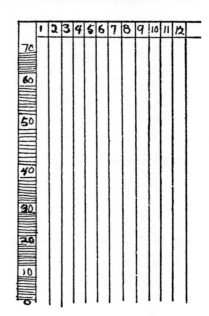

the children more aware of their environment. This, of course, would lose its effectiveness if it were a daily routine all through the year. The months of January and March are months of contrast. If the children keep a record of the daily weather, these months would be good for study purposes.

A large calendar made on poster board and mounted on the wall down on the children's level will make it easy for the children to record their daily observations. Symbols representing sunny weather, rain, snow, and cloudy weather may be made and kept available for the kindergarten "weatherman" of the day to mount on the calendar.

The group would also be interested in keeping a daily record of the temperature.

As the children note the outdoor temperature on a large thermometer, they might make a simple graph showing the daily temperature.

The teacher needs to draw the lines for the graph. The 24" × 36" size of one-inch ruled paper is easy to use. The lines needed for marking off the days are already printed.

With red crayon the weatherman can fill in the temperature for the day. The record should be made at approximately the same time each day. (The temperatures recorded above are: January 1, 22°; January 2, 30°; January 3, 24°; January 4, 40°.)

The song "The Weatherman," page 88, is excellent to use with this activity because the class asks the question, "What is the weather?" to which the weatherman answers, "I say it's *sunny.*"

COLLECTIONS

Seeds

Seeds of all kinds can be categorized in several different ways:

A. *Ways seeds travel*

1. Seeds that fly through the air—pine, maple, catalpa, ash.
2. Seeds that float through the air with parachutes—dandelion, cattail, milkweed.
3. Seeds that steal rides on animals' fur and peoples' clothes—beggar-ticks, cockleburs.
4. Seeds that are carried by birds—small fruits and berries.
5. Seeds that float—water lily and coconut.
6. Seeds that are scattered when the seedpod bursts—okra, beans, peas, touchme-nots, pansies.
7. Seeds that roll and are carried away by squirrels—nuts of various kinds.

Note-paper boxes with acetate tops are good containers for larger seeds. Plastic sandwich bags and pill bottles are useful for displaying smaller seeds.

B. Seeds people eat

corn	peanut
bean	sunflower
pea	tomato
squash	strawberry
rice	coconut
pecan	walnut

C. Seeds people do not eat

peach	grapefruit
apple	avocado
orange	prune

D. Seeds ground up for food

wheat (flour)
soybean (cooking oil)
corn (corn meal)
oats (oatmeal)
peanuts (peanut butter)

Abandoned Birds' Nests

These will show the different types of construction as well as the building materials used by different species of birds.

Feathers

These can show shape, color, and size, and can range from feathers from small song birds to turkeys and even a peacock (if you are that fortunate). Collecting feathers might be one objective of a trip to a farm.

Leaf Collections

It will be interesting to the group to collect leaves in the fall of the year (if you live in a section of the country where the leaves of deciduous trees turn bright colors). They can be enjoyed for their color, then can be pressed for a week or so between layers of newspaper. They may then be placed between two sheets of plastic food wrap to preserve them.

The children may then categorize them by shape, putting together the leaves shaped alike: white oak, sugar maple, tulip tree, linden, elm, etc.

In the spring the children may enjoy the new green leaves from the same species. Adults will probably have to collect the leaves in the spring. These collections might be made early in spring while the leaves are still quite small, to see whether or not the children can match them by shape to the leaves collected in the fall.

Rock Collection

Pebbles and rocks are especially fascinating to young children. They will gather them wherever they are to be found.

The children will be interested in the smooth, round rocks and pebbles and how they differ from the rough, sharp-edged ones. They will enjoy finding different colored rocks.

Fossils intrigue children. These might be borrowed from a parent who is a collector. When parents are informed of the group's "rock collection" interest, they can help their children find specimens when on camping trips or family excursions.

A parent or friend of the group who is a "rock hound" might be willing to bring some of his or her collection for the children to see.

The rock collection is one that can be added to all during the year, although the collection would not be in the science center continuously.

Caterpillar and Cocoon Collections

In the fall caterpillars may be brought into the kindergarten for observation. Care should be taken to provide each caterpillar with fresh leaves from the tree or bush on which it was found. Place the caterpillars in insect cages with a twig or two included from which a caterpillar may suspend its cocoon.

In the spring, when the moth emerges, the children will witness the miracle of change (metamorphosis). If the moth is a female (antennae will be wide, fern-like), she will lay eggs. In this case the children will have seen the complete life cycle of the moth.

Note: The cocoons should be sprinkled lightly with water every few weeks, or "on days that it rains" could be used as a reminder.

Seashell Collection

This is another type of collection which could be added to as families make trips to the beach or as friends living near a beach send shells to the kindergarten.

A very good activity for kindergartens in different geographical areas is to make collections of items native to each area and exchange with kindergartens in other geographical locations.

A growing seashell collection will include shells of all shapes, sizes, and colors, as well as starfish, sea biscuits, coral, sea horses, and other items.

Books about seashells should be available with this collection so that the children may match a shell to a picture of it.

Note-paper boxes with acetate tops are good for displaying the items in the collection.

BOOKS HELPFUL IN IDENTIFYING ITEMS

Leaves

Parker, Bertha M., *et al. Leaves.* New York: Harper & Row.

Shells

Hutchinson, William M. *A Child's Book of Sea Shells.* New York: Maxton Publishers, Inc., 1954.

Low, Donald F. *The How and Why Wonder Book of Sea Shells.* New York: Wonder-Treasure Books, 1961.

Podendorf, Illa. *The True Book of Pebbles and Shells.* Chicago: Childrens Press, 1954.

Rocks

Hyler, Nelson W. *The How and Why Wonder Book of Rocks and Minerals.* New York: Wonder-Treasure Books, 1960.

FURTHER SCIENCE EXPERIENCES

For activities in discovery through sensory perception, see *Church Kindergarten Resource Book,* by Josephine Newbury, pages 219–220.

For activities relating to the seasons of the year and weather, refer to *Church Kindergarten Resource Book,* pages 220–221.

For further activities with the calendar, see *Church Kindergarten Resource Book,* pages 222–223.

The opportunities for science activities in the following are in no way suggested as an outline of a year's work, but are merely indicative of some of the science activities that center around the seasons:

A. Autumn

   1. Possible Observations:
     a. Weather:
      The days are cooler.
      The days are becoming shorter, the nights longer.
      Frost often forms on the grass and plants during the night.
     b. Animals:
      Some birds go to warmer places for the winter.
      Some animals store food for the winter.
      Fewer insects are seen in autumn.
     c. Plants:
      The leaves of many trees become brightly colored.
      Many trees lose their leaves.
      Seeds of many plants ripen.
      Different kinds of seeds travel about in different ways.
      Some seeds develop inside fleshy fruits.
     d. People:
      People must live to fit the season.
      People get ready for winter by harvesting crops and putting food away.

   2. Kinds of Group Activities
     a. Discussions of observations such as weather getting cooler, seeds blowing through the air, frost on the ground, etc.
     b. Collecting and examining seeds, cocoons, colored leaves, empty birds' nests, etc.
     c. Hearing stories and singing songs about autumn.
     d. Reporting on weekend trips to mountains or country with family, bringing in house plants at night to avoid frost, and buying warmer clothes.
     e. Excursions to parks to observe trees, birds, squirrels, etc. Walk in woods to collect nuts (watch squirrels gather nuts).
     f. Experiment with seeds to find out what is inside. (Use large lima beans; soak and open to see the baby plants.) Plant lima beans on cotton and watch them sprout.
     g. Look at picture books with illustrations about children's experiences in autumn; look at projected slides, filmstrips, and movies about autumn.
     h. Watch caterpillar spin cocoon.

i. Before frost, collect cuttings of geranium, coleus, and begonia, and place in plastic glasses of water to watch sprout.

j. Plant flower bulbs.

B. Winter

1. Some Essential Concepts:

   a. *Weather:*

   The days are cold and the nights colder.

   The days are shorter, the nights longer.

   Ice and snow become water when melted.

   b. *Animals:*

   People help take care of animals.

   Some animals eat food they stored up in the fall.

   Some cocoons live through the winter.

   It is harder for birds to find food in winter.

   Some animals hibernate all winter.

   Some animals grow warmer coats for winter.

   c. *Plants:*

   Some plants that lose their leaves have buds for next spring's leaves.

   Some plants die in winter, but they have seeds for new plants in spring.

   Some plants die, but their roots live under the ground and send up new plants in spring.

   d. *People:*

   People wear warm clothing when they go outdoors.

   People have fires to keep their homes warm.

   People walk carefully on ice and snow so they won't fall.

2. Kinds of Activities:

   a. Discussions about first freeze of the season: frost on the windowpanes; children's new warm sweaters, mittens, boots, etc.

   b. Making a feeding station for birds and keeping feed in it.

   c. Watching thermometer indoors and out and comparing.

   d. Keeping a weather chart, putting up pictures illustrating the kind of weather each day.

   e. Observing snow crystals through magnifying glasses.

   f. Experimenting with water in freezing weather (freezing water in a plastic jar with a lid on it, blowing soap bubbles outdoors and watching them freeze). Experimenting with evaporating water (in pan over radiator and in a milk bottle in closet). Boiling water in shallow pan or in tea kettle to observe vapor.

   g. Enjoying stories and songs about experiences of wintertime.

   h. Planting various kinds of plants in water—sweet potato, avocado seeds, tops of turnips and carrots, beets, etc.—and watching the growth.

   i. Enjoying pictures in books, in viewmaster, and projected pictures about activities of wintertime.

   j. Experiences connected with physical science: playing with magnets to observe which objects they will attract; striking glasses filled with varying amounts of water to note differences in pitch; playing with different sizes of drums to observe tone and pitch; playing with prism and mirror to observe reflection of sunlight and colors; observing machines in construction; using pulley and wheels in construction work in kindergarten.

C. Spring

1. Some Essential Concepts:

   a. *Weather:*

   It is growing warmer.

   The days are growing longer and the nights shorter.

   The sun warms the ground.

   There are usually more rainy days in spring.

   The wind blows very hard in early spring.

   b. *Animals:*

   Birds build their nests.

   Birds lay eggs and hatch families of baby birds.

   Baby animals of many kinds appear in spring.

   Moths and butterflies come out of their cocoons.

c. *Plants:*

Plants that live through winter begin to grow.

Seeds grow into new plants.

Buds on trees begin to open—fruit trees bloom.

Plants need sunshine, water, and air to grow.

d. *People:*

People wear lighter-weight clothes.

People do not have to heat their homes, and they can leave the windows and doors open.

People plant flower and vegetable gardens.

2. Kinds of Activities:

a. Plant a small vegetable garden and care for it.

b. Plant flower seeds in cups to transplant.

c. Raise tadpoles.

d. Set a hen and care for her (or use an incubator), keeping a record of days it takes the eggs to hatch.

e. Take walks to look for signs of spring —flowers, new little leaves, etc.

f. Observe cocoons hatching and moths laying eggs.

g. Take an excursion to a pet shop and to a greenhouse.

h. Observe birds building nests and getting food for babies. (Put out nesting materials for the birds.)

i. Observe an ant colony which has been caught and placed in a narrow glass container or use a commercial "ant farm."

j. Observe the thermometer, watching the mercury rise.

k. Enjoy hearing stories and singing songs about experiences in spring.

l. Experiment with wind, feeling it turn a pinwheel. Fly a kite.

m. Observe clouds, rain, and thunderstorms. Measure rain fall.

n. Collecting rocks—breaking them to see what they are like.

o. Enjoying audio-visual materials about experiences in springtime.

p. Keep a weather chart on a large calendar, putting up pictures of the kind of weather on each day.

RESOURCES

We need to take a fresh look at materials, considering them as a means not only of self-expression but also as a child's media for discovery about himself and about the world around him, as the apparatus for basic experimentation within the framework of a creative atmosphere. Materials, then, are among the tools with which the child works out concepts. Through these concrete experiences the intellectual concepts take form and prepare him for the comprehension of the abstract.[4]

Equipment and Scrap Materials
Useful for Science Experiences

animal cage (preferably metal)

aquarium

balloons

bicycle pump

cages for insects

calendars of different kinds

cigar boxes

clock

compass

copper wire

corks of different sizes and shapes

cotton

drinking straws (plastic)

dry cell battery—9 volt

egg cartons (molded type)

flower pots

funnels—plastic and of different sizes

gardening tools

hourglass

jars (widemouthed, gallon size)

kaleidoscope

lamp chimney

locks and keys

magnets of all kinds and shapes

magnifying glasses

mailing tubes (cardboard)

masking tape

measuring equipment (½ cup, cup, pint, quart—all plastic)

medicine droppers

mirror

paper cups

periscope

[4]Charlotte B. Winsor, *Creative Activities for Young Children* (New York: Bank Street Publications, 1953), p. 4.

plastic drinking glasses (clear)
plastic cooking baster
plastic pill bottles—different sizes
plastic squeeze bottles
prism
pulleys and rope
rain gauge
rotary egg beater
rubber sheeting
rubber tubing (½″ × 3′)
rubber bands (different widths and sizes)
rubber combs
ruler
scraps of materials of all kinds of textures
scales for weighing and measuring
scales (balance type)
screen wire
small boxes with acetate tops
sponges
silver dinner fork
stethoscope
string
terrarium
tissue paper
thermometer
tin cans (8 oz.)
trowel
tuning fork—"C"
watering can
water tub
yardstick

Children's Books

Blough, Glenn O. *Not Only for Ducks: The Story of Rain.* New York: McGraw-Hill, 1954.

———. *Water Appears and Disappears.* Evanston, Ill.: Row, Peterson & Co., 1943.

Brown, Margaret W. *Color Kittens.* Racine, Wis.: Golden Press, 1958.

———. *The Dead Bird.* New York: William R. Scott, 1958.

Bulla, Clyde R. *A Tree Is a Plant.* New York: Thomas Y. Crowell Co., 1960.

———. *What Makes a Shadow?* New York: Thomas Y. Crowell Co., 1962.

Busch, Phyllis S. *At Home in Its Habitat: Animal Neighborhoods.* New York: World Publishing Co., 1970.

Davis, Alice V. *Timothy Turtle.* New York: E. M. Hale & Co., 1940.

De Regniers, Beatrice S., and Gordon, Isabel. *The Shadow Book.* New York: Harcourt Brace Jovanovich, 1960.

Ets, Marie Hall. *Gilberto and the Wind.* New York: Viking Press, 1963.

———. *Play with Me.* New York: Viking Press, 1955.

Flack, Marjorie. *Tim Tadpole and the Great Bullfrog.* Garden City, N. Y.: Doubleday & Co., 1959.

Friskey, Margaret. *Johnny and the Monarch.* Chicago: Childrens Press, 1961.

Foster, Doris V. *A Pocketful of Seasons.* New York: Lothrop, Lee & Shepard Co., 1961.

Gans, Roma. *It's Nesting Time.* New York: Thomas Y. Crowell Co., 1964.

Garelick, May. *Where Does the Butterfly Go When It Rains?* New York: Scholastic Book Services, 1970.

Gibson, Myra. *What Is Your Favorite Smell, My Dear?* New York: Grosset & Dunlap, 1964.

Hazen, Barbara S. *Where Do Bears Sleep?* Reading, Mass.: Addison-Wesley, 1969.

Holland, Vicki. *We Are Having a Baby.* New York: Charles Scribner's Sons, 1972.

Howell, Ruth Rea. *Everything Changes.* New York: Atheneum, 1968.

Huntington, Harriet. *Let's Go Outdoors.* Garden City, N. Y.: Doubleday & Co., 1939.

Kay, Helen. *One Mitten Lewis.* New York: Lothrop, Lee & Shepard Co., 1955.

Keats, Ezra Jack. *Pet Show!* New York: The Macmillan Co., 1972.

———. *The Snowy Day.* New York: Viking Press, 1962.

Kelling, Furn. *Listen to the Night.* Nashville: Broadmen Press, 1957.

Larrick, Nancy. *Rain, Hail, Sleet & Snow.* Champaign, Ill.: Garrard, 1961.

Mabie, Peter. *The Little Duck Who Loved the Rain!* Chicago: Follett Publishing Co., 1950.

Marsh, Jessie Brown. *The New Little Fuzzy Green Worm.* St. Louis, Mo.: The Bethany Press, 1960.

McCloskey, Robert. *Make Way for Ducklings.* New York: Viking Press, 1941.

———. *Time of Wonder.* New York: Viking Press, 1957.

McKie, Roy, and Eastman, Philip D. *Snow.* Westminster, Md.: Random House, 1962.

Meeks, Esther K. *In John's Back Yard.* Chicago: Follett Publishing Co., 1957.

Miles, Betty. *A Day of Summer.* New York: Alfred A. Knopf, 1960.

Parker, Bertha M. *The Wonder of the Seasons.* Racine, Wis.: Golden Press, 1966.

Parker, Bertha M., et al. *Birds in Your Backyard.* New York: Harper & Row, 1959.

Podendorf, Illa. *Living Things Change.* Chicago: Childrens Press, 1971.

———. *Things To Do with Water.* Chicago: Childrens Press, 1971.

———. *The True Book of Insects.* Chicago: Childrens Press, 1954.

———. *The True Book of Pebbles and Shells.* Chicago: Childrens Press, 1954.

———. *The True Book of Pets.* Chicago: Childrens Press, 1954.

———. *The True Book of Science Experiments.* Chicago: Childrens Press, 1954.

———. *The True Book of Sounds We Hear.* Chicago: Childrens Press, 1955.

Pringle, Lawrence. *From Field to Forest: How Plants and Animals Changed the Land.* New York: World Publishing Co., 1970.

Schlein, Miriam. *Little Red Nose.* New York: Abelard-Schuman, 1955.

Selsam, Millicent E. *Seeds and More Seeds.* New York: Harper & Row, 1959.

———. *Terry and the Caterpillars.* New York: Harper & Row, 1962.

Showers, Paul. *Find Out by Touching.* New York: Thomas Y. Crowell Co., 1961.

———. *The Listening Walk.* New York. Thomas Y. Crowell Co., 1961.

Simon, Mina. *Who Knows When Winter Goes?* Chicago: Follett Publishing Co., 1965.

Tresselt, Alvin R. *The Beaver Pond.* New York: Lothrop, Lee & Shepard, Co., 1970.

———. *The Dead Tree.* New York: Parents Magazine Press, 1972.

———. *Hi, Mr. Robin!* New York: Lothrop, Lee & Shepard Co., Inc., 1950.

———. *Johnny Maple Leaf.* New York: Lothrop, Lee & Shepard Co., 1948.

———. *Rain Drop Splash!* New York: Lothrop, Lee & Shepard Co., 1946.

———. *White Snow, Bright Snow.* New York: Lothrop, Lee & Shepard Co., 1947.

Udry, Janice. *A Tree Is Nice.* New York: Harper & Row, 1956.

Van Leeuwen, Jean, ed. *One Day in Summer.* Westminster, Md.: Random House, 1969.

Watson, Jane Werner. *Wonders of Nature.* New York: Golden Press, 1958.

Webber, Irma E. *Bits That Grow Big.* New York: William R. Scott, 1949.

———. *Travelers All: The Story of How Plants Go Places.* New York: William R. Scott, 1944.

———. *Up Above and Down Below.* New York: William R. Scott, 1943.

White, Mary Sue. *Touch and Tell!* Nashville; Broadman Press, 1962.

Wolcott, Carolyn M. *God Gave Us Seasons.* Nashville: Abingdon Press, 1958.

Zion, Gene. *Really Spring.* New York: Harper & Row, 1956.

Zolotow, Charlotte S. *Over and Over.* New York: Harper & Row, 1957.

Bibliography of Teaching Resources

Science Books

Association for Childhood Education International. *Young Children and Science.* Washington, D.C.: A.C.E.I.

Blough, Glenn O., and Campbell, Marjorie H. *Making and Using Classroom Science Materials in the Elementary School.* New York: Holt, Rinehart & Winston, 1954.

Blough, Glenn O., and Schwartz, Julius. *Elementary-School Science and How to Teach It.* 4th ed. New York: Holt, Rinehart & Winston, 1969.

Brandwein, Paul, and Cooper, Elizabeth. *Concepts in Science: Teacher's Edition K.* New York: Harcourt, Brace and World, Inc., 1967.

Jacobson, Willard J., *et al. Looking Into Science.* New York: American Book Co., 1968.

Jacobson, Willard, and Cowe, Eileen. *Beginning Science: Teacher's Edition.* New York: American Book Co., 1966.

Mallinson, George, *et al. Science 1.* Morristown, N.J.: Silver Burdett Co, 1968.

Piltz, Albert, *et al. Discovering Science.* Columbus, Ohio: Charles E. Merrill Publishing Co., 1970.

Reader's Digest Editors. *Our Amazing World of Nature: Its Marvels and Mysteries.* New York: Funk & Wagnalls Co., 1969.

Kindergarten Texts

Heffernan, Helen, and Todd, Vivian. *The Kindergarten Teacher,* ch. 9, "The Child Enters His Scientific World." Boston: D. C. Heath & Co., 1960.

Lambert, Hazel M. *Early Childhood Education,* ch. 14, "Teaching Science." Rockleigh, N. J.: Allyn & Bacon, 1960.

Leeper, Sarah Hammond, *et al. Good Schools for Young Children,* rev. ed., ch. 14, "Science." New York: The Macmillan Co., 1968.

Newbury, Josephine. *Church Kindergarten Resource Book.* Rev. ed. Richmond: John Knox Press, 1970.

Rudolf, Marguerita, and Cohen, Dorothy. *Kindergarten: A Year of Learning,* ch. 6, "Science Experiences for Children and Teachers." New York: Appleton-Century-Crofts, 1964.

Todd, Vivian E., and Heffernan, Helen. *The Years Before School,* ch. 9, "Building Science Concepts." New York: The Macmillan Co., 1964.

Wills, Clarice, and Lendberg, Lucile. *Kindergarten for Today's Children,* ch. 9, "Science for Children Under Six." Chicago: Follett Publishing Co., 1967.

Sources of Teaching Resources

American Nature Association
1214 Sixteenth St., N.W.
Washington, D.C. 20006
    Publishers of *Nature.* Write for catalog of free and inexpensive materials.

National Audubon Society
1130 Fifth Ave.
New York, N.Y. 10028
    Write for catalog of materials.

National Dairy Council
111 North Canal St.
Chicago, Ill. 60606
    Write for a catalog of health education materials and for the address of your local Dairy Council.

National Wildlife Federation
1412 Sixteenth St., N.W.
Washington, D.C. 20036

Filmstrips

Family Filmstrip Kit No. 1—Stories About the Seasons (available from denominational audio-visual centers):
    "God's Autumn World"
    "God's Care in Winter"
    "Playing in the Rain"
    "Picnic in the Country"

Society for Visual Education, Inc.
(Singer Education and Training Products
1345 Diversey Parkway
Chicago, Ill. 60614):
    "A Visit to the Zoo"
    "Fall Adventures"
    "Winter Adventures"
    "Spring Adventures"
    "Summer Adventures"
    "Farm Animals and Pets"
    "Autumn Is Here"—color
    "Winter Is Here"—color
    "Spring Is Here"—color

D. C. Heath & Company
Boston, Mass.
    "Seeds Grow Into Plants"
    "Magnets and Electricity"

Coronet Filmstrips: Discovering Your Senses
    "Your Eyes Are for Seeing"
    "Your Ears Are for Hearing"
    "Your Skin Is for Feeling"
    "Your Tongue Is for Tasting"
    "Your Nose Is for Smelling"
    "Your Senses Work Together"
    (6 filmstrips with 3 records)

Films

Wonders in Plant Growth. Ten minutes; color. Produced by Churchill Films.
    Two children grow plants from a bean and a squash seed, a geranium stem, and a sweet potato root. The growth processes are illustrated in time-lapse photography.
    Spring Comes to the Pond. Thirteen minutes; color. Coronet Instructional Films.
    Shows the birth and life habits of ducks, birds, frogs, insects, turtles, in and around a pond in New England in early spring. The recorded voices of these creatures make the film very realistic.
    Monarch Butterfly Story. Eleven minutes; color. Encyclopaedia Britannica Educational Corporation.
    Shows the successive phases of development from caterpillar through chrysalis to butterfly, illus-

trated by the use of closeup and time-lapse photography.

Encyclopaedia Britannica Films
(1150 Wilmette Ave.
Wilmette, Ill. 60091):
    "Children in Autumn," 11 min., color.
    "Children in Winter," 11 min., color.

Coronet Instructional Films
(65 East South Water St.
Chicago, Ill. 60601):
    "Spring Is an Adventure," 10 min., color.
    "Summer Is an Adventure," 11 min., color.
    "How Animals Live in Winter," 10 min., color.

Recordings

Carrot Seed by Ruth Krauss. Children's Record Guild.
    Muffin in the City, a recording of *The Noisy Book* by Margaret Wise Brown. Young People's Records.
    Muffin in the Country, a recording of *The Country Noisy Book* by Margaret Wise Brown. Young People's Records.
    Wait Till the Moon Is Full accompanies the book by the same title by Margaret Wise Brown. New York: Harper & Row, 1948.

Pictures

Picture Foldouts

The picture foldout is a new type of visual for use in teaching children to categorize and thus understand important concepts. Each of the foldout sets available in the science program contains six picture foldouts in full color. Each opens to a 14" × 28" picture.
    The science foldouts are entitled:
    "Animal Homes"
    "Animals That Help Us"
    "Plants That Provide Food"
    "Pets"

Study Prints

    "Baby Animals of the Wild"
    "Insects and Spiders"

Sequence Charts

These charts show the events in the life cycle in the correct time sequence. Each chart consists of six panels, 11" × 14" each. The chart when unfolded is 6 feet long. Resource materials are printed on the reverse side of the chart.
    The four charts available are:
    "Life Cycle of a Robin"
    "Life Cycle of a Monarch Butterfly"
    "Life Cycle of a Frog"
    "The Story of Corn"

The above picture foldouts, study prints, and sequence charts are available from:

The Child's World
P.O. Box 681
Elgin, Ill. 60120

Teaching Picture Sets
Lyons, Department N
430 Wrightwood Ave.
Elmhurst, Ill. 60126
  Sets of 12 pictures each:
    "Seasons"
    "Science Themes" No. 1
    "Science Themes" No. 2
    "Plants and Seeds"

Society for Visual Education, Inc.
1345 Diversey Parkway
Chicago, Ill. 60614
  Picture-Story Study Prints: Basic Science Series
    SP-101—Common Insects, Group 1
    SP-102—Spring Wild Flowers, Group 1
    *SP-103—Wild Animals, Group 1
    *SP-104—Common Birds, Group 1
    *SP-105—Pets

    *SP-106—Farm and Ranch Animals
    *SP-112—Zoo Animals
    *SP-117—Familiar Birds—Their Young and Nests

Sets marked with an asterisk have a record that accompanies the set. Records are priced extra. A catalog is available.

Magazines

Arizona Highways
2039 West Lewis Ave.
Phoenix, Ariz. 85009

Audubon Magazine
National Audubon Society
Audubon House
1130 Fifth Ave.
New York, N.Y. 10028

National Wildlife
Ranger Rick's Nature Magazine
1412 Sixteenth St., N.W.
Washington, D.C. 20036

12
Math Experiences for Young Children

I hear, and I forget—
I see, and I remember—
I do, and I understand.
　　　　　　　—*Ancient proverb*

The materials presented in this chapter are not intended as a mathematics curriculum for kindergarten, but rather a source of suggestions which have been found helpful in developing mathematical concepts with young children.

No formalized period is scheduled in the nursery school, kindergarten, or child development center school day for teaching number concepts. However, the experiences and activities are so planned and organized that the teaching is developed through *incidental* and *not accidental* experiences which provide opportunities for learning.[1]

Mathematical activities integrated throughout the daily sessions will provide the kindergarten child with opportunities to develop such abilities as:

acquiring meaningful math vocabulary related to shape, size, time, weight, and distance, and including quantitative words such as more, many, short, etc.;

learning to understand one-to-one relationships;

being able to recognize small sets of objects without having to count them (a set of five objects would probably be the largest group the child could recognize without counting);

beginning to understand the meaning of cardinal numbers o through 6 (how many *more* or *less* is a part of this understanding as well as the concept of *how many*);

using ordinal numbers situationally with the calendar and in lining objects up in building—or in recognizing turns in playing games ("Tommy is *first*. Jay is *second*. Ellen is *third*, and Anne is *last*.");

recognizing geometric shapes—circle, square, triangle, and rectangle—in the child's environment;

becoming aware of different means of measurement—of space, time, weight, volume, and temperature—situationally in experiences that occur in the group;

discriminating spatial relationships and making comparisons.

NUMBERS PERMEATE DAILY LIVING

Numbers permeate the life of the kindergarten child. In fact, number concepts may be found in nearly everything he does.

Jocelyn Bursten says that teachers "should encourage the child's awareness of all these concepts in order that he may have a solid foundation upon which he can build. Mathematical concepts do not just appear; they develop in growth."[2] Analyzing the school day, we see where opportunities exist within the program for solving mathematical problems and practicing mathematical understandings.

MATH ACTIVITIES AND THE DAY'S PROGRAM

Action Songs

"Triangle, Circle, or Square"
"One Shape, Three Shapes"
  Source: Recording—*Learning Basic Skills Through Music*, Vol. 2, by Hap Palmer.

"Listen and Do"
"Walk Around the Circle"
  Source: Recording—*Learning Basic Skills Through Music—Building Vocabulary*, by Hap Palmer.
Records available from
Educational Activities, Inc.,
Freeport, Long Island,
New York, N.Y. 11520

Rhythms

Materials needed: Large geometric-shaped pieces of colored plastic (discarded plastic tablecloths or shower curtains may be cut into the basic shapes).

Place these shapes about on the floor. The children may move around the shapes to music or the beat of a drum. Through this activity they will be helped to realize the properties of each shape—points, sides, and continuous curve of the circle.

If plastic is not available, heavy cord or rope may be used to outline the shapes on the floor.

Recognizing Geometric Shapes

Geometric collages may be made, using either colored paper or cloth shapes of different sizes (circle, triangle, square, and rectangle).

Geometric mobiles may be made by tying small colored shapes on a coat hanger.

Stippling may be done with pieces of cellulose sponge cut in geometric shapes. The sponge is pressed on a "stamp pad" (of tempera paint on felt-lined aluminum pie pan), then printed on paper to make interesting designs.

Object printing may be done with small

[1]Sarah Hammond Leeper, *et al.*, *Good Schools for Young Children* (New York: The Macmillan Co., 1968), p. 219.
[2]Jocelyn Bursten, "Mathematical Concepts for Young Children," from *Young Children*, March 1966, p. 229.

objects having geometric shapes. The "stamp pad" is the same as above.

Sometimes the art paper which the children use for such art activities as blow painting, blotto, and string painting may be cut in large circles, squares, or triangles. This will add interest to the activity and help the children be aware of the properties of the geometric shape.

Making Things from Paper Squares and Triangles

Discovering Shapes[3] (See diagrams.)

Use squares to make a kite and a sailboat. Use a triangle to make a cat and another one to make a dog.

Finger Plays and Poems

The following are examples of finger plays and poems which help in developing number concepts for young children.

THE CHICKENS

(Point to fingers on left hand, one for each little chicken.)
Said the first little chicken,
   With a queer little squirm,
"I wish I could find
   A fat little worm!"

Said the second little chicken,
   With an odd little shrug,
"I wish I could find
   A fat little bug!"

Said the third little chicken,
   With a sharp little squeal,
"I wish I could find
   Some nice yellow meal!"

Said the fourth little chicken,
   With a small sigh of grief,
"I wish I could find
   A little green leaf!"

Said the fifth little chicken,
   With a faint little moan,
"I wish I could find
   A wee gravel stone!"

---

[3] From *Discovering Shapes.* Copyright © 1963 by Western Publishing Company, Inc. Used by permission.

"Now see here," said the mother,
   From the green garden-patch,
"If you want any breakfast,
   Just come here and scratch."
        —Author unknown

TWO MOTHER PIGS

Two mother pigs lived in a pen
   (hold up thumbs),
Each had four babies, and that made ten
   (raise all fingers on both hands).
These four babies were black as night
   (extend four fingers of one hand),
These four babies were black and white
   (hold up four fingers of other hand).
But all eight babies loved to play,
And they rolled and rolled in the mud all day
   (wriggle fingers over each other).
At night, with their mothers, they curled up in
   a heap,
They closed their eyes and they went to sleep.
        —Author unknown

To make this finger play more interesting, make finger puppets to represent the two mother pigs and the eight little pigs. Make circles of masking tape and attach to back of puppets, making it easy to stick them to fingers.

ONE, TWO, BUCKLE MY SHOE

One, two, buckle my shoe;
Three, four, shut the door;
Five, six, pick up sticks;
Seven, eight, lay them straight;
Nine, ten, a big fat hen.
        —Old nursery rhyme

BAA, BAA, BLACK SHEEP

Baa, baa, black sheep, have you any wool?
Yes, sir, yes, sir, three bags full:
One for my master, one for my dame,
And one for the little boy who lives in our lane.
        —Old nursery rhyme

TEN LITTLE INDIANS

One little,
Two little,
Three little Indians,

Four little,
Five little,
Six little Indians,

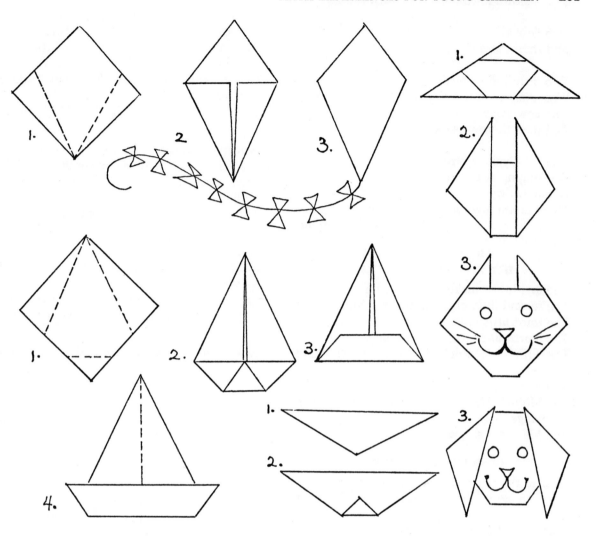

Seven little,
Eight little,
Nine little Indians,

Ten little Indian boys.

Ten little,
Nine little,
Eight little Indians,

Seven little,
Six little,
Five little Indians,

Four little,
Three little,
Two little Indians,

One little Indian boy
                    —*Old nursery rhyme*

One, two, three, four, five,
I caught a hare alive.

Six, seven, eight, nine, ten,
I let it go again.

                    —*Mother Goose*

Five little yellow birds
Were singing at the door.
One flew away
And then there were four.

Four little yellow birds
Were singing for me.
One flew away
And then there were three.

Three little yellow birds
Were singing for you.

One flew away
And then there were two.

Two little yellow birds
Were singing in the sun.
One flew away
And then there was one.

One little yellow bird
Was singing at the door.
One flew away—
There aren't any more.

—Old rhyme

MOTHER HEN AND
HER FIVE LITTLE CHICKS[4]

The first little chicken chased a bug.
The second little chicken just watched.
The third little chicken slept in the sun.
The fourth little chicken scratched.
The fifth little chicken cried, "PEEP! PEEP!
PEEP!"
As a hawk came sweeping low.
But Mother Hen gathered them under her
wings
And hid them all safely so!

OVER IN THE MEADOW

Over in the meadow in the sand in the sun
Lived an old mother turtle and her little turtle
one.
"Dig," said the mother. "I dig," said the one,
So he dug all day in the sand in the sun.
Over in the meadow where the stream runs
blue
Lived an old mother fish and her little fishes
two.
"Swim," said the mother. "We swim," said the
two,
So they swam all day where the streams run
blue.

Over in the meadow in a hole in a tree
Lived an old mother owl and her little owls
three.
"Tu-whoo," said the mother. "Tu-whoo," said
the three,
So they tu-whooed all day in a hole in a tree.

Over in the meadow by the old barn door
Lived an old mother rat and her little ratties
four.
"Gnaw," said the mother. "We gnaw," said the
four,
So they gnawed all day by the old barn door.

Over in the meadow in a snug beehive
Lived an old mother bee and her little bees five,
"Buzz," said the mother. "We buzz," said the
five,
So they buzzed all day in a snug beehive.

Over in the meadow in a nest built of sticks
Lived an old mother crow and her little crows
six.
"Caw," said the mother. "We caw," said the six,
So they cawed all day in a nest built of sticks.

Over in the meadow where the grass grows
even
Lived an old mother frog and her froggies
seven.
"Jump," said the mother. "We jump," said the
seven,
So they jumped all day where the grass grows
so even.

Over in the meadow by the old mossy gate
Lived an old mother lizard and her little lizards
eight.
"Bask," said the mother. "We bask," said the
eight,
So they basked all day by the old mossy gate.

Over in the meadow by the old Scotch pine
Lived an old mother duck and her little ducks
nine.
"Quack," said the mother. "We quack," said the
nine,
So they quacked all day by the old Scotch pine.

Over in the meadow in a cozy little den
Lived an old mother rabbit and her little rabbits
ten.
"Hop," said the mother. "We hop," said the ten,
So they hopped all day in a cozy little den.

—Old nursery song

---

[4]From *Ten Busy Fingers*, by Elsie S. Lindgren (Fortress
Press, 1955), p. 28. Used by permission.

HOW MANY?

(As the teacher reads this jingle, the children may fill in the italicized number.)

One mischievous puppy
    Chewing on a shoe,
Along came his sister
    And that made *two*.
           (One and one make two.)

Two baby squirrels
    In a hole in a tree,
Their mother came home·
    And that made *three*.
           (Two and one make three.)

Three fat turkeys
    By the barn door,
Another one strutted up
    So that made *four*.
           (Three and one make four.)

Four young bullfrogs
    Learning to dive,
Kerplunk! jumped another
    And that made *five*.
           (Four and one make five.)

Five busy beavers
    Looking for sticks,
One came to help
    And that made *six*.
           (Five and one make six.)

Six boys and girls
    Having lots of fun
Counting the numbers left
    When they took away one.

Six boys and girls
    Found a beehive
One ran away home
    And that left *five*.
           (One from six leaves five.)

Five busy beavers
    Gathered sticks—lots more—
But one lost his way
    And that left *four*.
           (One from five leaves four.)

Four young bullfrogs
    As noisy as could be,
One fell off the log
    And that left *three*.
           (One from four leaves three.)

Three fat turkeys
    Showing what they could do,
One strutted in the barn
    And that left *two*.
           (One from three leaves two.)

Two baby squirrels—
    My, how they could run—
One scampered out of sight
    And that left *one*.
           (One from two leaves one.)

One little puppy
    Romping in the sun,
He followed a neighbor boy
    So then there was *none*.
           —*Josephine Newbury*

Snack Time Activity

Crackers shaped like circles, squares, triangles, and rectangles may be served with the juice occasionally. The children will enjoy identifying the shapes and eating them as well.

Water Play and Math

Take five one-pound cottage cheese cartons or yogurt containers and punch holes of the same size in the bottoms of the containers. In one container punch one hole, in another punch two holes, in another three, in another four, and leave one without any holes. The children can fill each container full of water and watch it drain out into the water-play tub. They can count the streams of water and watch to see which of the containers empties first, next, etc.

NUMBER VOCABULARY

Number vocabulary emerges from many experiences. Let's look at one of the daily routines, snack time, and listen to the mathematical vocabulary that is being used.

As one of the hosts was helping to prepare for midmorning snack, the teacher said, "You will need to serve six people at your table. Put the right number of chairs at your table; then you can set the table properly." The child counted the six chairs and placed them at the table. Then he was heard to count out the place mats as he placed one *in front of* each chair. Talking to himself, he added, "One napkin *beside* each place mat." After pouring the juice in the cups, he set them around one at a time at the places, chanting quietly, "A cup of juice on each place mat. A cup of juice on each place mat." (One-to-one correspondence and relationships in space: *in front of, beside, on.*)

The following are examples of typical table conversation at snack time:

"The hostess didn't pour *as much* juice in my cup as she did in her's," complained one child. "She's got *more than* I have."

"Look, my cracker is square, and my cup is round at the top," explained Joyce. "My place mat is a rectangle," chimed in Ted. Then folding his napkin cornerwise, he added, "Now my napkin's a triangle." All this conversation at the snack table showed an interest in verbalizing understandings and relating them to new situations.

All these math concepts were evident at snack time on one morning! The alert teacher will give whatever reinforcement she thinks is needed for individuals in such situations. Children learn from each other in such small group experiences as having snack together with a few friends around the table.

At other times of the morning such statements as this may be heard: "My building is taller than yours," comes from the block center.

Two children were standing in front of the large class calendar in early January. One of the children, pointing to the picture of a birthday cake marking the 23rd, commented, "It's a long time till my birthday. I don't believe it will ever come." His friend replied, "Don't worry. It will come soon. The days in winter are real little" ("five-year-old logic" based only upon what he can perceive).

As the time drew nearer to his birthday, counting the days on the calendar helped this child to begin to see how time is measured.

As the children's height was measured in May, the teacher showed each child how much taller he was than when he was measured in September. She used a simple ruler to measure on paper the difference. Each child marked his growth in inches.

The children compared their heights on the chart with each other and used such terms as *taller than, the same as, shorter than.*

The following are words that can have mathematical significance for the young child. They will take on meaning for him as they are used functionally in the kindergarten in the various activities in which he becomes involved (block play, dramatic play, routines, creative movement and dance, finger plays, and songs):

above	large	short	before
below	larger	shorter	after
	largest	shortest	
under			circle
over	big	small	triangle
	bigger	smaller	rectangle
inside	biggest	smallest	square
outside			curved line
	many	wide	
alike	few	narrow	whole
different			half
	first	less	
few	last	more	shape
fewer			size
fewest	long	penny	none
	longer	nickel	
	longest	dime	
zero		quarter	minute
one	first	cent	hour
two	second		day
three	third	corner	week
four	fourth	money	month
five	fifth	count	year
six	sixth	one-to-one	
seven	seventh	next	top
eight	eighth	matching	bottom
nine	ninth	side	between
ten	tenth	ring	
		around	edge
		through	set
		point	
		on	taller than
		ruler	tallest
			more than
			as many as
			fewer than
			behind
			in front of

TEACHING RESOURCES

No one can make sense of mathematical symbols unless he has carried out actions with materials.[5]

The teacher selects those materials that are readily available and functional in the daily living of the group. He or she will be guided to a great extent by the needs and the readiness of individuals in the class.

Concerning this, Evelyn Pitcher says:

> Academic learnings, even more than other content, at the pre-school level must be "tailor made" for the particular child; and we must bear in mind his degree of readiness and his immediate and long-term needs. Always these learnings must flow from actual experiences the child has had with objects and events.[6]

Manipulative Materials and Equipment

balance scales
bead counting frame
calendars of varying kinds—wall, pocket, desk, revolving, book, engagement
checkers
clocks—large primary clock
dominoes—number and picture
flannel board
geometric shapes of felt, cardboard, plastic
geometric solids
hourglass
large numbers (0 through 10) of rubber or wood or printed on tiles
large wooden beads
large thermometer
maps of different kinds
magnetic board
measuring cups (plastic)
milk cartons—quart, pint, and half-pint
number puzzles (individual, interlocking)
number sorter
pairs of socks, mittens, gloves, shoes, etc.
parquetry blocks
pegboard
plastic jars—pint and quart size
pinch clothespins (plastic)
puzzles
rain gauge
scales for weighing and measuring children; kitchen scales
table games that require movement by counting spaces around a playing board
unit blocks
water-play equipment
world globe
yardstick, tape measure, ruler

Scrap materials:

All kinds of small objects having geometric shapes (fruit jar ring, small square rug protector, rectangular box, etc.)
corks
egg cartons
empty spools
empty thread cones
large buttons, bottle caps, tongue depressors, poker chips
pint and quart plastic ice cream containers
plastic bottle tops
small boxes of varying sizes

Equipment

Geometric Shape puzzles. This is a commercial product made of rubber. The puzzles are made of concentric pieces of each shape which fit tightly one into the other. The shapes are made in two colors. This allows the child to fit the pieces together to make different color patterns.

Number puzzles. Sets of ten two-piece puzzles, usually made of wood. One part of each pair has a number printed on it. The other part has the number of objects which corresponds to the number on the matching piece. For example, the "6" puzzle might have six balls pictured on it. These individual puzzles fit together in only one way, each puzzle being different. Therefore, they are self-correcting.

Kitchen scales are useful in weighing small objects. Balance scales with a fulcrum allow the child to compare weights of different objects. This activity helps the child deal with the concept of relative weight.

---

[5]Leonard Marsh, *Alongside the Child: Experiences in the English Primary School* (New York: Harper & Row, 1972), p. 53.

[6]Evelyn Goodenough Pitcher, *et al., Helping Young Children Learn* (Columbus, Ohio: Charles E. Merrill, 1966), p. 95.

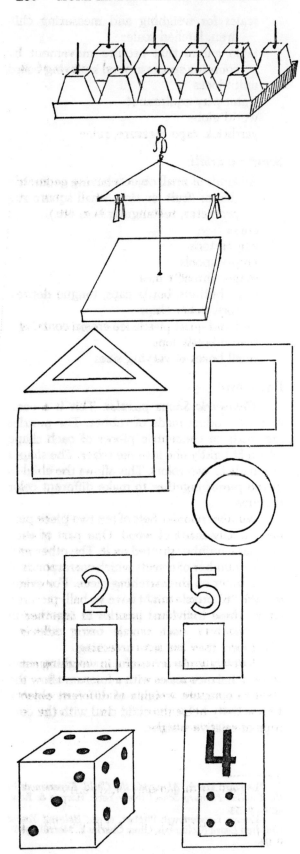

Number Counter

Materials needed: Egg carton, ¼" dowel cut into 12 lengths of 5" each. Six of the dowels may be left the natural wood color. The remaining six may be painted red or green. *Be sure to use a nontoxic paint.*

Directions: Turn the egg carton upside down and punch a hole just large enough to hold a dowel in each of the 12 compartments. Arrange the colored dowels along one side and the unpainted dowels along the other side.

Activity: The child can use this material for counting, one-to-one equivalence, and discovering number combinations.

Large Wooden or Rubber Numbers

Large wooden and rubber numbers are available commercially from equipment supply houses. The children will manipulate them and find various uses for them.

They may line them up in order, checking their order with the large classroom calendar. They may also collect small objects—beads, blocks, bottle caps, etc., and under each number arrange the corresponding number of objects.

The teacher may draw around the numbers on a piece of cardboard and let the children match the number with the outline of it, placing it within the outline.

Young children usually recognize the printed number names before they understand the number values.

GAMES

Tenpins

Detergent bottles of the same size and brand can be used to make a game of tenpins. A small rubber ball about 5" or 6" in diameter will serve well for knocking down the bottles. The child counts the bottles he knocks down and the ones that remain standing. This helps him to better understand the meaning of numbers and to become familiar with combinations for the number of "pins" he is using. Early in the year the number might be only 6 pins. As the children develop skills and number understandings, the number of "pins" may be increased.

Dominoes

The large (3″ × 6″) wooden dominoes available commercially are an excellent game. At first the children may just manipulate them and match up the dots.

As the children become more skilled in observing likenesses and differences, they will enjoy playing the game. Playing dominoes is a good activity for developing perception and helping the children understand the meaning of number names 0 through 6.

Simple Balance

All that is needed to make this are two coat hangers and a block of wood 4″ square and about 2″ high.

Leave one coat hanger intact. Cut the long, straight part of the other coat hanger and bend one end into a small hook, just large enough for the other hanger to rest on. Drill a fine hole in the wood block and stick the hooked wire into it.

When the hanger is in balance, indicate with paint the center of coat hanger where it lines up with the rod that holds it. This will show when it is in balance. *(See diagram on p. 236.)*

The children may then use small plastic clothespins to hang on either side of the balance. They will soon note how they can keep the coathanger even. They will be counting the clothespins, and they will be *adding* and *taking away.*

Sandpaper Shapes

From rough sandpaper cut circles, squares, triangles, and rectangles of different sizes. Paste each shape on a piece of heavy cardboard.

Let the children close their eyes and try to identify the shapes by feeling them.

Outlines of Geometric Shapes

Out of long plush-covered "pipe cleaners" make the outlines of a triangle, circle, square, and rectangle.

Out of heavy cardboard cut large outline shapes of a triangle, square, rectangle, and circle. The children may use these to draw around, both inside and outside the figure. *(See diagram on p. 236.)*

Outlines of the shapes may also be attached with black thread to a coat hanger to make a mobile.

Number Match

Materials needed: Large rubber or wooden numbers, cardboard, counters (buttons, bottle tops, etc.), small wooden cube block, plastic cup.

On the cardboards draw around the numbers 1 through 6 with a felt pen. Beneath each number outline a square for the counters.

With felt pen put dots on each side, just as dice are marked. The child shakes the die in the cup and places the right number of counters on the correct number board. *(See diagram on p. 236.)*

Sorting Objects

Materials needed: Plastic quart ice cream containers; materials for counting—pebbles, buttons, tongue depressors, bottle caps, etc.

Number the containers, always beginning with 0. At first the child may be able to match only through four or five. Add numbered containers as the child recognizes numbers up to 10.

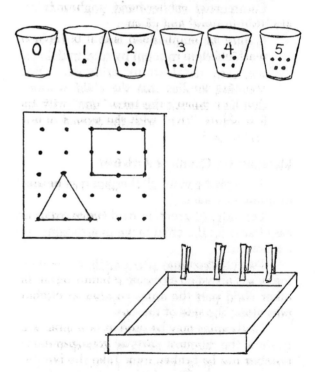

The child places the correct number of counters in each container.

Sorting Geometric Shapes

Materials: Cut from felt or colored cardboard a number of each of the geometric shapes. It makes it more difficult for the child to sort if there are different sizes and colors of each shape.

The child may sort them by the shapes or by sizes of each shape or by colors of each shape.

The child will find other ways of using these shapes.

Felt shapes may be used on a flannel board; cardboard or paper shapes may be worked with either on a table or on the floor.

Nail Pegboard

Materials needed: One-inch boards cut 10" × 10", finishing nails 1½" long, and colored rubber bands of different sizes.

Mark off the board for 25 nails to form 5 verticle and 5 horizontal rows, spaced at equal distances.

Drive the nails in securely, about half way.

The child stretches the rubber bands over the pegs, making as many different geometric shapes as he can.

Commercial rubber-band pegboards are available in wood and plastic.

It must be emphasized that it is futile to teach children to count by rote: in doing so they are not learning arithmetic. Real counting implies that the child is aware that he is pairing the term "one" with the first object, "two" with the second object, and so on.[7]

Materials for Counting Activities

Small plastic pinch clothespins may be used in numerous ways.

The sides of greeting card boxes make an easy frame for the child to use in arranging the clothespins.

Two children may play together, one moving beads across on a counting frame while the other child puts the same number of clothespins along the side of the box.

Clothespins may be used in this same way to show the different parts or arrangements a number can be broken into. Take the number six, for example. The child can discover by re-arranging the clothespins that he can have 5 and 1, 4 and 2, 3 and 3, 2 and 2 and 2, etc. He will discover that no matter what way he re-

arranges these six clothespins along the edge of the box, he will still have six clothespins.

Other materials may be collected for the child to use in developing his understanding of the attributes of numbers: tongue depressors, bottle tops, small sea shells, checkers, empty thread spools, smooth pebbles.

Caution: Be sure that all collections are of materials too large for the child to swallow!

MEASUREMENT

Time—Use of the Calendar

The informal use of the calendar in the kindergarten can help children begin to understand something of the meaning of time in their lives. They will begin to recognize the sequence of the days of the week and the months of the year. The terms *yesterday, today, tomorrow, last week,* and *next week* will have some meaning as events are recorded on the class calendar and referred to from time to time.

A large calendar can be made for each month. It should be placed on the level of the children, so that they can work with it on their own as their interest dictates or as the group is checking the current date and recording class or seasonal data.

The daily use of the calendar in the group will vary from month to month. For example, the October calendar would feature Halloween. The teacher could make orange paper jack-o'-lanterns and tape one over each date of the month. Each day the children could remove a jack-o'-lantern, thus exposing the date. This would be an interesting way of building the October calendar. It would not overwhelm the children with all 31 numbers at once.

The November calendar might be used in a similar way; cover each date with a paper turkey to be removed daily. Or the group might prefer to place small pictures of things for which they are thankful over each date as the days come and go.

The December calendar might be made like an advent calendar. A small picture of something appropriate for December could be pasted on the calendar, covering each day of the month. Red cards with the numbers 1 through 31, when taped over the pictures, make an advent calendar. Each day a child raises the

[7]Kenneth Lovell, *The Growth of Understanding in Mathematics: Kindergarten Through Grade Three* (New York: Holt, Rinehart & Winston, 1971), p. 35.

numbered paper and exposes the picture beneath. Used Christmas cards are an excellent source of the type and size of pictures needed: snow scenes, snowman, Christmas greens, Christmas tree, candles, churches, etc.

January is a month when new calendars are available everywhere. This is an appropriate time to present the entire year at once, using calendars of all types available. Pictures showing special events occurring in the months and the four seasons help the children to see what makes up a year and to begin to understand about the measurement of time.

For a more complete discussion of the use of the calendar, refer to the *Church Kindergarten Resource Book* by Josephine Newbury, pages 222–223.

Clock

It is good to have a large cardboard clock with moveable hands to use in setting time to match the clock in the kindergarten room. Special attention may be paid to the set times in the day's program which have to be scheduled, such as lunchtime and dismissal.

No formal attempt is made in the kindergarten to teach the children to tell time. But time is dealt with situationally as it is meaningful to the children.

Egg Timer

A plastic three-minute timer will be of interest to the children and helps them get the feel of minutes as a measure of time. It can be used by the children in timing themselves in the performance of an activity or in determining the length of "turns" each child has in a game or other activity. It might be used to warn the children that clean-up time is "almost here." Three minutes warning is helpful to the children in this routine.

Volume and Linear Measure

Experiences in linear measurement and volume will include the functional use of such manipulative materials as:

Plastic measuring cups in water and sand play and in such activities as making gelatin dessert, cookies, or churning butter.

Milk cartons of different sizes for use in water play. The children will begin to acquire related vocabulary that becomes meaningful as they discover the different capacities of the containers. Some will discover that a pint container filled twice will fill the quart container, etc.

Rain gauge. The use of a rain gauge to measure the amounts of rainfall will be of interest to the five-year-olds, particularly if a record is kept, from time to time, for comparisons.

Ruler, yardstick, tape measure. Distances and lengths begin to take on more meaning for the child when he uses measuring tools to "find out." And the words *inch, foot, yard, longer, shorter, as far as,* become more useful to him. He may want to measure the paper chain he has made, the wood or paper he is using in construction, the height of his block building, or how far he threw the beanbag. Rulers with only the inches recorded are easier for him to read and are less confusing.

TEMPERATURE

Indoor and Outdoor Thermometers

The use of thermometers, especially during seasonal changes, helps the young child become more aware of the variations in temperature. In the winter it will be interesting for the group to record the temperature of the kindergarten room and compare it with the temperature outdoors. A large, easy-to-read cardboard thermometer with a ribbon, part red and part white, running up to represent the mercury in the real instrument is a useful piece of equipment to have available. The children can move the ribbon up or down to correspond to the thermometer readings. With these experiences will come a more meaningful vocabulary of *hot, cold, cool, warm, freezing, thermometer,* and *temperature.*

Make a Graph

More mature fives will enjoy making a daily graph of the temperature. Large chart paper marked off in one-inch lines makes good graph paper. The temperature may be indicated along the left side of the paper. The vertical lines may indicate the days of the month. Each day as the temperature is read it can be recorded on the graph with a red crayon. If such a record is made in January, it will be interesting to make a graph of the temperatures in March or April. Each morning the group can compare the temperature to that of the same day in January. (See page 219 in chapter 11.)

WEIGHT

Scales

Young children are interested in how much they weigh and how they are growing. Periodic weighing and measuring and recording of the data can be very meaningful to the child because it is so personal.

Balance Scales

Experimenting with balances can lead the child to many discoveries about judging weights of different objects. He can begin to realize that size and weight can differ. (For example, a very small block at one end would tip the scale with a big box of cotton on the opposite end.) Experimenting with clay can help the child in conservation. An example would be taking two balls of clay the same size and putting them on the balance scale. Then weigh again after one ball is divided into two small balls. Because the one ball became two, the child is apt to guess that the two balls would weigh more than the other large ball. By placing them on the scale, he can test his judgment.

The clay can be rolled back into two equal balls again. The child sees that they are the same. Roll one into a "hot dog," and ask the child which he thinks weighs more. Again, he is apt to say the long roll of clay is heavier. He can test himself by weighing.

In using small kitchen scales, the child can be more accurate. In these activities he is building a more meaningful vocabulary of such words as *heavy, light, weigh, weight, scales, balance, pound, ounce,* and others such as *lighter* and *heavier.*

ACTIVITIES INVOLVING MATHEMATICAL CONCEPTS

Number Matching Cards, 0 Through 6

Materials needed: 14 pieces of heavy cardboard, 4½″ × 6″.

Directions for making: With a felt pen draw two sets of cards, leaving one card in each set blank, and arranging small circles or squares to represent the numbers 1 through 6.

Make the arrangement of these perception card sets different. *(See diagram across.)*

On the back of each card print the number which corresponds to the number of dots on the card.

Directions for using: These cards may be used in several ways. One set may be spread on the table with the number side up, and the child can match the figure set to the number set. *(See diagram.)*

When all are matched, he may then arrange them in order, being certain there is one more circle on each card in the progression of 0–1–2–3–4–5–6. This may be done in reverse, beginning with the figure cards, to which the child matches the number-name card.

These cards may be used in still another way. All 14 cards may be spread out, number-pattern side up. The child matches the cards, pattern for pattern, according to the number of circles on the cards.

Adaptation of Number Match

Materials needed: 2 boxes of checkers; 14 pieces of heavy cardboard, 4½″ × 6″, with one side left blank; marked sets of pattern cards as made for previously described activity.

Directions for making: On one side of 7 of the cards, print the numbers 0 through 6.

Directions for using: Using the marked sets with the patterns of circles, the child makes the identical patterns by placing checkers on the blank cards to correspond to the patterns on the printed cards.

The child may also use the blank card sets and checkers to make his own pattern of checkers on one set of blank cards to correspond to the numbers printed on the other set.

These activities, as well as giving meaning to numbers, aid in the development of the child's perceptiveness, and if the individual cards are recognized as *sets,* the idea of equivalent and non-equivalent sets can be shown.

It will be hard for some five-year-olds to recognize and match the patterns in these matching activities because of the differences in the spatial arrangements of the circles, but for those who are ready for such understand-

ings, this is a "fun activity" with mathematical values.

Recognizing Incomplete Shapes

Materials needed: Several pieces of heavy cardboard 10″ × 14″, marked off in incomplete shapes. *(See figure 1 and figure 2, page 242.)*

If you are making the materials for seriation given in the directions above, you may use the same cardboard cutouts. This will eliminate making more of the same materials, but it will mean that the patterns for the cutouts must be used to make the outlines on the cards.

Make four cards like figure 1 or figure 2, mixing the shapes about differently on each card.

These cards, with the corresponding cutouts (8 of each shape of matching size), will provide another type of table game—"Find the Shape Lotto." The cutouts are put in a box, and the player reaches in and draws out a shape. If he can use the shape on his playing board, he does. If not, he tries to find another player's board where the shape is needed. This insures that the game will move faster, and it encourages cooperation rather than competition, which is hard for some young children to handle.

Note: The children are not to draw in lines needed to complete the shapes on the playing boards of figures 1 and 2. All of the cards are to be used again and again as individuals choose to play with them.

Matching Shapes in Series

Materials needed: 12 pieces of cardboard about 10″ × 14″, marked off in differing series. *(See diagram, page 242.)*

Each card has a different series.

Cut shapes of the same sizes and of differing colored cardboard for each geometric shape.

The child matches the shapes in series on each card.

Provide enough of the cutout shapes so that the child can continue the series beyond or without the card model.

Small boxes with acetate tops (greeting card boxes) are good for storing the cutouts.

When the child finishes the seriation, he should place the cutout shapes in their proper boxes. This involves the child in another important activity of categorizing the shapes.

Outline Picture Charts

Materials needed: Cardboard cut in pieces 10″ × 14″. Draw in outline form simple objects with which the children are familiar. Have them find all the different shapes in each picture. *(See page 243.)*

Making Mysterious Shapes

Cut a circle one inch in diameter in one end of a shoe box. In the opposite end of the box cut a circle three inches in diameter. Cut a three-inch slit in the lid of the box near the larger circle. Give the children cards on which tiny holes have been punched to outline different geometric shapes. Children place a card in the slit and hold the box to the light, looking

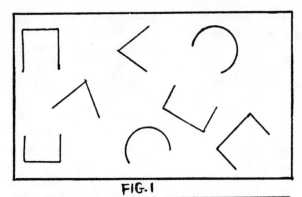

FIG. 1

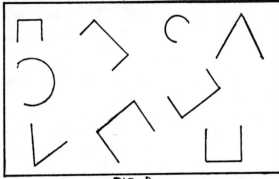

FIG. 2

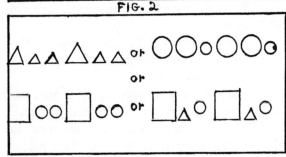

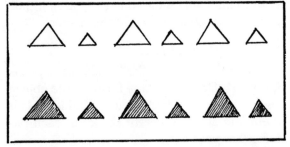

or

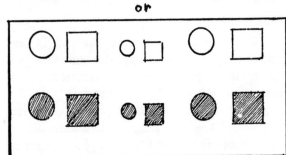

through the small circle in the box to identify the shape.[8]

Recognizing Pairs

Collect pairs of things known to the children and place them in a large box, mixing them up.

Let the children match up the pairs of objects.

Such things as the following might be included:

several pairs of socks of different sizes and colors
child's bedroom slippers
pair of tennis shoes
pair of sandals
pair of baby shoes
pair of rubbers
pair of galoshes
pair of driving gloves
pair of child's gloves
pair of child's mittens

Judging Weight

Young children need experience in perceiving likenesses and differences in weight.

1. Materials such as a rock, cotton, a feather, a wooden block, a small plastic box, a rubber ball and a baseball (both about the same size) may be collected for this manipulative activity.

   Children may sort them into boxes marked "light" and "heavy."
2. Identical plastic or cardboard containers may be prepared, pairs of them containing material of identical weight. The child lifts and judges the containers which are alike and places them together.

   To aid in this, one set might be marked with a red circle on top, the other set marked with a blue circle.

   The containers might have the following materials:

   20 cotton balls
   ½ lb. of sand
   1 lb. of rice
   ¾ lb. of rice

---

[8]From *Kids' Stuff*, by Mary Jo Collier, Imogene Forte, and Jo MacKenzie. Incentive Publications. Copyright © 1969. Used by permission.

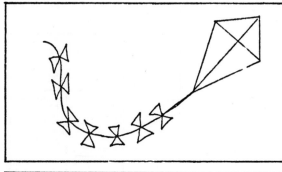

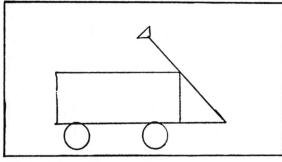

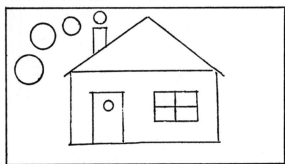

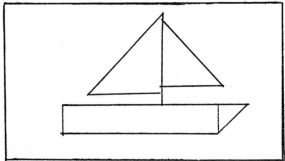

The containers could be covered with attractive contact paper. This will eliminate the possibility of the child seeing the amount of material within a container.

3. Children need experiences in judging the lightness or heaviness of objects of varying sizes and weights. Examples: a large roll of cotton and a small wooden block; a large sack filled with empty cereal boxes and a small bag with a can of rocks, etc.

The child needs to discover that size does not determine the weight of differing materials.

TABLE GAMES

Many number concepts are developed through the use of games.

Shapes Lotto

Materials needed: Four pieces of cardboard, 9″ × 9″. Rule off each piece into nine three-inch squares. Draw with a felt pen the true basic geometric shapes—circle, triangle, and square (one in each 3″ section), mixing them about on the card. Have an equal number of each shape on each of the four cards, but arrange them differently. Cut thirty-six three-inch squares of similar cardboard and draw the identical shapes, twelve of each shape, to match those on the playing boards. To make the game more durable, cover the boards and playing pieces with clear contact paper. *(See below.)*

Each player in turn draws a small card and places it on his board, covering the matching shape. Cards which a player cannot use are turned face down in another pile to be drawn later in the game when necessary. The game continues until all playing boards are filled.

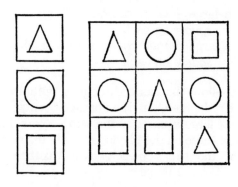

Colored Shapes Lotto

Materials needed: Cut four pieces of heavy cardboard 9" × 9" and rule them off in nine equal squares. Cut 36 squares of cardboard 3" × 3".

From colored construction paper cut the following shapes to fit into the 3" × 3" squares:

6 *large red* circles, triangles, and squares
6 *large green* circles, triangles, and squares
6 *large blue* circles, triangles, and squares
6 *large orange* circles, triangles, squares
6 *small blue* circles, triangles, squares
6 *small yellow* circles, triangles, squares
6 *small orange* circles, triangles, squares
6 *small black* circles, triangles, squares

Paste the small shapes on the larger ones in this order:

2 large *red circles* with a small *blue circle* on each
2 large *green circles* with a small *orange circle* on each
2 large *blue circles* with a small *yellow circle* on each
2 large *orange circles* with a small *black circle* on each

2 large *red circles* with a small *blue triangle* on each
2 large *green circles* with a small *orange triangle* on each
2 large *blue circles* with a small *yellow triangle* on each
2 large *orange circles* with a small *black triangle* on each

2 large *red circles* with a small *blue square* on each
2 large *green circles* with a small *orange square* on each
2 large *blue circles* with a small *yellow square* on each
2 large *orange circles* with a small *black square* on each

Follow the same directions with the 24 large red, green, blue, and orange triangles and the 24 large squares of the same colors. Paste half of these on the playing cards being careful to mix the shapes on each board. Mix the colors as well as the shapes.

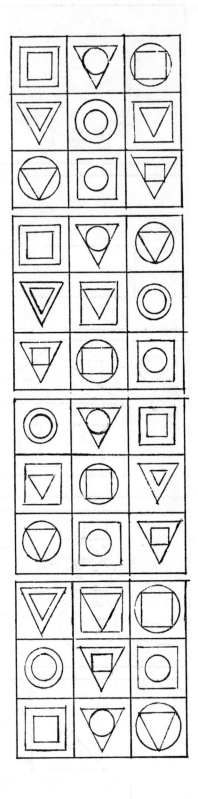

Now make duplicates of each pattern on the 3″ × 3″ playing cards.

After this is completed, cover the four playing boards and 36 playing cards with clear contact paper to make the game more durable.

Rules of the game: Four players can participate. Mix the 36 playing cards well and place them in a stack, face down. The player draws a card which, if it matches a place on his board, may cover it. If it does not match, he places it in a stack beside the other cards until it is needed.

If the children have difficulty maintaining interest in the game, let each child place the card which does not match his playing board on another child's playing board. This will speed up the game and lessen the chance of too much competition.

In any event, the game continues until all playing cards are used.

Number Lotto

Materials needed: Four playing cards made of heavy cardboard cut 10½″ × 10½″. Divide each card into six equal spaces 3½″ × 5¼″. With a felt pen draw in the figures as arranged below, using either small triangles or circles as the shape. From the same weight cardboard, cut 24 cards 3½″ × 5¼″ and duplicate the figures on the playing board. There will be four cards with no figures to match the blank spaces on the playing boards. In this game the children are working with the "numberness" of 0 through 5.

Cover the playing boards and playing cards with clear contact paper to make them more durable.

Number Bingo

Materials needed: Four pieces of heavy cardboard cut 9″ × 9″. Cut 50 cards 3″ × 3″ from matching cardboard.

Rule the large playing boards into nine equal squares, using a felt pen. Print the numbers 1 through 5 on each card, being sure to arrange the numbers differently on each card. Print the same numbers on the small cards, making 10 of each number. Cover all cards with clear contact to preserve them.

Two boxes of checkers are needed as markers (buttons or bottle caps may be used). *See diagram for sample marking.*

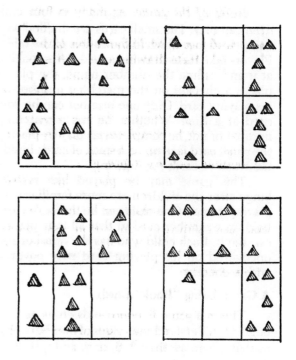

Rules of the game: As many as four children can play. The small cards are shuffled well and placed face down in the center of the table. Players take turns drawing a card. After looking at it and calling the number name, the player places a checker on the matching number on his playing card. Only one number can be covered at a time. Whether he has a matching number or not, he completes his play by placing the small card face up on a stack of cards beside the stack of cards for drawing.

This game may be played like regular bingo after the children are more familiar with playing games. One child can be the leader and hold up a number card so that all four players can see it. Each child who has the number still uncovered on his playing card may cover it with a checker.

A Game Using "Rook" Cards

This is a game five-year-olds enjoy as they begin to understand the values of numbers, that is, that 9 is more than 8, 6, or 7, and 5 is more than 4, 3, 1, 2, etc.

When the children first begin to play this game, it is best to remove all the number cards above 10. They may be added to the deck as the children have more experience with them in real-life situations.

Three to six children can play. Shuffle the cards well and deal them face down until all cards have been dealt. One child is selected to begin the game by taking the top card from his pile and laying it face up on the table. Each child around the table (clockwise) lays his top card out so that all the numbers are visible. The child having played the largest number picks up the cards on the table and starts another stack—his winning cards. He may then start the next round by laying out his top card, face up. In the event that two children lay down the same number, they each lay down another card, the largest number taking all the cards.

It makes the game more interesting if the children call the name of the number as they lay it down.

Shapes-Matching Game

Paper shapes are given out to a small group of children who are sitting in a circle. The teacher holds up one shape of the duplicate set, repeating the following jingle:

Look, look,
What do you see?
If you can find its twin,
Bring it here to me.

After the children become familiar with the jingle, they can lead the game.

To make the game more involved, the paper shapes may be of different sizes so that the child has to match both shape and size.

A third characteristic may be added—color—so that the cutout must be the right color, shape, and size.

Jack-o'-Lantern Lotto

Materials needed: Four large orange jack-o'-lantern-shaped playing cards about 10" × 12".

Outline on each with felt marker eyes, nose, and mouth, using geometric shapes. Each playing card should be different. (*See examples below.*)

Cut shapes out of yellow cardboard to match those outlined on the jack-o'-lantern-face playing cards.

Each player reaches into a sack and draws a shape. He first tries to fit it to his playing card, but if he cannot use it, he may play it on another child's card.

If the children are mature five's and are adept at playing table games, the child drawing a shape which he cannot use on his playing card may drop it back into the sack to be drawn later by another player.

Sorting Activity

Materials needed: Cut 6 cards 2″ × 3″ and number them 0, 1, 2, 3, 4, and 5.

Collect small objects such as 1 door key, 2 plastic pill boxes, 3 dominoes, 4 checkers, 5 wooden beads (of same shape, size, and color).

The child places the cards before him on the table and then tries to find the objects of the right number to go with each number card.

Several sets may be made with different objects for matching.

Scrap materials make interesting counters: empty spools, large buttons, corks, plastic drapery rings, clothespins, smooth stones, and plastic screw-on bottle tops. A few miniature toys from the dime store or from cereal boxes will add a bit more interest to this sorting activity.

Matching Shapes Activity

Materials needed:
16 pieces of heavy cardboard cut 5″ × 7″
16 pieces of the same cardboard cut 2½″ × 3½″

Cut from colored construction paper the following shapes:
4 colored circles 3″ in diameter
4 colored triangles 3″ × 3″ × 3″
4 colored squares 3″ × 3″
4 colored rectangles 3″ × 4″

4 colored circles 1½″ in diameter
4 colored triangles 1½″ × 1½″ × 1½″
4 colored squares 1½″ × 1½″
4 colored rectangles 1½″ × 2″

Paste the small shapes on the large ones, mixing the colors and being certain that each large basic shape has one each of the four basic shapes pasted in the center. Then paste the patterns of shapes on the large cards *(See diagram.)*

The small cardboards are to be matched to the large ones by shapes only, so with felt pen draw the 16 different matching patterns of shapes. For permanence cover all cards with clear contact paper.

This is a bit more difficult for the child than the colored-shape lotto, for there are no colors to help in the matching—only the geometric patterns.

One child may use this resource, matching the patterns to the large cards spread out on the table. Several children may work together,

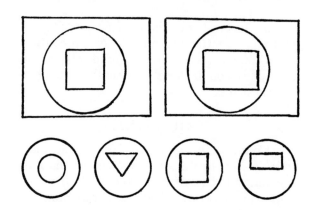

sharing in the matching, or it may become an activity much like a lotto game.

Categorizing Objects by Shape

Collect small objects of geometric shapes such as:

circular shapes—bottle tops, bracelet, large buttons, checkers, fruit jar ring, small paper plate, circular box, bottle caps, napkin ring, drapery ring;

triangular shapes—triangle (rhythm instrument), triangular-shaped building block, prism;

square shapes—small square boxes of different sizes, building block, square rug protectors, small floor tile;

rectangular shapes—domino, small boxes, soap dish, small cleaning sponge, small picture frame (without the glass), rectangular rubber eraser.

Label four shoe boxes, each with a different shape drawn in outline on one end of the box.

Uses:

1. Let the children categorize the objects by placing them in the boxes according to their shapes.

2. Play a game using two objects of each geometric shape. Place them on a table or on the floor before a small group of children. Ask one child to leave the group; ask another child to remove one object. The child who left the group is called back to guess which shape is missing.

3. Have the children sit in a circle on the floor with their hands behind them. Place an object in a child's hand and let him try to guess what shape it is by feeling it behind his back.

4. The teacher holds up a drawing or cutout of a square, a triangle, a circle, or a rectangle, and a child is asked to find one of the objects (on the table or on the floor) that has the same geometric shape.

COUNTING

Counting for the kindergarten child must involve him in the manipulation of things— touching the objects as he counts. He then begins to find more meaning than in rote number-name calling.

He comes to have a more adequate conception of what he is doing. He can then begin to make comparisons based on numbers. In this regard, Deal and Maness, in *New Horizons in Kindermath*, make the following observation: "The child moves from basing his thinking solely on the basis of what he sees to more abstract, logical ways of reasoning."[9]

BUTTON COLLECTION

Family button boxes have provided many young children with hours of satisfying rainy-day play experiences as they counted buttons, lined them up on the floor by color, made a train, or made designs and interesting arrangements with them.

A good collection of buttons of differing sizes, shapes, and colors can be used by the children in the kindergarten in a number of ways which will:

>   add to their understanding of the "numberness" of the number names;
>   give them experiences in sorting and categorizing;
>   offer them a different medium for creating designs;
>   help them in understanding the concepts of "more than," "the same as," "less than"; and
>   provide opportunities for the children to arrange the buttons in sets.

Caution: Use only buttons too large for children to swallow.

---

[9]Therry N. Deal and Jeannine P. Maness, "New Horizons in Kindermath," *Young Children*, September 1968, p. 357.
[10]*Ibid.*, p. 355.

Just "playing around" with a box of buttons has value for the kindergarten child. He may have a better experience if he plays with them on the floor. A square of rug sample makes a well-defined area for him.

Provide the child with large pieces of colored art paper and let him arrange the buttons in designs, laying them on the paper to make outline pictures. They can very easily make geometric shapes. Some of the children will "write" numbers or "spell" their names with the buttons.

Provide large plastic pill bottles (available from the druggist) for the child to categorize the buttons by size or by color.

The child may match buttons to cards which have been prepared for this activity. For example, make a group of cards showing the invariance of four buttons, regardless of their arrangement. *(See diagram.)*

Counting buttons: Cards with numbers 1 through 10 may be layed out, and the child places the correct number of buttons by each card: *(See diagram.)*

Arrange sets of buttons: Provide large wool rope loops (tie together lengths of rope to make loops of 10" in diameter). The child may work with sets of buttons in these rope outlines. *(See the diagram.)*

Here he can match the one-to-one relationship and see which has "more than" or "fewer than" or the "same as" buttons in the sets.

When a teacher labels and categorizes, and when she encourages her students to do so, she is fostering the child's ability to think, to reason, to sort, to see the whole and separate components of the whole and to communicate more effectively.[10]

CHILDREN'S BOOKS

Berkley, Ethel S. *Ups and Downs*. Eau Claire, Wisconsin: E. M. Hale & Co., 1951.

_____. *The Size of It*. Eau Claire, Wisconsin: E. M. Hale & Co., 1950.

Borten, Helen. *Do You See What I See?* New York: Abelard-Schuman, Ltd., 1959.

Bradfield, Joan and Roger. *The Big Happy 1-2-3*. Racine, Wisconsin: Whitman Publishing Co., 1965.

Budney, Blossom. *A Kiss Is Round*. New York: Lothrop, Lee & Shepard Co., 1954.

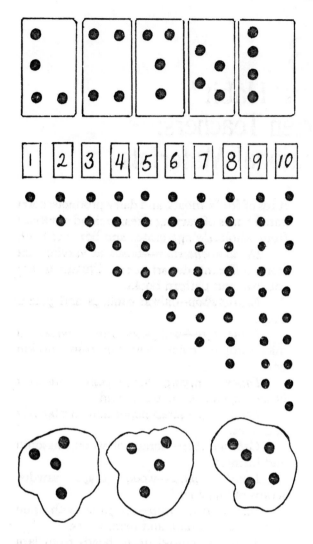

Kaufman, Joe. *Big and Little*. Racine, Wis.: Western Publishing Co., 1966.

Kay, Helen. *One Mitten Lewis*. New York: Lothrop, Lee & Shepard Co., 1955.

Keyser, Sarah. *Up, Down and All Around* (Changing Picture Book). Bronx, N.Y.: Child Guidance Products.

Krauss, Ruth. *The Growing Story*. New York: Harper & Row, 1947.

Langstaff, John, and Rojankovsky, Feodor. *Over in the Meadow*. New York: Harcourt Brace Jovanovich, 1967.

Meeks, Esther K. *One Is the Engine*. Chicago: Follett Publishing Co., 1956.

Moore, Lillian. *My Big Golden Counting Book*. Racine, Wis.: Western Publishing Co., 1957.

Oswald, Edith, and Reed, Mary M. *The Golden Picture Book of Numbers*. New York: Simon & Schuster, 1954.

Schlein, Miriam. *Fast Is Not a Ladybug*. New York: William R. Scott, 1953.

_____. *How Big Is Big? From Stars to Atoms*. New York: Scholastic Magazine, Inc.

_____. *It's About Time*. New York: William R. Scott, 1955.

_____. *Shapes*. New York: William R. Scott, 1952.

Schneider, Herman and Nina. *How Big Is Big?* New York: William R. Scott, 1946.

Sherman, Diane. *My Counting Book*. Chicago: Rand McNally & Co., 1960.

Slobodkin, Louis. *One Is Good But Two Are Better*. New York: Vanguard Press, 1956.

The Three Little Kittens. Ill. by Masha. New York: Golden Press, 1962.

Tudor, Tasha. *One Is One*. New York: Henry Z. Walck, 1956.

Wolff, Janet. *Let's Imagine Thinking Up Things*. New York: E. P. Dutton & Co., 1961.

Wright, Betty, and Wylie, Joanne. *Elephant's Birthday Party—A Story About Shapes*. New York: Western Publishing Co., 1971.

Young, Miriam. *Five Pennies to Spend*. New York: Golden Press, 1955.

"Adventures in Discovery" Series:
Discovering Shapes
Learning About Sizes
Time and Measuring
Understanding Numbers
New York: Western Publishing Company, 1970.
    For Encyclopaedia Britannica
    Educational Corporation
    425 N. Michigan Ave.
    Chicago, Ill. 60611

Duvoisin, Roger. *Two Lonely Ducks: A Counting Book*. New York: Alfred A. Knopf, 1955.

Emberley, Ed. *The Wing on a Flea*. Boston: Little, Brown & Co., 1961.

Friskey, Margaret. *Chicken Little, Count-To-Ten*. Chicago: Childrens Press, 1946.

_____. *Seven Diving Ducks*. Eau Claire, Wis.: E. M. Hale & Co., 1940.

Hymes, James L. *The Lightning Bug*. Evanston, Ill.: Row Peterson & Co., 1959.

Ipcar, Dahlov. *Brown Cow Farm: A Counting Book*. Garden City, N.Y.: Doubleday & Co., 1959.

13
The "Squirrel Habit" for Kindergarten Teachers: Sources of Educational Materials

One very important habit which teachers working with kindergarten children need to develop is known as the "squirrel habit." It can spark the creativity of all involved in the kindergarten—children and adults alike. The results of the employment of this habit can enrich many different kinds of experiences the children have and at the same time cut the budget for equipment and art materials.

There is a wealth of discarded materials of all kinds just waiting to be saved from the incinerator or garbage can—materials which may be used in art, music, science, math, and dramatic play activities.

It just takes a little imagination and a little time to transform discards into something interesting and useful in the classroom. Some items need recycling, while others may be used as they are. For example, items of adult wearing apparel would need altering to make them fit the children, while scraps of yarn, rickrack, cloth, styrofoam packing (the little tubes, disks, and peanut shaped kinds) are usable just as they are in making collages.

When young children participate in collecting and using scrap materials constructively, they are learning a valuable lesson in stewardship of their environment. And it's good for the ecology as well.

Wherever the kindergarten teacher goes, he or she should keep alert for scrap materials which would be useful in the kindergarten. Most of these materials are free. Merchants are usually glad to find someone who can use the things they discard. Some items, although scrap in nature, may carry a nominal price.

The following are typical of places from which discarded materials are frequently available and items which they may yield:

Grocery store—advertising, including pictures of fruits, meats, and dairy products; corrugated boxes of varying sizes; molded cardboard from wholesale egg crates and boxes of fruit.

Department store—boxes of varying sizes from different departments; Christmas card catalogs and pattern books.

Fabric shop—fabric catalogs and pattern books.

Paint store—wallpaper sample books, formica samples, color charts for paint, packing boxes.

Paper company—scrap paper and cardboard (often sold by the pound).

Print shop—scrap paper and cardboard of odd sizes.

Cabinet shop—scraps of wood, masonite, and formica.

Lumber yard—wood scraps, sawdust, scraps of wallboard.

Upholstering shop—scraps of cloth upholstery, plastic, braid, and foam rubber.

Music store—old drum heads from large drums.

Plumbing repair shop—nickel-plated pipe and fittings.

Automobile used parts dealer—brake drums and hubcaps.

Venetian blind and drapery company—scrap lengths of drawcords, sample books of drapery materials.

Kindergarten parents should also be alerted to keep a watchful eye for scrap and discarded materials. They will be glad to know what materials are needed and the uses which might be made of them. Some teachers mimeograph such lists and distribute them to the children's parents, suggesting that the kindergarten children might enjoy helping to search for and bring in the "treasures." It is surprising and quite gratifying to see the variety of materials which will be discovered and brought into the kindergarten as a result of such requests.

The following list suggests some of the kinds of scrap and discarded materials and some of the uses which can be made of them in the kindergarten:

Discarded adult clothes renovated to fit the children for dramatic play—skirts, jackets, small aprons, hats (men's and women's), scarves, pocketbooks, necklaces, etc.

Men's small and medium-size sport shirts, to be used as smocks for art activities.

Small train and attaché cases for dramatic play.

Discarded pony saddle or racing saddle from a harness shop or pony ranch. This can be attached to a wide-top sawhorse or a barrel for "riding."

Large fiber drums with one end removed for making drums; with both ends removed smoothly for making tunnels for outdoor play.

Wallpaper sample books for use as decorative paper, for collage making, and as pages for individual books for the children's dictated stories.

Sample fabric catalogs for touch books and for making collages.

Christmas card catalogs for making scrapbooks of picture and original stories.

Seed, flower, and travel catalogs as sources of pictures.

Dressmaking pattern books as a source of the types of clothing worn in different seasons of the year; as a source of pictures of children and adults for use as paper dolls and for making individual posters of the members of the children's families.

Catalogs from mail-order houses as sources of pictures for categorizing and organizing activities.

Large advertising posters with cardboard stands attached for displaying teaching pictures or children's art work.

Scrap cardboard and paper for creative art activities.

Gift wrapping paper.

Scraps of cloth for a touch book: felt, corduroy, linen, silk, burlap, nylon net, fur, denim, velvet, satin, double-knit, etc.

Scraps of lace, rickrack, net, artificial flow- *ers, feathers, and ribbon* for use in art activities.

Egg cartons (molded type) for use in making collections, for exhibiting small nature specimens, for use in art and math activities, and for making scissors holders.

Molded cardboard separators used in wholesale egg crates and fruit cartons for use in art activities.

Cardboard rolls from paper towels for art materials, box constructing, etc.

Scraps of styrofoam for art activities.

Thread spools, plastic bottle tops, corks of all sizes, scrap junk of all kinds that could be used for object printing.

Nickel plated plumbing connections and lengths of pipe for musical activities.

Horseshoes for making "triangles" with ten-penny nails for use in rhythms.

Discarded silk scarves and large turkey feathers for use in creative rhythms and movement.

Automobile brake drums and hubcaps to use in rhythms.

Carpet samples for sit-upons.

Discarded flashlight for dramatic play.

Camera (that no longer operates) for dramatic play.

Discarded plastic tablecloths and shower curtains to cover table for water play and for making aprons to be worn in water play and finger painting.

Aluminum frozen food containers to be used in the home center for making dish gardens, to be used as stamp pads (with scrap felt saturated with paint serving as the pads).

Widemouthed gallon jar with screw top for making terrarium.

Plastic medicine bottles for displaying small objects of interest (seeds, shells, pebbles, etc.); also for making "sniff bottles" (punch pin holes in the caps and place a piece of cotton in the bottle to secure the materials—perfume, peanut butter, vanilla, orange juice, lemon flavoring, etc.).

Plastic squeeze bottles for water play.

Large liquid detergent bottles of the same kind for use as "pins" for the game of tenpins.

Large buttons for math activities.

Family magazines as a source of pictures.

Milk cartons (cut down) for paint containers.

Food cans (bottoms removed smoothly) for

use in home play and grocery-store play.

Cottage cheese containers for storage of small materials and for water play.

Short length (4 or 5 feet) garden hose for dramatic play of "firemen."

Half-inch rubber tubing four feet long for water play (siphoning).

Wooden boxes and crates for making pet cages and for use in woodworking.

Scraps of soft wood for woodworking.

Boxes of all kinds:

Shoe boxes for storing materials and making valentine post office.

Hat boxes for making peep boxes, storing play hats, and making insect cages (cut out panels around the box and insert a roll of screen wire to fit the box).

Blanket boxes for storing children's art work.

X-ray film boxes for filing pictures (available in several sizes—10″ × 12″, 11″ × 14″, and 14″ × 17″—from hospitals and clinics).

Large corrugated boxes for use in dramatic play and for large pieces of cardboard for mounting pictures or making easels.

Small plastic boxes or note paper and Christmas card boxes with acetate tops for use in exhibiting nature specimens.

Corrugated mattress boxes for making large easels, puppet stages, bulletin boards, etc.

It is surprising how much money can be saved and what a variety of activites can be provided for the children when there is a wealth of "beautiful junk" available for use in the kindergarten at all times. The extensiveness of the creative use of scrap materials is limited only by the imaginations of the children and adults working with them.

AUDIO-VISUAL EQUIPMENT

Filmstrip Projector

Filmstrips appropriate for kindergarten are listed with resources at the end of several chapters of this text.

The filmstrip projector may be used other than for the total group viewing of a filmstrip.

For individual or small group viewing, place the projector on a table and project the pictures on a screen made by lining a grocery carton with white paper. Focus the picture so that it fits inside of the box. This can be done in a room with the lights on. The picture will be clear and bright.

The projector may be used for shadow play with hands or objects. A projection screen or a sheet hung up on the wall will do for this.

Color slides bought commercially or produced by the teachers and parents may be used. Five-year-olds can also take pictures to use with the group. A good "Instamatic" camera will usually insure satisfactory results.

Two-inch by two-inch acetate may be used to make blank title slides. Transparency pencils or pens may be used. This is not an activity for the child, but the teacher may sketch illustrations for a child's dictated story or may prepare counting materials.

The teacher may make slides by using a slick magazine picture cut to the 2″ × 2″ size. To lift the picture, follow these directions:

1. Use transparent *contact* vinyl which is sold in hardware and dime stores. Cut the contact vinyl 2″ × 2″.
2. Place the vinyl, sticky side down, on the picture to be lifted off.
3. Rub the vinyl carefully with the back of a spoon to press out any air bubbles and to make certain that the entire picture adheres to the contact vinyl.
4. Soak the paper off the contact vinyl in water to which a small amount of laundry detergent has been added. Peel off the paper carefully and blot the transparency dry.
5. You will have the picture on the vinyl. If the vinyl remains sticky, spray with lacquer.
6. The picture is then ready to mount on a blank slide.

Movie Projector

There are many excellent short movies useful for young children. A wide range of subjects is covered in the area of children's literature, science, and social science. Most state libraries have movies for loan.

Sound-Filmstrip Projector

This instrument projects a filmstrip on a flip-top projection screen and operates either manually or by remote control. The instrument has standard phone jack output connections, so that a group of children can enjoy a sound filmstrip without disturbing children in other learning centers.

Overhead Projector

A small overhead projector is certainly not a necessary piece of equipment in a kindergarten, but if one is available it can be useful. The teacher can make transparencies with the use of transparency pens or felt markers or can use the method of lifting slick magazine pictures described in the section on making 2" × 2" slides.

The pens and markers come in many colors and are either washable or permanent.

Some five-year-olds could draw on the film and would enjoy seeing their creations on the screen.

Color Print Viewer

This is a relatively new piece of equipment. It is designed to show color prints 3½" × 3½" and enlarge them on a 10" × 10" screen. It is simple enough for a child to operate.

For a kindergarten this piece of equipment could be used to show color prints of the children's families. But a more flexible use would be pictures mounted on tagboard 3½" × 3½" for the children to look at and talk about. The teacher has all kinds of possibilites for creative use in sketching materials on 3½" × 3½" tagboard squares.

Hand Viewers

Three-dimensional picture viewers have always been popular with young children. Vue Master produces a wealth of picture reels for the viewer. There is also a projector for showing these pictures on a screen.

Filmstrip viewers are available at a reasonable price for individual viewing of a film.

Cameras

As previously stated, kindergarten children can have good experiences in taking color slides with an automatic camera. It is interesting to discover the things that impress individual children when they are on a field trip. They will enjoy seeing on a screen pictures of the scenes, persons, or objects they have observed on a trip. This is also a good way to encourage young children to recall and talk about experiences.

Tape Recorder

A tape recorder can be used for recording children's conversations, stories, and music. The children thrill at hearing their own voices.

The teacher can record materials he or she would like the children to hear. These may be recordings of short excerpts of instrumental music, or of simple picture storybooks. The child may then enjoy looking at a book as he hears it "read" to him on tape.

The tape recorder may be connected to the "listening post" so that several children may enjoy a story at one time. Several copies of the book would make it possible for each child to listen to the story and keep up with it by "reading the pictures" in the book.

Record Player

A good record player is essential in a kindergarten. It will be much more versatile if it has a standard phone jack output for a headphone or listening center accessory.

Listening Center

A listening center with a built-in jack panel for headphones is very versatile. As many as six or eight children may listen individually to a recording without being distracted by noises in the room. They may also listen without disturbing children who are involved in other learning centers.

FLAT PICTURES

Flat pictures are a very important teaching tool. Every teacher should have a file of easily accesible pictures to use as learning situations arise which call for clarification or enrichment of the spoken word or firsthand experience.

The following are sources of teaching pictures for preschool children:

Bowmar
622 Rodier Dr.
Glendale, Calif. 91201
    Picture study sets in 3 categories:
        I. About Myself
        II. The World About Me
        III. I Talk—I Think—I Reason

Child's World, Inc.
120 N. Weston St.
Elgin, Ill. 60120
    Foldout and study prints in social science
    and science.

National Dairy Council
111 North Canal St.
Chicago, Ill. 60606
    (Contact your local Dairy Council if there
    is one in your community.)

Society for Visual Education, Inc.
1345 Diversey Parkway
Chicago, Ill. 60614
    Picture-story study prints, talking picture-
    story study prints. Records accompany
    prints. Science and social science.

Webster Division
McGraw-Hill Book Co.
Manchester Road
Manchester, Mo. 63011
    Tell-Again Story Cards, Level II (large pic-
    ture story cards for each story).

Standard Publishing
8121 Hamilton Ave.
Cincinnati, Ohio 45231
    "Present Day Pictures"—No. 2603 by
    Frances Hook.

A.B.C. School Supply, Inc.
P.O. Box 13084
Atlanta, Ga. 30324
    24 teaching picture sets in science, social
    studies, health, etc. Pictures 10 3/4″ × 13
    3/4″ in full color.

PERIODICALS

Arizona Highways
2039 West Lewis Ave.
Phoenix, Ariz. 85009

National Wildlife and
Ranger Rick's Nature Magazine
1412 Sixteenth St., N.W.
Washington, D.C. 20036

MOVIES ON KINDERGARTEN EDUCATION

The following films are available on free loan from Modern Talking Picture Service, 2323 New Hyde Park Road, New Hyde Park, N.Y. 11040, or from the nearest regional office:

A Chance at the Beginning. 16 mm, black and white, 29 minutes.
This film describes a program of preschool training for children from deprived backgrounds in a Harlem school. Dr. Martin Deutsch, head of the Institute for Developmental Studies, leads a discussion with a group of teachers.

Discipline and Self-Control. 16 mm, black and white, 25 minutes.
Demonstrates how teachers help children gain control of themselves in a friendly climate; discusses adequate supervision and the dangers of over- and under-control.

Organizing Free Play. 16 mm, black and white, 22 minutes.
This film focuses on the facet of early childhood education called "free play." The film shows children and their teachers in their physical surroundings and discusses such questions as: What is free play? How do children learn from free play? How does one facilitate free play?

Head Start to Confidence.
The film illustrates the vital need for every child to have a sense of his own worth as a person. It shows a teacher's various means of building self-confidence in preschool children through achievement, language, and the performance of useful tasks.

Four Children. 16 mm, black and white, 20 minutes.
This is the story of four young children, so alike as human beings, yet so different as people. It offers an intimate look at the children and the homes from which they come.

Early Expressionists. 16 mm, color, 15 minutes.
A delightful film of two- to four-year-old children, recording their spontaneous and rhythmic movements with various art media. Filmed at the Golden Gate Nursery Schools in San Francisco.

Jenny Is a Good Thing. 16 mm, color, 18 minutes.
This film reveals some of the excitement and feeling that results when staff and volunteers care

about children and their parents and what happens to the children when the curriculum is imaginative and richly varied.

The following films must be ordered from the distrubutors, as indicated:

Little World. 16 mm, color, 20 minutes.

This shows a typical program in a day care center for four-year-olds. Some of the activities shown are free play, block building, finger painting, a picture book session, and an excursion to see a fire engine. The film points out the kinds of equipment and activities essential to a good program for young children.

Available from:
Office of Public Relations
Office of Economic Opportunity
1200 Nineteenth St., N.W.
Washington, D.C. 20506

Primary Education in England. 16 mm, color, 17 minutes.

This film explores the highlights of a successful experiment in non-graded education in the early years. Very helpful in showing the uses of learning centers as an approach to early childhood education.

Available from:
IDEA, Inc.
P.O. Box 446
Melbourne, Fl. 32901

Learning in the Kindergarten. 16 mm, black and white, 39 minutes.

In following a day's activities at the Eliot-Pearson Children's School, this film presents key concepts of its innovative program.

Available from:
Anti-Defamation League of B'nai B'rith
315 Lexington Ave.
New York, N.Y. 10016

Learning Through the Arts. 16 mm, color, 22 minutes.

The viewer sees the natural reactions of kindergarten children as they explore the arts, showing experiences with language arts, music, movement, paint, clay, and clean-up time.

Available from:
Audio-Visual Services
Kent State University
Kent, Ohio 44240

The Purple Turtle. 16 mm, color, 14 minutes, free-loan.

Kindergarten children are photographed as they work creatively with easel paints, crayons, and clay. A number of interesting techniques are shown.

Available from:
The American Crayon Co.
P.O. Box 2067
Sandusky, Ohio 44870

FILMSTRIPS ON KINDERGARTEN EDUCATION

The Good Life in Kindergarten. 90 frames, color.

The pictures are candid shots taken in the Demonstration Kindergarten of the Presbyterian School of Christian Education. The purpose of the filmstrip is to provide a teaching tool for persons concerned about early childhood education. It is organized into the following groupings: arrival and dismissal, dramatic play, small group activities, block play, games, conflict situations, art and music experiences, routines, special days, expanding horizons, and outdoor activities.

Available from:
Director, Demonstration Kindergarten
1205 Palmyra Ave.
Richmond, Va. 23227

A Good Day in Kindergarten, 40 frames, color, sound.

This filmstrip shows the day's program indoors and out. Many of the activities are carried on in the spacious outdoor area of the kindergarten pictured in the film.

Available from:
Bureau of Elementary Education
California State Department of Education
Sacramento, Calif. 95801

The Nursery School. 82 frames, color, sound.

This filmstrip shows a planned program of experiences for three- and four-year-old children. Teachers and parents will find this comprehensive view of nursery school providing them with a much better understanding of the types and varieties of equipment necessary and the methods used in coping with behavioral patterns.

Available from:
Atlantis Productions, Inc.
894 Sheffield
Thousand Oaks, Calif. 91360

Teaching Deprived Kindergarten Children. 90 frames, color, sound.

This filmstrip shows approaches for presenting key concepts to young children. The filmstrip concentrates on the social studies and mathematics.

Let's Visit Kindergarten

Three color, sound filmstrips depicting the kindergarten "in action": *A Typical Day.* 80 frames. *Methods and Techniques,* Part I, 77 frames. *Methods and Techniques,* Part II, 64 frames.

The children's voices in the script make the experiences viewed on the screen come alive.

Available from:
Pollican Educational Services
1108 South 8th St.
Goshen, Ind. 46526

Nursery School and Kindergarten. 82 frames, color, sound.

This filmstrip suggests principles and practical procedures which may be applied in the classroom, since it is based on research findings from the booklet *What Research Says to the Teacher—Nursery School and Kindergarten,* by Sarah Hammond Leeper.

Available from:
National Education Association
Publication-Sales Section 87
1201 Sixteenth St., N.W.
Washington, D.C. 20036

I Am a Teacher Aide. 13 minutes, color, sound.
This filmstrip shows how a teacher's aide works as a part of the teaching team in a Head Start program. The voice of the narrator is that of the aide, so the viewer has the feeling that he is a part of the situation.

Available from:
National Audio-Visual Center
Washington, D.C. 20409

A Piaget Preschool Program in Action. Color, sound.

Part I—*Number*
Part II—*Measurement and Space*
Part III—*Seriation*
Part IV—*Classification*

In these four filmstrips one sees classroom sessions in which Dr. Lavatelli demonstrates how to apply Piaget's theories to develop the concepts listed as the titles. Interpretations are made in the discussion between the narrator and Dr. Lavatelli so that the viewers understand why the materials are used as they are and why certain questions are asked of the children.

Available from:
Knowledge Tree Films
Box 203, Department CE
Little Neck, N.Y. 11363

Hand Puppets. 54 frames, color, captioned.
This filmstrip shows teachers how to construct sock, envelope, stick, box, paper bag, and wire puppets. A number of simple puppet stages are shown.

Available from:
Society for Visual Education, Inc.
1345 Diversey Parkway
Chicago, Ill. 60614

Painting, I. 46 frames, color, captions,
Techniques demonstrated include: brush painting, cord painting, wet chalk painting, roller painting, sponge painting, straw painting, finger painting, monoprinting, and blot painting.

Print Art. 62 frames, color, captions.
The print making process is explained. Everyday materials are used to show gadget printing, roller printing, relief printing, monoprinting, texture printing, among other types. Both of these filmstrips demonstrate art activites in which kindergarten children can participate.

They are available from:
Western Publishing Co., Inc.,
Education Division
150 Parish Drive
Wayne, N.J. 07470

PROFESSIONAL BOOKS

(not appearing in individual chapter bibliographies in this text.)

Almy, Millie, *et al. Young Children's Thinking.* Columbia University, New York: Teachers College Press, 1966.

Anderson, Robert H., and Shane, Harold G. *As the Twig Is Bent: Readings in Early Childhood Education.* Boston: Houghton Mifflin Co., 1971.

Association for Childhood Education International. *Feelings and Learnings,* Washington, D.C., 1965.

Association for Childhood Education International. *Readings from Childhood Education,* Washington, D.C., 1966.

Auleta, Michael S. *Foundations of Early Childhood Education: Readings.* New York: Random House, 1969.

Axline, Virginia. *Dibs: In Search of Self.* Boston: Houghton Mifflin Co., 1966.

Baker, Katherine Read, and Fane, Xenia. *Understanding and Guiding Young Children.* Englewood Cliffs, N.J.: Prentice-Hall, 1967.

Biber, Barbara, *et al. Promoting Cognitive Growth—A Developmental-Interaction Point of View.* Washington, D.C.: National Association for the Education of Young Children, 1971.

Biber, Barbara. *Challenges Ahead for Early Childhood Education.* Washington, D.C.: National Association for the Education of Young Children, 1969.

Blackie, John. *Inside the Primary School.* New York: Schocken Books, 1971.

Brearley, Molly, and Hitchfield, Elizabeth. *A Guide to Reading Piaget.* New York: Schocken Books, 1969.

Brearley, Molly, ed. *The Teaching of Young Children: Some Applications of Piaget's Learning Theory.* New York: Schocken Books, 1970.

Bronfenbrenner, Urie, and Condry, John C. *Two Worlds of Childhood.* New York: Russell Sage Foundation, 1970.

Chauncey, Henry, ed. *Soviet Preschool Education: Volume I—Program of Instruction.* New York: Holt, Rinehart & Winston, 1969.

Chauncey, Henry, ed. *Soviet Preschool Education: Volume II—A Teacher's Commentary.* New York: Holt, Rinehart & Winston, 1969.

Christianson, Helen M., *et al. The Nursery School: Adventures in Living and Learning.* Boston: Houghton Mifflin Co., 1961.

Chukovsky, Kornei. *From Two to Five.* Berkeley: University of California Press, 1968.

Cook, Ann, and Mack, Herb. *The Teacher's Role* (Informal Schools in Britain Today). New York: Citation Press, 1971.

Croft, Doreen J., and Hess, Robert D. *An Activities Handbook for Teachers of Young Children* (a companion book to *Teachers of Young Children* by the same authors). Boston: Houghton Mifflin Co., 1972.

Department of Elementary-Kindergarten-Nursery Education, National Education Association. *Kindergarten Education*. Washington, D.C., 1968.

Dittmann, Laura L., ed. *Curriculum Is What Happens*. Washington, D.C.: National Association for the Education of Young Children.

Elkind, David. *Children and Adolescents: Interpretive Essays on Jean Piaget*. New York: Oxford University Press, 1970.

Engstrom, Georgianna. *Open Education—The Legacy of the Progressive Movement*. Washington, D.C.: National Association for the Education of Young Children, 1970.

Fraiberg, Selma H. *The Magic Years*. New York: Charles Scribner's Sons, 1959.

Frost, Joe L. *Early Childhood Education Rediscovered—Readings*. New York: Holt, Rinehart & Winston, 1968.

Furth, Hans G. *Piaget for Teachers*. Englewood Cliffs, N.J.: Prentice-Hall, 1970.

Grugeon, David and Elizabeth. *An Infant School* (Informal Schools in Britain Today.) New York: Citation Press, 1971.

Headley, Neith. *Education in the Kindergarten*. 4th ed. New York: Van Nostrand Reinhold Co., 1966.

Heffernan, Helen, and Todd, Vivian. *The Kindergarten Teacher*. Boston: D.C. Heath & Co., 1960.

———. *The Years Before School: Guiding Preschool Children*. New York: The Macmillan Co., 1964.

Hertzberg Alvin, and Stone, Edward F. *Schools Are for Children: An American Approach to the Open Classroom*. New York: Schocken Books, 1971.

Hess, Robert D., and Croft, Doreen J. *Teachers of Young Children*. Boston: Houghton Mifflin Co., 1972.

Hildebrand, Verna. *Introduction to Early Childhood Education*. New York: The Macmillan Co., 1971.

Holt, John. *How Children Fail*. New York: Pitman Publishing Corp., 1964.

———. *How Children Learn*. New York: Pitman Publishing Corp., 1967.

———. *What Do I Do Monday?* New York: E. P. Dutton & Co., 1970.

Hymes, James L. *Teaching the Child Under Six*. Columbus, Ohio: Charles E. Merrill Publishing Co., 1968.

Hymes, James L., Jr. *Behavior and Misbehavior*. Englewood Cliffs, N.J.: Prentice-Hall, 1955.

———. *A Child Development Point of View*. Englewood Cliffs, N.J.: Prentice-Hall, 1955.

Hymes, Jesild. *The Child Under Six*. Englewood Cliffs, N.J.: Prentice-Hall, 1963.

I.D.E.A. Early Childhood Series, Volume One. *The British Infant School*, 1969. (Available from IDEA, P.O. Box 446, Melbourne, Florida 32901.)

Leeper, Sarah H., *et al. Good Schools for Young Children*. 2nd ed. New York: The Macmillan Co., 1968.

Leonard, George B. *Education and Ecstasy*. New York: Delacorte Press, 1968.

Le Shan, Eda J. *The Conspiracy Against Childhood*. New York: Atheneum Publishers, 1968.

Marsh, Leonard. *Alongside the Child: Experiences in the English Primary School*. New York: Harper & Row, 1972.

Miller, Mabel Evelyn. *A Practical Guide for Kindergarten*. West Nyack, N.Y.: Parkes Publishing Co., 1970.

Murrow, Casey and Lisa. *Children Come First: The Inspired Work of English Primary Schools*. New York: McGraw-Hill, 1971.

Newbury, Josephine. *Church Kindergarten Resource Book*. Rev. ed. Richmond: John Knox Press, 1970.

Newman, Sylvia. *Guidelines to Parent-Teacher Cooperation in Early Childhood Education*. Brooklyn, N.Y.: Book-Lab Inc., 1971.

Nimnicht, Glen, *et al. The New Nursery School*. New York: General Learning Corporation, 1969.

Parker, Ronald K. *The Preschool in Action*. Boston: Allyn & Bacon, 1972.

Piaget, Jean. *The Child's Conception of Number*. New York: W. W. Norton & Co., 1965.

———. *Play, Dreams, and Imitation in Childhood*. New York: W. W. Norton & Co., 1962.

Pitcher, Evelyn, and Ames, Louise. *The Guidance Nursery School*. New York: Harper & Row, 1964.

Pitcher, Evelyn, *et al. Helping Young Children Learn*. Columbus, Ohio: Charles E. Merrill Publishing Co., 1966.

Pulaski, Mary Ann Spencer. *Understanding Piaget: An Introduction to Children's Cognitive Development*. New York: Harper & Row, 1971.

Read, Katherine H. *The Nursery School, A Human Relationships Laboratory*. 4th ed. Philadelphia: W. B. Saunders Co., 1966.

Robison, Helen, and Spodek, Bernard. *New Directions in the Kindergarten*. New York: Teachers College Press, 1967.

Rogers, Vincent R. *Teaching in the British Primary School*. New York: The Macmillan Co., 1970.

Rudolph, Marguerita, and Cohen, Dorothy H. *Kindergarten—A Year of Learning*. New York: Appleton-Century-Crofts, 1964.

Salot, Lorraine, and Leavitt, Jerome. *The Beginning Kindergarten Teacher*. Minneapolis, Minn.: Burgess Publishing Co., 1965.

School Mathematics Study Group. *Mathematics for the Elementary School, Book K*. 1965. Distributed by School Mathematics Study Group through A. C. Vronman, Pasadena, California.

Schulman, Anne Shaaker. *Absorbed in Living—Children Learn*. Washington, D.C.: National Association for the Education of Young Children, 1967.

Taylor, Barbara J. Rev. ed. *A Child Goes Forth*.

Provo, Utah: Brigham Young University Press, 1970.

Wadsworth, Burry J. *Piaget's Theory of Cognitive Development.* New York: David McKay Co., 1971.

Wann, Kenneth D., *et al. Fostering Intellectual Development in Young Children.* New York: Bureau of Publications, Teachers College, Columbia University, 1965.

Weber, Evelyn. *Early Childhood Education: Perspectives on Change.* Worthington, Ohio: Charles A. Jones Publishing Co., 1970.

———. *The Kindergarten: Its Encounter with Educational Thought in America.* New York: Teachers College Press, 1969.

Weber, Lillian. *The English Infant School and Informal Education.* Englewood Cliffs, N. J.: Prentice-Hall, 1971.

Weikart, David P., *et al. The Cognitively Oriented Curriculum.* An ERIC-NAEYC Publication in Early Childhood Education. Urbana, Illinois: University of Illinois, 1971. (Available from Publications Dept., National Association for the Education of Young Children, Washington, D.C.)

Wills, Clarice, and Lindberg, Lucile. *Kindergarten for Today's Children.* Chicago: Follett Publishing Co., 1967.

Yamamoto, Kaoru, ed. *The Child and His Image: Self-Concept in the Early Years.* Boston: Houghton Mifflin, 1972.

SOURCES OF EDUCATIONAL PAMPHLETS

Association for Childhood Education International
3615 Wisconsin Ave., N.W.
Washington, D.C. 20016

Bureau of Publications
Teachers College
Columbia University
1234 Amsterdam Ave.
New York, N.Y. 10027

Child Study Publications
The Child Study Association of America, Inc.
9 East 89th St.
New York, N.Y. 10028

Department of Elementary-Kindergarten-Nursery Education, National Education Association
1201 Sixteenth St., N.W.
Washington, D.C. 20036

National Association for the Education of Young Children
1834 Connecticut Ave., N.W.
Washington, D.C. 20009

New York State Council for Children Publication Center
The Carousel School

173–53 Croydon Rd.
Jamaica, N.Y. 11432

Play School Association, Inc.
120 West 57th St.
New York, N.Y. 10019.

Public Affairs Pamphlets
381 Park Ave., S.
New York, N.Y. 10016

Science Research Associates, Inc.
259 East Erie St.
Chicago, Ill. 60611

U.S. Department of Health, Education, and Welfare
Children's Bureau
P.O. Box 1182
Washington, D.C. 20013

PERIODICALS

Childhood Education. Journal of the Association for Childhood Education International
3615 Wisconsin Ave., N.W.
Washington, D.C. 20016

Child Study. Child Study Association of America
9 East 89th St.
New York, N.Y. 10028

Children
U.S. Department of Health, Education, and Welfare
Government Printing Office
Washington, D.C. 20402

Early Years
P.O. Box 13306
Philadelphia, Pa. 19101

Offspring
Michigan Council of Cooperative Nurseries
P.O. Box 4432
Detroit, Mich. 48228

Parents' Magazine
52 Vanderbilt Ave.
New York, N.Y. 10017

The PTA Magazine
700 North Rush St.
Chicago, Ill. 60611

Today's Child
92A Nassau St.
Princeton, N.J. 08540

Young Children. Journal of the National Association for the Education of Young Children
1834 Connecticut Ave., N.W.
Washington, D.C. 20009

MANUFACTURERS AND DISTRIBUTORS

ABC School Supply, Inc.
437 Armour Circle, N.E.
P.O. Box 13084
Atlanta, Ga. 30324

Bowmar
622 Rodier Dr.
Glendale, Calif. 91201

Childcraft Education Corporation
964 Third Ave.
New York, N.Y. 10022

Children's Music Center, Inc.
5373 West Pico Blvd.
Los Angeles, Calif. 90019

Children's Record Guild
100 Sixth Ave.
New York, N.Y. 10013

Child's World, Inc.
P.O. Box 681
Elgin, Ill. 60120

Community Playthings
Rifton, N.Y. 12471

Dick Blick
P.O. Box 1267
Galesburg, Ill. 61401

Educational Activities, Inc.
Freeport, L.I.
N.Y. 11520

Educational Record Sales
157 Chambers St.
New York, N.Y. 10007

Family Filmstrips, Inc.
Dept. of Audio-Visual Aids
TRAV
341 Ponce de Leon Ave., N.E.
Atlanta, Ga. 30308

Folkways Records and Service Corporation
117 West 46th St.
New York, N.Y. 10036

The Greystone Corporation
100 Sixth Ave.
New York, N.Y. 10013

Judy Company
General Learning Corporation
310 North Second St.
Minneapolis, Minn. 55401

Lyons
430 Wrightwood Ave.
Elmhurst, Ill. 60126

National Dairy Council
111 North Canal St.
Chicago, Ill. 60606

Peripole
P.O. Box 146
Lewistown Rd.
Browns Mills, N.J. 08015

Play-Art Educational Equipment Co.
20 Maplewood Ave. (Germantown)
Philadelphia, Pa. 19144

Scholastic Book Services
904 Sylvan Ave.
Englewood Cliffs, N.J. 07632

R. H. Stone Products
18279 Livernois
Detroit, Mich. 48221

S.V.E.—Society for Visual Education, Inc.
1345 Diversey Parkway
Chicago, Ill. 60614

"Threshold"
School Division
The Macmillan Company
Riverside, N.J. 08075

Weston Woods
Weston, Conn. 06883

SPECIAL RESOURCES FOR DAY CARE PERSONNEL

Pamphlets

What Is Good Day Care? Children's Bureau Folder No. 53. Available from Superintendent of Documents, U.S. Government Printing Office, Washington, D.C. 20402.

The Child's Right to Quality Day Care, by Annie L. Butler. Association for Childhood Education International, 3615 Wisconsin Ave., N.W., Washington, D.C. 20016.

The Children Are Waiting, by Ruth Gilbert. Order from Central Distribution Service, P.O. Box 7286, St. Louis, Mo. 63177.

Other Resources

How to Operate Your Day Care Program. Ryan Jones Associates, 906 Penn Ave., Wyomissing, Pa. 19610.

The Office of Child Development, Department of Health, Education, and Welfare (P.O. Box 1182, Washington, D.C. 20013), publishes the following:
Federal Interagency Day Care Requirements
No. 1: *Day Care—A Statement of Principles*
No. 2: *Day Care—Serving Infants*
No. 5: *Day Care—Staff Training*
No. 6: *Day Care—A Guide for Project Directors and Health Personnel*

Cohen, Monroe D., ed. *Helps for Day Care Workers — A Lap to Sit on—Much More.* Association for Childhood Education International, 3615 Wisconsin Ave., N.W., Washington, D.C. 20016.

C.W.L.A. Standards for Day Care Service. Child Welfare League of America, 44 E. 23rd St., New York, N.Y. 10010.

Bogulawski, Dorothy B. *Guide for Establishing and Operating Day Care Centers for Young Children.* Child Welfare League of America.

The National Association for the Education of Young Children (1834 Connecticut Ave., N.W., Washington, D.C. 20009) publishers: *The "Politics" of Day Care,* Vol. 1 *Day Care As a Child Rearing Environment,* Vol II

Evans, E. Belle, *et al. Day Care: How to Plan, Develop and Operate a Day Care Center.* Boston: Beacon Press, 1971.

Windows on Day Care: A Report Based on Findings of the National Council of Jewish Women. By Mary Dublin Keyserling. New York: National Council of Jewish Women, 1972.

Day Care for America's Children. By E. Robert La Crosse. Public Affairs Committee, Inc., 381 Park Ave., South, New York, N.Y. 10016.

Day Care As a Child-Rearing Environment. By Elizabeth Prescott and Elizabeth Jones with Sybil Kritchevsky. Washington, D.C.: Publications Dept., National Association for the Education of Young Children, 1972.

OTHER ORGANIZATIONS PUBLISHING INFORMATIVE MATERIALS

Bank Street College of Education
69 Bank St.
New York, N.Y. 10014

Canadian Welfare Council Research Branch
55 Parkdale Ave.
Ottawa 3, Ontario, Canada.

Child Study Association of America
9 East 89th St.
New York, N.Y. 10028

National Committee for the Day Care of Children
114 East 32nd St.
New York, N.Y. 10016

Day Care and Child Development
Council of America Inc.,
1426 H St., N.W.
Washington, D.C. 20005

PROFESSIONAL ORGANIZATIONS

Association for Childhood Education International
3615 Wisconsin Ave., N.W.
Washington, D.C. 20016

National Association for the Education of Young Children
1834 Connecticut Ave., N.W.
Washington, D.C. 20009

National Education Association
Department of Elementary-Kindergarten-Nursery Education
1201 16th St., N.W.
Washington, D.C. 20006

National Kindergarten Association
23 East Sixteenth St.
New York, N.Y. 10003

Southern Association on Children Under Six
1070 Moss Ave., N.E.
Orangeburg, S.C. 29115

Index

About the Author

JOSEPHINE NEWBURY is beloved alike by the many hundreds of children she has taught and the many teachers she has guided to more successful roles in the classroom. Through her writings she has inspired and given practical help to countless others.

Miss Newbury is a graduate of Oglethorpe University and holds a master's degree from George Peabody College for Teachers. She has also done graduate work at Emory University and the University of Maryland.

She has served as a public school teacher and assistant principal for the Fulton County Board of Education, Atlanta, Georgia. Since 1952 Miss Newbury has been professor of Christian education of the Presbyterian School of Christian Education, Richmond, Virginia. She was instrumental in planning for the Demonstration Kindergarten there, and, as director, she has guided its development since it opened in 1957. She is active in local and national professional teachers' organizations, and she has been involved for many years in teaching children in church school.

Other writings by Miss Newbury include *Nursery-Kindergarten Weekday Education in the Church* and *Church Kindergarten Resource Book*. She has also written graded curriculum materials and numerous articles in periodicals.